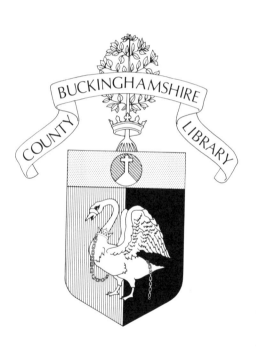

L. 29

A New History
of Cyprus

A New History
of Cyprus

From the earliest times to the present day

Stavros Panteli

Introduction by C. M. Woodhouse

East-West Publications
London and The Hague

To my father in
profound gratitude

First published in Great Britain in 1984
by East-West Publications Ltd
Jubilee House, Chapel Road
Hounslow, Middlesex, TW3 1TX

© 1984 Stavros Panteli
Introduction © 1984 C. M. Woodhouse
Cover design by Renos G. Lavithis

Panteli, Stavros
    A new history of Cyprus.
    1. Cyprus—History
    I. Title
    956.45   DS54.5

ISBN 0 85692 127 0
Typeset in 11 point Baskerville 1 point leaded
by Tellgate Typesetting, London WC2.
Printed in Great Britain by
The Camelot Press Ltd., Southampton.

Contents

Introduction

The history of Cyprus has been for the most part a series of foreign occupations – Phoenician, Persian, Egyptian, Roman, Crusader, Venetian, Turkish, British. The conquerors' motives were often obscure, sometimes inexplicable. Some occupied the island merely to prevent others from doing so; the Crusaders did so more or less by accident; the British hardly ever used it for the ostensible purpose of establishing a *place d'armes*. Yet the importance of the island's situation is undeniable. When it was suggested in 1915 that Cyprus should be ceded to Greece, the objection was raised by the Russians that this would make Greece the preponderant power in the eastern Mediterranean.

Only one thing has remained certain and invariable throughout three thousand years of history. Whoever ruled the island, the overwhelming majority of the population was Greek. Nothing could be more absurd than the fashionable slogan of the 1950's, that 'Cyprus never has been Greek.' What else has it ever been?

In the circumstances of the island's long history, it is not surprising that few Cypriots have had the chance to make a name for themselves in the outside world. Perhaps the one exception before the twentieth century was Zeno, the founder of the Stoic school of philosophy. But in our own lifetime two Cypriots have made a notable, if sometimes controversial, impact on international attention. They were Archbishop Makarios III, the National Leader (Ethnarch) of the campaign for *enosis* (union with Greece), and first President of the Republic of Cyprus; and General George Grivas, known as Digenis, the commander of the National Organization of Cypriot Combatants (EOKA).

These two men put Cyprus and its people on the map in their own right for the first time. It was a striking achievement, marred only by the irreconcilable disagreements between the two on the tactics of the struggle. Both believed in the goal of *enosis*, but not on the methods and the timing. Makarios believed in the power of diplomacy and bargaining, and he was profoundly uneasy about Grivas's conviction that the matter could be settled by force along. Hence the outcome was what neither of them originally wanted – not *enosis* but an independent Republic. And this outcome was again subjected to a partial foreign occupation in 1974, through the criminal folly of a military dictatorship in Athens, the aggressive voracity of an unstable government in Ankara, and the feeble indecision of the allied governments in London and Washington.

These were only the most recent of many lost opportunities. The prospect of uniting Cyprus with Greece has been frustrated by events again and again, and all the interested parties have been to blame in turn. Many British Ministers have declared themselves willing to concede *enosis*, but seldom when they were in office with the power to do so. The great Turkish leader, Mustafa Kemal, would have raised no objection to *enosis* in his last years, when he was encouraging the Turkish Cypriots to emigrate to the Anatolian mainland. Nor have the Greeks been guiltless of missing their opportunities. The government in Athens refused the offer of Cyprus as the price of alliance in 1915; and Makarios himself rejected the chance of winning self-determination in 1956. They had their reasons, of course; but Cyprus would surely have been better off today if they had seized their opportunities.

Not only the history but also the historiography of Cyprus has been contentious. Histories of the island, like sovereignty over it, have been mostly the work of foreigners. Not surprisingly, in the eyes of their subjects foreign historians have not always been objective. Their record does not fully satisfy Ranke's test of history: *wie es eigentlich gewesen.* Do we know, for example, exactly what Winston Churchill said during his memorable visit to Cyprus as Under-Secretary of State for the Colonies in 1907? The *Cyprus Gazette* and the *White Paper* of the time both agree that he said: 'I find it only natural that the Cypriote people, who are of Greek descent, should regard their incorporation with what may be called their mother-country as an ideal to be earnestly, devoutly and fervently cherished.' But when Sir George Hill wrote his authoritative *History of Cyprus*, two changes had occurred in the text: 'the Cypriote people, who are of Greek descent' had become 'the Cypriote people of Greek descent'; and 'what may be called their mother-country' had become 'what they call their mother-country'. Evidently an anti-enosist gremlin had been at work.

Evidently, too, it is high time for the Cypriots to undertake their own historiography as well as to take charge of their own destiny. Mr Panteli has done so, boldly and firmly, but also fairly. Naturally his conclusions do not pretend to be a final judgment; but when he passes judgment, he shows no favouritism. The 1959 settlement which established the Republic of Cyprus, for example, is characterised as a 'rogues' deal'; but the 'rogues' are as much Greek as British or Turkish. The same is true when he comes to the tragedy of July 1974. Although Mr Panteli does not hesitate to apportion blame, the positions of all the contending parties are defined with equal clarity.

It is right that a people's history should be written by itself and not left in the hands of foreigners. Indeed, it is normal; it is unusual only in the case of a subject people, which the Cypriots – most of them, at any rate – no longer are. What is still more unusual is that it should be written, as is the case with Mr Panteli, with complete facility in a language which is not his mother-tongue. This is indeed a new history of Cyprus, written from a new and much-needed point of view.

C. M. Woodhouse

Preface

The problem of historical analysis, interpretation and evaluation is full of pitfalls. One such pitfall is that of objectivity. There can be no doubt that all of us bring to our work inborn instincts, prejudices and subjective thoughts. The present writer is no exception. By frankly expressing his ideas in print on this sensitive period of history, he has tried to face up to this difficulty; in the following pages, he offers his personal views to open and critical evaluation, for only by free, unrestricted and rational discussion can objectivity be approached.

Thus, in presenting my version of Cypriot history (a study which has given me many headaches since 1977), I will sleep much easier if I can be persuaded to believe that I have succeeded in offering not only an easy to read unbiased narrative for the general reader but also a more precise and detailed analysis for the serious student to enable him to explore further the several lacunae that still exist. If I succeed in generating debate and further research, then I believe that my endeavours will have been fully justified.

I have concentrated on the unexplored years between 1877 and 1950 of which very little has been written. The post-1950 period has been tackled by various authors in the last decade or so and does not need elaborate comment. I am under no illusions that I have exhausted the subject in all its aspects. There are still many gaps and, where no concrete evidence is put forward, the facts are presented as they seemed at the time. In truth, certain events are very enigmatic not only to the uninformed but also to the informed such as the historian and politician.

Acknowledgements

While it is impossible to acknowledge everyone, I am grateful to a large cross-section of individuals for the help they have given me while I was preparing this book. A sizeable number of personal friends and relatives (listing their names would take at least half a page and even then some may be offended for not being mentioned), my colleagues G.V.S. Peiris and J.R. Wood, that great Oriental novelist J. Vijayatunga and several Turkish friends (who have expressed their desire to remain anonymous) have all read parts of the typescript and given the benefit of their suggestions and experience. Above all, I am indebted to C.M. Woodhouse who read the whole of the first draft and made some penetrating and helpful criticisms. The Introduction bears witness to his great wisdom and scholarship.

I sincerely thank all the Greek-Cypriot political and religious leaders who were kind enough to grant me, on several occasions, some of their most precious hours, to discuss and debate some of the controversial issues of the last forty years.

I should like to express my appreciation for unfailing help to the staffs of the British Museum Reading Room, Public Record Office and University of London Library.

I owe a lot to the Chairman of my publishers, L.W. Carp, for giving me this great opportunity to write such a massive work on Cyprus. I would also like to thank Peter Found and Matthew Reisz.

I am forever grateful to Penny and Tracy, my two beautiful typists who between them have made my life more bearable.

Finally, I wish to record my deepest gratitude to my wife Floria, not so much for assisting me in completing this study but more for her sense of understanding, respect and patience during my six-year ordeal.

To conclude, however, I wish to reiterate that the shortcomings of the book remain entirely my own.

Part I

THE EARLY YEARS

1 *Cyprus through the centuries*

The island of Cyprus, latitude 35°N, longitude 33° 30′ E, is some 3,572 sq.m. (9,250 sq. km.) in area and is situated in the north-eastern corner of the Mediterranean sea. It is the third largest island in the Mediterranean after Sicily and Sardinia. Its greatest length including the long narrow peninsula of Cape Andrea is 140 miles and its greatest breadth 59 miles; its area is 7 per cent that of England.

At all times Cyprus has been what she is now – the watchtower and outpost of three continents. The island's strategic location has made her the envy of her neighbours, who have, from ancient times, practised a policy of territorial expansion at her expense.

The history of Cyprus, derived from its geography, begins with the neolithic (or new Stone) age, going back to the middle of the 7th millennium BC and lasting for approximately three millennia. It is now widely accepted that the first inhabitants of the island came from the nearby Syropalestinian coast. The most important neolithic settlements were in the south at Khirokitia, Kalavasos, Erimi and Sotira; on the north coast at Petra tou Limniti and in the centre of the island at Ledra (Nicosia). Scholars and students of this period are greatly indebted to the Cypriot archaeologist Dr Porphyrios Dikaios for his marvellous work on the island's Stone Age civilization.

During this period the inhabitants lived in low circular domed stone houses, similar to igloos, and were very fond of hunting. Their settlements were usually near the coast or near streams, but they had little contact with any of their continental neighbours during those years. This, of course, is not altogether surprising considering that mastery of the sea lay far in the future, as also did the technological advances which were to drive these self-sufficient food-raisers into a position of dependence upon their neighbours for certain rare and precious commodities.

The Bronze (or Copper) Age which lasted from approximately 2500 to 1500 BC characterized the next distinct stage of the island's development. Human settlements began to spread towards the centre of the island; homes with right-angled corners and interior walls which divided them into several rooms replaced the domed, igloo-like stone huts of the neolithic period. The dead were no longer buried in their homes; cemeteries or necropolises were used. The worship of divinities was introduced, and organized community life was henceforth practised.

However, the most important event in the Bronze Age was the arrival of the Achaean-Mycenaeans around the middle of the second millennium BC. At the end of the thirteenth century many of the Mycenaean settlements were afflicted with disaster, in the course of which Pylos was overwhelmed and Mycenae grievously harmed. A considerable dispersal of the mainland population took place, which resulted in the establishment of refugee settlements at widely separated points, from the Ionian islands and Achaea in the west to Chios in the east. At least one substantial group of these people (estimated at around 1,200) fled to Cyprus, where their establishment in a number of places, including Engomi, Kition and Kouklia, was of incalculable significance for the future history of the island, and true Mycenaean pottery began to be produced in sizeable quantities.

The arrival of the newcomers was important in two respects: firstly, the island's civilization was transformed and the ethnological composition of the population changed. From their Peloponnesian home, the Achaean settlers introduced into Cyprus not merely a language but names of places, institutions and cults. Secondly, the island turned towards the west and began to draw away from the east.

By the end of the second millennium more Greek colonists arrived to live in Cyprus – the island which they at first called 'Makaria' ('blessed'). (The island was also called 'Aeria', probably from the Latin word for copper, *aes*.) They came mainly from Asia Minor and their chief occupations were farming and the fine arts. Both historians and poets spoke highly of the wealth and culture of the island under kings such as Kinyras, Pylagoras, Onasagoras and Philokypros, King of

Soli, who entertained Solon, the famous Athenian statesman and lawgiver in 570 BC.

In the meantime large settlements of Phoenicians arose on the island, concerned more with trade than colonization, who came mainly from the Syrian coast. The Phoenicians favoured Persia, and so extended their sway in Cyprus at the time of the Persian domination. Kition and Amathus (in that order) were considered as having the strongest Phoenician character. After the end of the second millennium Cyprus became predominantly Greek. Colonists came from Crete, Thessaly, Macedonia and Asia Minor. The older inhabitants, i.e. the indigenous population, called 'Eteocyprians', and the Phoenicians played only a secondary part in the life of the island.

Near the end of the eighth century BC Cyprus, after an independence lasting several centuries, came under the domination of the Assyrians. The island was described as divided into city-kingdoms – Salamis, Kition, Amathus, Kourion, Paphos and Lapithos being capitals in their own right. The Cypriots, who lived in true Mycenaean fashion, fared well under the Assyrian domination and the kings enjoyed full freedom in domestic affairs.

In fact the Assyrian occupation of Cyprus was aimed at the defence of the western borders of the Assyrian empire along the coast of Syria and southern Asia Minor – political domination of the island was not intended. The Assyrian domination was very brief (it probably lasted for 50 years), but the *stele* of Sargon II, found at Kition and now in the Berlin Museum, is an interesting reminder of Assyrian supremacy. Around this time Cyprus was known as 'Iatanana'. For the next 100 years or so the Cypriots enjoyed full political independence.

The next major power to control Cyprus was Egypt. The Egyptians hold the distinction of being the first to capture the island by recourse to war. From rather scanty records we find that Hophra (reigning from 588 to 569 and known to the Greeks as 'Apries') conducted an expedition, with a strong army and fleet, against Cyprus and, after defeating the combined Cypriot and Phoenician fleet in a great sea-fight, returned to Egypt with much spoil. The island, however, was not conquered.

Amasis, who succeeded Hophra and reigned from 569 to 525,

took the island around 560. He was however a great believer in Greek culture and traditions and he proceeded to decorate many religious buildings. It was also during the reign of Amasis that another Greek settlement was established by the Milesians. The traces of Egyptian conquest are scanty and it seems to have left little impression on the island; it was probably limited to the payment of tribute and the acknowledgement of dependence.

The Egyptian hold over Cyprus was soon over. At the time of the expedition of Cyrus the Elder, King of Persia, against Babylon in 538, the Cypriots voluntarily placed their forces at his disposal. In acknowledgement of their support the Cypriots were allowed to retain their own rulers. Cyprus therefore became the western seaward link of the great Persian empire. The kings of the island were obliged to pay tribute to the King of Persia and to supply him with an army and ships for his foreign campaigns.

The greatest King of Cyprus in these times was Greek, Evelthon of Salamis, grandfather of Onesilos. He was not only the first king of the island to strike his own coins but he maintained considerable independence under Persian suzerainty. He maintained close relations with the kings of Cyrene in Africa and entertained the exiled Queen Pheretime in 530, but denied her the pleasure of raising an army to help her return to Cyrene.

Ten kingdoms in all were in existence in the middle of the fourth century: Salamis, Kition, Soli, Paphos, Kourion, Lapithos, Kyrenia, Marium, Amathus and Tamascus. Under the Persians satisfactory progress was made in the arts and general culture of the island and a particular style in sculpture, the so-called 'Cypriot character', appeared, only to suffer a severe setback a few years later in the Onesilos revolt of 499-8.

It is unnecessary here to describe in detail the course of that rising. Suffice it to say that, following the outbreak of the Ionian revolt, Onesilos, the younger brother of the pro-Persian King Gorgos of Salamis, tried to persuade him to take up arms against their rulers. There was, it is true, a strong anti-Persian faction, particularly at Soli, which had close ties with Athens. The pleading of Onesilos was in vain, but when Gorgos left the city Onesilos shut the gates against him. He persuaded all the

Cypriots, except those of the predominantly Phoenician city Amathus, to join the revolt against the Persians.

At the battle of Salamis the Greeks were their own worst enemies. During the engagement the contingent from Kourion went over to the Persians and the chariot corps from Salamis followed suit. In the ensuing rout Onesilos was killed and, as the Ionian fleet now sailed home from an apparently hopeless venture, the insurgents were left without a leader. The capitulation of Salamis spread like wildfire, although the endeavours of cities such as Soli, which held out for five months, caused myriad problems for the Persians and their allies.

Thus the Cypriots after a year of freedom were again enslaved by Persia. Onesilos, however, became a symbol of heroism after his death at Amathus. Aristokypros, son of Philokypros, was also slain by the Persians.

The kings of Cyprus continued paying tribute to Persia and fulfilled all their obligations arising from the treaties. For this reason they contributed 150 ships (the most sizeable contribution to the fleet of any Greek city, bar Athens) and fought (allegedly wearing turbans) with Xerxes in 480 when he invaded Greece. One of the first acts of Xerxes after succeeding his father Darius I was to subdue the rebellious Egyptians, who were in active revolt at the time of his accession; then he assembled a vast army from all parts of his empire, believed to be composed of 46 nations, and, with the addition of an enormous fleet furnished by his allies (especially the Phoenicians), started upon the third attempt to subjugate Greece.

At the battle of Salamis (an island just off the coast of Piraeus, the port of Athens) in 480 BC the Greek fleet of 370 galleys faced a Persian fleet of around three times its strength. The Greeks were victorious. Xerxes and his army witnessed the rout from the shores of Salamis and he was forced to postpone his land offensive. However, included in the number of distinguished commanders on the Persian side were two Cypriots – Gorgos, King of Salamis, and the wealthy Timonax, son of Timagoras, of whom nothing else is known. Nevertheless the Cypriot contribution to the expedition appears to be of minor importance.

A high point in the good relations between the Athenians and the Cypriots came with the efforts of the distinguished general, Kimon (son of the victor of Marathon, Miltiades), to end Persian domination along the coastline of south-western Asia Minor; if it were successful the liberation of Cyprus would follow. In the year 466 BC Kimon set off and encountered the enemy at the Pamphylia region, situated on the south coast of Asia Minor. He launched his attack while his opponents were still waiting for a reinforcement of 80 vessels from Cyprus. Kimon followed up his success at sea by landing his troops and engaging the Persian army, which was completely routed. The victory was rendered even more decisive by Kimon's success in capturing the 80 ships which the Persian commanders had been waiting for. The victory of the river Eurymedon must rank as one of the most glorious in the annals of Greece.

Even though this victory secured the adherence of the south and south-west of Asia Minor to the Delos (Athenian) Confederacy, and marked the climax of Kimon's career, the expedition did not lead to an attempt to 'liberate' Cyprus. However, in the summer of 450 BC Kimon, accompanied by Anaxicrates, set sail for Cyprus with a fleet of 200 triremes (ancient warships with three banks or rows of oars). The Athenians and their allies won a decisive victory, on both sea and land, at Salamis, but both leaders died and in 448 the Athenians entered into a peace agreement with Artaxerxes according to which they abandoned Cyprus to the Persians.

Cyprus played a part too in the later Greco-Persian wars and under Evagoras I (King of Salamis from approximately 411 to 374 BC) the Cypriots were again temporarily 'liberated'. Evagoras, a Greek captain of fortune, wrested the city of Salamis from Abdemon, its Phoenician king, by a daring *coup de main*. Evagoras justified his own assumption of royal authority over Salamis by tracing his genealogy back to the founder of the city Teucer, brother of Ajax. He was, by all accounts, the greatest King of Cyprus, who nurtured the Greek civilization of the island and spread it to the surrounding 'barbarian' countries. During his reign many Athenians came and settled on the island.

Evagoras united the cities of Cyprus under his leadership and then declared war on Persia. It was however an uneasy alliance because of the internal dissensions within the Greek cities – Greek against Greek, Greek against Phoenician, Phoenician against Phoenician. Nevertheless he amassed a fleet of 200 triremes and a large and well-appointed army and had as allies Athens, Egypt and Tyre. For ten years (390 to 380) he was at odds with Persia, continuing a most unequal conflict with quite exceptional heroism.

Evagoras is one of the most famous characters in the history of Cyprus; he is described as having excelled all his contemporaries in his beauty, his military ability and the ardour of his patriotism. Thus Isocrates, his friend and admirer as well as the tutor of his son Nicocles, considered Evagoras the model of the ideal ruler. He described him as such in the three orations which he presented to Nicocles.

The intervening Peace of Antalcidas in 386 is worth a brief mention. Although Evagoras was not a party to it, the Athenians recognized the claim of the Persian king Artaxerxes that all the cities of Asia and the islands Clazomenae and Cyprus should be subject to him. Yet, 54 years after Antalcidas, Alexander the Great freed Cyprus. The battle of Issus in 333, with 35,000 Macedonians fighting a vast horde of Asiatics and 30,000 Greek mercenaries under Darius, King of Persia, was decisive. Alexander then received 120 ships from Cyprus to help in the siege of Tyre in 332. This strongly fortified city, built on an island separated from the mainland by a channel 1,000 yards wide, was finally taken after seven months. Eight thousand Tyrians fell and about 30,000 were sold into slavery, which reduced Phoenician chances of dominating Cyprus. In his *Alexander's Anabasis* the historian Arrian described in detail the siege of Tyre and the active participation in it of the kings of Cyprus, particularly Pnytagoras of Salamis, who won great glory for his resilience and valour.

Thus between 332 and 323 the kings of Cyprus retained sovereignty over their own cities. Alexander left them in undisputed possession of their own little kingdoms, honoured them with his friendship and, later on, entrusted them with important duties. Thus Stasanor of Soli became governor of the Persian province of Drangiana. Furthermore the kings of Salamis and Soli, Nicocreon (who succeeded and followed the pro-Hellenic policy of Pnytagoras) and Pasicrates, were well spoken of. The only administrative change of any significance was that Cyprus became part of the huge system of Alexandrine coinage. Another point of major importance was that commercial relations between Greece, particularly Athens, and Cyprus were very active. The Cypriot economy reached new heights.

Because of its geographical and economic importance Cyprus was involved in the scramble for power between Alexander's successors – Antigonus and Ptolemy. After a struggle which lasted for nearly 29 years, Ptolemy obtained Cyprus. The Ptolemaic period lasted from 294 to 58 BC – nearly two and a half centuries.

During that period the island achieved a fairly high degree of culture and prosperity, with the cities preserving a certain amount of autonomy. In practice, the masters of the cities were the commanders of the garrisons who gave their orders to the elected organs of native government. The island was however administered by viceroys and regarded as one of the most valuable possessions of the Egyptian Crown. In fact the revenues which the Ptolemies drew from Cyprus were enormous. Hence came the copper that Egypt needed so much; here too were built many ships for the Egyptian navy and mercantile fleet.

Even though the age of the city kingdoms was over, the Cypriots participated in the regulation of their cultural affairs. Besides 'To Koinon ton Kyprion', the League of the Cypriots, a federation of semi-autonomous communities, was a powerful force making for cohesion.

Next, for nearly 300 years, from 58 BC to AD 330, the Romans were the rulers of the island, although for several years, probably from 47 BC to the death of Cleopatra in 30 BC, Cyprus returned to Ptolemaic rule. It is interesting to recall that Mark Antony, who met Cleopatra at Tarsus in 41 BC and married her at Antioch four years later, presented Cyprus to his wife and her sister Arsinoe because it was, he explained, 'supreme in beauty and well above all other places'.

Cyprus became part of the province of Cilicia (Roman from 103 BC), which was governed by a proconsul. Porcius Marcus Cato became its first governor. Under Octavian (called Augustus from 27 BC) the island became first an imperial province (31 BC) and then, nine years later, a senatorial province again governed by a pro-consul. The capital was henceforth transferred from the ancient site of Salamis to Paphos, the centre for the worship of Aphrodite.

Under the Romans Cyprus was not only robbed of its treasures (especially those of Salamis) but was made a place of banishment for the debauched nobles of the Re, who, having disgusted the not-too-sensitive susceptibilities of Roman morality, were sent to Paphos to finish their 'sensual' studies. On the whole, however, the material lot of the Cypriot showed a slight improvement. Here, as everywhere, the Romans paid great attention to road-making. For example, they encircled the main part of the island with a road running from Salamis in the east diagonally to Kyrenia in the north and from there roughly following the west and south coasts round, and so back to Salamis.

The general peace of the island during those years was disturbed only a few times. Around AD 45-6 Christianity was introduced into Cyprus by Paul, Barnabas and his nephew Mark. The conversion of the proconsul Sergius Paulus to Christianity at Paphos in AD 46 marked the beginning of the penetration of the new religion into the Roman administration. This was an important event, accompanied by radical changes in the life of the Cypriots and, of course, others. The island's history, so deeply affected by the new religion, was to be dominated thereafter by Christianity.

In spite of the evident difficulties (for example, the island's Jews were faithful to their religion and system of worship and the Greeks or Gentiles had their own deeply entrenched deities and methods of worship), the spread of Christianity continued steadily during the first three centuries of our era. By the fourth century the new religion had an undisputed dominance. Among those who contributed to this triumph were: Lazarus, who according to tradition was raised from the dead by Christ and later became the patron saint of Larnaca; Spyridon of Tremithus, who took part in the First Ecumenical Council in AD 325; and St Epiphanius of Constantia (Salamis), who though not a native of Cyprus distinguished himself as a scholar and played an important part in the various church controversies of the fourth century.

The religious zeal of the Cypriots expressed itself in the

establishment of monasteries (those of Chrysorrhoyiatissa and Machaeras date from the twelfth century), the building of churches and the beautification of both with frescoes and icons of the highest artistry. The Byzantine period and the years immediately following are notable in this respect. Important frescoes survive in the mountains dating from the eleventh century: St Nicholas of the Roof (*tis stegis*) in Kakopetria; St Mary of Araka in the Pitsillia region; St Neophytos Monastery in Paphos, and so forth.

Barnabas visited Cyprus for a second time and was again accompanied by Mark. He was martyred by the Jews at Salamis and was buried by Mark with a copy of the Gospel of St Matthew which he had always carried with him. The discovery of the tomb by Archbishop Anthemius in the reign of Zeno (474-91) was of paramount importance. Attempts by the Church of Antioch (claiming that it was the first see of St Peter and thus superior to Cyprus) to put the island under its administrative control were countered by his findings, which proved that Cyprus was just as much an apostolic foundation. The Cypriot Church became autocephalous (independent); this was again confirmed in AD 691-2 at the Quini-Sext or Trullan Council at Constantinople.

Towards the end of the reign of Trajan, around 115-16, a widespread insurrection of the Jews broke out in Cyrene, Egypt and Cyprus. In fact when Jerusalem fell in AD 70 many banished Jews had fled to Cyprus. The revolt spread from country to country and was marked by ghastly atrocities. The trouble must have arisen in the usual way, with racial conflict between Jews and Greeks, but it rapidly developed into a desperate struggle of the Jews against the imperial government. In Cyprus the revolt was led by Artemion. Around one million lost their lives in the three countries. The suppression of the Jewish revolt is the sole recorded military operation in the history of Roman Cyprus.

From rather inconclusive historical evidence it is deduced that the dead on the island numbered about 250,000 (estimated at around 15 per cent of the total population), of which 24,000 are said to have been massacred in one day. Salamis was utterly destroyed and its non-Jewish population practically exterminated. The settlement of Jews in the island was henceforth forbidden, and even those driven there by adverse winds were, it is believed, put to death. Entry was allowed again only after 1160.

The tranquillity of the island was again disturbed in AD 269. After the failure of the Gothic invaders (who came from the western Black Sea area) in Moesia, part of their fleet made a series of raids through the Aegean, attacking Greece, the Cyclades, Crete, Rhodes and then Cyprus. The damage to the island however was slight and the expedition, ravaged by disease, eventually came to a sudden end.

Further incidents, with several Byzantine rulers, failed to bring any change of masters to the island. But its cities were repeatedly ruined by seismic convulsions. Especially serious were those of 15 BC, which destroyed Paphos (a flourishing and sacred metropolis during the Roman period), and AD 76-7, when several cities, amongst them Salamis and Paphos, were destroyed.

From 330 to 1191 Cyprus was part of the Byzantine complex. Five major events must be briefly mentioned:

1   The earthquakes of 332 and 342 which destroyed Salamis, Paphos (not rebuilt for some time) and other cities and the 30- to 40-year drought and famine of the first half of the fourth century (when Cyprus was depopulated) left their ugly scars on the island. Salamis was rebuilt a few years later through the material aid given by Constantine, the son and heir to Constantine the Great, who renamed the city Constantia. The new city replaced Paphos as the island's capital and became the seat of the first bishop, who thus became Archbishop of Cyprus. His name was Epiphanius (later to be called Saint Epiphanius) and he led the Cypriot Church from 368 to 403.

2   In 488 Emperor Zeno the Isaurian declared the Cyprus Church autocephalous. Further imperial privileges were granted: to this day the archbishops sign with red ink (a distinction which none but the emperor enjoyed), wear a purple cloak at Church festivals and carry an imperial sceptre instead of a pastoral staff.

After two centuries the independence of the Church of Cyprus was again confirmed. Justinian, in his struggle with the Arabs, broke the compact of 689 between Byzantine and Islam by which the tribute of Cyprus was divided and in 691 removed a large proportion of the island's population to the Hellespont (Dardanelles) and other districts in the south and west of Asia Minor. Just as Justinian I had founded Nova Justiniana in the previous century, so in 691 Justinian II founded the city of Nea Justinianopolis for the Cypriots. The synod of the same year recognized the Metropolitan of Cyprus, now Bishop of Nea Justinianopolis, as Metropolitan of the Hellespont and enacted that he should enjoy the same independence of the patriarch as in Cyprus. Once again therefore the autocephaly of the Church of Cyprus and the prerogatives of its archbishop were recognized and definitely asserted. A few years later (before the close of the century) Cyprus was repeopled when most of the inhabitants of Nea Justinianopolis were sent back to the island by Leontius, the new emperor.

3   Also of great significance were the Arab raids between the seventh and tenth centuries, which brought great destruction to the island. In contrast Cyprus enjoyed a peaceful existence during the fifth and sixth centuries. Especially severe were the raids of 647, led by Muawiya, the Emir of Syria, who commanded 1,700 ships, and of 653, when Muawiya despatched a second force of 500 ships under Abu'l-Awar. The Arabs carried out a systematic policy of senseless cruelty, brutality and desecration. Although the garrison established in the island was withdrawn by the Caliph Yazid around 682, Cyprus continued to pay tribute.

Thus from 653 on, for about a generation, very little is heard of Cyprus. It is probable that the island, having been twice plundered within a few years, offered little prospect of further booty, and the tribute seems to have been continuously collected by the Arab authorities. There were, however, further raids in 743, 747, 772, 790 and 806. The last, under Harun-ar-Rashid, was the most destructive. Alleging that the Cypriots had violated the treaty of neutrality which since 698 had regulated their relations with both Byzantium and Islam, the Arabs landed in Cyprus, laid waste the island and took back to Raqqa (a town on the Euphrates) 16,000 prisoners, including the archbishop, other ecclesiastics and many archons. Once the neutrality treaty was renewed most of them were allowed to return.

The Arabs, it may be noted, never made any organized attempt to become permanent rulers of Cyprus. They were content with the loot and prisoners their raids yielded. The raids however caused a marked movement of the population from the coastal towns to the interior of the island, where they sought refuge in caves and fortifications. Thus the three principal castles on the Kyrenia range, St Hilarion, Kantara and Buffavento, were erected during the Arab raids as a defence against the 'barbarian' onslaughts. Nevertheless, in spite of all these difficulties, Cyprus was still considered a place of refuge by the Christians of Syria and Palestine.

In 965, Emperor Nicephorus Phokas sent General Nikitas Chalcutzes to Cyprus to repel the Arab raiders once and for all. The Byzantine fleet achieved the final conquest of the island and the defeat of the Egyptian fleet in August 965. Cyprus soon recovered from the suffering inflicted on her by the Arab raids and was turned quietly into a Byzantine *theme* or military province.

4   The two risings of 1042 and 1092 and the attack on Cyprus which began in 1156 were also significant. Both risings were attempts by local governors to proclaim Cyprus independent. The first was led by Theophilos Eroticos and the second by Rhapsomates. Both revolts had been planned in collaboration with Tzachas, the Emir of Smyrna who had been raiding the Aegean islands, and both had been vigorously suppressed by the Grand Duke John Ducas, brother-in-law of Emperor Alexios Comnenos. Nicosia, which played an important part in the second revolt, became the capital of Cyprus in the eleventh century.

In 1156, Reynald of Chatillon (since 1153 husband of Constance, Norman princess of Antioch), together with the Armenian prince Thoros, led a devastating and unprovoked attack on Cyprus from Armeno-Cilicia in southern Asia Minor. It failed and the island remained a Byzantine province. In 1158 it suffered yet another raid from the organized Arab bandits of Egypt. In 1160 it was raided, once more, by Raymond III, Prince of Antioch. Cyprus, by reason of its geographical position, size and economic potential, has always been a target for more powerful neighbours.

5 Isaac Ducas Comnenos, nephew of the old Emperor
Manuel Comnenos, reached Cyprus in 1184 with a small body
of armed men from Isauria (now southern Turkey directly to
the north of Cyprus) and by showing forged letters of
appointment made himself independent ruler of Cyprus. He
succeeded through sheer force and intrigue in becoming the
tyrannical emperor of the island. Isaac was justly accused of
wanton murder, ravishing of virgins and reducing the wealthy
to beggary and starvation by robbery. According to a
chronicler, 'the island groaned beneath this scourge of fate, and
he reduced the Cypriots to such a state of despair that all were
ready to welcome anything which afforded a means of escape
from such tyranny'. Their prayers were soon answered.

In 1191, Cyprus fell into the hands of Richard I, the great
crusading warrior, King of England. The first king to adopt
arms consisting of three lions 'passant guardant' was Richard
'Coeur-de-Lion'. Perhaps more by accident than by design he
reached Limassol on 6 May 1191, but did not go ashore. His
fleet, whilst around the Cretan waters, encountered a severe
storm and its ships were separated. Among the 25 or so missing
were the three dromonds (large medieval ships for war or
commerce) which carried Berengaria (his future wife), Joan
(his favourite sister), the greater part of his treasure and the
Great Seal. Trying to reach the shores of Cyprus, some of the
ships were driven on to the rocks by adverse waves and wind.
Part of the crew, including Richard's signet bearer, were
drowned, but those who managed to swim to safety were
harshly treated by Isaac.

Richard sent a courteous message to Isaac requesting him to
make amends for the evil that had been done to the shipwrecked
pilgrims. The king's emissary was duly insulted. Richard at
once shouted 'Aux armes!' After a brief but costly skirmish, the
port of Limassol (then at Amathus) was taken. Isaac retreated,
but from his stronghold in Kolossi castle sent an insulting
message to Richard demanding that he should quit the island
without delay. Kolossi was attacked and captured. Richard
returned to Limassol with immense booty, including the
imperial standard of Isaac which he dedicated to the memory of
Saint Edmund. On his return to England he deposited it upon
the tomb of the martyr prince in Suffolk.

In the meantime Richard was joined in Limassol by a number of lords from Syria accompanied by around 160 knights. Amongst them was Guy de Lusignan, who came to seek support for his claim to the crown of Jerusalem. On 12 May 1191, Richard married Berengaria, daughter of the King of Navarre, in the chapel of Saint George at Limassol and she was crowned Queen of England by John Fitz, bishop of Evreux. The king had earlier been crowned at Westminster on 3 September 1189.

At the end of May, Isaac at last surrendered after suffering a humiliating defeat at Tremethousha – the ancient Trimythos, principal town of Mesaoria. The career of the self-styled 'Emperor of Cyprus' was at an end. The Anglo-Normans under Richard were henceforth in complete control of Cyprus and easily subdued resistance even in the remotest parts of the island. A revolt under the leadership of a monk, a relative of Isaac, ended in failure.

With the conquest of Cyprus, the provisioning of the crusading forces once more became possible and for many years the island proved indispensable to the Christian armies. Richard continued on his way eastwards, leaving Cyprus on 1 June, and, after visiting Tyre and Tripoli *en route*, arrived at Acre seven days later.

Richard, however, like all his predecessors, had robbed the island of most of its treasures. Archbishop Constantius of Sinai, writing in 1766, rather unfairly described him as a 'bloodthirsty beast' and explained that the 'poor Cypriots little knew that they had escaped the wolf to fall into the jaws of the bear'. The English king, furthermore, passed the island over to the Order of the Knights Templar for 100,000 byzants (or besants, the great gold currency of Europe in the Middle Ages), of which 40,000 was to be paid at once and the remainder by instalments.

The arrogant and vicious Templars, however, soon found their new burden a heavy one. The war with Saladin was already absorbing all their energies in Syria and the small garrison they were able to maintain in Cyprus could barely cope with the impoverished Cypriots. Accordingly in May 1192 (following the Easter massacre) they begged Richard to buy back the island on the same terms as he had sold it, but Richard, who was not prepared to lose the cash he had received, induced Guy de Lusignan to acquire the island as some compensation for the loss of his kingdom of Jerusalem. He took possession of his realm towards the end of May.

From 1192 to 1489 the island passed into the hands of the Lusignans, and Cyprus became a Frankish kingdom, successor to the Kingdom of Jerusalem, though the title of King of Cyprus was first assumed by Guy de Lusignan's brother Aimery, who succeeded him on his death in 1194. (Three hundred French noblemen, a personal guard of 200 and many soldiers accompanied Guy and settled in Nicosia.)

The Lusignans ruled the island on the feudal system – all privileges belonged to the nobles, with the masses reduced to serfdom. Before 1192 the Cypriots were harshly taxed and the peasants were not allowed to leave the land on which they worked. Otherwise they were neglected by their imperial rulers. After 1192 the Cypriots were even worse off than before. Their lands were distributed among the barons and knights, to whom they were attached as serfs, and, in the words of Porcacchi, a Venetian historian, 'the tyranny of the masters grew so fiercely insolent that some bartered their slaves unblushingly for dogs or other animals'.

What many Greeks saw as a retrograde step was the establishment in the island of the Catholic Church as the official Church. The *Constitutio Cypria* or *Bulla Cypria* of Pope Alexander IV (3 July 1260) confirmed the superiority of the Latin Church but did not put an end to the troubles. This edict, which reorganized the Roman Catholic Church on the island, forbade the election of a new Orthodox archbishop and ensured the subjugation, both ecclesiastical and economic, of the Orthodox bishops to the Catholic ones.

The Latins therefore persecuted the Greek Orthodox Church of Cyprus, robbing it of its revenues, controlling its ordinations and burning its bishops as heretics. Hence in 1231 13 Greek monks were condemned to death at Kantara because they refused to accept certain Catholic beliefs. Yet the Orthodox Church thrived under persecution and its monasteries, particularly those in the remote mountain ranges where the painted churches may still be seen today, continued to prosper. The Cypriot Church had undoubtedly become a focus for the islanders' obstinate sense of Greekness in an alien Latin world.

However, the lot of the Orthodox Cypriot was improved in the fifteenth century by the passionately Orthodox queen of John II, Helen Paleologa. Helen was the daughter of Theodore II Paleologus, ruler of the Morea. Helen's daughter Carlotta also followed a pro-Hellenic policy.

Rulers such as Hugh II and Hugh III (called 'the Great') in the thirteenth century, Hugh IV and Peter I in the fourteenth century, contributed immensely towards the stability and financial prosperity of the island. The years between 1320 and 1360 were especially prosperous. However, rivalries, claims and counter-claims, feudal disputes and the inefficiency of other rulers, caused the decline of the island.

During the reign of Peter I Turkish vessels twice attacked Cyprus. Taking advantage of the seriousness of the plague (the Black Death of 1348-9 took the lives of something between a quarter and a half of the inhabitants), and of the king's absence in France, these vessels landed first near Pentayia and then near Rizokarpaso. Looting and senseless destruction followed. The Cypriots however retaliated, pursued the Turkish vessels and landed in a Turkish town called Anemouri. The place, directly to the north of Kyrenia, was pillaged and many hostages were taken, just as the Turks had done earlier.

Following a quarrel dating from 1364, Famagusta was taken by the Genoese from Peter II in 1374. The town continued to be a colony of that commercial republic until 29 August 1464, when it was reconquered by James II, the illegitimate son of John II.

At the beginning of the fifteenth century the island suffered a series of disasters. It was ravaged successively by plagues (the one of June 1438 resulted in many deaths and lasted for 17 months), locusts and droughts; in the midst of such misfortunes the Sultan of Egypt, accusing the Cypriots of allowing the roaming pirates to pillage the Saracens and then buying the booty, declared war and invaded the island in 1424. The Cypriot forces were defeated at Khirokitia and King Janus was taken prisoner and carried to Cairo in 1426. (He obtained his freedom by consenting to a ransom plus an annual tribute of 5,000 ducats to the Sultan.) To this day the site of the battle can be seen. It is called 'Kremmos tous Frangous' – the cliff of the Franks.

The island was then overrun by the Egyptian troops;
Nicosia, the capital, was occupied, its fortifications destroyed
and its palaces reduced to ruins. The churches, monasteries
and houses of Christians were pillaged and many of them were
taken prisoner by the Saracens. All this was followed by a
peasant insurrection when many rose in rebellion and pillaged
everything belonging to the Christian inhabitants; many
Christians were killed. Leontios Machairas, secretary to King
Janus, gave a first-class account in his *Chronicle of Cyprus* of the
fortunes of the Lusignans in Cyprus from 1359 to 1432. He
stated that 'they did many ill deeds which God would not
endure'.

The Republic of Venice, by a stroke of diplomatic craft,
succeeded in inducing James II to marry Katherine Cornaro,
daughter of the Venetian patrician Mark Cornaro. James did
not long survive this marriage. After his death, which was
attributed to poison, the republic succeeded in placing Queen
Katherine under a most humiliating tutelage. Furthermore, the
crafty Venetian senators did not limit their acts to this
unjustifiable interference. In 1489, having poisoned her son
James III, they compelled Katherine to yield to them the
kingdom of Cyprus.

The Lusignans, though deprived of their royal rights,
remained in Cyprus even after the expulsion of the Venetians
by the Turks in 1571. This is borne out by the number of
languages spoken on the island, French following Greek as the
second language for many years. During the 297-year Lusignan
rule, the following were the monarchs of Cyprus. For almost the
same number of years they carried the empty titles of King of
Jerusalem and, from 1368, of Armenia:

Guy de Lusignan (Lord of the Island)	1192-4
Aimery	1194-1205
Hugh I	1205-18
Henry I	1218-53
Hugh II	1253-67
Hugh III	1267-84
John I	1284-5
Henry II	1285-1324
Hugh IV	1324-59

Peter I	1359-69
Peter II	1369-82
James I	1382-98
Janus	1398-1432
John II	1432-58
Carlotta (Queen)	
Louis of Savoy (King Consort)	1458-60
James II	1460-73
James III	1973-4
Katherine Cornaro (Queen)	1474-89

After nearly 300 years of the Lusignans, the Cypriots had to contend with the Venetians for another 82 years. The Venetian period was characterized by intolerable misrule. The persecution of the Church and people was intensified and culture on the island sank to very low depths. 'We have escaped from the grasp of the dog to fall into that of the lion,' wrote a Christian abbot.

The Venetians regarded Cyprus primarily as a military post. They built magnificent fortifications at Nicosia, Famagusta and elsewhere, but contented themselves with drawing from the island as large a revenue as its impoverished province could supply. With the exception of an ill-timed abortive rising in 1546, of which very little has been recorded, the history of Venetian rule is a mere chronicle of decay. Droughts, floods, locusts and earthquakes added to the distress caused by misgovernment. Trade languished, manufactures practically ceased and all who could afford to do so emigrated.

Hence between 1489 and 1571 the Venetians exhibited little but an insatiable lust for commercial gain and an overbearing, unsympathetic spirit towards the native population. In fact the treasury of the island was in a chronic state of depletion – as it had been under the Lusignans. Following the pattern of their predecessors, all sorts of devices were used to 'ease' the situation: for example, the sale of freedom to the serfs and the sale of entire villages belonging to the royal domain to private persons. Both instances gave ample opportunities for corrupt dealings by officials. Martin von Baumgarten, on his return from the pilgrimage to the Holy Land and Mount Sinai, visited Cyprus in 1508 (staying from 8 February to 28 March), and confirms the misery that existed:

All the inhabitants of Cyprus are slaves to the Venetians, being obliged to pay to the state a third part of all their increase or income, whether the product of their ground, or corn, wine, oil or of their cattle, or any other thing. Besides every man of them is bound to work for the state two days of the week wherever they shall please to appoint him: and if any shall fail, by reason of some other business of their own, or for indisposition of body, then they are made to pay a fine for as many days as they are absent from their work. And which is more, there is yearly some tax or other imposed on them, with which the poor common people are so flayed and pillaged, that they hardly have wherewithal to keep soul and body together.[1]

The Venetian dominance of this most noble island came to an end in 1571. The Venetians, who obtained it mainly by extortion, shamefully lost it by the negligence, jealousy and cursed pride of those to whom the preservation of it had been entrusted. In the main the guilty ones were Dandolo, who had assumed the supreme command, and Eugene Sinclitico, Count Roucha, who according to Alexander Drummond, a British diplomat, was 'a brave but empty madman'.

Following their capture of Syria in 1516, Egypt in 1517, Rhodes in 1522 and Constantinople in 1543, the Turks directed their energies towards Cyprus. The Sultan, Selim II ('the Sot'), prompted by the renegade Joseph Miquez Nasi (see page 51), a Portuguese Jew, who held in fief the island of Naxos and hoped for the investiture of Cyprus, set himself to attempt its conquest. Selim, also known as 'the Drunkard', ignored the considerations which had weighed with his predecessors that the enterprise was difficult in itself and certain to stir up against his empire the forces of the Christian princes joined to the powerful armaments of the Venetians.

By late May 1570 the Turks carefully prepared a well-equipped fleet at Constantinople. Under the command of Mustapha Pasha (perhaps the toughest but certainly one of the most far-sighted Ottoman commanders, whose nickname 'Lala' meant 'tutor'), with Piale Pasha as admiral of the fleet, the Turkish invading force, which consisted of well over 220 long vessels ofwhich 160 were galleys, the rest galliots, and about 80 ships of burthen of various kinds, set sail on 27 June.

On 1 July the Turkish forces landed near Limassol. The town automatically capitulated. At once the Turks set fire to Limassol and to a few villages in the neighbourhood which had been abandoned by their defenders and with fire and pillage laid waste the surrounding countryside. The next town to be pillaged was Nicosia. The defenders of the capital numbered just over 11,000 of which:

1,500 were Italian paid soldiers, many of whom were disabled by illness,
3,000 were cernide or island militia,
2,600 were armed citizens,
2,100 were natives paid either by the state or by private persons,
1,000 were gentlemen adventurers and others of noble blood,
  500 were Albanian horsemen,
  200 were Albanian infantry,
  200 were native artillery men and
   60 were Italian artillery men.

Uberto Foglietta, a leading authority of the period, says: 'The government had collected also within the walls about 8,000 villagers, fit only for manual labour. Of women, children and others unfit for service there were 56,000, so that the total number of mouths to be fed reached 76,000.'[2]

Against this pitiful Cypriot number, the Turks had over 100,000 of which half were paid infantry. The inhabitants however were confident of outright victory. Such confidence was raised even higher by their belief in heavenly aid. A smart skirmish soon ensued between the besiegers and two companies of soldiers who came out of the city. Captain Andrea Cortese, an Albanian, fought long and splendidly. He had charged however too recklessly into the heart of the enemy, who soon surrounded him. The Turks were astounded at the valour of a single man fighting against such odds. He was taken prisoner on 9 August and according to F. Falchetti, a chronicler of the time, himself taken prisoner and then sold, 'his head was cut off'. The heroic resistance of other captains such as Ercole Podocataro and Andrea Speglio helped to inflict heavy losses on the invaders. Nicosia nevertheless soon fell. The siege had lasted 48 days.

Gio. Sozomeno, who served as an engineer during the siege and was then made a prisoner at its fall, wrote that the slaughter which lasted six days was so great that 'the nobles who survived were some 25 or 30, with no great number of citizens'. Elaborating on the above, Paolo Paruta, a prominent Venetian statesman and historian, recorded the following:

> The Turks ran without any order or discipline all over the City, plundering the houses, destroying the churches, dishonouring matrons, violating virgins, and putting all to the sword, without any distinction either of sex, age, or condition. So as the Turks slew that day above 20,000 persons; and those whose lives were spared by the cruel army, rather for their greater punishment, than out of any charity, were tied in chains, dragged over the dead carcasses of their parents and friends, and carried away prisoners.[3]

Hence owing to the incapacity and disunity of the Venetian leaders, the victors had made an easy conquest of the capital, but the Turks dishonoured their success by scenes of savage butchery and spoliation. The nobility were slain and the whole town was delivered up to the fury and lust of the troops. Giacomo Diedo, a Venetian senator, wrote: 'The victorious soldiery, satiated with booty, blood and lust, gave further vent to their execrable savagery by tearing from their graves the bones and dust of the dead, and scattering them in fiendish rage over the streets.'[4]

With Nicosia burning, it was now the turn of Famagusta. The main strength of the town consisted of 2,500 Venetians, 2,500 Cypriot soldiers and 200 Albanian horsemen. Marco Antonio Bragadino, the town's leader and governor-general, endeavoured with spirited speeches to bolster the courage of the inhabitants, explaining that the time had come for them to prove the true courage of which for months past he had seen indications. 'No glory', he said, 'that warriors had earned in any age could be greater than that which is reserved for you who, in defending against the might of the Ottoman Empire a fortress so far from other Christian lands, will ensure the preservation of our flourishing kingdom from enslavement by barbarians'.

Throughout the siege Bragadino organized scores of sorties

from the walls of Famagusta, thus giving his attackers the impression that his defending garrison was much larger than it really was. The purpose of these forays was not only to harass the enemy but to obtain more food for all those who sheltered within the walls. After a blockade of ten months Famagusta fell on 1 August 1571. It was in fact prolonged in the vain hope of receiving help from Venice.

With the siege at an end, the terms of surrender were not respected and the massacre of Nicosia was repeated. The treatment meted out to the gallant Bragadino (his three lieutenants Baglioni, Martinengo and Quirini were executed in his presence) topped all other atrocities. After being subjected to the most excruciating public tortures, which he bore with great fortitude, (Mustapha three times made him hold out his neck under the axe; he cut off his nose and ears; stretched him on the ground and trampled on him using all kinds of insults), he was flayed alive and his skin was stuffed with straw and, suspended to the yard-arm of a vessel, sent to Constantinople. His skin was then exposed in the prison in which the Christian prisoners and slaves were confined. It remained there for 25 years until redeemed by his brother Antony and three sons, Mark, Hermolaus and Antony, for a great price and laid in its present resting place in the church of Saints John and Paul at Venice.

The siege of Famagusta however was costly. It has been estimated that the Turks lost over 50,000 men, amongst them many prominent nobles and commanders, such as the Pasha of Anatolia, Suleiman Bey, and the Sanjaq of Antippo. This fact alone spurred the invaders on to even greater atrocities. Paolo Paruta, in his most lucid account of the sieges of Nicosia and Famagusta, recorded the deeds of Mustapha: 'It was mere madness which stirred him to rage even against the dead. He entered the Episcopal Church of Saint Nicholas, caused the graves to be opened and the bones scattered. He destroyed the altars and the images of the saints, and committed other bestial and cruel acts for which he was much blamed even by his own people.'[5]

With the fall of Nicosia and Famagusta the rest of the island was occupied without opposition. However, there was also the battle of Lepanto (now known as Návpaktos) in the Corinthian

Gulf. The forces of Don John (not yet 25 years of age) representing Spain, Venice, Genoa, Malta and the Papal States, inflicted a crushing defeat on a massive Turkish-Algerian fleet. The Christian alliance lost around 8,000 men and their opponents around 25,000. Some 12,000 Christian slaves were rescued from their galleys.

However, the effects of the victory in 1571 were moral rather than material. Following the abortive campaign by the Christian armada in 1572, a treaty was signed at Constantinople on 7 March 1573 by which it was agreed that the Sultan should retain Cyprus and that the expenses of his expedition should be refunded to him. Consequently only Crete, Paros and the Ionian islands remained in Venetian hands.

The Cyprus War of 1570-3 was over. It exacted however from the Turks and their allies a large expenditure and no inconsiderable loss of men and munitions, and the almost total destruction of their effective naval forces at Lepanto. This caused the Turks to commit unheard-of barbarities in all parts of the island. Thus the old of both sexes with the ugly women and children unfit for service were built up within one funeral pile in the market place of Nicosia and there burned alive. Thousands were carried off the island and sold as slaves and two of the largest vessels were filled with jewels, plate and furniture of prodigious value.

Acclaimed as the conqueror of Cyprus, Mustapha returned to Constantinople with 21 galleys. On board one of these ships he put the nobles and most beautiful of the young Cypriot women, to grace his own triumph and to enrich the seraglio of his master. But one of the ladies, Maria Sinclitiki, having procured a lighted match crept down into the powder room and blew up the ship. Together with another ship close by it was instantly destroyed.

Thus Europe's bulwark against the Ottomans and the most important base of the Venetians in the east had fallen. Cyprus remained in Turkish hands until 1878 when it was conditionally ceded to Great Britain. For 307 years the Cypriots suffered under their new rulers. The period was marked by misgovernment, earthquakes, epidemics and plagues of locusts. Sir George Hill wrote:

The war had reduced Cyprus to a sorry state. It was all the worse because from the capture of Famagusta until the next harvest there was a great dearth . . . the island was almost desert, the only part cultivated being the hilly country of the west. The desolation which too often followed in the wake of Ottoman conquest was already evident. Those of the upper classes who had ransomed themselves and remained in the island were reduced to extreme poverty, and had to make a living as muleteers or pedlars.[6]

It was often said that nature seemed to have combined with man to accomplish the island's ruin. Serfdom however disappeared and after the expulsion of the Latin priests the Greek Orthodox Church was restored. The Greeks of the island were recognized as a 'millet' or nation under the leadership of the Church of Cyprus and its archbishop who was, especially since 1660, the 'millet bashi' or ethnarch. The Church in fact was the upholder and protagonist of the continuous existence of a well-defined Greek Cypriot national community. Moreover, for many years of Turkish rule a certain measure of autonomy was granted to the Christian population.

Generally speaking, the administration of the island was in the hands of the governor called a Mutassurif, assisted by a council over which he presided. It was composed of the Mufti, or highest mussulman religious authority, the Greek archbishop, the Evcaf-Nazir, or administrator of mussulman religious property, three mussulmans and two Christian notables. The council usually met once a week and its decisions were embodied in documents called 'musbatas', which were signed by all the members present. From its membership it can be seen that all initiative came from the Mohammedan majority.

Cyprus was then divided into 17 cadelisks, or administrative districts (reduced to six during the nineteenth century), each having its agha or governor and cadi or minister of justice. Turkish administration and personnel varied tremendously over the years. Favouritism and corruption, the twin cankers of Ottoman rule, determined the choice of the highest officers in the state. With total population declining, the composition was also radically altered. Sir Harry Luke explains:

The conquest of 1571 had introduced into Cyprus, the bulk of whose inhabitants had hitherto been Greek in religion and language, a considerable number of Ottoman Turks. The original Turkish settlers were principally drawn from Lala Mustapha's soldiers, who were given fiefs in the island by Sultan Selim; but they were supplemented from time to time by Turkish immigration from Anatolia and Rumelia. The Turks thus became a permanent element of the population of Cyprus; they maintained relations with their Greek Christian neighbours which, if not intimate, were on the whole quite amicable.[7]

In addition the Turkish population of Cyprus originated from the Franks and to a smaller extent from the Greeks, who in order to escape the massacre or enslavement which followed the Turkish conquest of the island adopted Islam in order to enjoy greater quiet but continued secretly to observe the numerous customs of the Greek Orthodox Church. These were often called renegades, cryptochristians, or were simply known as *linobambakoi* (linen-cottoners). Niven Kerr, the British consul in Cyprus, observed in a letter to Sir Stratford Canning on 4 June 1844 that 'there are several villages whose inhabitants, although professedly mussulmen, secretly embrace the Greek religion and attend the services of that Church'.

From several accounts we find that before 1571 Cyprus contained 14,000 villages but after the Turkish invasion and the successive rebellions in 1580 and 1593, of which very little is known, the greatest part of the inhabitants were either killed or exterminated. Moreover, the pestilence of 1624 was so severe that the number of villages were reduced to around 6,000. The plague of 1691 caused the death of around 30 per cent of the population. Dr Ioannis Cotovicus, a Venetian traveller to Cyprus in 1599, wrote: 'The present condition and appearance of the island is far different, oppressed by barbarian rule and stripped of its old grace and glory; much of it is uncultivated, neglected, deserted. Cities once famous and populous, and full of stately buildings, are now ruinous, squalid and thinly peopled: towns and villages lie desolate and forsaken, for it is the way of the Turks to lay waste city and field, to destroy ancient splendour.'[8]

The economy of the island and general well-being of the inhabitants were further paralysed by unjust taxes. Successive changes in its administration meant that the people were harassed with exactions of all kinds, enough to reimburse its rulers after one year in office. Both mussulmans and Christians had equal cause to be dissatisfied with the maladministration that continued unhindered. Insurrections and mass protests were therefore joint affairs.

The first serious uprising appears to have occurred in 1680 under the leadership of Mehmed Agha Boyaji-Oghlu and lasted for seven whole years. It was a protest against harsh taxes and maladministration. After some difficulty the rebellion was crushed and Oghlu, together with some of his closest followers, was executed. After this protest the island became for some time the personal possession of the Grand Vizier.

The second revolt of 1765-6 had wider repercussions. As soon as Chil Osman had entered on his post as agha in July 1764, he issued an order compelling the payment by each Christian subject of 44½ piastres and by each Moslem around half that amount. Osman, described by Kyprianos, writing in 1788, as 'that rock of offence, that cause of all our ills, over head and ears in debt', had managed within several months to extort 350,000 piastres over and above the legal assessment. A special mission to Constantinople (believed to be led by Hadji-Vasilis of Mia Milia) was successful in persuading the Sultan to order Osman not to demand the half of what was collected. A special envoy was also sent to Cyprus to see that the order was enforced. The bishops and around 300 other leading personages assembled at Osman's palace on 25 October 1764 to hear the order read. The assembled crowds suspected that Osman was plotting to kill all the notables in his own house and when part of the floor collapsed they rushed the palace. Osman and about 18 others were murdered. The incident was patched up but a commission was sent by the Porte (the Ottoman court at Constantinople) to inquire into the events that led up to it.

A considerable amount of money was thus required to cover the expenses of the commissioners, the blood-money of the victims, the rebuilding of the Saray, the thefts from the treasury and other demands. Hafiz Efendi was left to arrange for the settlement of the account for all the damage that had been done Because of his greed the expenses were overestimated. This placed the tax collectors in great difficulties and when they visited the Mesaoria villages they had to fly for their lives. The exactions were however pressed and open rebellion ensued.

In April 1765 (on Easter Tuesday), around 300 Turks from the Mesaoria and Famagusta districts seized Kythrea with its water-mills and thus cut off the capital from its supply of flour. Although some concessions were made the tax continued to be collected. Some months later, at a fair in Myrtou, Khalil Agha, commandant of the fortress of Kyrenia, was chosen to lead the rebellion against tax injustices. The revolt was supported by Turks and Greeks, and by August over 3,000 armed men were under his orders. The authorities completely lost control of the situation but Archbishop Paisios and the bishops of Paphos and Kyrenia escaped to Constantinople to plead for help.

Khalil withdrew to Kyrenia when the authorities promised that excessive taxes would not be levied and that all the insurgents would be pardoned. But it was not long before Hafiz decided once more to collect the taxes. Khalil's men now numbered over 5,000. He therefore made attempts against Famagusta and Nicosia. Meanwhile the Porte sent Ibrahim Bey with two caravels and a quite inadequate force of 150 men to deal with the rebellion. By June 1766 the Porte further sent Kior Ahmed with 2,000 troops and 500 horse in 16 ships and Kyrenia was blockaded. After a three-week siege Khalil was forced to surrender and by August the revolt was over. Khalil was garrotted, Emir Ahmed, his lieutenant, was impaled and around 200 were beheaded. Their heads were sent, according to custom, to the Sultan.

The result was that the island's debt amounted to more than 500,000 piastres and the unfortunate people who had to pay it off hardly numbered 15,000. Even so maladministration continued and Hadji Baki, believed to be a native Turkish peasant, managed to get himself appointd chief of the treasury in 1771. A one-eyed, quite illiterate woodcutter, he had been banished from Cyprus in 1767 for 'indescribable trickery, deceit, treachery and persecution of many people'. In 1775 he poisoned the new Turkish governor, Hadji Ali Agha, and amongst others poisoned was the governor's second in command who died 40 days later. Two years later this villain was appointed governor, calling himself Hadji Abdul Baki Agha.

The same story is repeated many times in the annals of Turkish rule over Cyprus. Even the Turkish troops mutinied in 1799, and in 1804, together with the Turkish civilian population of Nicosia, they rose in revolt against the governor, archbishop and Hadjigeorgakis the dragoman, or interpreter, who served as liaison between the island's Hellenic population and the Ottoman government in Constantinople, and was perhaps the wealthiest person in the island. The insurgents gained possession of Nicosia and behaved, according to Ali Bey, who visited the island in 1806, 'atrociously, and they even killed those who refused to give them money'. Hadjigeorgakis Kornesios appealed to the Porte and the revolt was suppressed.

The Turks however resented the powers of the dragoman and in 1806 enlisted the help of Altiparnak ('six fingers'), a colonel at Tarsus, to champion their cause. They laid waste the countryside, murdered Christians and raided churches and monasteries. But Altiparnak was soon taken prisoner and flayed alive. However, in 1809 Hadjigeorgakis, on charges of malversation, was executed in Constantinople and in the following year Archbishop Chrisanthos was exiled to Euboea. Cyprus had thus lost two intellectual and cultural benefactors.

In 1806 an adult Greek population of around 30,000 paid a yearly tribute to the Porte of 500,000 piastres to provide for the garrison kept in Cyprus. A further tax on cotton and other products was raised by the Sultan which yielded around 250,000 piastres and as much again was raised by the governor-general and local governors. The Greek bishops also received the same amount and perhaps even more.

The position of the bishops was greatly enhanced in 1660 when the Porte assigned to Archbishop Nikiforos and to his successors the responsibility of collecting taxes from both the Greek and Turkish inhabitants. This was in accordance with the customary procedure of the Porte in using the leaders of a country's majority to act as tax collectors and thus keeping the displeasure of the people within manageable bounds. By following this practice the archbishop was recognized as the leader of the well-defined Greek Cypriot nation. This position was often exploited, and the oppression of the priests found in many objective accounts was well brought out by William Turner, a British diplomat and traveller, who after staying in the island for over one month in 1815 wrote, perhaps rather harshly: 'In short, these Greek priests, everywhere the vilest miscreants in human nature, are worse than usual in Cyprus from the power they possess. They strip the poor ignorant superstitious peasant of his last para, and when he is on his deathbed, make him leave his all to their convent, promising that masses shall be said for his soul.'[9]

Nevertheless, despite their enhanced and seemingly omnipotent position, the status of the Church leaders was difficult and delicate. As mentioned above they often became victims of intrigue, plots and rebellions. The events of the early 1820s were indicative of that trend.

Another characteristic of Turkish administration in the eighteenth century, which brought much controversy, was the creation of the position of dragoman. With the dragoman directly in control of affairs and the Greek archbishop enjoying immense prestige, the Greek population became in effect, for many years, self-governing, a unique experience for the islanders.

As if these anomalies were not enough the inhabitants were further punished by acts of nature. A severe pestilence in 1624 resulted in thousands of deaths and the plague of 1691-2 wiped out a large proportion of the population. The two earthquakes of 1741 and 1756 (the former damaging the cathedral of Saint Sophia) brought great material destruction. The great dearth of 1757-8, being the outcome of the drought and the locusts, meant that a great number fled to Syria and Asia Minor. The year 1768 was also one of famine. Another drought, followed by famine between 1870 and 1874, once more threatened the life of the inhabitants. To these misfortunes was added the stark reality that the Mohammedan lords, who possessed considerable areas of land, seldom engaged in farming but simply sucked what they could from the impoverished peasantry.

The nineteenth century was dominated by three major events:

1   The abortive reforms of 1821 to 1856. The island benefited slightly by the liberalizing reforms of the Hati-Sherif of 1839 and the Hati-Humayun of 1856 (in fact a confirmation of the earlier charter), and by a change in the administration. For the most part however the promises of both charters were practically meaningless. Nevertheless relative prosperity showed mild signs of emerging and a sizeable increase in population was the outcome.

2   The disturbances of the 1820s associated with the Greek rising. On a charge of conspiring with the insurgents in Greece, the Turks hanged on 9 July 1821 Archbishop Kyprianos and Meletios, his archdeacon, beheaded three other bishops (Meletios of Kition, Chrisanthos of Paphos and Lavrentios of Kyrenia) and many laymen. A number of Cypriots were members of Philike Hetairia, the Greek revolutionary society, and many fought at Messolonghi, Roumeli and the Morea. Kyprianos issued an encyclical on 16 May 1821 advising his flock to remain calm. Open revolt in the island was definitely not wanted.

   The Porte was in great trouble at the time and did not approve of Kutchuk Mehmed's (the island's governor's) intentions of putting to the sword leaders of the Greek 'insurrection'. It finally sanctioned the killings and the taking over of the property and houses of the accused. G.I. Kepiades, in his *Reminiscences of 1821 in Cyprus*, described the massacre as 'the most monstrous spectacle ever seen'. Vasilis Michaelides, perhaps the finest of the Cypriot dialect poets, described the events in his magnificent 56-verse narrative poem 'The Ninth of July 1821'. The common grave erected at Phaneromeni church in Nicosia in 1872-3 honoured Kyprianos, his archdeacon and three bishops, together with Joseph, the abbot of Kykko monastery, and many prominent laymen.

   The above killings, of course, were followed by looting, rape and other atrocities. General Thomas Gordon, a British historian of some repute, wrote in 1832 that 10,000 Syrian troops, 'the scum of that barbarous country', brought to the island to put down the non-existent revolt, 'gave themselves up to every species of villainy'. From another account we learn more of the fatal shocks experienced by the Christian Cypriots:

Daily the Governor has no other care than to bring from all parts of the island innocent and unhappy persons, that even more blood of Christians, monks and priests may be shed, making diligent enquiry about them, and keeping by him an exact note, so as to have them at his bidding. Going further still, he has reached the unparalleled cruelty of murdering, between priests and laymen, ten, fifteen and even twenty a day. If he allows one day to pass without any such victims, on the next he doubles the number, to make things even. On this fiendish plan he has already destroyed the primates, the abbots, the archpriests; and to escape death some have disguised themselves as Franks, and embarked for Genoa, for Marseille or Leghorn . . . the island will then remain a den of wild beasts, rather than an abode of men.[10]

Thus many villages and hamlets had entirely disappeared. Many churches had been turned into mosques and a few into stables. Thomas Gordon emphasized that the whole of Cyprus was 'converted into a theatre of rapine and bloodshed'.

3   For the second time in its illustrious history, Cyprus became subject to the dominion of England. In 1191, of course, it was acquired by force of arms but in 1878 it was acquired by diplomatic agency. Hence, after 307 years of Turkish domination, described as 'a sad record of oppression and misgovernment', a new master had arrived.

The Turkish empire may have been decadent in the eighteenth and nineteenth centuries but it had nevertheless succeeded in crushing every revolt against its authority. The Cyprus rebellion of 1764 had fizzled out; the Morean revolt which Catherine II of Russia had encouraged in 1770 had ended in disaster and the rebels were sternly punished; the treason of the Wallachian and Moldavian princes in 1806 was ruthlessly crushed; the revolt of the Serbs which broke out under Karageorge in 1805 dragged on for many years before it reached success and the Greek rising of 1821 went through many ups and downs before it brought ultimate victory. In Cyprus there were further outbursts of rebellion in the 1820s and early 1830s. One worth mentioning was the so-called 'insurrection of the monk', led by Ioannikios, a fiery monk born at Ayios Elias and said to have fought in the Greek war of independence. Following the insurrections of Nicolas Theseus (brother of Archimandrite Theophilos and nephew of Archbishop Kyprianos) and of Giaour Iman in 1833, Ioannikios in the same year began to stir the Karpass, the eastern end of the island. From rather patchy historical evidence we find that he was encouraged by several European diplomats in the island and helped by Albanian troops to whom he promised lavish prizes. He proceeded to raise the insurgents' flag at Trikomo but the revolt was not serious and was crushed within four days. The defeated received no mercy. Many were hanged, hundreds were tortured and the surrounding countryside was laid waste.

Thus the expected collapse of the Ottoman empire never materialized until the early twentieth century. Yet as early as the sixteenth century many critics and scholars, including Lorenzo Bernardo, the Venetian Ambassador to Constantinople in the 1580s, predicted its eventual disintegration. Bernardo offered his analysis to the Venetian court in 1592 of the reasons why the decline of the Turkish empire 'may now be under way'. Like many others before and after him who speculated on this topic he stressed the weaknesses in the empire's leadership: luxury and dissipation, loss of control over the armed forces and the failure of the Ottoman will. But it is inescapable that the three basic qualities which had enabled the Turks to make such remarkable conquests and rise to such importance in a brief period were religion, frugality and obedience.

The Turks were tolerant in their treatment of the Christians. This was in no way a Turkish innovation; the Arabs of earlier days had set a precedent. Though they definitely regarded the Christians and people with other religious beliefs as 'lesser breeds without the law', they generally felt that Allah did not commend his faithful to convert them by force or exterminate them, as was the case with idolators. The Koran in fact forbids violence and force in the conversion of unbelievers. With very few exceptions this attitude of aloofness constituted the prevailing policy. However, in return for certain privileges, such as exemption from taxation, the Turks used the Orthodox Church to collect taxes for their administration and thus keep their subjects under control.

The privileges for obedience formula worked well for many years. Yet their much-spoken-of policy of religious toleration was erratic and haphazard and was conveniently ignored when new circumstances seemed to suggest a different course of action. The events of July 1821 in Cyprus bear full testimony to the above assertion.

Part II

THE BRITISH PERIOD

2 *European Diplomacy and Strategy: Britain Acquires Cyprus*

This chapter tells the behind-the-scenes story of how Britain, for the second time, came to hold Cyprus. A combination of factors, including European concern over the worsening state of the famous 'sick man of Europe' (the Ottoman Empire), the Russo-Turkish War of 1877 (leading to the Treaty of San Stefano in 1878) and above all, perhaps, Disraeli's 'forward' policy, led to possession of the island.

The purchase of Khedive Ismail's 176,602 Suez Canal shares for £4 million in mid November 1875, the Russian advance southwards following the San Stefano Treaty (causing a new shift in the fragile European balance of power) and the concerted urge of British industry to expand, meant that Disraeli (Prime Minister from 20 February 1874 to 21 April 1880) had to act fast. He had already shown an interest in the island – and not only for British reasons. While still in his twenties (he was born on 21 December 1804) he paid an extended visit to the Mediterranean area, including Cyprus, which he described more than once as the 'rosy realm of Venus'. In his subsequent literary career, Disraeli constantly harked back to Jerusalem and Cyprus. 'The English want Cyprus and they will take it as compensation,' one of his coffee house politicians was made to say in his *Tancred or The New Crusade* (1847); and another of his heroes, awakening in the Thames estuary, is made to register appropriate disappointment: 'The Isle of Dogs! It should at least be Cyprus.'

There is evidence to suggest that Britain's first Jewish Prime Minister, along with many others, regarded the island as a natural stepping-stone to Zion. (Palestine was a central preoccupation of his *Tancred*.) Agitation was fairly strong in England from the 1850s onwards for a Jewish state in Palestine to guard the route to India. Thus almost immediately after the

signing of the highly secret Anglo-Turkish Cyprus Accord of 4
June 1878, demands for a Jewish settlement on the island were
heard throughout the Jewish world. Among the first was that of
the London *Jewish Chronicle*, which set the tone and developed
the arguments found in all subsequent proposals. On 9 August
1878 it wrote quite emphatically that Cyprus had once been the
seat of a flourishing colony of Jews. (It is indeed true that the
Sultan had invited 500 Jews to settle in Cyprus in the early
1570s – and thus to help in consolidating Turkish rule there;
those who went were concerned with trade and the
manufacture of cloth.) Why could it not be so again? the *Jewish
Chronicle* asked. This demand was followed by many others,
notably by Davis Trietsch and Theodor Herzl in the 1890s.
Disraeli too, during the Berlin Conference (13 June to 13 July
1878), seems to have regarded Cyprus, under the British flag,
as a possible place of refuge for the Jews of the diaspora.

Britain's policy towards Turkey in the 1860s and 1870s was
not at all consistent. Two reasons suffice to explain this
inconsistency. First, control of British foreign policy alternated
between Gladstone, a pacifist Prime Minister who cared very
little for the imminent collapse of the Porte (the publication of
his pamphlet, 'The Bulgarian Horrors and the Question of the
East', on 6 September 1876 resulted in tremendous agitation in
Britain against Turkish misrule), and Disraeli, who, after 1874,
reversed many aspects of policy. An analysis of British foreign
policy belongs to another study. What I wish to reiterate is the
marked difference of perception between the two leaders about
Britain's global interests.

This shift and hence inconsistency in policy was, in the
second place, the result of the ever-changing European balance
of power – the collapse of Austria (leading to the unification of
Germany and Italy), the advance of Russia and the emergence
of international competitors in industry such as France, Japan
and the United States. Dwight E. Lee, in his excellent account
of the Cyprus Convention, wrote:

> In fact in 1875 England had stood at the parting of the ways
> in her policy toward Turkey. Was she to bolster up the
> Ottoman Empire or partition it and take her share? The
> exigencies of imperial interests and the constellation of the
> foreign powers had led Beaconsfield to proclaim the

traditional policy but had not prevented partition, although England's share was disguised by the Cyprus Convention and by lip-service to the old shibboleth of the independence and integrity of the Ottoman Empire.[1]

The Russian advance in 1877 spread terror not only in Turkey but in all the European nations. By 10 December the Turkish strategic stronghold of Plevna had been starved out and Osman Pasha had capitulated. The end was approaching, and the Treaty of San Stefano (signed on 3 March 1878) reduced the 'sick man of Europe' to a 'stunted torso' and revived the fortunes of Tsarist Russia. However, the war continued unchecked and so peace terms were dictated to Turkey. The Porte therefore had a grievance since, in what was considered probably their gravest crisis, they had stood alone with no allies. Sir Austen Henry Layard, the British Ambassador in Constantinople, wrote to Beaconsfield on 9 January 1878 expressing the Turkish concern: 'We must not conceal from ourselves that the state of affairs in Turkey is extremely critical. The Turks are greatly disappointed at what they call our "desertion" of them and very bitter with us for the advice we have given them to make their own arrangements with Russia for an armistice.'[2] And, to the Earl of Derby, Layard wrote on 30 January as follows: 'The Sultan and his Ministers spend their days and nights in council and in expectation of the armistice. All business at the Porte is suspended. The Turks have lost all heart, finding themselves deserted and abandoned by everyone.[3] The greatest anxiety, of course, was the future of Constantinople. The Turks dreaded a Russian seizure of their main city, and especially the Sultan, since that would have cost him his throne and possibly his life.

At this point it will not be out of place to comment on the so-called 'spontaneous zeal of war' that existed in Britain. Military leaders were now busy preparing their battle plans, believing that their country's honour was at stake. As early as 20 June 1877 Layard transmitted his *modus operandi* to Beaconsfield. He proposed the following:

1   Turkey should be given money, officers and troops.

2   Use should be made of Hungary and Galicia to prevent the active interference of Austria on behalf of Russia or, if

necessary, to incite the Hungarian and Galician Poles to take up arms against Russia.

3   The Islamic states in central Asia, occupied or threatened by Russia, should be incited against her.

4   Greece should not be allowed to move against Turkey or to encourage insurrections amongst the Greek populations.

While Plevna held, there was little desire for war. But after it fell in December 1877 and the Russians were pressing forward in their headlong advance across the Balkans towards Constantinople, war fever took hold. The very foundations of British interests seemed to be in jeopardy.

The government however ignored this desire for war and thus accepted the Russian advance in Asia Minor, in spite of the threat it involved to the British position in India. The reason, according to Lord Salisbury, was simple: his government had already made preparations for 'the erection of another dyke behind the shattered Turkish break-water'. Thus, after various places (such as Crete, Mytilene, Lemnos, Alexandretta, Acre, Haifa and Alexandria) had been considered, Britain decided on the acquisition of Cyprus, which Beaconsfield described to Queen Victoria on 5 May 1878 as 'the key of western Asia'. Indeed he always depicted the acquisition of Cyprus in the most glowing and romantic colours. However, this was characteristic of the partition of the globe in the last quarter of the nineteenth century, when the world was 'shared' by the major powers in complete disregard of the wishes of the native inhabitants.

Hence the myth of the takeover of Cyprus became a reality and a necessity. On 10 May the outlines of an agreement had been sent to Layard, with instructions to proceed with the negotiations as soon as word arrived from London. Six days later the British cabinet approved the projected convention and, as soon as it became clear that Russia would insist on the retention of Kars and Batum, Layard was instructed (on 23 May) to submit the draft agreement to the Sultan – who was given forty-eight hours to take it or leave it. How could he refuse? Four days earlier, in fact, he had sent a telegram to London asking for help, money and an alliance.

On 25 May, during an interview with the British

Ambassador, the Sultan (who was suffering from great depression), relieved to hear that only Cyprus was demanded, gladly conceded it. According to the Layard Papers, Abdul Hamid II on that occasion, unlike all previous audiences with the British Ambassador, had a host of guards around him because he had heard that Layard was about to assassinate him. At all events, in view of the English threat to desist from further opposition to the Russian advance and from further efforts to postpone the partition of his Empire – at one stage in June 1878 the Turks suspected that there was a secret understanding between England, Austria and Russia for the dissection of their country – the Sultan made no objection and the Convention was signed in secret on 4 June. Its publication during the Berlin Congress came as a 'thunder-clap' upon the diplomatic world.

Before giving the context of the Convention, a brief account of the character and aims of Abdul Hamid II must be given. Through brute force and intrigue he had obtained his wish and become undisputed Sultan of Turkey on 31 August 1876. He held this position for 33 years. He was totally opposed to westernization and, in effect, succeeded in putting back the clock for an appreciable time. His methods were simply to repress and if possible liquidate all westernizing elements he could. The unfortunate Armenians were perhaps the chief sufferers. Unlike the other nascent nationalist groups of the Ottoman Empire, they did not possess any territory in the Balkans which could serve as a geographical nucleus for their state-to-be. They lived largely in Anatolia and so were at the mercy of the Sultan, the anti-westernizing true Ottomans and the peasants. The massacres of August 1896 earned Abdul Hamid the titles 'Great Assassin' and 'Red Sultan'. A Turkish publication (*The New Turkey*) described his character as follows:

> Turkey fell under the domination of a suspicious despot who conceived that the best way of maintaining the old regime was to isolate his people from European influences and to use his position as Caliph to excite the Moslem world against potential European enemies. His reign was marked by the demoralization of public life, and the conversion of the Empire into a 'Police State', where fanatics, concession-hunters, court favourites and spies played a sinister role.[4]

Thus an anti-western, suspicious despot was left alone to face the Russians. By December 1877 his defeat was complete – just 16 months after he had ascended to the highest and most lucrative position in Turkey. It is perhaps not surprising then that according to Layard he was 'spitting blood continually' after August 1877. His so-called allies however did not abandon him completely. Mainly for self-interested reasons they managed to salvage considerable areas for Turkey, although future sources of tension were created at the same time. The terms of the San Stefano Treaty were strongly Pan-Slavist, which meant that neither Britain nor Austria-Hungary could stomach them. European nations therefore demanded a 'revising' conference and on 27 March 1878 Beaconsfield persuaded his cabinet to call up the reserves immediately and summon to the Mediterranean a large body of Indian troops. The outcome was the Congress of Berlin, which opened on 13 June 1878 in the famous Radzivill Palace.

It was the most imposing gathering of diplomats Europe had seen since the Congress of Vienna 63 years earlier, while the choice of meeting-ground marked the continental primacy which Germany had attained as a result of its successful war with France in 1870. Britain sent three representatives – Lord Beaconsfield, her Prime Minister, Lord Salisbury, her Foreign Secretary, and her able Ambassador to Berlin, Lord Odo Russell. Since Salisbury took A.J. Balfour, his nephew, with him as secretary, three successive Premiers of England were among those present. The list similarly included three Chancellors of Germany – Bismarck, Hohenlohe and the youthful Bülow. The principal representative of Turkey was Alexander Pasha Caratheodory, a Phanariot Greek (a Hellenic official, usually a member of the mercantile oligarchy, in the service of the Sultan). Of quite exceptional ability, he struggled to defend the interests of his master as stoutly as any man could. He was, however, constantly and rudely snubbed by Bismarck, who told him in so many words that he was there only to accept what the Powers dictated.

The success of the Conference was largely though not wholly assured by secret conventions concluded between the Powers beforehand. Britain signed three of them: with Russia on 30 May, with Turkey (the Cyprus Convention) on 4 June and with

Austria-Hungary on 6 June. The Congress of Berlin destroyed the San Stefano Treaty without the cost of war; in pursuit of his major aim – to fend off the Russians from Constantinople – Beaconsfield succeeded remarkably: the Congress sanctioned strategic annexations by Russia at the south-east corner of the Black Sea and the transfer of Cyprus to British occupation and administration, as had been arranged earlier by the two countries; Austria won a protectorate over Bosnia and Herzegovina; and France secured recognition of her claims in north Africa.

Beaconsfield's return from Berlin was a veritable triumph. In a characteristic phrase he told his cheering fellow countrymen that he brought back 'peace with honour'. It was indeed the climax of his career. A major war was averted for 36 years and he secured for the British Crown the 'Mediterranean jewel'. However, the Berlin agreement also contained the seeds of the First World War: it left the Balkan countries dissatisfied, Turkey seriously weakened, Russia and Germany permanently estranged; it sharpened the rivalry between Russia and Austria and provided no long-term solution to any of the problems of Near or Middle East.

The first step in the transfer of Cyprus from Turkish to British rule was the signature of the 'Convention of Defensive Alliance between Great Britain and Turkey with respect to the Asiatic Provinces of Turkey' (commonly known as the Cyprus Convention) in the following terms:

> If Batum, Ardahan, Kars, or any of them shall be retained by Russia, and if any attempt shall be made at any future time by Russia to take possession of any further territories of His Imperial Majesty the Sultan in Asia, as fixed by the Definitive Treaty of Peace, England engages to join His Imperial Majesty the Sultan in defending them by force of arms.
>
> In return, His Imperial Majesty the Sultan promises to England to introduce necessary reforms, to be agreed upon later between the two Powers, into the Government, and for the protection of the Christian and other subjects of the Porte in these territories; and in order to enable England to make necessary provision for executing her engagement, His Imperial Majesty the Sultan further consents to assign the

Island of Cyprus to be occupied and administered by England.[5]

That was Article I of the Cyprus Convention, signed on 4 June 1878 at the Imperial Palace of Yeldiz. Furthermore, an Annex containing six conditions was signed on 1 July. The two most important (the third and sixth) read as follows:

That England will pay to the Porte whatever is the present excess of revenue over expenditure in the Island; this excess to be calculated upon and determined by the average of the last five years.

That if Russia restores to Turkey Kars and other conquests made by her in Armenia during the last war, the Island of Cyprus will be evacuated by England, and the Convention of 4 June 1878 will be at an end.[6]

Thus, in return for the protection of his bankrupt Empire, a tribute of around £92,800 and, as it turned out, 4,166,220 okes (or 10,865,416 lb) of salt per annum, the Sultan agreed that Great Britain could occupy and administer Cyprus. Furthermore, according to the sixth condition, the island was to return to him. This however was a 'hollow' condition, which few took seriously. Even Earl Granville, himself sceptical of the strategic value of Cyprus, stated on 18 July 1878: 'The promise that Cyprus is to go back to Turkey if Russia gives back what she has got is of a perfectly illusory character. Looking at it as men of business, we must see that the cession of Cyprus is a virtual cession of a portion of the Porte's Dominions.'[7]

In fact on 16 March 1921, when Russia transferred to Turkey two of the three Armenian territories (Ardahan and Kars but not Batum) referred to in the 1878 Convention, Britain still retained control over Cyprus. Moreover, in 1923 both Greece and Turkey acknowledged British sovereignty over the island, and two years later it was declared a Crown Colony.

As we have seen, Britain agreed to pay Turkey the average excess of revenue over expenditure in the island for the past five years. G.W. Kellner, appointed financial commissioner of Cyprus, proceeded to put the revenues of the island into some kind of order. In his Estimates of Revenue and Expenditure for 1878/79, he predicted that the current revenue would not only cover the annual payment to the Porte and the expenses of administration but would also permit a fair outlay on roads and sanitary improvements. However, all was not well, because Kellner failed to take into account the role of Turkish financial officials and troops in the collection of taxes. Sir Garnet Wolseley (the first British Administrator for Cyprus) wrote to Layard on 1 August 1878 in the following terms: 'It seems to me that they have no intention of going away at present, and I suspect they are desirous of remaining as long as there is anything to be sucked out of Cyprus in the way of taxes.'[8]

Wolseley confirmed the pitiful behaviour of the Turkish officials in another letter to Layard on 4 September. He stressed that 'the Turkish treasurer walked off with a sum of money to which he had no right whatever'. Similar complaints were transmitted to Layard by Wolseley's successor, Sir Robert Biddulf. On 18 June 1879 he wrote: 'I am much disgusted with the way the Porte has behaved. They are lost to all sense of shame, and are full of tricks and deceit.'[9]

The acquisition of Cyprus however was not well received in Britain. MPs, military strategists and students of imperial and mercantile interests failed to agree with the government's policy. The main exponents of this policy were Beaconsfield and Salisbury. In a forceful speech on 18 July 1878 Lord Beaconsfield told the House of Lords that:

> The Treaty of San Stefano was looked on with much distrust and alarm by Her Majesty's Government – they believed it was calculated to bring about a state of affairs dangerous to European independence and injurious to the interests of the British Empire. . . . In taking Cyprus the movement is not Mediterranean; it is Indian. We have taken a step there which we think necessary for the maintenance of our Empire and for its preservation in peace. If that be our first consideration, our next is the development of the country.[10]

Lord Salisbury, in a speech at Manchester on 17 October 1879, echoed the Prime Minister's words:

> The occupation of Cyprus was merely following out the traditional policy of the English Government for a long time past. When the interest of Europe was centred in the conflicts that were waged in Spain, England occupied Gibraltar.

When the interest of Europe was centred in the conflicts that were being waged in Italy, England occupied Malta; and now that there is a chance that the interests of Europe will be centred in Asia Minor or in Egypt, England has occupied Cyprus.[11]

What advantages did Cyprus offer? B. Bordone, writing in 1528, emphasized that 'the situation of this most noble island yields to no other in merit'. With Gibraltar in the west of the Mediterranean and Malta in the centre, Cyprus formed one of a series of strong places which gave to Britain a preponderance of power in every direction. It directly commanded the entrance to the Suez Canal, the coasts of Palestine and Syria and the southern provinces of Asia Minor. The process of converting the Mediterranean into a distant British lake was now complete. Cyprus, then, possessed the great naval advantage of situation and was to serve Britain as a *point de départ* and a *place d'armes* for controlling and protecting the route to India and beyond.

Politically too Cyprus was a great gain. With Constantinople now easily accessible, Britain was henceforth in a position to take over from the other Powers the key role of 'adviser and comforter' to the Porte. Britain's moral influence among all the nations of the east, and especially the people of India, was considerably increased.

Economically and commercially, then, Cyprus once more brought many advantages to Britain. The opportunity was there to develop its many resources and work its gold and silver mines and its caves of jaspar and agate – immense resources which had been utterly neglected under the desolate Turkish system of government. Hence one important effect of the occupation and improved administration of Cyprus was the immediate and rapid increase of the island's population by immigration – Greeks, Syrians and other Arabs came to Cyprus to acquire land and establish commercial and industrial enterprises which had earlier languished and decayed under ruthless Turkish taxation. Thus in 20 years between 1881 and 1901 the island's population increased by around 28 per cent.

So the Cyprus Convention, regarded as a 'side-show' quite outside the Congress of Berlin (that grandiose assembly of European statesmen), secured for Britain an outstanding acquisition – the key to the continents of Europe, Asia and Africa.

Because of the island's strategic importance opposition came from several quarters. Gladstone, the great British Liberal leader, called the agreement an 'insane covenant' and declared that the Cyprus deal was 'an act of duplicity not surpassed and rarely equalled in the history of nations'. Addressing the electors of Midlothian on 11 March 1880, he stated that the Conservatives had dishonoured the name of Great Britain by, among other things, 'filching the island of Cyprus from the Porte under a treaty clandestinely concluded in violation of the 1854 Treaty of Paris'. Gladstone in fact attacked on several occasions both the Cyprus Convention and the Treaty of Berlin because, as he saw it, the British government had loaded itself with three responsibilities: first, the occupation and administration of Cyprus, which were morally wrong; second, the defence of Turkey in Asia against Russian designs – a country that was over 2,000 miles away; and third, the good behaviour of 'what is perhaps the worst governed country in the whole world'.

Others pointed out that the Cyprus Convention was deficient in so far as it did not allow Britain to use her naval force in the Black Sea against Russia. It was, they believed, a hasty decision, based on imperfect information; mature deliberation would have selected a position in the Persian Gulf instead. Some went as far as to say that, like Corfu, Cyprus was 'commercially and politically useless', and as a naval station and a place of arms 'worse than useless'. Part of a speech delivered by Earl Granville on 18 July 1878 deserves quoting: 'I believe that Cyprus is farther from the Dardanelles than Malta. I believe if we fight Russia for Turkey, Turkey will not be slow in putting every facility in our way at Constantinople. Therefore, if you put Cyprus in a proper state, it will be perfectly useless to send troops there.'[12]

In the end however the sceptics were outnumbered and, as the *New York Times* commented in July 1878, 'Cyprus has now become another Malta'. Traditional British policy once more prevailed. Even Gladstone and his colleagues, who, out of office, strongly denounced the treaties of 1878, persistently upheld and made use of them as soon as they came to power. In fact Gladstone made it clear during his Midlothian speeches in the winter of 1879-80 that in the event of victory at the polls in April 1880 the specific engagements entered into by the Conservative government would not be repudiated, although 'prudence, care and diligence, may do much in the course of time'. In the first year or so of Liberal rule however there was talk of surrendering the island, since 'it could never bring any military or political advantage to the Crown'. G.J. Goshen, one of the leading members of the Liberal party, proposed such a scheme in February 1881, but such was the opposition (Queen Victoria was firmly set against retrocession) that the idea was finally abandoned. The Cabinet also decided against an evacuation policy and even Gladstone indicated that he would make no change of policy. This was endorsed by the House of Commons following its Cyprus debate on 19 August 1881.

Dwight E. Lee, in his lucid account of European diplomacy in 1878, records: 'While the Treaty of Berlin represented a compromise of the conflicting European views and aims, the Cyprus Convention between Great Britain and Turkey, and the policy and ambitions which it involved, were attempts to safeguard and develop what Englishmen considered to be peculiarly British interests.'[13]

There was a strange coincidence concerning the last two occupations of Cyprus – by Turkey in 1571 and by Britain in 1878. Cyprus was conquered for Turkey by João Miques (later known as Joseph Nasi), a Jew, on the former occasion and was taken over by Beaconsfield, also a Jew, for Britain 307 years later. Both occupations were combinations of careful planning and mere chance.

The story behind the first Jewish connection is as follows: Nasi, born in Portugal, was descended from a family of merchants and bankers who had fled from Spain (from which a decree of 30 March 1492 expelled all Jews) to Portugal, and there had been victims of the forced conversion of 1497. With his aunt Beatrice De Luna (she became known later as Gracia Mendesia) Nasi fled to the Low Countries, where the family owned a banking establishment. From there they fled to Lyons (where their bank was confiscated) and then Venice (where Gracia was temporarily imprisoned for her Jewish beliefs), and finally they arrived at Constantinople in 1554. (Turkey was then the main haven of refuge for persecuted Jewry.)

He married his cousin Reyna, a woman of dazzling beauty, and was henceforth called by his ancestral Hebraic name, Joseph Nasi. He already had influential friends in Constantinople, among them the court physician Moses Hamon, who introduced him to the Sultan. Hence, with characteristic ambition and acuteness, he threw himself into the whirl of Turkish domestic politics and espoused the cause of Prince Selim, the younger son of Suleiman, as candidate for the succession to his father's throne. Selim in due course became ruler of Turkey in 1566 and Nasi received his reward in a shower of favours and dignities which took him into the highest rank of Turkish public affairs. For many years to come his career knew no check. He rose to such a high position at court that he was virtually the ruler of the Turkish Empire for a time.

Nasi planned the conquest of Cyprus and, as a reward for his earlier services, had been created Duke of Naxos and Prince of the Cyclades. His designs on Cyprus, though serving the ambitions of Turkey, were largely inspired by his desire to take vengeance on Venice, as he did against Spain and France, for the ill-treatment suffered by his aunt and mother-in-law Gracia Mendesia (perhaps the most benevolent and most adored woman of her day) and himself when they sought asylum in the Republic. (The Venetians, of course, were the rulers of Cyprus from 1489 to 1571.)

It is conceivable that Nasi had some vague idea of using the island to help solve the Jewish refugee problem, which was acute in the sixteenth century. (The Sultan granted Nasi a stretch of land around Tiberias, where a substantial Jewish population assembled. An important settlement had even come into existence in the Holy Land itself.) Nevertheless, far from helping his co-religionists, Nasi's intervention in Cyprus nearly proved catastrophic to those who lived under Venetian rule. Jews of both sexes and every rank were ordered to leave the city of Venice. The order was revoked on 7 July 1573, only a few months before the fatal day. Nasi died in 1579 and hence failed to become King of Cyprus, as had once seemed possible. The island, almost continuously peopled by around 80 per cent Greeks and 20 per cent Turks, remained under Turkish control until 1878.

In that year the occupation of Cyprus by Britain's first Jewish Premier was designed, above all, to serve the interests of the British Empire. The island was taken over by diplomatic agency (often referred to as the 'Cyprus bribe') and there was no question of personal vengeance – just personal ambition, pampered by the greatest military and naval power of the 1870s. It has already been shown that powerful and well-informed Jewish quarters regarded the island as a natural stepping-stone to Zion. In fact soon after Cyprus passed from Turkish to British rule voices were heard in the Jewish world for the establishment of a Jewish settlement on the island. Hence in 1883 an attempt at agricultural settlement was made by a group of Russian Jews. In 1885 and 1891 similar attempts were made by Rumanian Jews. Then in 1897 a small settlement of Russian Jews was founded at Margo Chiflik under the auspices of the Jewish Colonization Association and the Ahavat Zion Settlement Society of London. In the following year Davis Trietsch, an early adherent of the Zionist movement, advocated the Jewish colonization of Cyprus, which was to form part of a Greater Palestine. Such was the beauty and position of Cyprus that its tiny acreage was desired by many and for different reasons.

Cyprus, then, became a British responsibility in 1878. What was needed next was for a British contingent to land on the island. On 1 July Vice-Admiral Lord John Hay, commanding in his flagship the *Minotaur* the channel squadron lying at Suda Bay (Crete), received secret orders from the Admiralty to collect the scattered units of his fleet and sail for Cyprus. It was not then known that Turkey had handed the island over to Britain for occupation and administration. The squadron left Suda Bay on 2 July.

On 4 July Lord John Hay, with four officers, one doctor and 50 marines, arrived at the bay of Larnaca. By next morning the British naval strength had been increased to six ships. However, Cyprus and its inhabitants were an unknown quantity both to Hay and to his crew. Captain Harry Rawson was sent on shore on the 8th and 9th to test the situation. He was well briefed by Watkins, the British consul, and following his second visit he laid an informative but short report before Hay on all the leading points, not only as to Larnaca but as to every corner of the island. He described the townsfolk as 'quiet and sociable, very lazy and given to pleasures of every sort'. He went on to say that 'since they were not fanatical they would not fight' and though 'robberies, assassinations and brigandage were nearly unknown, drunkenness was not uncommon'. However, the inhabitants of Nicosia, being chiefly Turkish, were described as, 'fanatical; men devoted to their religion and faithful to their caliph; in other words, men who might possibly turn out to fight'.

On 10 July HMS *Salamis* arrived, bringing Sami Pasha, the representative of the Porte, bearing the imperial firman, and Walter Baring, the second secretary of Her Majesty's Embassy at Constantinople, who brought a copy of the Convention. Next day Hay sent Baring and Sami Pasha to Nicosia to negotiate preliminary proceedings and either present the firman himself or let Sami Pasha do it. Rawson went with them to examine the defences of the place while they dealt with the governor. Rawson returned at night to Larnaca and reported to Hay. Almost immediately he was sent to Nicosia with 50 bluejackets and 50 marines to guard the flag. Hay followed within the hour, driving in a wagonette with no military guard, and entered Nicosia by the Famagusta gate at 11.30 a.m. on 12 July.

As it was Friday and the hour of prayer, nothing could be done until later. At the Saray (the Turkish governor's official residence), where Hay called on Bessim Pasha, he found Sami Pasha anxiously waiting to read the firman. This he did and Bessim formally handed over the administration to Hay. In his brief address the transitory guardian of Cyprus explained that as a result of the convention that had been concluded between Her Majesty Queen Victoria and the Sultan, and now enforced by an imperial firman, he was commanded by Her Majesty's government to occupy the island of Cyprus in the name of the Queen and to assume its temporary administration until a governor appointed by Her Majesty arrived. He went on to promise justice, progress and the equality of all the inhabitants before the law.

This very plain and businesslike address, spoken in English, was of course not understood by those present. Only the words 'Queen Victoria' were comprehended and were soon echoed by the crowd amidst tumultuous cheering. All this took place within the palace and when Hay and his staff emerged on their way to the flagstaff they were followed by large crowds. The marines were drawn up and Rawson hoisted the Union Jack, which was then saluted. As soon as this brief ceremony was over Hay formally announced to the people that Her Majesty Queen Victoria now reigned over Cyprus. The crowds applauded enthusiastically. Hay was then followed to the rostrum by George Kepiades, a prominent Greek and the historian of the massacres of 1821, who expressed the joy of the Cypriots and their hopes for prosperity and full political liberty.

On 22 July 1878 Sir Garnet Wolseley arrived in HMS *Himalaya*, landing at Larnaca at around 6.00 p.m. accompanied by some 1,500 troops. On the following day he issued a proclamation in which he gave assurances of the Queen's wishes for the prosperity of the island and her desire to take measures for the promotion and development of commerce and agriculture, and to endow the people with the benefits of liberty, justice and security. According to a letter from Wolseley to Salisbury (dated 28 July and written on board HMS *Himalaya*), the edict, which was read in English, Greek and Turkish, was greeted with cheers. Wolseley also enclosed two copies of the ordinance – one in English and the other in Greek. Kyprianos, the Bishop of Kition, is said to have welcomed Wolseley's sincere assurances and then explained that the inhabitants gladly accepted the change of government and trusted that Britain would help Cyprus, as it did the Ionian Islands, to be united with Mother Greece, with which it was naturally connected.

In fact the substitution of a Christian empire for a Mohammedan one was seen as the golden bridge which would ultimately unite Cyprus with Greece. It is interesting to point out however (from rather patchy historical evidence) that when Wolseley arrived in Nicosia on 30 July Archbishop Sofronios in his address of welcome stressed the protection of liberties and so forth but gave no clear-cut indication of any desire for union with Greece. Nevertheless the leading Greeks of the island (mainly professional and ecclesiastic) welcomed the British occupation as a break in Cypriot affairs and proceeded to set their sights on even higher achievements – self-government, autonomy, self-determination and finally union with Greece. The 1950s especially, and beyond, reflected the visions of the nineteenth-century enlightened few.

3   1878-1914: From Occupation to Annexation

By the so-called thieves' deal, Great Britain acquired *de facto*, if not *de jure*, sovereignty of Cyprus. Britain, of course, never disputed the legal sovereignty of Turkey. British citizenship was not acquired by the Cypriots until after 1914, when the island was annexed by Britain. Cyprus however, as Winston Churchill emphasized on 19 October 1907, came under British rule 'ruined and prostrate from centuries of horrible ill-usage'; consequently improvements all round were necessary. The problems of settlement were as follows:

1   *The Sultan's lands*. According to Sir Robert Biddulph, the Sultan's lands were 'greatly staggered [*sic*] in the titles', and he complained that the Turkish behaviour over this problem was 'simply childish', since they claimed 'neither more nor less than all land in Cyprus for which the inhabitants showed no title'. There was of course also dispute about the interpretation to be given to the Convention of 1878, especially to Article 4 of the Annex which referred to the above problem. In the end large areas were ceded by the Turkish officials and a settlement, which took several years to finalize, was reached.

2   *Tax problems*. Sami and Bessim remained in Nicosia until 23 August 1878, since the process of clearing up the accounts of the administration was complicated by the endeavours of the Turks to present as large a balance as possible in the Treasury. It was in their interest to do this, since the annual tribute was to be based on the average surplus of the last five years. Moreover, to meet the expenses of the Russian war taxes had been doubled. This created further problems for the tax collectors, who had the difficult task of extracting more and more from Cypriot peasants who could hardly make ends meet. Reflecting on the virtual collapse of the Turkish administrative machinery, Wolseley wrote to Layard on 10 February 1879:

'What a pity it is that the Sultan does not place his finances in the hands of some able Englishman: the Turk is such a child in all money matters. . . . A few honest officials with full powers sent into any province of the Empire would soon restore its prosperity. But I suppose the Sultan would not be made to understand this: the Turk is so proud that he does not like to be told he is ignorant of the art of governing.'[1]

3   *Law and order*. Wolseley's first request was for a judge and he proposed a Mr Phillips, whom he had known in Natal and who was in his view 'a first-rate lawyer of a rough-and-ready type'. Wolseley asserted that impartial justice was his motto and mentioned as illustration that he had, in the first three months, imprisoned one tax collector for robbery, one Greek churchman for refusing to pay tithes and one Maltese antiquity hunter for breaking the law. He also insisted on the immediate deportation of a large number of Turkish convicts (around 314) whose presence on the island was as undesirable as it was dangerous. In a letter to Lord Salisbury on 6 August 1878, Wolseley explained that Cyprus 'under Turkish rule was made the receptacle for the worst criminals in the Sultan's empire'. He was also convinced that Turkish *cadis* should be removed from their posts as judges instantly, although he believed they should be retained as expounders of the existing law while verdicts should be delivered by a British judge or commissioner. He further emphasized that if they were retained the Greeks – the mass of the population – would never feel satisfied that justice was being done to them. A year later Biddulph confirmed that the people had lost all faith in native judges.

4   *The question of privilege*. Biddulph in an explanatory letter to Layard on 29 March 1880 wrote: 'The peasantry are quite satisfied. The real difficulty is with the privileged classes, those who had exemptions from taxation etc., and the Greek church no doubt feels the want of the pressure of the Executive to compel their community to pay the church dues. But this is a matter in which we cannot help them, though I am very sensible of the expediency of keeping the Bishops on our side.'[2]

The bishops, appointed during the Turkish occupation as tax collectors, amassed a great fortune for themselves out of the poor villagers. This came to an end after 1878. A new grievance was thus born, which played a major role in increased agitation for union with Greece. The same fate befell other privileged classes such as lawyers, merchants and bankers.

5   *The problem of the corrupt office holders.* Nepotism, bribery and corruption had been allowed to grow and flourish without check. Wolseley, in a letter to Layard on 4 September 1878, remarked that officials, once appointed, became untrustworthy, dishonest and arrogant. On another occasion he complained that 'scarcely a day passes without my finding out some fresh pieces of rascality on the part of Turk officials here'. Wolseley saw that the island had subsided into utter stagnation under protracted Turkish rule and that a strong hand was needed to stir her energies and set forward her welfare. However, following a strong hint from the government at Westminster, he set about purifying rather than abolishing Turkish institutions. The British excuse, of course, was uncertainty of settlement. One of his first acts therefore was to nominate six British officers – of whom the first was Colonel Robert Biddulph (eventually his successor) – to take the places of the Turkish kaimakans, who had administered the six districts into which the island had been divided.

6   *Health.* Obviously acts of nature such as earthquakes could not be prevented but the poor health of the inhabitants and afflictions such as cattle disease (an outbreak occurred in 1879/80) and locust destruction to crops (to prevent which a considerable amount of money was spent between 1881 and 1885) could, with the right men and resources, he alleviated.

7   *Education and language.* Illiteracy and therefore apathy were the rule rather than the exception. The language problem meant slower progress. Thus at the first, and quite successful, meeting of the legislative council (established by Order in Council of 14 September 1878), which met on 9 December, the languages spoken were English, French, Turkish and Greek.

8   *Miscellaneous problems* included customs duties, currency, climate, refugees, religious property, harvests and finance. At one stage Cypriots were even liable for conscription in the Turkish army unless they paid a poll tax.

These and many other problems faced Wolseley, in addition to the usual difficulties which always face an incoming administration. In the summer of 1879 Kyprianos, the Bishop of Kition, in two letters to Colonel F.G.E. Warren and Sir Garnet Wolseley, elaborated on the current ills of the island, which in brief were:

1   Cypriot farmers were facing crippling difficulties, even though the soil of Cyprus is generally very fertile.

2   Progress had been hindered by the countless evils of the decadent Turkish administration.

3   The clergy were enduring serious hardship and humiliation.

4   The inequitable legal and taxation systems were unbearable.

The bishop expressed hope of progress under a Christian liberal empire.

The period between 1878 and 1914 (from occupation to outright cession) was dominated by four major themes:

the Hellenic ideal or *megali idhea* (Great Idea);
the emergence of the Constitution;
great expectations but slow economic progress; and
Church disputation.

The Hellenic ideal

The Hellenic ideal of course was much older than the British occupation. Before the close of the sixteenth century several attempts had been made by the Greeks of Cyprus to free themselves and decide their own destiny. Immediately after the Turkish occupation in 1571 a Cypriot delegation left for Constantinople to plead for the granting of the rights promised by Mustapha, the leader of the Turkish forces in the capture of the island. Freedom of worship was thus secured. At around the same time the Duke of Savoy, Filivertos Emmanuel, instructed his ambassador in Constantinople to find out if the Sultan was willing, in return for a tribute, to free Cyprus. In 1578 many discontented Turks joined the Greeks in raising the standard of revolt. Thanks to Venetian intrigue, Ahmed Pasha was killed by his own soldiers, whom he had not paid and had exasperated by his brutality. The revolt however collapsed and appeals for help despatched to Spain and Venice met with no response. Yet the history of this abortive revolt was to repeat itself many times.

In 1583 a letter from Evgenios Benakis addressed to the Duke of Savoy, Charles Emmanuel I, pleading that Cyprus must be freed, also came to nothing. In 1587 a secret meeting at the archbishopric took place. It was resolved that an appeal for help should be addressed to Philip II, King of Spain, and Gabriel Nomikos was chosen to deliver the letter. The Greek hopes were again dashed. Three years later Markos Memos of Paphos was sent to Rome and then Turin to try to get help from the Duke of Savoy. By the turn of the century the House of Savoy expressed its wish to help Cyprus. First however it needed up-to-date information and Don Frangisko Akidas was chosen to obtain it. On his way to the island he visited Alexandria and then Jerusalem, where he explained his mission to Patriarch Sofronios IV. Sofronios expressed great joy over the projected 'Cypriot Bill of Rights' (a list of fundamental freedoms) and prayed that God might help 'this operation' and decide it in favour of 'our long-suffering Cypriot brothers'.

Don Frangisko, on his arrival in Cyprus, discussed with Archbishop Veniamin the projected plan called 'Operation Easter Day'. He found however that elaborate plans for a revolt had already been prepared. The 'Capitulation', containing the terms on which the Cypriots would acknowledge Charles Emmanuel (Duke of Savoy) as their king, was also drawn up and duly signed. Yet nothing happened before 1607, apart from the Turkish governor strengthening his defences against the possibility of a Spanish and Maltese attack in 1605. The threat of 1607 was more serious. Ferdinand I, Grand Duke of Tuscany, conceived a plan for a grand expedition to the Levant, which was to include the conquest of Cyprus. The 'invasion' was not only ill-timed but ill-prepared and the few Greeks that rebelled were massacred.

However, the notorious Norman corsair Jacques Pierre, known from his great experience as 'the Captain', was asked by Ferdinand I to report on the failure of the expedition. This he did in 1608, at the same time making recommendations for a second attempt. But the Grand Duke died on 7 February 1609 and 'il Capitano's' plan was not put into effect.

From time to time the rulers of France and Venice also circulated plans for the purchase, lease or occupation of the island. The Cypriots made further appeals to Savoy in October 1609 and April 1611, and a last in 1670. Appeals were also sent to Spain. In fact appeals flowed from all quarters in Cyprus to all foreign countries known for their adventurism or love of the island. In the beginning of the seventeenth century the Duke of Savoy again incited the Christian Cypriots to rebel, but in the end he failed to take any decisive steps and the archbishop who inspired the movement lost his life in 1638. From further inconclusive evidence we find that in 1630 Henri duc de Rohan made a remarkable proposal to buy the island to set up a kingdom which should be a refuge for all persecuted Protestants. It is also recorded that a certain Vittorio Zebeto raised a revolt shortly before 1617 and killed a number of Turkish soldiers. He was forced to flee to Savoy.

Several lukewarm attempts in the eighteenth century also proved abortive. But following the Russo-Turkish War of 1769-70, two events important for Hellenism took place. First, Cyprus showed some signs of recovery, both economically and politically, and second, the concept of Hellenism found political expression in the Philike Hetaireia founded by Constantine Rhigas at Bucharest in the early 1780s. Although the movement received a check with the execution of Rhigas in 1798, it was revived in Odessa in 1814. From 1818 onwards several Hetaireia emissaries visited the island (known by the secret code number of 13) and the part of Cyprus in the coming struggle was determined.

The revolt in Greece broke out on 25 March 1821. The Cypriot connection was a reality and the Turkish governor Kuchuk Mehmed feared a full-scale revolt in all the territories which either had, or had once had, Greek majorities. The visit of Constantine Kanares to Cyprus between 19 June and 1 July increased the fears of Kuchuk Mehmed. (He called at a small harbour near Aghios Serghios, then at Asprovrysi near Lapithos, and in both places was greeted by Cypriots who brought him money and three shiploads of sheep, cattle, corn, barley and other provisions.) Kuchuk Mehmed promptly reported to Constantinople, stating that the Cypriots were implicated in the Greek revolutionary movement, urging that troops should be sent to forestall the expected insurrection and recommending, as the only effective way to suppress the movement, the execution of all the leading Christians from the archbishop downwards. The first request was promptly complied with. Over 4,000 ill-disciplined troops were sent over from Syria (described as the 'off-scourings' of that country), but their behaviour was appalling. Hence whilst marching through Larnaca in May they fired on the flags of the foreign consuls, especially the French, who later demanded and obtained satisfaction from the Porte. Concerning the second request, the Sultan at first hesitated, but with a Russian attack on Istanbul imminent he ordered the disarming of the Empire's Christians. What followed has already been described on page 33.

After the success of the Greek insurrection, Count Capodistria, who had come to power in 1828, immediately expressed a desire for the *enosis* of Cyprus. A small revolt was suppressed in 1830. Three years later two Greek-led revolts took place, in addition to the one led by the Giaur Imam, a well-to-do Turk of Trimithousa (less than ten miles south-east of Polis in the Paphos district), who resented the payment of taxes and who managed to 'rule' Paphos for several months. Of the two Greek-led revolts, one was led by Nicholas Theseus and inspired partly by dissatisfaction about taxation. Having failed, Theseus, with the help of the French consul Bottu, escaped on board a Greek ship to Rhodes. The French poet Lamartine, who spoke of Theseus as being 'good-mannered and intelligent', took him to Constantinople to plead his case. Having failed in his mission he left the Ottoman dominions. In 1839 he returned to Greece and was appointed consul at Beirut – a post which he held for a few years.

The third rebellion of 1833 had a much stronger enosist element. It began in the Karpass area in July and was led by Ioannikios, a monk (*kalogeros*) who promised liberation from the Turkish yoke. (See pages 34-5.) It has been estimated that the cost of the suppression of these three risings was over one million piastres.

The movement for *enosis* with Greece, therefore, had begun before the British occupation. Furthermore, the provisional

character of the Cyprus Convention and the precedent of the
Ionian Islands (Britain took them from the French during the
Napoleonic Wars of the early nineteenth century and, following
enosist unrest in 1849, ceded them to Greece in 1864) fostered
the belief that it was only a matter of time before a similar
gesture would be made over Cyprus. Resolutions, memoranda,
deputations, protests and riots in favour of union with Greece
are to be found with great frequency in the annals of Cypriot
history since 1878.

The Greeks formed 80 per cent of the population. The largest
minority – descendants of the Ottomans, who ruled Cyprus
from 1571 to 1878 – were the Turks who formed around 18 per
cent. These were direct descendants of those left on the island to
serve as a garrison or brought there as settlers. The
approximate number was 20,000. The other minorities were
the Franco-Levantines, descendants mainly of the Lusignans,
who ruled the island from 1192 to 1489; Armenians, Maronites
and some British, who settled in Cyprus after the occupation of
1878.

For over 2,000 years the 'Greekness' of Cyprus was beyond
doubt. When the Turks conquered the island in 1571 it had a
population of just over 150,000 Greeks and several thousand
others. They proceeded to institute a policy which directly
created the Cyprus problem. It was very similar to that which
the English government was pursuing, about the same time, in
Ireland, and it had similar results. This was the so-called
'policy of plantation' – importing Moslem Turks, speaking a
foreign language and practising a different religion, to form an
ascendancy and help keep the native Greeks under control.

The struggle to unite Cyprus with the Greek mainland was
from the outset a Greek-Cypriot affair – the struggle of the
majority. Only certain elements of the Turkish minority, as we
shall see in later chapters, objected; contrary to what has been
written elsewhere, the vast majority of the Turkish population
did not support the repressive measures imposed by the British
to check the agitation of the enosists.

As already stated, leading Cypriot personalities in 1878
declared their desire to join Greece to Sir Garnet Wolseley. In
the first year of occupation there were anti-British protests
following the incident of the two Christian monks. According to

evidence both scanty and unclear, two very old monks were first shaved and then imprisoned. During the second year of occupation a wave of enthusiasm swept Cyprus as Greece mobilized for war against Turkey. Scores of volunteers, mules and a letter to the King of the Hellenes from Archbishop Sofronios II expressing solidarity with mother Greece were the Cypriot contribution. The archbishop wrote as follows on 30 October 1880: 'The Greek people of the Island charged me to send to Your Majesty by colonel Hadji Yianni – he too a son of Cyprus – one hundred and seven mules. Be pleased to accept in the name of our nation this modest gift from our now impoverished Cyprus, with my ardent prayers for the fulfilment of her Pan-hellenic longings.'[3]

King George I replied on 2 December, praising the Cypriots for their devotion – notwithstanding the changes they had undergone over many years, and their distance from Greece – in never forgetting their duty to their dear country. He saw the Cypriot contribution as clear proof of the true strength of Greek feeling – Hellenism – an indissoluble bond based on descent, religion and tradition.

Britain proceeded to pass the Cyprus Neutrality Order in Council of 18 May 1881, which empowered the High Commissioner to control recruitment of the islanders. But the Greekness of Cyprus was further proved when the Greek inhabitants gave an enthusiastic welcome to a Greek warship *Admiral Miaoulis* when it visited the island. This event, together with the general attitude of the Greeks, alarmed the British authorities. On 12 April 1881 Biddulph sent a telegram to Lord Kimberley, the Colonial Secretary, informing him that a 'report has spread here that the British government has offered Cyprus to Greece'. On the following day Biddulph's fears were eliminated when Kimberley telegraphed that 'there is no truth whatever in report that the British government has offered Cyprus to Greece'. There had simply been a proposal in Parliament for the handing of the island to Greece.

Before embarking on the arduous task of outlining the most important Cypriot moves for *enosis*, three of the references made by Gladstone (the great Liberal leader and four times Prime Minister of Great Britain between 1868 and 1894) to the Cyprus problem should be noted. Speaking at Penicuik,

Scotland, on 25 March 1880, he emphasized his desire that sooner or later Cyprus should be united with Greece because, apart from other considerations, 'the bulk of the people are Greek'. On 17 December he suggested to Glanville (another leading Liberal politician) that Cyprus should be handed to Greece by Britain and Turkey 'in sovereignty not in mere occupation'. Gladstone was here enlarging on Bismarck's (the German Chancellor's) wish to cede Crete to Greece. Crete, with its Greek majority, had repeatedly stated that union with Greece was not only desirable but essential. Gladstone's words were seized upon by the Cypriots, who promptly despatched a memorandum to the Colonial Secretary in 1881 expressing their long-held wish for union with the mainland. The Cypriot Association of Nicosia had earlier (16 February 1880) sent a letter to Gladstone expressing its sincere gratitude to him for his genuine concern for the desires of the Greeks. Gladstone also received in April 1881 three telegrams from the people of Nicosia, Larnaca and Limassol thanking him and reiterating their desire for ultimate union 'with our motherland Greece'.

His third reference to the Cypriot problem was on 13 March 1897. From the château Florence, Cannes, he wrote to the Duke of Westminster a long exposition of his half-century's experience of the eastern question. Of Cyprus he wrote: 'While I subjoin the satisfaction I should feel, were it granted me, before the close of my long life, to see the population of that Hellenic island placed by a friendly arrangement in organic union with their brethren of the Kingdom and of Crete.'[4]

Meanwhile, another resolution was sent to the Colonial Secretary in 1885; two years later the celebration of Queen Victoria's Jubilee was boycotted by the Greeks, who went on to advocate union in all the churches and arranged sports meetings so that the British celebrations failed for lack of attendance. However, the celebrations of the Diamond Jubilee in June 1897 succeeded beyond all expectations. These festivities marked the sixtieth anniversary of Her Majesty's accession. On 25 June, the High Commissioner wrote in a despatch to Joseph Chamberlain, the Colonial Secretary: 'I confess however that I was not prepared for the universal and spontaneous outburst of loyalty which took place on the 22nd of June, and which will make that day a memorable one in the history of Cyprus.'[5]

The years 1893 and 1895 saw a renewed burst of agitation; every expression of opinion by non-Greeks in favour of union with the motherland was eagerly seized upon by the Christian leaders of Cyprus. In January 1893 a Turkish deputation headed by the Mufti complained to Sir Walter Sendall of the publication in the *Phoni tis Kyprou (Voice of Cyprus)* of letters written by two English Members of Parliament about the political situation in Cyprus. The correspondence in question consisted of letters exchanged between Dilke and George Siakali, a member of the legislative council, and letters alleged to have been written by Labouchere to Harvey, a correspondent in Ireland. The letters suggested that as Britain could not relieve Cyprus of the tribute (see page 80-81), the Greeks of the island should work for the cession of it to Greece by Turkey, in return for a cash payment, and that Britain might be willing to guarantee a loan for the purpose. The Moslem delegation pleaded for the continuance of the status quo and urged that the very stringent Turkish press laws should be enforced to prevent the publication of similar material.

The reduction of the garrison decided on in 1894 and carried out in 1895 also caused rumours of the coming evacuation of the island. However, it was announced that there was no intention of relinquishing Cyprus and that the movement of troops was purely a matter of military convenience and had no political significance. Further agitation was occasioned by the discussions held at Westminster during a debate on the supplementary estimates which covered the Cypriot grant-in-aid. It was deduced from the debate that Cyprus, described in 1878 as the 'bright jewel of the English Crown', was now not wanted. Sir Charles Dilke, the chief instigator of the debate, explained on 8 March 1895: 'With regard to Cyprus generally, it was originally occupied as a military station, but there is now no great military or naval authority who says it is of any military value to this country. . . . Cyprus must be looked upon as the whitest of white elephants.'[6]

The Cypriot reaction was prompt and certain. Lively demonstrations were organized on Greek Independence Day and Sir Walter Sendall, the High Commissioner, received a letter, dated 22 April and signed by Archbishop Sofronios and a number of Christian politicians, stating that they proposed to hold public meetings on 28 April to assert that the condition of the island made it impossible for the people to go on paying taxes. Above all, they reminded the High Commissioner that if the British government wished to withdraw and forget Cyprus, then it was the ardent wish of the Greek element to be united with Greece. The proposed meetings took place (usually called the 'Anti-Tax and Tribute Demonstrations'), and resolutions, including one on union, were adopted in Limassol and Nicosia.

The feeling excited by this debate prompted Sendall to send confidential despatches to the Marquis of Ripon (Colonial Secretary) on 7, 8 and 23 April requesting permission to repeat the assurance, conveyed to him in September 1894, that 'Her Majesty's Government has no intention of relinquishing the administration of Cyprus' since, amongst other things, it was 'causing much disquiet amongst the Moslems'. In a letter addressed to the archbishop and the other organizers dated 26 April, Arthur Young, the Chief Secretary of the Cyprus Government, consented to the meetings of 28 April, pleaded for order and declared that 'England has absolutely no intention whatever of withdrawing from the Island'.

Two years later the Christian element of Cyprus demonstrated yet again their Hellenic feelings by sending probably over 1,000 volunteers to fight in the so-called 'Thirty Days War' between Greece and Turkey. They were commended for their heroism, especially at Velestino. Sendall, on 30 March, asked whether he should take action under the Cyprus Neutrality Order in Council of 18 May 1881 to stop attempts at recruiting volunteers for the Greek army. In the previous year aid to the Cretans had been prevented by the Cypriot authorities. On 2 April Sendall reported that some Greeks had already left and that Moslem meetings were being held and subscriptions raised to aid the military operations of the Porte. On 7 April he stated that around 1,000 Greek Cypriot volunteers were on the move and on the 16th he reported once more to Joseph Chamberlain that although recruitment was still proceeding the situation was not dangerous and the taking of repressive measures might therefore have the effect of stimulating rather than checking the movement. On several occasions he also acknowledged that action could not be taken against persons who recruited or who offered themselves as volunteers, but only against those who induced others to take service or who aided and abetted them in so doing. He pointed out that the chief aider and abettor in this matter was the recently appointed Greek consul Philemon, who was regularly greeted by the Christian population as the representative of 'our king' but, paradoxically enough, was regarded by the British authorities in Cyprus as a 'sincere gentleman' and 'especially friendly to England and the English'.

Nevertheless the High Commissioner issued a proclamation on 23 April calling on the inhabitants to abstain from acts likely to cause disturbances. He also informed the Colonial Office that excitement still prevailed and that grounds for anxiety arose partly from the composition of the police force. He was of course referring to the loyalties of Christian and Moslem policemen in the event of clashes between the two communities. By 6 May Sendall was able to report that 'the most perfect tranquillity prevails everywhere'. Yet two notable incidents during the Greek Easter celebrations, which very nearly set the patriotic embers of the two sides alight, are worth recalling. The first incident occurred at a Famagusta church where an explosion injured thirty-five persons and killed a child and an old man. Although several Turks were arrested, the motives, if any, for this reckless act were not established by the authorities. The second incident took place in Limassol, where another incident in a church nearly provoked violence. In this case, during the ceremony of the 'Judas bonfire' (lit in the precincts of churches on Easter eve) a native Turkish police officer was seen to enter the church smoking a pipe. Once more the moderating influences prevailed and there was no violence. In fact political violence was a rarity in the island.

Even before the above hostilities the Greeks of Cyprus had sent another memorandum to the High Commissioner (17 February 1897) stating quite explicitly that 'our hopes which were raised in 1878 are now worthless – we now believe that Great Britain occupied Cyprus for her own political motives and is now turning a deaf ear to our wishes and desires'. Further protests came in 1899. These followed a speech by Joseph Chamberlain (Secretary of State for the Colonies) during a discussion on Civil Service estimates in the House of Commons.

Chamberlain did much, compared to his predecessors, for the economy of Cyprus but, following a suggestion by the Liberals that the island should be handed to Greece, said on 4 August:

> I have no doubt that in some respects that would appeal to the sentiments of the Grecian population in the island; but I have no reason to believe that the Mahomedans in the island, who are equally worthy of our good-will and care, would at all like any such transfer. I am not certain that even the Greeks themselves would, considering the financial disabilities under which they would immediately be placed, feel that these would be compensated for by sentimental considerations'.[7]

This insinuation infuriated the Greek Cypriots, who went on to declare for the thousandth time that union with mother Greece was their ardent and inextinguishable desire. Three years later Chamberlain's speech, again during a debate on Civil Service estimates, once more prompted the Greeks to retaliate. Speaking in the House of Commons on 26 May 1902 he said: 'I say the Cypriots have nothing whatever to complain of. . . A suggestion has been made tonight that this island be transferred to Greece. . . I do not think that any change in the occupation of the island could be possible.'[8]

While meetings were held and resolutions passed by the Greeks the Turks held counter-meetings and thanked the Colonial Secretary for his wisdom in not transferring Cyprus to Greece. A resolution signed by the organizers and 600 others emphasized that union or a change in the status of the island would bring about the annihilation of the Moslem community; if the island were to be abandoned, then it should be restored to the Ottoman empire, the lawful owner of the island.

The Greek members of the legislative council, however, passed a resolution expressing their profound distress at the inaccuracies of Chamberlain's statements and his 'insults' to the Greek Cypriots' personal and national sense of honour. On 12 February 1903 a similar protest was sent to Chamberlain from the legislative council, embodying resolutions from Nicosia, Larnaca, Limassol, Famagusta and Kyrenia. The memorandum centred on three main issues:

1   The tribute, which was considered excessive and the cause of all the economic misfortunes of the island. As a protest the elected members of the legislative council attempted to throw out the estimates in both 1902 and 1904.

2   The safe keeping and preservation of antiquities. It may be recalled that in the years 1885-6 a syndicate which carried out excavations at Polis tis Chrisohous sold the contents at an auction in Paris.

3   The sacred and steadfast will for the union of Cyprus with mother Greece, which was once more emphasized.

The memorandum was printed in Greek and English and was sent to many British Members of Parliament and leading newspapers. The Greek version was signed by Kyrillos, Bishop of Kition, Th. Theodotou, G. Siakallis, N. Rossos, F. Zannetos, I. Bonditsianos, S. Frangoudis, I. Kyriakides and Ch. Sozos. It must also be recalled that the accession of King Edward VII and Queen Alexandra to the throne of Great Britain was received with joy, although the nine Greek members of the legislative council in their telegram of congratulation expressed their permanent wish for union with the motherland. The year 1903 also witnessed resolutions and counter-resolutions for union with Greece or Turkey in the legislative council. In July the Greek elected members carried by a majority (the three elected Moslem members being absent) the insertion in the reply of the legislative council to the High Commissioner's opening speech a statement to the effect that their just claims would be met with full satisfaction. The resolution expressed the wish of the whole island for the restoration of Cyprus to Greece. (This refuted Chamberlain's earlier statement of 26 May 1902 that most Cypriots would rather be governed by a rich government than annexed by a poor state.) The Moslem members subsequently introduced a resolution opposing any such idea.

The Greek politicians of Cyprus received excellent support from organizations outside the island. Particularly effective was the national club in Athens styled the 'Patriotic League of Cypriots' formed on 14 November 1898. Its president was G. Frangoudis and its chief clerk A. Kyrou. From the minutes of its foundation we can see that it had three principal objects:

the national re-establishment of Cyprus;
the improvement of ecclesiastic and educational standards
and the amenities of the island;
the protection of the material interests of Cyprus, which
meant first and foremost the abolition of the tribute.

This clamour for *enosis* alarmed Sir William Frederic Haynes-
Smith, the High Commissioner, who in a letter to Chamberlain
on 12 May 1903 named Andreas Themistocleous, the Director
of the Limassol Gymnasium, as one of the prominent unionist
leaders and suggested that the open flaunting of political
emblems and flags should be restricted by an Order in Council.

The Greek-speaking, Greek-thinking, Greek-feeling
Cypriots continued their agitation for *enosis* by all available
means. It was consequently no surprise when a Greek cadet
training ship *Admiral Miaoulis* visiting Limassol in 1906
occasioned fervent enosist demonstrations. Further outbursts
resulted from the visit of Winston Churchill in 1907. The
Parliamentary Under-Secretary of State for the Colonies
arrived in Famagusta on the morning of Wednesday 9 October
and departed on the evening of Sunday the 13th. A confidential
despatch from Sir Charles King-Harman to the Earl of Elgin,
Secretary of State for the Colonies, dated 21 October, records
Churchill's reception: 'While the wharf and the streets of the
town were gay with the colours of Greece, the air was rent with
shouts for the Union. The display was at one time in danger of
being marred by the Turks of Famagusta who, in their
indignation at the Greek demonstration, fell foul of some of the
processionists and began what might have developed into a
very considerable affray.'[9]

Nevertheless, an address was given by the mayor of the town,
who gave prominence to the national aspirations of the Greeks.
The Turks were also ready with their address of welcome, in
which they repudiated the pretensions of their Greek
compatriots. Churchill also received a memorandum from the
Greek elected members on behalf of the Greek population of the
island. It emphasized the three cardinal points: union with
Greece, abolition of the tribute and wider political liberties for
the representatives of the people. Concerning *enosis*, Churchill
commented significantly that 'such a desirable consummation
will doubtless be fulfilled in the plenitude of time and that, in

the meantime, the people of Cyprus will be content to remain under the British flag'.

Churchill of course did not discuss the *enosis* issue, but on 19 October he presented a memorandum to the British Cabinet on the appalling condition of Cyprus (part of the memorandum is quoted on page 82), and in his reply to the Greek elected members he said: 'I think it is only natural that the Cypriot people, who are of Greek descent, should regard their incorporation with what may be called their mother-country as an ideal to be earnestly, devoutly and fervently cherished.'[10]

To Churchill such a feeling was an example of the patriotic devotion which so nobly characterized the Greek nation. His government however had to consider also the views of the island's Moslems and the fact that a British occupation of Cyprus should not lead to the dismemberment of the Ottoman Empire. Furthermore, as to the alleged precedent of the Ionian Islands, they had actually been in the possession of the British government, as Cyprus was not. So ended Churchill's reply.

The Greeks however persisted with further protests, letters, telegrams and deputations. A statement from the Athens Society of Students to Lord Gladstone (written in Greek on 15 December 1909 and signed by its president P. Christodoulides and its secretary A.M. Triantafilides on the occasion of the centenary of his father's birth) expressed once more the Cypriots' wish for the fulfilment of their eternal passion for union with mother Greece. Similar memorials were sent to the High Commissioner, Sir Hamilton Goold-Adams. One was dated 1 December 1911 and another 5 February 1912. Telegrams sent to the King and Queen on their coronation in 1911 by the archbishop and mayors of Cyprus expressed yet again their steadfast desire for national restoration. The same wish was expressed later when the royal couple passed near the island on their way to India. On 28 April approval was given by the members of the legislative council, who resigned *en masse* on 17 April 1912, to the formation of a central committee, under the presidency of the archbishop, for carrying on the national struggle. The resolution adopted declared that 'no power in the world, no oppression could alter the national sentiment and will to be annexed to Greece'.

The Turco-Italian War of 1911-12, which brought a Turkish

defeat, caused some excitement in certain towns in Cyprus. The disturbances in Nicosia and in a few other villages were not serious, since there were only a few minor injuries. However, serious trouble occurred at Limassol on the night of 27 May 1912. The primary cause of the riot was the incident at the little mosque (*jamouda*) in the Katholiki quarter, where some Greeks stoned two carriages full of Turks coming from the village of Malia. One of the Turks immediately drew a knife and stabbed two Greeks. The bells of the Katholidgi church began ringing and Greeks, sensing trouble, arrived in large numbers. A brawl developed, but when the police opened fire the crowds dispersed.

On 15 June a mixed commission consisting of Major W.N. Bolton, Mustapha Sami Yorghanzi Bashizade Efendi and Mr S. Stravrinakis was appointed to carry out a full enquiry into all matters relating to the Limassol riots. The commission was unable to come to a unanimous conclusion as to the cause of the disturbances (the British and Greek members stated that the riot was certainly not premeditated, whilst the Turkish member insisted that it was), but they were all of the opinion that the local police commander was justified in firing on the rioters. The casualties reported by the commission were as follows:

> 3 killed and 100 wounded, caused by the rioters to civilians;
> 1 officer and 14 men wounded, caused by the rioters to police;
> 2 killed and 9 wounded, caused by rifle fire of the police.

At least 18 persons were sentenced, using the outdated Ottoman penal code, to imprisonment ranging from nine months to 15 years. These sentences were reduced considerably in June 1913. Disturbances of this nature were rare and caused by certain irresponsible elements, both Greek and Turk, usually flaring up on the spur of the moment. A typical example occurred in 1909 when, following some excitement caused by several meetings of Greeks, over 680 Moslems assembled in one corner of Nicosia and armed themselves with swords and knives; but nothing happened.

Another Greek delegation (composed of three members) was sent to London in the summer of 1912. Lewis Harcourt, the

Colonial Secretary, in a confidential despatch on 20 August informed Sir Hamilton Goold-Adams of his interview with the deputation about matters affecting the constitution and administration of Cyprus. Harcourt suggested an increase in Christian representatives on the legislative council and the introduction of new procedures to afford elected members greater opportunities for examining amendments to the annual estimates. The Colonial Secretary therefore considered that the constitution should be radically changed. The High Commissioner's confidential reply of 3 October urged that nothing whatever should be done, since it would be seen as a sign of weakness: the success of the Greeks' recent agitation would not only spur them on to further demands but would infuriate the Moslem element.

Before the year was over both Moslems and Christians presented further petitions via the High Commissioner to the Colonial Secretary. On 13 December the Moslem members of the legislative council (Mehmed Shevket, Mustapha Hami and Mehmed Ziai) praised in their petition the life of the Turks under the British, expressed their concern that if Cyprus was annexed to Greece the Moslems would be annihilated – an eternal disgrace to civilization – and suggested that if a change in the status of the island was contemplated it should be ceded to Great Britain or annexed by Egypt. The Greeks, on the other hand, following a meeting at the Archiepiscopal Palace on 6 December, expressed the wish, in a petition dated 19 December, that the Liberal British government might, in the present favourable circumstances (i.e. during the Balkan Wars and the following settlement), finally settle the Cyprus issue in accordance with their eternal aspirations.

The Greeks were also aware of the suggestion of Lloyd George (Chancellor of the Exchequer and perhaps the strongest British political figure) in the winter of 1912-13 that Cyprus might be ceded to Greece in return for the right of Britain to use Argostoli in Cephalonia as a base in case of war. This prompted the archbishop, who chaired a meeting of notables and provincial delegates on 7 January 1913, to 'proclaim' the union of the island with Greece. On 18 January the Cypriot newspaper *Eleftheria* published an article to the effect that Cyprus was shortly to be handed over to Greece and that Constantinos Papamichalopoulos had been designated by the Greek government as its first Governor of Cyprus. The Turks were once more alarmed, but the High Commissioner assured them that their interests would be safeguarded if and when such a change occurred.

Hence although the Greeks of Cyprus reacted strongly to Lloyd George's lukewarm proposition, that is as far as it went – nothing more was heard of it. Nevertheless, further pressure was exerted on the British authorities. A memorandum was sent to the Colonial Office on 30 May and another on 10 June 1913. In the latter, the nine Christian members of the legislative council repeated that 'from Great Britain, this powerful advocate of the rights of nations, we expect, in the near future, the fulfilment of the national rights of this most Hellenic and historical island'. Furthermore, on 21 November 1914, following the annexation of the island by Britain, a delegation headed by the archbishop informed the High Commissioner once more of the one and only desire of the Greek inhabitants.

Thus language, tradition, race and religion prompted the Greeks of Cyprus to struggle for union with Greece. Stanley Casson, the Oxford archaeologist, wrote in 1942 that 'Cyprus is still populated by Greek stock which can claim a more direct descent from pre-Dorian Greek strains than most parts of the mainland of Greece'. Sir Ronald Storrs, governor of the island from 1926 to 1932, wrote in 1937 that 'no sensible person will deny that the Cypriot is Greek-speaking, Greek-thinking, Greek-feeling, Greek, just as much as the Canadian is French-speaking, French-feeling and French, hence the Greekness of Cyprus is in my opinion indisputable'. The feelings of the Greeks of Cyprus therefore were only natural. There was however another factor that kept this desire alive – the voice of the clergy and of the educated professional classes. Professor Douglas Dakin in his thorough study of Greek affairs says: 'Before the Balkan Wars of 1912-13, large numbers of Greeks from the unredeemed lands – Constantinople, Asia Minor, Macedonia, Thrace, Crete, Epiros, Cyprus, and other islands – found their way to the University of Athens, whence they returned to their territories as apostles of the *megali idhea*.'[11]

For years the Greeks had been dreaming of a Greater Greece in which all Greeks, especially those living under foreign governments, would be united under one flag. No Greek thought however of bringing his compatriots in Egypt, the United States or Britain into this Hellenic fold, but nearly every Greek thought in terms of rescuing his enslaved brothers from Turkish rule. The most concern was shown for those in the Smyrna district, the Bulgarian littoral, Macedonia, Epirus, the Dodecanese islands and Cyprus. This Great Idea, the hope for a Greater Greece, was a national ideal that transcended party lines. Hence the desire to expand, to liberate more and more Greeks from Turkish rule, became the motivating force of Greek foreign policy. Indeed, from the time of the independence of Greece, the Greek people were passionately attached to a foreign policy inspired by the *megali idhea*.

Greece obtained the Ionian Islands in 1864; Thessaly and one district of Epirus in 1881; Crete, southern Epirus, a large portion of Macedonia and most of the Aegean islands came to her as a result of the Balkan Wars in 1912-13. By the end of these wars the majority of the Greeks were finally united under the Greek flag. Greece increased its territory by 68 per cent and its population from approximately 2,700,000 to around 4,800,000. This was a powerful incentive for the other Greeks to aspire to join the motherland, aspirations which were greatly encouraged by President Woodrow Wilson's plea for government with the consent of the governed. All subject peoples took new hope.

Yet around 2,500,000 'unredeemed' Greeks were left scattered in Bulgaria, Turkey, the Dodecanese islands and Cyprus. Only in the last two territories did they constitute majorities. In the decade which followed the Balkan Wars Greece obtained western Thrace and an exchange of population agreement with Bulgaria. But her renewed struggle with Turkey ended in total defeat. Following the conflict of 1919-22, the legitimate desire to protect the national interest and the romantic dream of an imperial Greece with its capital at Constantinople (Istanbul) became fatally fused in the Greek mind. The price Greece paid for its Anatolian venture was the mass expulsion of over 1,250,000 Greeks from their ancestral homes in eastern Thrace and Anatolia. The 1923 Treaty of Lausanne put a stop to the Greek dream. Yet four years earlier, at the Paris Peace Conference, E. Venizelos received specious promises that, once the Greek question as a whole was settled, Cyprus would also become part of Greece; and by the Treaty of Sèvres (1920) the Allies duly awarded to Greece almost everything the Greeks wanted. Only Cyprus, Constantinople and the Dodecanese islands were denied them. Venizelos told the assembled statesmen: 'We will win among the family of free nations and hand down to our children a Greece such as generations past have dreamt of, a Greece such as we ourselves foreshadowed in our recent victories of 1912 and 1913.'

Next to be received into the fold of Hellenism were the Dodecanese islands. Italy had occupied the islands in her 1911-12 war with Turkey and had thereby prevented Greece from occupying them during the Balkan Wars. She continued to hold them, in spite of the repeated pleas of the Dodecanesians for union with Greece, until her defeat in the Second World War. At the 1946 Paris Peace Conference the islands were awarded to Greece in recognition of her heroic struggle against Mussolini and Hitler. Turkey, for several reasons, did not contest the award. In the first place she had remained neutral during most of the war; secondly, the Balkan Pact of 1934 meant that one of the most notable trends in Turkey's policy was her cordial attitude towards the liberated Greeks; thirdly, apart from Turkey's genuine admiration for the courage and tenacity of the Greek people the attitude was due, no doubt, to a vague hope of preparing a Graeco-Turkish counterweight, under the aegis of Britain and America, to a possible Yugoslav-Bulgarian-Macedonian federation, under the aegis of Russia; and lastly, Turkey had announced prior to the termination of the war that she had no territorial claims to bring forward since her predominant interest was the security of Anatolia. Turkey preferred therefore that the islands should be handed to Greece – her neighbour and ally.

The emergence of the Constitution

The second major trend between 1878 and 1914 was the emergence of the Constitution. Less than two months after the arrival of Sir Garnet Wolseley, an Order in Council (14 September 1878) established a legislative council and an executive council to run the affairs of the island. The latter was constituted as might be directed by instructions addressed from time to time to the High Commissioner by the British Government.

The legislative council consisted of the High Commissioner and not less than four and not more than eight other members – half being officials and the other unofficial: Those present at its first meeting on 9 December were the High Commissioner, C.A. Cookson, Colonel Biddulph (who succeeded Wolseley in 1879), Colonel G.R. Greaves, Richard Mathei (an Italian long resident on the island), Mustapha Fuad Efendi (a Turkish Cypriot) and George Glikys (a Greek Cypriot merchant). It met again on 16 December and at its third meeting on 19 December took into consideration a proposed ordinance regarding the sale of land to subjects of foreign countries. Following a discussion it was passed, with opposition from Mathei, Fuad and Glikys.

The freedom which Britain promised the Cypriots turned out to be the autocratic (*monokratoria*) rule of the High Commissioner, who possessed practically unlimited powers. Protests began to pour in – those of 1881 being particularly effective. In the meantime Cyprus was transferred, on 6 December 1880, from the Foreign Office to the Colonial Office; by late 1881 or early 1882 the British government contemplated changes in the Constitution. An Order in Council dated 30 November 1882 modified the existing form of administration. The subsequent elections brought out certain long standing divisions. Thus the so-called 'Old Turkish Party' objected at first, believing that the elections and the formation of the legislative council would stabilize the British regime, thus giving the non-Moslem majority a chance to impose its will on them.

However, the elected legislative council assembled for the first time at 5.00 p.m. on Thursday 21 June 1883. Those present were the High Commissioner and six British official members, eight Greeks (including Kyprianos, the Bishop of Kition) and three Turks. The High Commissioner had a casting vote. Consequently the British government not only had power to legislate for the island by Order in Council but could amend or revoke decisions reached by the legislative council. In fact, although some form of representative government was given, there was no provision for majority rule. In reality it was a very thinly disguised form of authoritarian rule. This undemocratic form of colonial administration (communal representation was first formulated in Cyprus) meant that those areas of business not decided solely by the High Commissioner were handed to the legislative council. This, however, worked on the principle that the British and Turkish members at least equalled, or exceeded by one, the number of Greek members, with the High Commissioner (or governor after 1925) having the casting vote. An Anglo-Turkish combination, therefore, could carry any measure against the united opposition of the Greeks representing 80 per cent of the total population of the island.

This system was maintained, especially after Cyprus became a colony in 1925, through a process of privileges for the Turkish members, antagonizing the Greek Cypriots and providing therefore the basis for 'divide and rule'. The *Edinburgh Review*, reviewing events in Cyprus from 1878 to 1891, remarked:

> The Cyprus constitution was a sham gift. The giver gave nothing. The recipient received that which he did not want, and was unable to put to any good use. And the gift has had the fate of all shams. It has made the giver contemptible and the receiver ungrateful. Cyprus in 1881 had asked for bread, and we gave her, in response to her petition, not a stone – nothing so substantial – but a very feather, a plume of finery to stick into her poor and ragged turban. The Cypriot is as hungry, nay hungrier, than ever for the bread that might satisfy him; and when he looks at the valueless and inappropriate ornament that flutters uselessly over his head, he feels not only hungry but ridiculous.[12]

This so-called constitution was unchanged when Britain annexed Cyprus in 1914; was modified in 1925 when the island became a colony; and was eventually abolished in 1931. An advisory council set up in 1931 replaced the legislative council.

The economic situation

The third major trend of the period was the economic situation. The Cypriots were assured by Wolseley in 1878 that measures would be taken to promote and develop commerce and industry. The inhabitants were given to understand that half a century's peace and good management would push the island to as high a position as it had occupied in the time of its greatest glory. As *The Times* commented on 22 July 1878, 'Englishmen will not prove inadequate' to the development of the island. Once more however man and nature combined to inflict severe blows on the already retarded Cypriot economy.

As early as 1879 there were protests about the acute economic situation and the persecution of the priests. In 1877-8 there was a drought, in 1880 a plague, and there were bad harvests in 1877 and 1889. On 12 November 1892 a disastrous flood in Limassol caused 22 deaths and a loss of over £50,000. An earlier flood in the same town, on 24 December 1880, caused more than five deaths.

The publication of certain Parliamentary Papers about the affairs of Cyprus in June 1881 caused considerable excitement and ill-feeling in the island. Resolutions were passed and telegrams sent to Lord Kimberley. Secretary of State for the Colonies. Kimberley's minute of 18 July 1881 virtually announced the complete abandonment of the policy which may be called 'recognition of responsibility'. A national petition in 1882 signed by the archbishop, bishops and all the leading Christian merchants called attention to certain administrative shortcomings in the past and set out the people's wishes and hopes for the future. In fact towards the close of the year 1882 the people of the island became fully aware that they were dissatisfied with British rule. A letter dated 22 November 1882 from Archbishop Sofronios to Gladstone, the British Prime Minister (forwarded by Biddulph the High Commissioner together with an official translation), expressed his heartfelt congratulations and blessing on his fiftieth political anniversary (he became the Member for Newark in 1832 at the age of 23), and pleaded for the long-awaited promised reforms: 'Hoping therefore that your Honour will favourably accept these simple congratulations, expressions from myself as well as from all my Christian flock who wish impatiently to see the application of new reforms.'[13]

The Cypriots at the time were in fact asking for material help for:

>schools of agriculture, and the introduction of new seeds, plants, stock and agricultural machinery;
>an agricultural bank;

irrigation works;

replantation of trees in the forests;

encouragement of the growth of tobacco by the removal of fiscal restrictions of an obviously oppressive character; and

the abolition of the tithe (i.e. a tax on produce and stock).

Another Greek Cypriot deputation led by the archbishop arrived in England in 1889 to plead in person for some remission of the fiscal burdens facing the inhabitants. The memorandum, described by the High Commissioner as being 'of some importance', related mainly to:

the general financial condition of the island;

the system of taxation;

payments made under the Cyprus Convention of 1878;

the value of landed property;

the poor condition of education;

the police force;

the agricultural interests of the island;

the constitutional powers of the legislative council and the constitution of the executive council; and

the condition of the independent Eastern Orthodox Church in Cyprus.

The archbishop was received by Queen Victoria and was created Doctor of Divinity by the University of Oxford. The deputation however received no encouragement from the Conservative government of Lord Salisbury.

Further protests to the High Commissioner in August 1894 and April 1895 strongly emphasized the humiliation of the Cypriots, who were often compelled to sell their household goods to meet their tax and other payments. Joseph Chamberlain promised to relieve the Cypriots of their burden, but nothing much was done. Dissatisfaction and hunger led to violence. The *Edinburgh Review* said: 'One of the most remarkable, and certainly one of the most discouraging, results of British government in Cyprus is the great increase in crime, more especially of serious crime, since the occupation.'[14]

The tribute was perhaps the most important factor in the fortunes of Cyprus. Britain, in return for the occupation of the island, undertook to make good to Turkey the average difference between the island's revenue and expenditure in its last five years as an Ottoman province. Since Turkey had spent nothing on the island but had, on the contrary, taken what it could get out of it, the difference worked out at £92,799 11s. 3d. a year, a sum which was debited annually from its revenue. Usually British governments had voted a grant-in-aid of a fluctuating amount, which in 1910 was fixed at £50,000 a year. In November 1926 the elected members of the legislative council unanimously rejected the budget as a protest against the continued payment of the tribute. The budget of course was passed by an Order in Council, but the elected members had made their point. Successive High Commissioners and Colonial Secretaries had criticized the payment of tribute. L.S. Amery, the Secretary of State for the Colonies, in a secret memorandum to the Cabinet (dated 14 July 1927) on the political situation in Cyprus, spoke of the tribute in the following unequivocal terms: 'We must face the fact that in taking up their stand on this particular issue, the Elected members are in a strong moral position. The payment against which they are protesting is, in my opinion, one which can no longer be justified by His Majesty's Government.'[15]

In the same year the persistence and persuasiveness of Sir Ronald Storrs induced the British authorities to take over the whole charge, i.e. to abolish the tribute. As Amery said, it was simply an act of elementary justice to abolish it.

Turkey did not receive a single penny of the Cypriot tribute. It was retained by Britain to be paid to the bond-holders, mostly British and French, of a loan on which Turkey had been in default since 1855. Accordingly the government made over as interest on the 1855 loan the required annual amount of £81,752, offering to the Porte only the balance of the tribute. This the Turks declined to accept, and the British invested the annual balance in consols as a contribution to the sinking fund of the loan.

Development of the island's economy was therefore held up, and the Cypriots kept on protesting. They found an ally in Winston Churchill, who insisted that all taxation raised should be used for the benefit of the island's inhabitants. As Parliamentary Under-Secretary of State for the Colonies, he reported to the Cabinet on the condition of Cyprus, stressing that although the most grinding economies were enforced, although all public works were neglected and the whole administration was cut down to starvation point, Britain never succeeded, any more than the Sultan, in squeezing the full tribute out of the island. He continued:

> This iniquitous and immoral arrangement lasted for twenty-seven years, during which time we succeeded in extracting from this wretched island about £60,000 a year on the average or about £1,600,000 altogether. . . . But the fact stares me none the less in the face that we have no right whatever, except by *force majeure*, to take a penny of the Cyprus tribute to relieve us from our own just obligations, however unfortunately contracted. There is scarcely any spectacle more detestable than the oppression of a small community by a great Power for the purpose of pecuniary profit; and that is, in fact, the spectacle which our financial treatment of Cyprus at this moment indisputably presents. It is, in my opinion, quite unworthy of Great Britain, and altogether out of accordance with the whole principles of our colonial policy, in every part of the world, to exact tribute by force from any of the possessions or territories administered under the Crown. Let the figures be juggled by any sophistry or artifice within the wit of man, these two root-facts remain – that Cyprus pays £42,800 a year, and that Great Britain receives £42,800 a year for her own benefit, namely, to pay a portion of her own debts. And that, I say, constitutes a blemish upon Imperial policy of a peculiarly descreditable kind.[16]

Churchill of course did report improvements but stressed that 'an improvement upon Turkish standards is not a sufficient or suitable defence for British policy'. Britain justified the poor economic progress of Cyprus by the fact that the island was held in trust and indeed was the only British possession in the strange position of not being either inside or outside the British empire. It was claimed that the peasant was now protected and that money had been spent on medicine and education. It was further claimed that just over £25,000 was paid out of the tribute between 1882 and 1886 for the ransom of Colonel Synge and H. Suter, who were captured (not in Cyprus) by brigands. Another 'forceful' argument put forward was that, since the population of the island increased from 186,173 in 1881 to 237,002 in 1901, Cyprus was on the road to recovery. Joseph Chamberlain was able to claim in 1899 that 'the island is better off now than it ever was'. To sum up, the economic story of the island can be described as one of great expectations but small beginnings. The already quoted *Edinburgh Review* criticized the British authorities for lacking 'foresight' and 'liberalism' and emphasized that 'England alone has chosen to leave the work undone'.

Not surprisingly therefore the Christian deputies of the legislative council reacted strongly. On 12 April 1910 a special resolution expressing their views on the financial position of the island was introduced by Th. Theodotou and agreed to after three days' debate. On 5 February 1912, following proposals by the High Commissioner to alleviate some existing injustices, the Greek elected members emphatically stated that 'there is but one strong and unalterable will' on the part of the people of Cyprus, 'to be politically united with its free mother'. On 17 April 1912, after presenting a written protest addressed to Sir Hamilton Goold-Adams, the nine Greek members unanimously resigned and left the chamber. This was followed by local unrest and a demonstration in Nicosia on 28 April. The protests concerned four major issues:

1   The defectiveness of the Constitution should be rectified so that the people could duly participate in the administration of their own affairs.

2   Their representation on the legislative council should be in proportion to the sizes of the two communities. It was stressed that the council as constituted formed a constitutional parody.

3   The surplus obtained from the financial administration of the island should be restored to Cyprus since it stood in great need of additional finance.

4   The taxes paid by the people of Cyprus should be used only for their own benefit.

Church disputation

Another issue which helped to raise Greek passions was the 'squalid schism' within the Church between 1900 and 1910 brought about by the death of Archbishop Sofronios II on 22 May 1900. What was called 'an undignified contest between two parties' resulted in the archiepiscopal see remaining vacant until the election of Kyrillos II, Papadopoulos, on 21 April 1909. Epifanios, the Bishop of Paphos, who had precedence over the other bishops, had died on 5 February 1899; hence the island was left in 1900 with no archbishop and only two bishops, those of Kition, Kyrillos Papadopoulos, and of Kyrenia, Kyrillos Vasiliou. The former was a fiery and active politician, the latter almost the reverse – and consequently widely regarded as the one more likely to succeed.

The Holy Synod of Cyprus, which consisted at the time of six dignitaries of the Church, took over the administration of the throne and made preparations for the election of a successor to Archbishop Sofronios II. The above two bishops were members of the Holy Synod and the only candidates. The election took place in September 1900, but its validity was disputed and the tranquillity of the island was disturbed by disputes between the highest functionaries of the Christian Church.

Several attempts were made to resolve the dispute. In the autumn of 1901 a delegate from the Oecumenical Patriarch, the Archimandrite Georgiades, arrived in the island. The first conclusion he arrived at was that the Holy Synod was not, ecclesiastically and according to canon law, a synod at all, and he then persuaded the two opposing parties to sign separate requests to the Oecumenical Patriarch to arbitrate in the dispute. Unfortunately, subsequent correspondence stated that the Oecumenical Patriarch failed to find a solution to the difficulty.

The contest eventually involved the whole population, with charges and counter-charges put forward by the supporters and opponents of the two candidates, declarations of support and so forth. At one stage in 1903 charges were brought by 600 persons against the Bishop of Kition for alleged ecclesiastical offences. Demonstrations and riots were also common. The early months of 1908 were particularly eventful. The High Commissioner, C.A. King-Harman, alarmed at the disturbed state of public feeling in Nicosia, requested troops to be sent from Limassol. Accordingly an officer and 50 men of the Yorkshire Regiment, stationed at Polemidia, near Limassol, arrived on 16 March and, following the municipal elections of 25 March, returned there on 6 April. Meanwhile the government had occupied the Archiepiscopal Palace. The riots of April were even more serious and some evidence exists that they were not spontaneous. On the night of the 9th the disorder culminated in a serious riot, in the course of which firearms were freely used. On the following day the High Commissioner issued a proclamation that, in order to put an end to the disorder, Nicosia would be occupied by the police and attempts to disturb the peace would be forcibly suppressed; he warned peaceable people to avoid scenes of disturbance. Although considerable damage was done to property and some serious injury inflicted on individuals, there was no loss of life.

In April 1909 the Bishop of Kition was elected archbishop under the Archiepiscopal Election Law, although the Bishop of Kyrenia was appointed archbishop by the Church of Constantinople. However, in early 1910 the Bishop of Kyrenia at last consented to recognize his opponent as archbishop and resumed his own see with the title 'His Beatitude the President of Kyrenia'. The dispute was finally resolved in April 1910, following the elections to the sees of Paphos and Kition. The High Commissioner, in a letter dated 10 March 1910 to the Earl of Crewe, the Secretary of State for the Colonies, showed his relief: 'Thus closes what I hope and believe to be the last chapter of the history of the Cyprus Archiepiscopal dispute, a dispute which has lasted for close on ten years, which has rent the Greek population of the Island in twain, has retarded the moral and, possibly also, the material progress of the people and which has occasioned scandal and disgrace to the Greek Orthodox Church.'[17]

The Church of Cyprus acquired a constitutional charter, drawn up by the Holy Synod in 1914, regulating its administration on the basis of the sacred canons and prevailing practice, thus preventing the recurrence of any similar conflicts. It provided for an electoral body of 66 elected general representatives (22 clerical and 44 lay), voting jointly with the Synod which was reinforced at archiepiscopal elections by seven abbots and certain other dignitaries. The total was to be 77 members.

When Kyrillos II died in 1916 he was peacefully succeeded by his opponent Kyrillos III, Vasiliou, who led the Church until 1933. Foremost among those who had laboured to promote the unity of the Cyprus Orthodox Church had been Photios, the Patriarch of Alexandria.

1. Soli Theatre

It appears to be Roman and to belong to the end of the second or beginning of the third century. The theatre was excavated in 1930 by Einar Gjerstad's Swedish expedition.

2. Bellapais Abbey

Possibly the most important medieval monument in Cyprus, the abbey was founded late in the twelfth century as a house of Augustinian Canons by Aimery de Lusignan and got its name from the French 'Abbaye de la Paix' (Abbey of Peace). Dramatically situated on a rock escarpment, half-way up the Kyrenia mountains, it commands magnificent views over much of the northern coast.

3. Emmanuel Tsouderos

Born in Rethimnon, Crete, in 1882, Tsouderos was destined to become one of the most important national figures of Greece after 1924, when he served as Minister of Communications under Eleftherios Venizelos. He was Prime Minister of his country from 21 April 1941 to 13 April 1944.

4. Ismet Inönü and Eleftherios Venizelos

Two protagonists of Turco-Greco friendship during the early 1930s: Ismet Inönü (left), Atatürk's lifelong friend and closest collaborator, who served his country for 17 years as Prime Minister and 12 years as president between 1923 and 1965, and Eleftherios Venizelos, whose political life in the first 30 years of this century is justifiably referred to as 'the history of Greece'. He served his country as Prime Minister for nearly 13 years between 1910 and 1932.

5. Leontios Leontiou, Metropolitan of Paphos

He acted as *Topoteretes (locum tenens)* from 1933 to 1947 during the
vacancy of the archiepiscopal see. As archbishop his reign was very
brief. Elected on 20 June 1947, he died on 26 July.

6. Initialling of the Cypriot Constitution

This took place at Government House on 6 June 1960. Sir Hugh Foot
is in the centre with Archbishop Makarios to his right and Dr
Kutchuk second from his left.

7. President Makarios with President Kennedy during his trip to the USA in 1962.

To their right is S. Kyprianou, Minister of Foreign Affairs, and to their left Zenon Rossides, Permanent Representative of Cyprus to the United Nations.

8. Top secret discussions on the Cyprus problem

Archbishop Makarios, General Grivas, Spyros Kyprianou (Minister
of Foreign Affairs) and Polycarpos Georgadjis (Minister of the
Interior) at the Grande Bretagne Hotel, Athens, on 14 April 1964.

4 1914-1925: *Cyprus becomes a British Crown Colony*

The Cyprus (Annexation) Order in Council of 5 November 1914 was generally received with great enthusiasm. Britain announced that the Cyprus Convention, the Annex and the Agreement of 1878 had become null and void since Turkey had joined the Triple Alliance (Germany, Austria and Hungary) and was therefore in direct conflict with Great Britain and her allies. A telegram sent by the High Commissioner and received by the Colonial Office at 7.58 p.m. on 2 November shows that even the most senior Turkish officials of the island rejoiced at the change in the legal status of Cyprus:

> Before publishing the statement relating to Anglo-Turkish affairs, I summoned the chief Cadi, the Mufti and Irfan Bey, the senior Muslim elected member of the Council, and read the statement to them. After hearing the same they expressed the view that Great Britain was now fully justified in taking any action against Turkey which was thought fit and spontaneously added that Cyprus should be annexed by England and the inhabitants so released from Constantinople intrigues.[1]

Yet in a letter to Harcourt on 4 September, Gould-Adams was alarmed by the fact that local Moslem newspapers, like those of mainland Turkey, had been inciting their readers against Great Britain following the taking over of two ships being built for Turkey. He further confided that the dominant Old Turkish Party was then facing the Young Turks who were at that very moment 'being led astray by the German advisers in Constantinople'.

Following its annexation, Cyprus formed part (both *de facto* and *de jure*) of His Majesty's Dominions. Hence the advent of the First World War gave the inhabitants British citizenship. This was finally settled on 27 November 1917 by an Order in

Council. Furthermore on 10 March 1925, by Royal Letters Patent (which, like other royal instruments such as Orders in Council, Proclamations and Writs, simply provide a convenient mechanism for implementing important governmental decisions), Cyprus was proclaimed a Crown Colony.

Between 1914 and 1925 two problems dominated Cypriot affairs. The political movement among the Christian majority for union with Greece was the most powerful force in Cypriot politics. By and large, however, agitation for *enosis* was successfully contained – sometimes even suppressed by force of arms as in 1931 – until the 1950s, when a successful guerrilla campaign ousted the British. The second major issue was the economic problem.

There were two British 'offers' (of Cyprus to Greece) in 1912 and 1915 and two 'promises' in 1919. After the first phase of the Balkan Wars the combatants met in London (from 16 December 1912 to 6 January 1913) to discuss peace terms. At the head of the Greek delegation was Eleftherios Venizelos, 'the maker of modern Greece', who holds the distinction of being the first Greek Prime Minister to raise the question of Cyprus in an international gathering. Venizelos met Lloyd George, the Chancellor of the Exchequer, Winston Churchill, the First Lord of the Admiralty, and Prince Louis of Battenberg. Britain at the time feared a major confrontation with Germany and her allies, and was therefore seeking allies itself. Lloyd George asked Venizelos whether Britain could use the naval facilities provided at Argostoli in return for Cyprus. This unofficial request and offer was accepted by Venizelos in principle. Lloyd George of course added that an official offer could be made only by Sir Edward (later Viscount) Grey, the Foreign Secretary, who was not present at the meeting. Grey had always been in favour of giving up Cyprus; in a letter to Sir Francis Bertie on 29 October 1908 he wrote: 'I believe Cyprus is of no use to us and the Convention respecting it is an anachronism and encumbrance. I would therefore give the island away in return for any better arrangement we could obtain. Indeed bargain or no bargain we should be better without Cyprus.'[2]

As to the offer made by Lloyd George, Asquith, the British Prime Minister, was in favour of the proposal. However, neither the Greek nor the British government pursued the proposal to any sort of conclusion in 1912 or 1913.

Further offers however were transmitted to Greece in 1914 and 1915. On 22 November 1914 the Entente powers offered North Epirus to Greece in return for 'immediate participation'. On 24 January 1915 Britain suggested concerted action in the Balkans 'in return for very important territorial concessions on the coast of Asia Minor'. On 6 March the pro-German King Constantine refused such overtures, Venizelos resigning in protest. From the private papers of Sir Edward Grey we learn that the Queen of Greece declared in 1915 that if a single German soldier was killed by a Greek she would immediately leave Greece for ever. In fact the British officials in Athens, frustrated at Greece not joining the Allies in 1915, believed that the only way to get Greece in was to get the king out.

The new ultra-right government of Gounaris assured the Bulgarians on 30 July of Greece's neutrality. However, the Allies continued to press for the participation of the Balkan countries in combating the German 'menace'. Sir Edward Grey, in a telegram to Sir Francis Elliot (Envoy Extraordinary and Minister Plenipotentiary) in Athens, said on 12 October that 'the moment has now come when the Greek Government must definitely choose whether they will fulfil their treaty obligations or not'. On the following day Grey informed Elliot that 'if Greece joins now her territory will be guaranteed and she will receive proper territorial acquisitions at the end of the war'. The offer of Cyprus to Greece was telegraphed on 16 October by Grey to Elliot. The relevant parts read as follows:

> His Majesty's Government are asking the support of Greece for Serbia believing that it is especially in the interests of Greece to prevent Serbia from being crushed. If Greece is prepared to give support as an Ally to Serbia, now that she has been attacked by Bulgaria, His Majesty's Government will be prepared to give Cyprus to Greece. Should Greece join the Allies for all purposes she would naturally have a share with them in advantages secured at the end of the war, but the offer of Cyprus is made by His Majesty's Government independently on condition that Greece gives immediate and full support with her army to Serbia.[3]

This telegraphic offer (No. 902) was approved by the King, the
Premier, Lord Kitchener, Bonar Law, Secretary of State for the
Colonies, Balfour, then at the Admiralty (after consulting the
First Sea Lord) and Chamberlain (then at the Indian Office).
On the following day Elliot replied to Grey that he had pointed
out this 'unique opportunity' for Greece, that 'Cyprus was
assured to her whatever was the result of the war'. Bonar Law
informed the High Commissioner of Cyprus of the British offer.
On 16 October he telegraphed the following:

> His Majesty's Government feel that in the present
> emergency no effort must be spared to induce Greece to go to
> the help of Serbia in accordance with her treaty obligations.
> They have therefore offered to give Cyprus to Greece on
> condition that Greece gives immediate and full support with
> her Army to Serbia. Please communicate this fact to the
> Archbishop or other leading personages in Cyprus and
> suggest to them that if they wish to take advantage of this
> opportunity for securing the union of Cyprus with Greece,
> which is unlikely to recur, they should immediately proceed
> to Athens and press their demand on the King and
> Parliament. You are authorised to give them any assistance
> in your power with this object.[4]

The October and other British promptings to Greece not only
included Cyprus but further concessions in western Thrace and
Asia Minor – both inhabited mainly by Turks and not British
sovereign territory. There was, furthermore, no mention of
naval facilities. Similarly there was no talk of the Turkish
minority in Cyprus being an obstacle.

The Zaimist government rejected the British offer. Zaimis,
often referred to as 'the handyman of Greek politics', had
become Premier with the express purpose of not applying the
Greco-Serbian Treaty. The pro-German Greek establishment
was adamant. The opportunity of acquiring Cyprus was lost.
Sir Edward Grey, replying to a question from Sir Philip
Magnus MP on 26 October 1915, explained:

> His Majesty's Government felt bound, in the very critical
> position in which their Serbian Allies were placed, to make
> every possible effort to obtain for them the only assurance
> which was immediately available. Accordingly, they made it

known that, if Greece would give full and immediate support to Serbia against Bulgaria, His Majesty's Government would be prepared to give Cyprus to Greece. As Greece has not seen her way to support Serbia, the condition on which the offer was made has not been fulfilled, and it has, therefore, lapsed.[5]

In Cyprus the offer was received with mixed feelings. On 1 November Irfan Bey, the Turkish member of the legislative and executive councils, sent a telegram to the Secretary of State for the Colonies stating that the Moslems of Cyprus were dismayed and angered at the news of Cyprus having been offered to Greece. A petition to the High Commissioner on the following day expressed the same concern. Irfan Bey repeated this to the Earl of Cromer on 13 November. On the other hand the Greek Cypriot leaders were perplexed by the Greek refusal. However, the archbishop and the members of the legislative council presented a memorandum to the High Commissioner on 8 November, asking for it to be transmitted to the Secretary of State for the Colonies, which expressed their deep emotion and profound gratitude to the British Crown, government and people for their magnanimous offer to cede Cyprus to Greece. Furthermore, arrangements were made for E. Hadjioannou, a prominent member of the legislative council and Mayor of Larnaca, to go to Athens via Alexandria on 13 November in order to agitate for the union of Cyprus with Greece and for the prompt intervention of Greece in the war.

The possession of Cyprus (with its population in 1921 of more than 250,000 Greeks) had long been an ideal of Hellenic nationalism and it had been expected that its cession to Greece would be welcomed with enthusiasm. The gift however was refused and its refusal was tantamount to an admission that King Constantine had received promises from the opposite camp of a still more alluring kind in the event of the German victory which he was persuaded would occur. This refusal must certainly be ascribed to the influence of the pro-German group of advisers, who were daily putting more and more pressure on the king, rather than to Zaimis the Prime Minister. The latter's policy was certainly one of genuine neutrality: during his term of office he maintained as far as he could friendly relations with the Entente, which even supplied him with a loan to bolster up

Greece's ailing economy. At all events, this wonderful opportunity of settling the Cypriot question once and for all was lost. In a speech delivered to the Greek Parliament in August 1917, Venizelos, elaborating on his pro-Entente policy, said:

> . . . I was instinctively aware, I was sure, I was convinced that the policy I was following would bring me at the end of the war yet another most valuable section of Hellenism, the island of Cyprus, which would to some extent compensate us for the growth of Bulgaria which I anticipated. That my provision and my confidence were not groundless was proved soon afterwards, when Cyprus was offered to us and was refused by the 'Saviours' who were in office at the time. . .[6]

The October offer, it may be added, was made by Britain in good faith and in pursuance of her established foreign policy; it had been made with the consent and knowledge not only of the Prime Minister but of the other senior ministers. Certain elements of the population however were alarmed. F.T. Piggott, in an article entitled 'The Integrity of the Empire', wrote: 'The offer by the British Government of Cyprus to Greece sent a wave of apprehension through the country. . . . When the offer of Cyprus to Greece was announced there must have passed through the minds of many the thought, "If Cyprus, why not Gibraltar?" Ministers may have misjudged the temper of the country; too certain of support in Parliament they may have recklessly agreed to the cession.'[7]

Greece eventually entered the war on the side of the Allies but by 1917 they were already on the road to victory and there was no reason to change the administration of Cyprus. Its contribution to the war effort however was, for so small an island, phenomenal. Its total population was only around 280,000 in 1914, yet over 13,000 between the ages of 18 and 41 served as auxiliary troops – mainly muleteers for the British Salonica Force. The participation of this large number of men naturally resulted in a shortage of labour at a time when the resources of the island were being strained to the utmost for the production of foodstuffs and other commodities to supply the needs of the Allies. This courageous contribution was acknowledged by the High Commissioner who, in a letter to

Viscount Milner, the Secretary of State for the Colonies, on 3 June 1919, said: 'All classes of the community combined in a cheerful and resolute manner to assist the Government of the island by willingly meeting the many demands made on them and by readily submitting to the restrictions imposed by the various regulations which military exigencies necessitated.'[8]

However, even though many sacrifices were made and the Cypriots distinguished themselves between 1914 and 1918, neither Britain nor Greece mentioned the problem during those years. The question was next raised by Venizelos during the peace conferences that terminated the war. Furthermore, according to the writings of Professor Paul Mantoux, the celebrated interpreter of the Peace Conference, a conversation between Lloyd George and Woodrow Wilson on 13 May 1919, during a meeting of the 'Council of Four' (composed of Woodrow Wilson, President of the USA; Lloyd George, Prime Minister of Great Britain; Georges Clemenceau, President of the Council of France; and V.E. Orlando, Prime Minister of Italy), went like this:

L.G.: It is my intention to give Cyprus to Greece.
W.W.: Excellent idea. (The latter's liberalism led him to sympathize with the various national movements.)
L.G.: (referring to the Turks) They have no right in a country which they had converted to mere desert.

This was the first 'promise'. It was not kept for several reasons:

1 Military tacticians of the early twentieth century believed that such a transaction was undesirable since there were strong strategic considerations for not giving up the island.

2 It was strongly urged by some officials that it was the duty of Britain to develop the island economically. In so doing the Cypriot authorities would find it much easier to convince the inhabitants that Britain regarded the island as an important part of the Empire and that it was not simply playing 'dog in the manger'. The Cypriot economy, like that of other countries, was on the road to recovery (thanks to the post-war boom); consequently the poverty was, at least temporarily, eliminated as a grievance.

3 British foreign and colonial affairs experts also believed that

the chief difficulty Britain had to face in handing Cyprus to Greece was the claims of Turkey, based not only on historical but on strategic and ethnological grounds. Much the same kind of problem had been faced in the handling of the Dodecanese islands. It was believed however that Turkey would prove far more intractable in the case of Cyprus than in the case of the Dodecanese. In the light of events since the First World War, this belief has proved totally correct.

4   The pressure applied by the Greeks was not strong enough; indeed, the problem was nearly forgotten altogether after 1920 with the Asia Minor disaster of 1922 (see pages 115-16) and the somewhat negative policies of the Cypriot leadership.

5   The British contended all along that the Cypriots were not yet ready to run their country entirely on their own.

6   After the lapse of the offer of October 1915, Great Britain had given France a veto over the disposal of Cyprus in the secret Sykes-Picot Agreement concluded in April/May 1916. This provision appeared as Article 4 of the Franco-British Convention signed at Paris on 23 December 1920, which stated that 'in virtue of the geographic and strategical position of the island of Cyprus in the Gulf of Alexandretta, the British Government agrees not to open any negotiations for the cession or alienation of the said island of Cyprus without the previous consent of the French Government'. There was also a secret clause in the Venizelos-Tittoni Agreement of 1919 by which Italy agreed to hold a plebiscite in Rhodes if Great Britain should be willing to cede Cyprus to Greece.

The second 'promise' was made by Ramsay MacDonald, the leader of the Labour Party, in February 1919. Speaking to 102 delegates from 26 countries at the Socialist International conference held at Berne, he emphasized that his party supported Cypriot self-determination and that, if he ever came to power, he would do everything he could to carry out his commitment. However, MacDonald, who led the short-lived minority Labour government of 1924 (22 January to 3 November), failed to honour his pledge.

The educated proponents of the *megali idhea* intensified their efforts to achieve national self-realization. They were spurred on not only by the promises already referred to but by the Cretan example of 1913. In that year Crete proclaimed its union with the mainland, action legalized when Turkey expressly abandoned her suzerain rights in a clause of the Treaty of London. A statement by the President of the United States also raised their hopes. Wilson, in his note to all the belligerent governments, called upon both parties to state 'in the full light of day' the 'aims' they had set themselves in prosecuting the war. The Allies, in their joint response made public on 11 January 1917, stated that they had no difficulty in meeting his request and offered a list of definite objectives. Among them were:

> the liberation of the peoples who lay beneath the 'murderous tyranny' of the Turks; and
> the expulsion from Europe of the Ottoman empire, which had proved itself 'so radically alien to western civilization'.

The Greeks of the island rejoiced. The 'masses' however, who in the post-war economic boom enjoyed unexampled prosperity, were not at the forefront of the *enosis* movement and perhaps indeed, as long as their bellies were full, cared very little, though their passions were roused on several occasions – in 1919, 1931 and of course in the 1950s. Greek nationalism is not an artificial conception of theorists, but a real force which impels all fragments of the Greek-speaking population to make sustained efforts towards political union with the national state. Under the British administration the political consciousness of the inhabitants had been awakened and had expressed itself in a growing desire of the Christian majority to realize its nationality. They also believed that the Moslem preference for the status quo and antipathy to union should not prove permanent. Arnold Toynbee, elaborating on Greek foreign policy since 1882, explains: 'However important the retention of Cyprus may be to Great Britain from the strategical point of view, we shall find that even in the balance of material interests it is not worth the price of alienating the sympathy of a united nationality.'[9]

Memoranda, petitions and deputations fill the annals of Cypriot history between 1914 and 1925, just as they had done since 1878. In their memorandum of May 1914, the Greeks pleaded for union with mother Greece. On 3 June 1914 the archbishop, three bishops and eight Christian members of the legislative council, on the occasion of the fiftieth anniversary of the union of the Ionian islands with Greece, sent a telegram to the Colonial Office praying His Majesty to fulfil the eternal and strong aspirations of the people of Cyprus by 'uniting us with our co-racial Hellenic Kingdom'. But following the annexation the High Commissioner informed Harcourt on 20 November of the Moslem desire that Cyprus should be permanently united with the British empire. Harcourt was also informed of the Christian support of Britain and her allies and hope that the island should be ceded to Greece in the near future. Four days earlier J.M. Triantafilides expressed the Maronite feelings and their loyalty to Great Britain.

In June 1915, on the occasion of His Majesty's birthday, the Greeks referred in their congratulatory address to their 'national rehabilitation'; the Turks expressed their joy at being assured of remaining under 'His Majesty's sceptre', while the Armenians stressed that they were 'infinitely happy and proud of enjoying the privilege of being in the rank of His Gracious Majesty's most loyal subjects'. However, Greek deputations on several occasions in 1914 and 1915 assured the High Commissioner that the Christians would cause no unrest among the people and asked for the continuation of the liberal attitude towards them by the British administration.

Nevertheless, the Greeks saw annexation as the last stage before achievement of national self-realization and kept up the pressure for union through their newspaper *Enosis*. With this aim in mind the nine Christian members of the legislative council addressed a long memorandum to the Colonial Office on 29 July 1917, confident that the promise of liberation to all nationals, embodied in the Allied declaration of 11 January, would bring them their final victory. They also explained that Cyprus had been offered to Greece in October 1915; that the Turkish suzerainty had come to an end; and that all Cypriots were, since annexation, British subjects.

On 26 August a memorandum by Irfan Bey on behalf of the Moslem population of Cyprus recorded the customary protests. It expressed and reiterated their loyal sentiments towards His Majesty's Government and protested most vigorously against any change in the status of the island. On 8 December the Pan-Cypriot assembly with the archbishop at the head passed a resolution sympathizing with England and the Allies and expressing once more its one and only unalterable desire – union with Greece. The High Commissioner however suppressed the telegrams to both Houses of Parliament, the Archbishop of Canterbury and the Anglo-Hellenic League in London as being somewhat misleading and embarrassing. On 19 December a meeting of Moslems unanimously passed a resolution protesting vigorously against the earlier Christian resolution for the union of Cyprus with Greece. The Greeks however continued their pressure. Towards the end of the year they sent telegrams to Venizelos, who was on a visit to Britain, to do everything in his power to resolve the Cyprus question once and for all and to complete the liberation of enslaved Hellenism. Unfortunately, even the Greek political genius could not secure such a promise from the British authorities in 1917.

On 5 December 1918 a deputation consisting of the archbishop and the eight Greek members of the legislative council left for London to press their demands on the British government. Their demands had also been expressed on 15 October, when telegrams were handed to the High Commissioner addressed to President Wilson of the United States and the Premiers of Britain, Greece, France and Italy, praying for the realization of their eternal aspiration of union with Greece. Clauson, the High Commissioner, informed Walter H. Long, the Colonial Secretary, on 20 October that he had approved the suppression of these telegrams as improper and possibly embarrassing.

The departure of the deputation prompted the island's Moslems to address a memorandum to the Secretary of State for the Colonies on 23 December, protesting 'on behalf of the 60,000 Turks of Cyprus' against the agitation of the Christian element for the union of Cyprus with Greece and praying for the continuance of British rule over the island.

After meeting Venizelos in Paris the deputation arrived in London on 3 January 1919. A telegram was despatched to Viscount Milner from Irfan Bey on 27 January reiterating the Moslem position and desire for the status quo. In fact there

were signs of unrest among the Moslems of Nicosia, who feared
that the island was about to be ceded to Greece. Consequently a
small party advocating the return of Cyprus to Turkey was
formed. Sir Malcolm Stevenson (the officer administering the
government of Cyprus, appointed High Commissioner on 31
July 1920), in a secret despatch dated 26 April, informed
Viscount Milner that the leaders of the 'Union with Turkey
Party' were Dr Mehmed Essad and Dr Hussein Behije. The
former arrived in Cyprus as a refugee in November 1914 and
'soon began to take an active part in local politics as a leader of
the anti-Greek section'. Dr Behije, a local practitioner
'generally drunk', was in the habit of touring villages. He was
fined 'quite recently' for creating a disturbance at Aphania, a
village in the Famagustà district. Stevenson further informed
Milner that associated with the above two persons was Hassan
Karabardak, a 'rowdy individual', the leader of the butchers
and *hamals* (native porters), who 'are a rough and undisciplined
section of the community'. Karabardak took a leading part in
the riots of 1912.

The Greek deputation, meanwhile, was received by Viscount
Milner on 3 February 1919. They appealed in the name of
British justice and the glorious traditions of Great Britain for
the return of the island to the 'motherly bosom of Hellas'.
Milner, who had been appointed Secretary of State for the
Colonies only on 10 January, stated that he appreciated and
respected the aspirations of the Greek population of Cyprus for
union with Greece. He thought that those aspirations were
natural, but that it was neither possible nor right for him to give
them a definite reply then. The Christian delegation also
appealed on 5 May to the British government, parliament,
Church, press and nation at large. An extract from the appeal
reads:

> Cyprus, an historically Hellenic Island, has one, only one
> and unalterable wish, to be reunited to the Kingdom of
> Greece, with which strong, common and indelible ties of
> blood, religion, history, language, character and national
> conscience unite her. . . . We are unshaken in our belief in
> you. We have implicit confidence in the application of
> British justice. We feel sure that the British honour will be
> upheld. The much-heralded principles of the war were

certainly not mere political orations, and we strongly believe that from the soil, which has been saturated with the human blood of millions, will spring up the tree of liberty for all, big or small, strong or weak. Convinced as we are of this we expect from you alone the realization of our national aspirations.[10]

Back in Cyprus, the expected Moslem disturbances did not take place and by May the symptoms of unease had disappeared. However, the situation remained critical. Sir Malcolm Stevenson received information from many quarters on the likelihood of disturbances. One such source was Said Efendi, a member of the legislative council. A secret despatch to Viscount Milner dated 6 May reads as follows:

> Reports had been received from certain ex-agents of the late military intelligence department in Cyprus and other sources that Doctor Essad, Doctor Behije and Hassan Karabardak contemplated the creation of a disturbance in Nicosia during Easter week, which was to be followed, on a signal if successful, by an outbreak of the Prisoners of War at the Camp at Famagusta who were to over-power their guards, seize their rifles and take part in the general rising.[11]

In London the delegation addressed further letters to Lieutenant Colonel L. Amery on 17 July and to Lloyd George on 15 September explaining in full their reasons for desiring union with Greece. The concluding appeal in their letter to the Prime Minister was as follows:

> Any other solution will cause the greatest despair to the Greek Cypriots. But we do not believe that Great Britain is capable of committing an injustice. We feel confident that the British liberal traditions will be followed; that the British honour will be upheld. Add, Right Honourable Sir, a new glorious page to the history of your magnanimous Nation and give new grandeur and splendour to the Crown of His Britannic Majesty by ceding Cyprus to Greece – a State deeply grateful to England for the valuable protection given in the past and bound to remain always a friend and trusted ally of Great Britain.[12]

The same plea for the realization of their national aspirations formed the conclusion of the telegram of congratulation sent by Kyrillos, Archbishop of Cyprus and President of the deputation, on the occasion of the King's birthday in June 1919. The delegation also informed Lloyd George on 21 October and 13 November of the resolutions passed on 12 October by the Pan-Cypriot National Assembly. This meeting of delegates (914 in all) representing almost all the Greek villages of the island was held at the Archbishop's Palace in Nicosia. The five resolutions, arrived at unanimously, expressed the familiar demands.

The Moslems of Nicosia, Limassol, Larnaca, Famagusta, Paphos and Kyrenia sent telegrams to the Prime Minister and others, protesting against the above resolutions and pleading for the continuance of British rule in Cyprus. Another petition to the British government in May contained the same wish. Furthermore, there were constant protests from the London Moslem League against any British cession of the island to Greece. A letter to the Secretary of State for the Colonies on 25 July pleaded with the British authorities and expressed the hope that 'His Majesty's Government will not countenance the Greek agitation or abandon the Moslems of Cyprus to the tender mercies of their Greek compatriots'. Telegrams from the Moslem members of the legislative council recorded the same concern. For entirely different reasons, the British-Israel World Federation, in a letter to the Secretary of State for the Colonies on 6 August, also pleaded against the cession of Cyprus to Greece, since 'its strategical position in relation to the near east and especially to Palestine, renders its occupation by Britain imperative'.

The island's Moslems were assured on several occasions that their interests would receive full consideration by the British government. They were also assured that there was a great body of opinion against the Greek petition and that Great Britain had no intention of relinquishing the island. His Majesty's Government therefore expressly stated that there was no hope of Cyprus being united with Greece. A letter from 10 Downing Street to the Greek delegation on 14 November 1919 confirmed this. It stated that the British government was 'fully aware' of the sentiment among the Greek population of Cyprus in favour of union with Greece and that the 'wishes of the inhabitants will be taken in the most careful and sympathetic consideration by His Majesty's Government when they consider its future'. However, owing to the uncertainty of the situation in the Middle East, Lloyd George was not able to give any definite reply to the petition of the Cyprus deputation. He also regretted that he was unable to meet them in person. The reply of 24 November trusted that the British government 'will relieve the prolonged anxiety of the people by announcing at an early date the happy solution of the Cypriot problem'.

So far the Cyprus deputation, whose members changed but whose policy continued unaltered, had very little to show for their endeavours. In Cyprus however a local committee, following the guidelines set by the deputation, called in August 1919 in a telegram to the Secretary of State for the Colonies for the satisfaction of their national aspirations and declared that they would be grateful if their wishes were ascertained by a plebiscite.

Evidently the cause was a lost one. Yet the Greeks continued to hope that their dreams would soon be realized. No avenue was left unexplored – Members of Parliament were lobbied, petitions were sent to both Houses of Parliament, letters were sent to leading politicians, churchmen, trade unions and the press. A letter to the Prime Minister on 3 June 1920 urged the early cession of the island to Greece. Another letter was sent to *The Times*, pleading for its support 'in a cause which is incontestably right and just'. This letter was dated 5 July and was signed by the archbishop, F. Zannetos and others.

Following the return of some members of the deputation on 24 September 1920, countless questions were asked about their work in London. One of them, Lanitis, addressed a meeting in the Hadjipavlou Theatre, Limassol, on 17 October. Protests and resolutions followed immediately on hearing the news that Britain 'will not relinquish Cyprus'. Furthermore, on 26 October, Amery, the Under Secretary of State for the Colonies, received the members of the deputation (on behalf of Milner) and informed them that His Majesty's Government could hold out no hope that the union of Cyprus with Greece would be sanctioned. The same answer was given by Amery to a Parliamentary Question from Major Barnes on 15 November.

The year 1920 witnessed the end of one era and the beginning of a new one in the history of Cyprus. The failure of the Cyprus delegation, which continued its work in London for nearly two years, led to bitterness, resentment and frustration. The Cyprus problem was thus born. The Greek inhabitants of Larnaca, Paphos and Nicosia held public meetings in the last two days of October and voted unanimously for a strong protest, declaring that they would use every lawful means and undergo any sacrifice to achieve the fulfilment of their national aspirations.

A far more decisive event occurred on 8 December 1920, when the Christian members of the legislative council resigned *en masse* and unanimously decided to initiate new forms of struggle. Their letter of resignation concluded: 'Under these circumstances and as a proof of the strong protest of the people against the unjust decision of His Majesty's Government we submit in a body our resignations as representatives of the people in the Legislative Council and declare that we will continue without yielding our struggle until the desires of the people and their national aspirations are satisfied.'[13]

The Cyprus problem therefore assumed new dimensions. The celebrated Foreign Office document of 7 July 1943 pointed out in the clearest fashion that 'these unsatisfied aspirations and unappeased grievances prepared the way for the disturbances of 1931'. The following year, 1921, was not only the centenary of Greek independence but the year in which a new political organization was set up to direct the *enosis* struggle. It also witnessed disturbances in Nicosia, the imposition of martial law and the deportation of Catalanos.

On 8 March the Christian deputies who had earlier resigned informed Churchill that, since no candidates were nominated to oppose them, they were once more elected, with a mandate to ask Britain to apply to Cyprus the right of nationality and the right of self-determination. Furthermore, like the local committees on the national question of Cyprus in 1919, they asked for a plebiscite to ascertain the wishes of the people regarding union with Greece. On 11 March the archbishop and the nine Christian deputies addressed a memorandum to Churchill, who was on a visit to Egypt, requesting that he should visit Cyprus personally.

On 6 and 7 April Greek Independence Day was the occasion

for a disturbance at Nicosia which the police succeeded with difficulty in putting down. Stevenson reported to the Colonial Office that temporary quiet had been restored but that he feared fresh disturbances during the Greek Easter, with the prospect of racial riots. He therefore enlisted 90 ex-policemen as a temporary addition to the force and asked the General Officer commanding Egypt to send two platoons of British troops. However, the disturbances, which partly originated in the legitimate Greek demand to demonstrate with Greek flags, were not serious, and the troops were not needed (indeed had not even arrived) since various Greek local committees decided to abandon further festivities planned for 8 May, the date of the Turkish feast of Bairam. However, HMS *Ajax*, on her way from Constantinople to Alexandria, was diverted to Cyprus on 6 May. The cost in fuel of this diversion was £2,230.

Meanwhile the British authorities imposed martial law and warned some of the leading nationalists that if they stepped outside the rules they would face deportation. Internal security was also tightened. On the night of 8 April, N. Catalanos (who came to Cyprus in 1893 from Mali, a village in Greece) allegedly addressed an inflammatory speech to a number of persons at the New Hellenic Club – a new political organization he had started. Stevenson, reporting to Churchill on 24 April, stated that a visitor to the club, 'a reliable government official', heard Catalanos speak of resisting the government in every way possible. Stevenson described him as a 'dangerous firebrand' who was 'liable to cause trouble' at any moment. On the 24th the High Commissioner ordered the deportation of Catalanos. On the same day another 'undesirable', an Australian journalist called Lloyd left 'on his own accord'. He was arrested by the Italians at Adalia, having previously been deported by them from Rhodes for causing disturbances there. Stevenson talked of him as 'an advanced Pan-Hellenist'.

The deportation of Catalanos provoked numerous protests. The Nicosia Reading Club, of which he was president, and the Christian Schools Committee of Nicosia voiced their concern. The archbishop and the nine Christian members of the legislative council addressed a long memorandum to Churchill, giving their own version of events and protesting against the action taken by the government. They pleaded for a special commission of enquiry to be sent to Cyprus 'in order that His Majesty's Government may be fittingly enlightened before it is too late'. On 3 June the archbishop further reminded Britain of the eternal Cypriot wish: a message for the King's birthday stated that 'in submitting our felicitations and prayers for a long and glorious reign, we pray that Your Majesty will listen favourably to the wish of the people of Cyprus for union with Greece'.

On Sunday 23 October a meeting of representatives from various villages of Cyprus, known as the National Assembly, was held in Nicosia under the presidency of the archbishop. It discussed in particular the dilemma facing the members of the legislative council. It also resolved to demand *enosis*. The National Assembly met again on 4 and 5 December in Nicosia – again under the presidency of the archbishop. The main item on the agenda was a discussion of what further steps should be taken to promote union of Cyprus with Greece. A new political organization set up on 5 December provided for the constitution of an elective body of 45 members known as the National Council. It was to take the place in the movement for union which had until recently been filled by the Central Committee of the National Cause. The function of the National Council, which was responsible to the National Assembly and thence to the people for its actions, was to direct the progress of the *enosis* struggle and to decide the policy to be followed in furtherance of the national aspiration of every Greek Cypriot.

After the creation of the National Council, the High Commissioner, reporting to Churchill on 25 December, remarked that, although the organization was ably planned and the rules were well drafted, it remained to be seen how it would work in practice and whether it would ever be more than a 'high-sounding charter'. Stevenson, reporting on 6 February 1922, claimed that the country was 'perfectly peaceful'. Yet on 19 March a memorandum from the archbishop, as President of the National Council, demanded the union of the island with Greece.

On 20 May the National Council passed further resolutions for union which expressed dissatisfaction with the unsympathetic reply of the British government in refusing justice to their national aspirations. A petition from the

Moslems followed on 11 December. The organizer was Dr Eyioub Mussa Nejm-Ed-Din, elected to the legislative council in 1921. He was apparently jealous of Irfan Bey who, as a member of the executive and legislative councils and delegate of Evkaf (the Moslem department responsible for religious foundations), was regarded in some quarters as being too pro-British. This was not far from the truth since even a Colonial Office minute of 29 November 1921 referred to him as 'our old friend' at the time of his election to the legislative council. The ostensible objectives of the petition were three:

1   The restoration of the island to the Ottoman empire or, in default of such a cession, the return to the status *ante bellum* in which Cyprus was administered by Britain while remaining part of the Ottoman empire.

2   The establishment of a Moslem council or central board to exercise control over certain Turkish affairs such as education.

3   Opposition to the grant of self-government to the native inhabitants of Cyprus.

On 16 December a memorandum addressed to the Duke of Devonshire, the Colonial Secretary, by the archbishop (for and on behalf of the National Council) contained a request for self-government pending the realization of aspirations for *enosis*. Regret was also expressed about the entirely inadequate and unjust Constitution. The reply was not encouraging.

   The tightening of internal security resulted, amongst other things, in the deportation of F. Zannetos in December 1922 according to an Order dated 31 October 1922 made under the Aliens Law of 1921. Zannetos was the Mayor of Larnaca, for many years a member of the legislative council and a doctor much loved for his philanthropic activities. Law XXIV stated that foreign subjects practising as doctors or schoolmasters had to sign a declaration that they would not concern themselves with politics in Cyprus. Zannetos, who had lived on the island since 1888, refused to sign the declaration but gave up his practice. Yet he was still deported. This decision puzzled and indeed infuriated a considerable number of people. On the day he left Larnaca a very large crowd, including women 'and children, were weeping and crying for union and for 'their' doctor. If this action of the authorities was designed to repress national sentiment, it had precisely the opposite effect.

The failure to achieve any concrete result or even renewed promises from the British caused a split in the Greek political organization and a feeling of despair. Even so further memoranda were sent in 1923. The ones sent on 21 January and 23 March contained the usual demands. The April memorandum asked for self-government. Of more significance was the one sent on 3 June. The third Pan-Cypriot National Assembly, formed of Christian representatives of the whole island, resolved that 'the Hellenic population of the island adheres unanimously and unshakably to its just demand to be united with its mother country Greece'. They also asked Venizelos to take up the case of the people of Cyprus before the British authorities. The gathering of the major powers at Lausanne in the summer of 1923 was seen as a suitable venue. But unlike Versailles (1919) and Sèvres (1920), when Greece entered the negotiations as an integral member of the victorious team, at Lausanne she arrived as a defeated power. Her voice, as we shall see in the next chapter, carried very little weight.

The above meeting of 3 June also protested against certain provisions of the Education Bill on the grounds that they interfered with the ancient privileges of the Church authorities. Whatever the merits of this protest, Spyros J. Araouzos was authorized to deliver the resolution personally to the Colonial Secretary. (The Elementary Education Law of 1929, incidentally, was widely believed to have precipitated the disturbances of 1931.) Araouzos was received by the Under Secretary of State for the Colonies, W. Ormsby-Gore, on behalf of the Duke of Devonshire on 30 July. Also present were Sir M. Stevenson and W.D. Ellis of the West African and Mediterranean Department of the Colonial Office. On the general political situation Araouzos, a Limassol lawyer of exceptional ability, stated that the Greek population were unanimously in favour of union with Greece. He demanded a revision of the Constitution, which would give the Greek population proportional representation with the Turks. He further demanded that the Turkish tribute which burdened the Cyprus estimates should come to an end: payments might be usefully devoted to the formation of an agricultural bank.

Lastly, he talked at length about the poor state of the Cypriot countryside – the backbone of the island's economy.

On 25 February 1924 a memorandum addressed to J.H. Thomas, Secretary of State for the Colonies, by Kyrillos, Archbishop of Cyprus, as President of the National Council, concentrated on three issues:

> the foundation of an agricultural bank;
> the granting of wider political powers; and
> the need for a commission to investigate the present situation in Cyprus.

It was the first appeal made to a Labour government and it concluded:

> In submitting, Sir, these just demands of the Cyprus people to the first Labour Government of Great Britain we nourish the unfailing confidence that the sound, lofty and humane principles of the Labour Party will exert their moral effect in general on the development of the public affairs of the British Empire, and in particular on the fate of our own country. The Cyprus people considers it a particularly happy coincidence that there is at the head of the British Government to which it addresses its demand, and from which it confidently expects the realization of its national restoration, the Right Honourable Ramsay MacDonald who at the Socialist Conference of Berne strongly supported the handing over of Cyprus to the Hellenic Kingdom.[14]

A similar plea was made in March to the Greek Vouli (Parliament). It was also pointed out that the British Labour government, which required Italy to hand over the Dodecanese to Greece, should do the same for Cyprus. Around this time there was also a movement for the autonomy of both Cyprus and the Dodecanese under the League of Nations. However, to a question in Parliament by Lieutenant-Commander Kenworthy on 14 April, who asked the Prime Minister about the policy of his government on the future of the island and whether the inhabitants had been consulted on their future destiny, the Prime Minister replied: 'His Majesty's Government are not contemplating any change in the political status of Cyprus.' Later in the month this statement was slightly modified by J. Clynes, the Lord Privy Seal, who promised that no change would be made without consulting the wishes of the inhabitants.

Once more the aspirations of the Christian inhabitants of Cyprus were frustrated. The National Council received another setback when a moderate merchant was elected on a programme of close co-operation with the government in the Larnaca-Famagusta district. A new line of attack was decided on. A memorandum dated 14 October was sent direct to both Houses of Parliament, reiterating the demand for union with Greece and elaborating on the maladministration of the island. They were informed in reply that the Speaker and the Lord Chancellor could not communicate the memoranda to their respective Houses – Commons and Lords.

The occasion of the official pronouncement declaring the island a Crown Colony (1 May 1925) was used by the archbishop to register a protest: his memorandum to Amery on 1 May reiterated the aspirations of the Greek-Christian population for union with Greece, but he was reminded that this question had been finally closed and could not be reopened. However, the National Council, in a resolution of 9 May, protested against Cyprus becoming a Crown Colony. The Letters Patent, bearing the date 10 March 1925, were the instrument henceforth regulating the government of Cyprus.

It is beyond doubt that under British rule Cyprus fared better than under its earlier rulers. A simple comparison of the period before occupation and the aftermath of the First World War will make this clear:

Pre-1878	1920
Communications were practically non-existent. Generally speaking, there were only mule and camel tracks.	Good roads and bridges existed and a railway ran from Famagusta to Nicosia.
Post offices hardly existed.	Over 65 existed, with about 200 rural mail stations dealing with 3 million letters, cards, newspapers, books and parcels.
Hospitals did not exist.	There was at least one in each district, usually under the supervision of government medical officers.

Printing presses did not exist.	Around 15 newspapers were published. This was 'an eloquent proof of material and educational advancement'.
Schools were very inadequate. Around 170 were in existence.	Around 740, with well-trained teachers, were to be found on the island.
Trade was minimal.	Imports showed an increase of 550 per cent and exports 500 per cent.

From the above brief but very superficial comparison, the positive aspects can be seen very clearly. This progress was labelled 'unexampled prosperity'. Speaking in the House of Commons on 25 March 1920, N.P. Jodrell, elaborating on the advantages of British rule, said: 'The bulk of the population are perfectly content, whether Greek-speaking or not, to remain under British rule, and not only that, but they live on very good terms with their Moslem compatriots. . . . I am convinced that the population of the island are thoroughly content with the present rule, which is prosperous.'[15]

But there were also many negative aspects, complaints which were regularly included in the memoranda sent to the British authorities. Cyprus was, and is, predominantly an agricultural country and it was here that least progress had been made. Furthermore, the people suffered high levels of taxation: the Turkish tribute and the Imperial Defence Tax were imposed over and above more usual taxes. Living standards were low, and poverty, accentuated by the malpractices of the money-lending few over the ignorant and uneducated, was widespread. There was a mass exodus from the villages to the towns, children worked long hours under intolerable conditions (it seemed as though the Britain of the seventeenth and eighteenth centuries was 'transplanted' on twentieth-century Cyprus), and wages were generally very low. Churchill, in his memorandum to the Cabinet quoted on page 82, admitted that although there was some progress, 'an improvement upon Turkish standards is not a sufficient or suitable defence for British policy'. This is the crux of the matter – Cyprus had been simply neglected.

A.J. Cunningham, for some time the Assistant Island Postmaster, in a letter to W.D. Ellis of the Colonial Office in

1917, enclosed a long paper entitled 'England's Duty to Cyprus' which he believed was useful reading for the Colonial Office administrators. He listed two main duties:

> to retain the island;
> to exploit the natural resources of the island and improve the standard of living of the inhabitants.

He was at pains to stress that Cyprus was being exploited by a handful of 'blood-sucking advocates' or 'legalized spiders' and several wholesale merchants, who not only controlled the legislative council but in practice controlled ecclesiastical decisions, schools and village councils. He suggestived five practical remedies:

(a)   the provision of £1 million to lift the mortgages off property in the agricultural districts;

(b)   the opening of an agricultural bank to make advances to villagers;

(c)   the enactment of a law forbidding the mortgage of property except to the agricultural bank;

(d)   that all existing mortgages after the passing of the law should bear interest at not more than 5 per cent;

(e)   that it might also be desirable to revise the present system of commissionerships; the duties of the appointed commissioners should be the enforcement of the laws relating to mortgaging of agricultural property, the prevention of litigation and the encouragement of agriculture and stock-breeding.

Cunningham saw the current socio-economic condition of the island as an affront to human existence and dignity. It was, he believed, a matter of life and death. He wrote: 'This is the outstanding duty of England to Cyprus, to bring about both by policy and legislation a normal and healthy livelihood for the inhabitants. The present bleeding of the agricultural inhabitant to the extent of a quarter of his wealth annually is in the nature of a haemorrhage. Money is to a country what blood is to the body; and such a continuous drain on the vital force of the country means stunted growth and early decay.'[16]

If Britain believed that the incorporation of the island into the Empire was to be permanent, she ought to seize an early opportunity to make this known. She must assert herself and initiate a new policy, seeking the co-operation and friendship of all. Criticism should be tolerated, Cunningham believed, but agitators, fanatics and troublemakers should not.

Although the contents were noted, nothing much was done to implement Cunningham's suggestions.

All in all, there remained many grievances, although certain improvements were acknowledged. (Critics rightly point out that the improvements made since 1878 were necessitated by the rapid advance of the technological revolution.) The Greeks continued to push for a reduction of their fiscal burden and an improvement in their standard of living. In 1925 the tithe was abolished and in 1927 the tribute (the Turkish debt of 1855) received the same fate.

It has already been made clear that the British offers and promises, the war efforts of the Cypriots, the support given to the 'sacred desire' by British newspapers and journals such as *The Times*, *Daily News*, *Sunday Times*, *Herald*, *Manchester Guardian*, *Daily Telegraph*, *Westminster Gazette* and *Contemporary Review*, especially when the Cyprus mission was in London in 1919, all helped to spur on the Greek demand for union. The early 1920s also saw the formation of new political groupings (such as the National Council, page 104) which demanded the independence of Cyprus. One such grouping was the KKK – the Communist party of Cyprus. While still in a formative state, it sent a statement to the British TUC on 26 February 1924. It greeted the access to power of the British Labour party and attacked the 'disgusting economic system' prevailing in Cyprus, with its exploitation of labourers and peasants. It also attacked the indifference of the British authorities to this situation and the self-interest of the wealthy classes and the so-called Unionist politicians. The letter concluded by expressing a double hope: if the Labour party ceded Cyprus to Greece, the KKK would 'join hands with the proletariat of Greece for the struggle against the Greek and international capitalists'. If however the Labour party decided to keep Cyprus, the party would enjoy 'the socialist regime and will celebrate the emancipation of the labourers and rural population of this island'.

The KKK was formed in 1925 and was succeeded by the

AKEL (the Progressive Party of the Working People) in 1941. Its first constitution was published in 1926. Although the work of the KKK was aimed primarily at solving the problems of the working class and impoverished farmers, it also stressed in 1927 the need for a united front 'against the common enemy of all the people – imperialism'. It called on all the inhabitants – Greeks, Turks, Maronites, Armenians – to fight for the island's self-determination.

Parties of the right were also formed. By 1931 two nationalist parties (KEK, Kypriakon Ethnikon Komma, the Cyprus National Party, and EPEK, Ethniki Rizospastiki Enosi Kyprion, the Cyprus National Radicalist Union) were in existence. Their target was of course union with Greece. Most of these parties were personal and ephemeral organizations: many violent clashes took place between leading personalities striving to win more support. Yet on the national issue, even if from different viewpoints, they appeared to be united.

5 1925-1931: Towards the First Major Popular Protest

The years between 1878 and 1914 witnessed a movement for union with Greece and efforts to secure greater rights of self-government. Following the treaties of Sèvres and Lausanne, the Cypriots demanded, in addition to *enosis*, autonomous and representative government. This was refused, and later on, after disturbances in many parts of the island in 1931, even such liberties and participation in government as existed were abolished. Hundreds were imprisoned and ten Church, nationalist and Communist leaders were deported. Thus the struggle assumed its second phase – the third was between 1946 and 1950, and the decisive fourth phase between 1955 and 1959. The British authorities always claimed that Cypriots had not yet attained a degree of political development such as would justify the grant of increased constitutional powers or self-government. When the history of British rule in Cyprus is carefully considered, it becomes clear how unfair this policy was.

The Treaty of Sèvres (near Paris), which developed from the San Remo Treaty of the same year, was signed on 10 August 1920. The three articles concerning Cyprus are numbers 115, 116 and 117. Article 115 states that the High Contracting Parties recognize the annexation of Cyprus proclaimed by the British Government on 5 November 1914; the next article states that Turkey renounces all rights and title to Cyprus, including the right to the tribute formerly paid to the Sultan; lastly, Article 117 says that Turkish nationals born or resident in Cyprus will acquire British nationality and lose their Turkish nationality, subject to the conditions laid down in local law.

The second agreement of 1923 deserves a closer examination. The Conference of Lausanne, which met (not continuously) from November 1922 to July 1923, was one of the most important diplomatic gatherings after the First World War.

Even the USA sent Senator Hamilton Levy to salvage something for the American oil companies. Thus a Foreign Office minute dated 25 July records that 'the Americans want to keep Ismet at Lausanne negotiating a separate treaty with them by which they shall obtain more favourable terms than we have been able to get'. The treaty was signed on 24 July and contained 143 articles of which four will be mentioned:

Article 15
Turkey renounces in favour of Italy all rights and title over the Dodecanese.

Article 16
Turkey hereby renounces all rights and titles whatsoever over or respecting the territories situated outside the frontiers laid down in the present Treaty and the islands other than those for which her sovereignty is recognized by the said Treaty.

Article 20
Turkey hereby recognizes the annexation of Cyprus proclaimed by the British Government on 5 November 1914.

Article 21
Turkish nationals ordinarily resident in Cyprus on 5 November 1914 will acquire British nationality subject to the conditions laid down in local law and will thereupon lose their Turkish nationality. They will, however, have the right to opt for Turkish nationality within two years from the coming into force of the present Treaty, provided that they leave Cyprus within twelve months after having so opted.

Hence, by Article 16, Turkey surrendered all titles and claims over Cyprus. Likewise, by accepting the agreements Greece endorsed and put her name to the cession of Cyprus to Great Britain. The Turks however reserved the right to receive into Turkey, during the following two years, any Cypriot Turk who wished to retain Turkish nationality. In the period up to 1925 only a small percentage of those living on the island were attracted to Asia Minor by the promise of grants of land. This clearly proved that Turkey considered her last legal links with Cyprus broken. In fact by 21 October 1927 only some 2,500 to 3,000 out of the 9,000 or so persons who opted for Turkish nationality had actually left Cyprus to return to Turkish territory. There was therefore, as the Foreign Office observed, 'a Turkish colony of some five to six thousand people in the island, who for this and the succeeding generation may be a source of anxiety to the authorities'. Yet the presence of the Turkish community in Cyprus was also described on many occasions by leading British officials as 'an asset from a political standpoint'. The British ploy of playing the two communities, with their distinct religious beliefs, against each other was seen as a way of perpetuating and British rule in Cyprus.

Greek nationalism was betrayed by Article 15, which gave the Dodecanese to Italy (this was acknowledged by Venizelos in his pact with Mussolini in 1928), and by Article 20, which gave Britain Cyprus. One may ask what happened to the spirit of nationalism created by Versailles in 1919: both the Dodecanese and Cyprus were assigned to foreign powers without even being asked.

Lausanne was important for three other reasons. First, it marked the definite triumph of Turkish nationalism under Mustafa Kemal Pasha (Atatürk, or Father of the Turks, born at Salonica in 1881). His chief military collaborator was Ismet Pasha (later Inönü), a fellow officer from the days of the First World War and a true Ottoman, who in his own way had perhaps become as westernized as Mustafa Kemal. Ismet headed the Turkish delegation at Lausanne; Turkey's search for a western European identity was at last a reality.

The Ottoman empire had ceased to be, but a new national state of Turkey had arisen in Anatolia under the guiding hand of Atatürk, who directed its destiny along the path of modernization. The new Turkey was liberated from antiquated financial and economic bondage and was ready to begin life anew in a revived and independent spirit. The long struggle of the Turks for national independence is one of the great epics of recent world history. That independence, won on the battlefields of Asia Minor, was to be finally achieved by no less notable victories in diplomacy at Lausanne. Ismet ominously intimated that Turkey would 'never' accept a Greek Aegean or a Greek Cyprus.

Second, Lausanne marked the disastrous defeat of Greece and the end of the Hellenic dream in Asia Minor. Greece was

humbled beyond all expectations. In fact on 28 April 1922 the
Cypriot archbishop telegraphed the British Premier to express
regret and indignation at the attitude adopted by the great
powers to the just and reasonable claims of Hellenism.
However, Lausanne formally registered the triumph of Turkish
aims and the failure of the Allied powers to maintain their
original peace settlement. The expulsion of the Greeks from
Asia Minor resulted in the death of some 15 per cent of the
Greek population and the permanent absorption of another
1½ million Greek refugees whose arrival increased the
mainland population by 30 per cent.

Lausanne was called by Lloyd George in his book *The Truth
about the Peace Treaties* an 'abject, cowardly and infamous
surrender'. It recovered for Turkey practically all the territory
which had been taken away at Sèvres for the benefit of Greece
and Armenia.

Third, it signified a victory of French over British policy in
the Near East. The French sphere of political and economic
influence in the region was not only consolidated but expanded.

For Cyprus the treaties had a twofold importance: first,
Turkey renounced all right to the island. Hence not even a
whisper was raised when Cyprus became a Crown Colony in
1925. Second, the Greeks of the island believed that the British
would sooner or later grant them their ultimate wish since
Turkey was now definitely out of the way. Britain's uncertainty
of tenure, especially between 1878 and 1914, was often cited as
a reason for not granting union with Greece and for not
carrying out necessary economic reforms.

On 1 May 1925 an official pronouncement declared the
island a Crown Colony and the High Commissioner gave way
to a governor. Almost immediately the legislative council was
reconstructed. An Order in Council dated 6 February 1925
provided that the council should be composed of the governor,
nine official members and 15 elected members, of which three
were to be elected by Mohammedan electors and 12 by non-
Mohammedan electors. The elections of October duly
provided the legislative council with 15 elected members.
Notable among those who failed to be elected was Theofanis
Theodotou, a fiery pro-union politician, who was defeated by
1,444 votes to 1,405 by the pro-government, almost illiterate

farmer from the village of Deftera, Hadji Eftychios Hadji Procopi. The failure of the Greek Cypriot politicians to achieve anything constructive towards their ultimate goal contributed to the defeat of Theodotou.

In addition to this increase in the size of the chamber, a unique restriction on its powers was imposed. The provision, which was contrary to the Colonial Laws Validity Act of 1865, stated that the council, despite its representative character, might make no law to alter the Constitution. In fact these so-called new arrangements were no different from those which already existed. The Greek members of the National Council, in a memorandum to the Secretary of State for the Colonies on 25 February 1924, explained:

> The Island has had since 1882 a constitution of a pseudo-parliamentary character, akin to those devised for the enslaved peoples, which aim rather at their corruption than at their culture. Because of these political systems none of the real blessings of true parliamentary constitutions are shed, while only the evils of discord and political recrimination result to the people . . . this system having fallen completely from the conscience of the people of Cyprus, has been condemned by them in a manner showing their unremitting determination not to acquiesce in this parliamentary mockery, by which on the one hand their will is trodden upon and annihilated and on the other, no real right of active participation in the administration of their public affairs is exercisable.[1]

It was a non-democratic form of colonial rule, since only those areas of business not decided solely by the governor were handed to the legislative council. Moreover, an Anglo-Turkish combination could carry any measure against the united opposition of the 12 Greek deputies representing 80 per cent of the island's total population. This system was maintained by granting privileges to the Moslem members, which antagonized the Christian element and provided the basis for divide and rule, a strategy deliberately applied in other areas. Figures provided by N.P. Jodrell (a British Member of Parliament) on 25 March 1920 showed that in 1919 out of 789 commissioned and non-commissioned police officers, 420 were

Moslems; in other words, 53·2 per cent came from 18 per cent of the population.

Hence the legislative council had no more power than before, and the issuing of Orders in Council was often used to override its decisions. When the budget was rejected by the council in 1927 it was put into execution by such means; in the same year, in order to cover a deficit, taxes were increased by £40,000 without its advice or consent. Seven such Orders were passed in 1927 alone. H.R. Cowell, of the Ceylon and Mauritius Department of the Colonial Office, was able, on 24 December 1928, to describe the use of such Orders as not only necessary but desirable: 'The practice of resorting to legislation by Order in Council has been so freely adopted that we are not likely to be seriously embarrassed by any action which the Councillors may take.'[2]

Apart from these problems about the Constitution, the British authorities faced a series of memoranda on *enosis* and economic issues. As mentioned in the previous chapter, the archbishop's memorandum of 1 May 1925 to Amery, reiterating the aspirations of the Greek Christian population for union with Greece, was rebuffed. Furthermore, when the archbishop on a later occasion used phrases such as 'an enslaved people with national aspirations', Amery, in a draft minute dated 21 July, stated that he deprecated the use of such disloyal expressions from a personage holding such a high position in a British colony.

The reconstituted legislative council met for the first time on Friday 6 November 1925. On the 17th, the 12 Greek members presented a memorandum demanding union with Greece or the granting of a greater measure of self-government. In the first two weeks of December counter-petitions came from the Mohammedans, Catholics, Maronites and Armenians. The Christian deputies were duly informed that the union question was definitely closed and could not be reopened. They were also reminded of their oath of allegiance to His Majesty. As to self-government, they were told that Cyprus had not yet attained a degree of political development such as to justify the granting of increased constitutional powers.

On 30 March 1926 the elected members of the legislative council unanimously passed two resolutions (proposed by the

Bishop of Kition and Michael H. Michaelides) concerning the share of Cyprus of the Turkish debt charge. Stevenson, reporting to Amery on 14 April, stated that the official members had abstained on his instructions. He also stressed that 'to relieve Cyprus of this heavy burden on its resources would be a most politic move at the present time'. In November, by a vote of 13 to 9, the deputies rejected the Appropriation Bill of 1927 and thus the Colonial Estimates of revenue and expenditure for the same year. Similar bills had been rejected in 1888 and 1911. On 29 November Amery was informed by R. Popham Lobb (the officer administering the government of Cyprus) that the elected members had 'chosen to stand or fall' on the question of the tribute and 'are within their rights in so doing'.

On 30 November Sir Ronald Storrs succeeded Stevenson as governor of the island. He was a self-confessed *philokyprios* and philhellene. When he arrived at Famagusta Storrs accepted from the mayor an address of welcome tied with the blue and white ribbons of Greece. He claimed on several occasions that his professed love of Hellenism was often taken advantage of. But, he emphasized, even political extremists must realize that he was not appointed to give away portions of the British empire. Thanks to him however the detested tribute was abolished in 1927. This pleased all Cypriots, who expressed their satisfaction in more than one way. Thus when Storrs returned to the island on 5 September 1927, he was greeted in Limassol and handed a document assuring him of their readiness to co-operate at all times in those measures which would serve the true prosperity and welfare of Cyprus.

On 7 February 1927 the Appropriation Bill and Colonial Estimates were passed by Orders in Council 176 and 177. The Orders provided for the appropriation of the revenues of Cyprus during 1927 and imposed certain new customs duties. On 21 March a memorandum from the 15 elected members of the legislative council regretted the continued impositions. The same feelings were expressed on 28 December 1926 in a reply to the governor's address to the legislative council.

The year 1927 was also important because it was then that the authorities began in earnest their anti-left campaign. The Seditious Publications Law of 1921 was used to prohibit publications such as the *Kratos kai Epanastasis* (*State and*

Revolution) and the *Red First of May*. By 11 December 1928 15 such publications were prohibited. In 1928 the government tightened up internal security and on 1 January 1929 the KKK went underground; its newspaper *Neos Anthropos* (*New Man*) was forced to close down, but it was replaced by a biweekly publication called *O Neos Ergatis* (*The New Worker*). In 1930 the KKK leader Haralambos Vatiliotis (nicknamed 'Vatis') was tried in an assize court for distributing Communist propaganda but was acquitted. This was the type of harassment the British began to direct at the Communists, who were finally acquiring, contrary to all expectations, a large following on the island. Despite its difficulties the KKK advocated a united anti-British front to include all Cypriots, all classes and all parties which for one reason or another did not want foreign rule, hoping to promote a spirit of co-operation and united action 'against the common enemy of the people – imperialism'.

By 1928 several issues troubled the authorities in Cyprus:

1   The worsening economic situation meant that more and more Cypriots joined the anti-British bandwagon.

2   The forces of the left continued to grow.

3   The loyalty of the Turkish members to the legislative council became questionable (see below), so that the constitutional machinery threatened to break down completely.

4   The Greek flag was flown all over the island and subscriptions collected for the Greek Air Force.

5   The teaching in Greek schools and to boy-scout troops was directed to the 'glorification of Hellenic ideals'. The Greeks were clinging to their ideal of a greater Hellas comprising within its territories the whole of the Hellenic race. The governor saw this problem as the most serious one facing Britain. In a secret despatch to Amery on 10 May 1928 Storrs requested the services of Mr Wynn-Williams (one of His Majesty's Inspectors of Schools) to enquire into and report on the educational system and prepare a scheme of reorganization.

The year 1928 was also the fiftieth anniversary of the British occupation, and the governor, after careful consideration, decided 'to extract from this jubilee something of that publicity which Cyprus so sorely needed'. Sporting activities were organized, a silver crown was struck and a set of jubilee stamps were issued, which brought to the exchequer a net profit over and above normal postage requirements, of £20,000. However, a circular issued by the bishops, the Greek members of the legislative council and the mayors not only protested against the British occupation but recommended that the celebrations should be boycotted. Venizelos and the Synod (council of Greek bishops) of Athens advised participation, but the Greeks refused to take part in any of the activities except the spring horse races, which, according to Storrs were the best attended since his arrival.

The politicians, furthermore, abstained from attendance at the birthday review of the troops and police and at the annual garden party, which was postponed from 30 May to 4 June. The latter date being the anniversary of the Defensive Alliance between Britain and Turkey in 1878, the Holy Synod, the Greek Cypriot politicians and the mayors in the national assembly addressed the Secretary of State for the Colonies, regretting that liberty had not been given to the island with the denunciation of the treaty of 1878. The memorandum asked for union with Greece, a continuation of the struggle and the protection of minorities. Iacovos (Bishop of Paphos), S. Stavrinakis (member of the legislative council) and G. Markides (mayor of Nicosia) were entrusted to present the memorandum to the Colonial Secretary's office in Cyprus, to be transmitted to the proper authorities in Britain.

The other inhabitants of Cyprus (the non-Greek minorities) protested against the memorandum and expressed their satisfaction with the present system of administration. Amery, replying to a written parliamentary question from Miss Wilkinson on 13 July, repeated in parrot-like fashion the phrase 'His Majesty's Government will continue to govern the island in the general interests of the inhabitants as a whole'. Once more Greek aspirations were rebuffed. Nevertheless in 1928 and 1929 scores of press articles appeared (especially in the Athenian *Proia* and *Eleftheron Vema*) advocating the union of Cyprus with Greece and criticizing the British administration. Parliamentary questions were also asked in Britain on the *enosis* issue.

The coming to power of the second British Labour government on 5 June 1929 prompted the delivery of a long memorandum on 20 July. This Labour victory was a source of particular gratification to the Greeks because of earlier promises and pronouncements by Labour leaders that national self-determination was not beyond the reach of the Cypriots. The memorandum emphasized the desire of the Greek people of Cyprus to be united with Greece, with which 'sacred and unbreakable ties of blood, religion, language, traditions and national conscience link them'. It also listed the main grievances of the people of Cyprus.

The Constitution, it was claimed, was worthless and examples were given to substantiate the criticism; the writers of the memorandum suggested several amendments. The economy was in a deplorable state and made even worse by the detestable taxation system: the burden of taxation had long since reached the highest possible limit of endurance of the Cypriot taxpayers. On top of all these grievances there were too many officials receiving very high salaries. The writers also expressed the opinion that the Moslem minority in Cyprus was only a pretext for the denial of national autonomy.

After explaining the state of the island and expressing the hope that it would not be allowed to continue, the writers requested that the British government should appoint a Royal Commission of Inquiry to investigate and report. The writers felt certain that such an inquiry would draw appalling inferences from the 50 years of British rule which 'must form a quite unique instance of British maladministration'. The memorandum was signed by the 12 elected Greek members of the legislative council headed by Nicodemos, the Bishop of Kition.

A three-man deputation led by Nicodemos arrived in London to put their case. They met Sir John Shuckburgh, the Under-Secretary of State for the Colonies, on 11 October 1929 and on 25 October had an hour-long interview with Lord Passfield, Secretary of State for the Colonies. Also present were W. Lunn MP, his parliamentary private secretary, Sir John Shuckburgh, and H.R. Cowell and A.J. Dawe, both of the Ceylon and Mediterranean Department of the Colonial Office. At the meeting the bishop explained that the reason the people of Cyprus wanted to be handed over to Greece was the natural law which makes people love liberty and desire to be ruled by people of the same language and traditions as their own. He concluded by reiterating that the national desire of the Greek Cypriots would always remain the same.

Lord Passfield replied on 28 November. He stated that the memorandum of 20 July had received his full attention and that he had listened carefully to the arguments put forward by the deputation. His reply touched on all the grievances, national, constitutional and economic, outlined by them. On their requests to grant the island union with Greece or some form of responsible government (i.e. dominion status) and to appoint a Royal Commission to inquire into the state of Cyprus, he had this to say:

> His Majesty's Government are unable to accede to it . . . the time has not yet come when it would be to the general advantage of the people of Cyprus to make a trial of a constitutional experiment in this direction. Those institutions already established in the Island which are subject in varying degrees to popular control, cannot be said to have attained that reasonable measure of efficiency which should be looked for before any extension of the principle is approved . . . this proposal has received my consideration, but after careful reflection I have formed the view that the appointment of such a body would at the present juncture, be of no real benefit to Cyprus.[3]

The Minister decided therefore that what Cyprus needed at the time was fewer opportunities for political discussion and more occasions for constructive work. Passfield's reply prompted the Greek inhabitants of Cyprus to send scores of telegrams to him and the Prime Minister, protesting against what he had said and demanding union with Greece.

Meanwhile the non-Greek Cypriots were also active. In September the Turkish members of the legislative council sent a memorandum to the Colonial Office protesting against the one presented by the Greek delegation. The Turks also expressed their full satisfaction with the answer given by Passfield. Yet once again the Greeks persisted and vowed to continue the struggle for *enosis.* Thus in January 1929 the archbishop sent memoranda demanding union to distinguished persons in England. Amongst the replies was one from Viscount Longford, who on 13 April published an article in the *Star* (the official paper of the Irish government) stating that he hoped the Cypriots would manage to get rid of the foreign ruler and succeed in achieving union with Greece. In the previous month an exchange of letters took place between M. Lanitis, a leading enosist, and T.P. O'Connor MP, who often raised questions with the British government on the island's political and economic situation. The former recalled Gladstone's hope that Cyprus would one day be reunited with Greece. The latter replied that he had no doubt that the desires of the Cypriot people would be fulfilled in the end.

A decisive step was taken in Nicosia on 26 January 1930, when the Pan-Cypriot National Assembly voted for the establishment of a national organization the object of which was to promote the cause of union. The assembly of the organization consisted of 37 members, all of whom were fervent enosists. They were able to co-ordinate their activities and thus proceed to penetrate the countryside, to bolster the faithful and convert or pacify those against. The resolutions passed on 3 June 1930 by the 'whole' Greek population in favour of union were sent to the Secretary of State for the Colonies. It was later found however that opposition existed, and some villages declared their disapproval and trust in British rule. Nevertheless, in the elections of 15 October the pro-unionists were triumphantly successful. The above resolutions, presented on the occasion of His Majesty's Birthday, prompted Passfield to reply yet again that Britain was unable to accede to the request for the cession of Cyprus to Greece.

With victory bells still ringing, the unionist politicians met Dr Drummond Shields, the Under-Secretary of State for the Colonies, on 20 October. Dr Shields, who visited Cyprus on his way home from Palestine, made it absolutely clear that *enosis* was out of the question. Moreover the Greeks were made to understand that the Turkish minority was strongly opposed to such a move. A memorandum addressed to him on 23 October by the representatives of the Maronite and Latin communities (through the Colonial Secretary of Cyprus since Shields and his party had already left the island) also expressed contentment at continuing to live under the British flag.

Further letters expressing the same desire, and replies containing the same phrases, flowed between the archbishop and the Colonial Office from November 1930 till January 1931. The mood of the Colonial Office was expressed by A.J. Dawe, who in a draft minute dated 8 December 1930 stated that 'any gesture of politeness towards the Enosis party is interpreted as weakness'.

In trying to achieve their goal, the enosists used everything they could lay their hands on. Thus from January 1931 onwards Zenon Rossides, the London representative of the national organization, conducted a campaign by letters addressed mainly to the *Manchester Guardian*, confident that his activities were gaining ground for the movement. Many other British sympathizers pressed for the achievement of the Cypriot ideal. Fenner Brockway and G. Mander were among Members of Parliament who pressed for an extention of self-government for the island. 'No such steps are at present in contemplation,' was the polite government response.

In Greece events in Cyprus were closely followed by the press. Articles and editorials in such newspapers as the *Proia*, *Eleftheron Vema*, *Hemerisios Typos* and *Hestia* appeared regularly. Irrespective of the political repercussions, the object was to keep alive the movement for union. Furthermore, Alexis Kyrou (the Greek consul whose father, the founder of the influential Athenian newspaper *Hestia*, was born in Cyprus) urged the Cypriots to insist on union and only union. However, Venizelos, after the Asia Minor collapse, was striving to achieve some form of peaceful co-existence with Turkey. Hence in June 1931 he promised the British Ambassador that he would recall Kyrou and intimated that the Cypriots should first achieve other freedoms and allow the union movement to mature with time. In fact both the political and economic policies of Greece at the time were decided for her by the west and particularly Britain, so Venizelos was unable to offer constructive proposals for Cyprus at diplomatic level. The advent of the Metaxas dictatorship on 4 August 1936 was a setback to Cypriot aspirations since Metaxas announced that there would be no change in the foreign policy of Greece, which would continue to be based on a close understanding with Turkey and the maintenance of the Balkan *entente*.

On arrival Storrs had remarked that Cyprus was 'financially

spoiled' and 'politically spoilt'. Why was the island financially spoiled? It is true that under British rule Cyprus had made some progress, but it had not been as rapid as the Cypriots had hoped for the following seasons:

1   The peculiar nature of the Constitution ensured that the majority were thwarted by the minority and the appointed officials.

2   Taxation and the tribute were unfair. The latter, abolished in 1927, 'from the beginning constituted a genuine, a bitter and an always remediable grievance', according to Storrs. It was in fact a heavy annual fine which prevented development. As already indicated, the final rejection of the Appropriation Bill in November 1926 showed that the elected members of the legislative council had chosen to stand or fall together on the tribute question. Apart from all the other customary and imperial taxes there was the salt tax, increased on 11 August 1931 from three piastres an oke (2·8lb) to four piastres. This was a genuine grievance that helped lead to the disturbances of that year.

3   British apathy produced further and worse evils. Agriculture, the island's principal source of wealth, was in a primitive condition compared to other countries. The Cypriots formed a community of small peasant proprietors without financial resources, without knowledge of how to sell their produce to the best advantage and without banking facilities. As Sir Philip Cunliffe-Lister, Secretary of State for the Colonies, said, 'that kind of man fell a very ready prey to the money lender'. It is however true that co-operative credit societies increased from 28 in 1925 to 50 in December 1926 and to 326 in 1930, catering for about two-thirds of the villages. Furthermore, an Agricultural Bank was established in June 1925 (Law No. 15) under the joint auspices of the government and the Ottoman Bank.

But while the peasant was crippled, the landlord was helped. Colonel Wedgwood MP, during a debate on the colonies on 13 July 1928, explained:

Cyprus has just escaped paying £50,000 a year, and I would draw the attention of my Honourable Friends on this side to what has been done with that £50,000. Cyprus got this £50,000 and used the money three or four years ago, in advance of getting it, before the advent of Sir Ronald Storrs, to relieve all the landowners of Cyprus of the taxes on their land values, putting the money straight into the pockets of the landlords of Cyprus – a very fine illustration of what always happens when a Tory Administration is in power and has a natural propensity to help its friends.[4]

He emphasized once more that 'the time has come when this absolutely forgotten colony should be taken in hand'. Storrs, elaborating on the above criticism, had this to say:

Cyprus is a purely agricultural country and three-quarters of the population is engaged in agriculture. Most of these are illiterate. Seventy per cent are chronically indebted to usurers and merchants whose actions for recovery (more than half the cases in the District Courts), afford employment to the numerous advocates, who derive the major part of their professional income from that source. I found on the Council eight advocates, three of whom were money-lenders; one landowner who was also a money-lender; one bishop of the Greek Church; one merchant and one farmer. Thus though the real interests of the Colony were those of the peasant producer, the interests represented in the Legislature were exclusively those of the numerically insignificant class of parasites who made a living out of him.[5]

The above arguments, needless to say, give weight to the criticism that Cyprus was merely occupied rather than administered or developed. They also illustrate the fact that the island, not being on the direct route to India (Britain, Gibraltar, Malta and Suez), was slowly acquiring the status of a second-class colony; hence the government was not particularly interested in its development. This prompted the Communist newspaper *Neos Anthropos*, in a leading article on 14 January 1928, to attack the jubilee celebrations of that year by stating that 'the conqueror has milked for fifty years the Cypriot cow which has therefore now ceased to yield'. The British failure to cure the evident economic grievances of the island was continually attacked by the press.

4   The Cypriots also suffered from that monstrosity of feudal and manorial domination – forced labour. On 23 June 1931 Fenner Brockway MP asked Dr Shields whether he was aware that forced unpaid labour was in operation for road-making and other purposes in Cyprus. The Under-Secretary of State for the Colonies replied: 'Amending legislation has been enacted to put an end to the system under which compulsory labour could be exacted for village road construction. . . .'[6]

Hence what the heroic French revolutionaries fought – in the name of liberty, equality and fraternity – to abolish in 1789 still persisted in Cyprus 142 years later.

5   The peasantry was dominated by the Church. This however was less in evidence in the twentieth century.

6   The anomalous and uncertain position of the island up to 1914 may explain to some extent the lack of interest in its development.

7   The First World War and the economic depression that followed (after an initial temporary boom) further retarded development and strengthened, in Cyprus as elsewhere, discontent among the population.

8   The Hellenic nationalism of the majority is claimed to have obstructed at times what the British called 'constructive measures' in the legislative council. This view is easily refuted. A forceful government could have passed any welfare or social measure it wished by the use of the Anglo-Turkish majority or the adoption of an Order in Council, a device widely used whenever the government wanted to impose its will on the populace.

Cyprus, then, was a mainly agricultural country and, according to the census of 1931, the rural population constituted 80·5 per cent of the total. Despite this only around three-fifths of the land was under cultivation, the rest being held by the government and the Greek and Turkish religious institutions. In 1928 a special government report recorded the plight of the peasantry. Storrs records in his reminiscences:

The lives of the very poor are in all countries the problem of the statesman and the opportunity of the demagogue. In order to put some check upon the ceaseless flow of uninformed comment upon the state of the Cyprus peasantry, I caused to be prepared a Survey of Rural Life in Cyprus. The Survey which was made ... revealed conditions of living preserved through the Ottoman Empire from a dim past and roughly equivalent to those of Tudor England. Though sad reading, it was to be the basis of much social legislation – as in the treatment of domestic servants – for many years.[7]

The Survey, which fixed a minimum level of subsistence, found that over 25 per cent of the rural population lived below that level, 50 per cent around that level, and the rest, the so-called 'wealthy', above that level. By 1934 the Cypriots were many times worse off because of the world economic slump. A general fall in commodity prices led to higher customs tariffs to safeguard the revenue; this increased the burden of rural indebtedness, which further boosted the exploitation of the peasant. In many cases the only reward for the toiling Cypriot was his daily bread and in most he worked for only an inhumanly low wage. On top of all these calamities, the 1930s witnessed a two-year drought which reduced the land to a barren burning desert.

The Cypriot therefore had to endure excessive and unfair taxation, an unworkable Constitution, political persecution, forced labour, exploitation, court actions, the world economic slump and the so-called 'initial uncertainty of permanence'. The period between 1929 and 1931 was dominated by political and economic unrest. The political outlook of the people was undergoing change and the labour movement was beginning to make its voice felt. The formation of trade unions was generally described by the authorities as being 'synonymous with Communism' and they were suppressed whenever they appeared. Nevertheless, a strike by 1,000 asbestos miners in 1927 induced the Asbestos Mines Corporation to reduce the working day from ten to nine hours. The strike was organized by the KKK. T.W. Adams, in a publication for the USA Hoover Institution on *War, Revolution and Peace*, says:

Although still young, and despite the police surveillance of many of its members, the new party was able to organize an

important island-wide strike in July 1929: 6,000 asbestos
miners left work the same day. They demonstrated in front of
their company offices and shouted slogans demanding
shorter working hours, higher wages and freedom to buy
bread from markets of their own choice. . . . The company's
management asked the workers to return to work and
promised to meet all their demands, but the workers would
not trust the company's promises and continued the strike.
Consequently many workers were arrested, tried, convicted,
and imprisoned; scores more were fired; and some
communists were exiled. Even though the strike of 6,000
asbestos miners was not successful, it was a turning point for
the entire labour movement in Cyprus, and the experience
strengthened the KKK for its later struggles.[8]

Apart from asbestos (of which, for its size, Cyprus is one of the
biggest producers in the world), the island is also rich in metals,
particularly copper and chromium.

Several other factors helped to cause unrest. After the
rejection of the Appropriation Bill for 1927 by the members of
the legislative council in November 1926, and the recourse to
Orders in Council, the Secretary of State for the Colonies stated
that Britain did not propose to govern Cyprus by such Orders
and that unless the legislative council co-operated alterations to
the Constitution would be necessary. But the estimates for 1928
received the same response and were passed by the same
method. In the following year Storrs urged that the legislative
council should be enlarged, with three-quarters of the elected
members actively engaged in agriculture. Money-lenders were
to be ineligible. But the Constitution was not amended and this
chance to bring peasant representatives into the legislative
process was missed.

Education in Cyprus was largely dominated by the Church
and its unionist supporters, and the authorities wished to
minimize this control. Storrs recollects:

I was strongly averse to diminishing the study of the Greek
language and classical traditions. But the method of
appointing, transferring and dismissing teachers, male and
female, by the Greek Members of Council was open to grave
objections. The politicians too often exercised their power for

political or petty personal aims. The teacher was usually the only educated man in the village; as a political agent he was therefore almost indispensable to the politicians, who were exclusively town-dwellers. Being dependent upon the politicians for advancement in his profession he had to serve the political purposes of his masters.[9]

Storrs introduced the Elementary Education Bill in 1929. Control of the appointment, promotion, transfer, dismissal and discipline of elementary teachers of all communities passed from the political committees to the government, and the salaries of all were greatly increased. The Bill in effect sought to prevent the use of schools for the glorification of Greek or Turkish ideals. Three Greek members, N. Nicolaides, P. Cacoyiannis and Eftychios Hadji Procopi, voted for it in the legislative council and the Bill was therefore passed. Storrs however was quite unfairly denounced as 'a traitor to the Greek cause' and 'the assassin of Hellenic education'; the Athenian press described him as 'a distinguished Philhellene who had abolished the tribute' but who had now turned into a 'fiend' and an 'imperialist dictator'.

The Cypriots were infuriated. The Educational Bill and Passfield's reply to the Greek memorandum on 28 November produced a crop of petitions and protests from Greek politicians and ecclesiastics. Further protests were received by Passfield on 11 and 17 December and the archbishop pleaded with the Premier to examine the issue further. None of the three members that had voted for the Bill presented themselves for election in 1930.

The island's educational system was regularly described in government circles as an unnecessary evil which needed reform. Yet the Annual Report for 1928 (sent to the Colonial Office on 4 December 1929) stated that everything was functioning satisfactorily. This caused an angry reaction. A minute dated 15 January 1930 from Sir John Shuckburgh to A.J. Dawe stated: 'Is it wise to talk about the "satisfactory results" etc, of the present system when we have just been engaged upon scrapping the system on the ground that it is intolerable? . . . If we are to be criticised for our recent educational proceedings, it will certainly furnish ammunition to our critics if they can point to the Annual Report as evidence that the old system was working admirably!'[10]

A statement by Philip Snowden in the House of Commons on 8 July 1931 also caused widespread dissatisfaction. The Chancellor of the Exchequer stated that the accumulated surplus from the payments made from the Cyprus revenue as tribute to Turkey under the Cyprus Convention of 1878 had been disposed of for the sinking fund of the Turkish loan guaranteed by Britain in 1855. Following that announcement the Cypriots expected taxation to be reduced; instead the governor proposed increases. A deficit in the budget of around £60,000 was envisaged and not more than £40,000 of this could be met immediately from reductions in expenditure. Meanwhile the world economic blizzard of the late 1920s and early 1930s was causing new problems. Because of the general fall in commodity prices the customs tariff was in need of readjustment and revision in order to safeguard the island's revenue. (Additional revenue of around £20,000 was required to avoid encroachment on the small reserve of £90,000.)

A committee of three British officials, three Greeks and one Turk was appointed to make recommendations for meeting the deficit. They proposed a temporary levy of 5 per cent on official salaries above £100 a year and the substitution of specific (based on the quantity purchased) for *ad valorem* (in proportion to the value of the goods purchased) customs duties. These recommendations were unanimous and were duly accepted by the governor, who proceeded to introduce a bill in the legislative council. The elected members however refused to agree to any legislative measure involving fresh taxation.

The governor knew that so long as the three Turkish members remained loyal to him the wishes of the Greek majority could be overridden. But the activities of Assaf Bey, the Turkish consul, the anti-colonial mood that prevailed in the island and, more important, the formation of labour organizations for both Greek and Turkish peasants and workers ensured the election of Misirlizade Nejati Bey, who could not be counted upon to support the government. In fact Munir Bey's successor had joined the Greeks. Storrs remarked that Nejati Bey was a 'man of straw' but he 'nevertheless possessed in effect the casting vote in the legislative council'. When the vote for the revised tariff was taken the Greeks solidly opposed it and the 'little Turk', the 'thirteenth Greek', voted with them. The measure was thrown out but the governor imposed it by an Order in Council. This procedure was described as a 'tyrannical flouting of the people's will'.

The activities of Nejati Bey deserve some comment. Almost immediately after his election he took his place with the Greek opposition; together this combination blocked the passage of the Customs Bill and the Village Authorities Bill, amongst other measures. This prompted W.R. Shipway, a senior Colonial Office official, to record on 16 June 1931 that the already creaking constitutional machinery now threatened to break down completely. Nejati Bey was referred to as 'worthless' by Shipway and as an 'elected Turkish nonentity' by Storrs. Nevertheless he travelled round the country speaking to large crowds, and assembled a meeting of Turks from all parts of the island on 1 May 1931 to appoint a Mufti (the official interpreter of the law) as political and religious leader and a committee to take over the Evkaf department.

This meeting, composed of some 140 people, declared itself a National Congress, with declarations of policy issued by the central committee and the new Mufti. A. Said Efendi, who took over that title, issued his manifesto on 6 May. A short extract will suffice: 'On this date a new era has been inaugurated in the life of the Turks of Cyprus. . . . Common grievances require common measures. . . . All communities which fell under foreign rule succeeded in maintaining and defending their existence and honour only by making such sacrifices and by close co-operation.'[11]

The governor, in a secret despatch to Lord Passfield on 4 June, acknowledged that a united and loyal Turkish community which had always been regarded as a useful safeguard in troubled times 'cannot at present be guaranteed'.

As already indicated, the Church, the nationalist politicians and the Communists were striving for the same ends – though from totally different motives. Yet in the summer of 1931 a violent quarrel and riots broke out between the right and the left as to what would happen if the struggle to overthrow the status quo were successful. On 25 March 1931, National Independence Day, the Communists held demonstrations.

Sir Ronald Storrs, in a detailed account (despatch No. 80,

paragraph 13) of the October events sent to the Colonial
Secretary on 11 February 1932, records:

> Minor disturbances had occurred at Nicosia and Larnaca in
> consequence of the opposition of the National party to the
> spread of communism. The Communist party had openly
> attacked the National movement and succeeded in gaining
> many adherents. The National leaders thereupon decided to
> suppress all communist meetings and they had secretly
> persuaded large bodies of the riff-raff in the towns to attack
> the communists. The disturbances were well handled by the
> Police and kept in check, and the leaders on both sides were
> severely   warned.   But   sufficient   assaults   had   been
> perpetrated   and   injuries   sustained   to   frighten   the
> communists. As your predecessor was informed at the time,
> the successful employment of mob violence by the National
> party was a disquieting factor in the general situation.[12]

However, at a meeting on 24 October at the archbishopric
(held to discuss what measures should be taken to force the
government to set free the ringleaders), a reconciliation
engineered by A. Emilianides was concluded between the
Communist leaders and the Church. Vatiliotis kissed the hand
of the archbishop and promised him the support of his party in
the immediate struggle against their colonial masters. On the
following day Vatiliotis was arrested in Nicosia while
addressing a crowd, and Costas Skeleas, another leading leftist,
suffered the same fate in Limassol on 26 October whilst
distributing pamphlets announcing the KKK's decision to join
in the protest but to demand autonomy rather than union. Both
men were deported along with other Greek political leaders.

Hence ill-feeling and total dissatisfaction prevailed in
Cyprus during the summer months of 1931. The general
discontent was brought to a head by the enosists, led by the two
nationalist movements KEK and EPEK. The latter, officially
formed on 18 October 1931 (it was originally set up as a secret
organization in Kyrenia in 1929), announced a comprehensive
ten-point programme (the union of Cyprus with Greece being
at the forefront) which the 21 signatories pledged to uphold.

It was also announced that its political wing would have, as
its official organ for regular communication with the public, the

newspaper *Irreconcilable (Adiallaktos)*, which would begin publication on 24 October. Another organization, the Pan-Cyprian Greek Association of ex-Service Men, was formed in December 1930. Its most active member was Theofanis Tsangarides, one of the CNRU leaders, and one of those deported after the October 1931 disturbances. These disturbances were actually precipitated by the passage of the Elementary Education Law and by a conflict of wills between the Greek representatives (ably supported by Nejati Bey) on the legislative council and the British authorities over the Budget for 1931.

On 12 September, three days after the publication of the Order in Council which introduced a new customs tariff, the Greek members were summoned by the Bishop of Kition (cousin of Archbishop Kyrillos) to a meeting at Saitta, a summer resort near Troodos, to decide on policy following the Chancellor's statement and the new tariff. No concrete proposals for future courses of action were agreed at Saitta, but it later became known, and was mentioned in the Press, that the participants had formally resolved to call upon all Cypriots to refuse to pay taxes and to boycott British goods. However, no action was to be taken until the resolution had been approved by the National Organization, a body first formed in 1922 under the title of the National Assembly, which claimed as members all Greek Cypriots living in Cyprus and abroad.

By this time the movement was well supported financially by subscriptions and by the Church. It employed a secretary in Cyprus and a representative in London (Zenon Rossides) to further the cause of *enosis*. In London pressure was exerted through the Press, particularly the *Manchester Guardian*, and through a number of pro-Greek Members of Parliament. In Cyprus all avenues were exploited, including the establishment of a number of national youth clubs in the villages to extend the movement and 'catch them young'.

On 3 October the Orthodox members of the legislative council and the members of the National Organization met at the archbishopric to discuss the Saitta resolution – in other words, to adopt a common front following the disposal of the surplus balances of Cyprus and the enforcement of the new customs duties by the Imperial Order in Council. No decisions

were arrived at, presumably because of the refusal of the
members of the council to resign immediately. Although some
contend that the meeting dissolved in uproar, a new meeting
was arranged for the following week. The meetings on 10, 11
and 17 October also proved abortive, and the extremists,
foreseeing retreat and unwilling to be involved in any sidetracking, resigned *en masse*. At the last meeting the Bishop of
Kition, Nicodemos Mylonas, read a manifesto he had drafted
which advocated resistance to British rule and demanded its
overthrow. He emphasized that 53 years of British occupation
(1878-1931) had proved most clearly that:

> Enslaved peoples were not liberated by prayers and appeals
> to the tyrants' sentiments.
> Such appeals led only to contempt and arrogance from the
> tyrants, who regarded them as dissatisfied slaves.
> Their only salvation was national liberation; the foreigners
> were there to further their own general and specific interests,
> which had as an inevitable result the moral and material
> misery of the Cypriots.

The bishop ended by appealing to youth to lead the way in the
struggles to achieve a free country. This manifesto was agreed
in principle, but the members decided that the draft should be
further considered at another meeting in a week's time.

On the following day it was discovered that exactly the same
manifesto had been published independently by the bishop on
the previous day and had been widely circulated with a letter
tendering his resignation from the legislative council. Several of
the other Greek members of the council immediately expressed
surprise at the bishop's secret resignation, which had, they
believed, badly shaken the unity of the Greek members. Eight
members of the council, St. Stavrinakis, Th. Theodotou, G.
Hadjipavlou, M. Shiakallis, D. Severis, K.P. Rossides, Chr.
Galatopoulos and Char. Nicolaides, denounced the bishop's
resignation as 'treacherous'. Moreover, a supplementary
attack on the bishop appeared in a broadsheet entitled *Above all
sincerity* under the signature of George Hadjipavlou (nicknamed
'Phonallas' or 'loud-mouth').

The bishop was now at the centre of a crisis as his advocacy of
illegal measures was hailed by the extremist elements. On the

18th he addressed a crowd at Larnaca, advising them not to be afraid of Britain's fleet and not to obey the laws; in the quest for union, blood should flow if necessary. On 20 October the bishop arrived in Limassol and raised what is now customarily called 'the fiery cross'.

He addressed a crowd of over 3,000 at the sports ground, and the terms used were inflammatory. 'In the name of God and the people,' he said, 'I declare the union with mother Greece and disobedience of and insubordination towards the illegal laws of the immoral, vile and reproachful regime'. At the *enosis* club he reiterated his demands and shouted 'Long live the union'. The bishop's speech at the stadium was followed by similar appeals from N.K. Lanitis and Zenon Rossides, who reminded the people that the policy of memoranda, delegations to London, local demonstrations with flags and processions, anti-British invective in the Press and on platforms, and non-co-operation and obstruction in the legislative council had come to nothing; they must look to deeds rather than words to achieve their object. Nevertheless, despite the polemical speeches, the crowd dispersed quietly. Nicosia was henceforth to be the focal point for discontent.

6 *October 1931: Violence Erupts*

The events of 21 October sparked the first outbreak of major violence in the island. The Bishop of Kition once more urged his congregation in a Limassol village church to disobey the laws and fight for union. Lanitis quickly dispatched a telegram (with a somewhat exaggerated account of the bishop's following in the Limassol district) to the secretary of the National Organization in Nicosia. It concluded by emphasizing that 'never before has there been a more panegyric approval'. The effects of the telegram were instantaneous.

By 5.30 p.m. it became known that the Orthodox members of the legislative council had decided to resign. In his letter of resignation Th. Theodotou emphasized that it was his imperative duty to declare once more that the one and only claim of Cyprus was to live free in the bosom of its mother country – Greece. K.P. Rossides stated in equally strong terms that the one and only aim of the forthcoming struggle was the termination of British rule in Cyprus. S.G. Stavrinakis pleaded with the governor to convey to the government in London the firm and unshakeable resolution of the Greek population of Cyprus to be united with its mother Greece.

The situation had by now become explosive and the 'humorous race', as Storrs described the Cypriots, were in a demanding mood. In Nicosia members of the new National Union met at the commercial club and immediately sent emissaries to cause the church bells to be rung to summon the people. Others went round the town telling the shopkeepers to shut their shops and assemble at the club. All prominent enosists, who were in fact the best known Cypriot politicians of the time, spoke to a crowd of over 3,000 and promised to settle their differences and work together for union and only union. The crowd repeatedly shouted 'To Government House'.

At that juncture Dionysios Kykkotis, chief priest of

Phaneromeni, the most important church in Nicosia, stepped forward and declared revolution. A Greek flag was handed to him and he abjured the people to defend it. One more speech was made, the speaker kissed the flag and the cry 'To Government House' was renewed with frenzy. The leaders seized the flag and at around 6.45 p.m. began to lead the crowd in the half-mile trek to their declared destination. Passing the government timber yard, the crowd, composed mainly of youths, helped themselves to sticks of various sizes and by 7.45 p.m. the 'exit' gate of Government House was reached. The police force consisted of one inspector, one sergeant major, seven mounted police and 12 foot police.

As set out by several despatches from the Cyprus government to London, the events leading to the burning of Government House were as follows:

7.45 p.m. The procession arrived at the exit gate. The declared intention was to present the governor with a petition on the island's grievances.

8.00 p.m. The crowd broke the police cordon at the exit gate and moved into the grounds of Government House.

8.20 p.m. The crowd surged up to the walls of the wooden bungalow and eight or nine of the foot police were lost in the crowd and consequently took no subsequent active part in the proceedings. By now the *enosis* chant drowned everything else.

8.20-9.30 p.m. Mr Hart-Davis, Commissioner of Nicosia, and Major Wright, Chief Assistant Secretary to the Government, spoke to the leaders of the crowd, which up to that time was good-tempered. The governor then informed the commissioner that if the crowd withdrew to a respectful distance he would see one or two of their leaders. But by now the noise had grown louder, desultory throwing of stones, mainly propelled by slings, began, and soon all the windows in the front of the building had been smashed. The rioters then climbed upon the roof and hoisted the Greek flag. At that juncture Inspector Faiz (the Turkish senior police officer) and 40 armed police arrived and took up their positions inside Government House.

9.30-10.00 p.m. Meanwhile the other policemen tried to keep

back the crowd by expostulation and pushing. Some of the leaders, who had condemned violence, had by now disappeared. The officials and several policemen who had been standing on the porch of Government House were driven inside by violent stone throwing. The police however concentrated their numbers in squares and beat up the 'top boys' (the most able-bodied) as an example to the others. A baton party was also ordered but was unable to form up. Major Wright's car, which was in front of the porch, was overturned and as petrol was running loose the crowd burnt it. The rioters, who simply believed they were out for the evening, did the same to three other police cars. At that juncture Inspector Faiz requested permission to fire but the commissioner refused because the crowd was composed almost entirely of young people and he considered that further efforts should be made to disperse the rioters by peaceful means. He confided to several colleagues later that bloodshed at that hour could have led to revolution and hence disaster.

10.00 p.m. The commissioner telephoned for reinforcements and a copy of the Riot Act. The crowd were by now throwing burning sticks and other blazing material as well as stones into Government House. Some rioters were inside the building. One of them, Karakoushis, an alcoholic from Ayios Dhometios, took a bottle of brandy and some meat from the kitchen and searched for the governor's chair. After several minutes he found it and sitting very elegantly with outstretched legs he cried 'Mother, come and see your son who is now the governor'.

10.35 p.m. Many of the electric lights were broken and the telephone was wrecked.

10.45 p.m. Inspector Yianni and 22 armed police arrived.

11.00 p.m. Government House was set on fire. Within half an hour this inflammable mid-Victorian military wooden bungalow, diverted at Port Said from its intended Ceylon destination to Cyprus by Sir Garnet Wolseley in 1878 for use as Government House, was burnt down.

11.15 p.m. Once more a baton charge was launched but it failed. The commissioner then addressed the crowd and read the Riot Act whose contents were shouted in Greek by a policeman. The bugle sounded and a further warning was shouted. The bugle sounded once more and a police firing party of 12 men was ordered to fire one round but to aim at the legs of the crowd. The police discharged a volley plus several scattered shots. The crowd melted away but was pursued by the police whose orders were to clear the grounds by charging.

11.35 p.m. Following the firing and the police charge the crowd dispersed. Fifteen civilians were injured, of whom an 18-year-old youth, Onoufrios A. Clerides, died shortly afterwards.

Meanwhile the governor, who had escaped with A.B. Wright, the Acting Colonial Secretary, and a guard of two policemen through a tunnel, headed in a motor car for the Secretary's Lodge. Storrs was certain that there would have been no trouble had the Colonial Office not rejected his three requests:

> the transfer of the troops to Nicosia, submitted in 1927;
> the modification of the Constitution, proposed in 1929 and 1930; and
> the removal of Kyrou, the Greek consul.

Nevertheless Storrs summoned the troops from Troodos (the permanent garrison consisted of three officers and 123 men), cabled for military and air reinforcements and applied the internal security scheme. The commissioner then issued large printed notices warning the public to remain within doors from sunset to sunrise, prohibited assemblies of more than five persons, the carrying of firearms and provocative conduct. The notices were posted in Nicosia early on 22 October and were part of the island's emergency scheme for disturbances.

The excitement caused by the Nicosia disturbances spread to the other parts of the island. In Limassol, as in other towns, excited gatherings took place, schools were shut and normal business suspended. A crowd, seeing that the market was opened specially for British soldiers, prevented the lorries loading food for the troops. Soon afterwards the church bells began ringing and the people were urged to assemble at the bishopric. The crowd, shouting 'union and only union', went on to burn the commissioner's house.

At Famagusta the leaders were repeatedly warned of their

responsibilities and informed that the police had orders to shoot if any burning or looting occurred. Speakers freely mentioned the need for 'sacrifice' and 'bloodshed' and the 'meanness of the English in fighting and suppressing unarmed people'. The situation in Famagusta, as in Paphos, was further complicated by the incursion of villagers. A crowd of over 8,000 heard further speeches demanding 'our rights' on 24 October. On the following day part of the crowd forced the proprietors of licensed premises to reopen. This was followed by a concerted attack on a police station. Windows and doors were smashed and police property and records were thrown into the street and destroyed. Police and marines from HMS *Colombo* (which arrived on the 25th and landed 30 marines) ultimately opened fire. One civilian (Haralambos Fili, an 18-year-old from Lefkoniko) was killed and two seriously wounded. Many more, on both sides, received minor injuries.

Demonstrations at both Paphos and Larnaca took place mainly outside police barracks. Police were stoned, property was destroyed and telegraph wires were cut. However, it was at Nicosia that most of the excitement occurred. A crowd of over 10,000 attended the funeral of Onoufrios A. Clerides. Representatives of all the political clubs, ex-service men, Boy Scouts, farmers and workers carrying banners and Greek flags attended and speeches were made urging the people to continue the struggle. Part of the crowd attacked the house of a police officer just outside the town but were driven off by troops.

On 24 October the archbishop sent his chaplain to seek an interview with Storrs. At the interview Storrs was accompanied by the Acting Colonial Secretary and the officer commanding the troops, the archbishop by his chaplain. The archbishop pleaded not only for the release of the Cypriot leaders arrested by the authorities, but also for the 'fulfilment of the sacred and just national aspirations of Cyprus which is unanimously demanded by the entire Greek population of the island'. The governor's reply was short. The ringleaders, he said, would not be released, the government was solely responsible for the preservation of law and order and the armed forces would not hesitate to take extreme measures to repress any further disturbance. Storrs also urged the archbishop to induce his people to obey the law and to warn them of the consequences of disobedience.

Later that evening the crowd again stoned the picket at the Nicosia new entrance and refused to move. Rumours of an impending attack on the electric plant and law courts caused the troops to fire. One man (Kyriacos Papadopoulos) was seriously wounded by a bullet and died the following day. The small crowd dispersed immediately.

On the same day the Bishop of Kition arrived at the outskirts of Nicosia, was stopped by a picket and, after a scene of violent protest, obeyed the order to return to Kyrenia where the scene was much quieter. At once he addressed a church congregation and informed them that he was stopped by bayonets as he was entering the capital. The usual phrases were used and the bishop ended his speech by saying that he 'shall hoist the Greek flag where it should be'. He led a crowd of over 300 to the government offices where the Union Jack was hauled down and torn to pieces and his own personal servant hoisted the Greek flag in its place. The commissioner repeatedly warned the crowd of the consequences. Heeding his warnings the bishop led his followers back to the town and the Greek flag was replaced by a new Union Jack. However, throughout the day the number of people at the bishopric greatly increased as villagers, some armed with heavy sticks and pieces of iron, continued to come in. They clashed with police and troops and many civilians received minor injuries. Three were seriously wounded of whom Michael Ioannou from Karavas died on 27 October.

Though the towns, especially Nicosia, were the main centres of discontent, scores of villages were also active. The lot of the peasant was worsened by the deterioration of economic conditions and the economic depression had strengthened the case of the discontented. W. Lunn MP, addressing the House of Commons on 22 April 1932, correctly pointed out 'that in Cyprus there is fearful poverty at the moment that there is famine in the land, and that such a condition of affairs will ferment disturbances in any community.'[1]

That was exactly what happened in Cyprus. Out of a total of 598 Greek Orthodox and mixed Orthodox and Moslem villages, 200 experienced excitement and demonstrations without serious breach of the law. In less than 70 villages was property destroyed. Where no disturbances were recorded it was because there were no police stations or other British authorities to serve as the object of such demonstrations or to report the matter to the government. Furthermore, some of these villages may have been too remote or their inhabitants may have joined their nearest neighbours of the larger settlements in the disturbances.

One of the most general offences was the theft of salt. For example, in the Famagusta magistrates' courts, out of the 405 persons convicted up to mid November 1931, 368 were found guilty of stealing salt. Of those convicted, 206 were fined £1 10s, 146 £2, 8 £3 and the remaining 8 received a heavier fine of £5. For those years these fines were very excessive. Salt was stolen because, firstly, it was very expensive owing to the tax on it and an alleged shortage; secondly, the government was piling it up to push the price even higher; and thirdly, government stores were easy to break into since they were generally not guarded.

The inhabitants of Pisouri, incited by Galatopoulos, an ex-member of the legislative council, destroyed some valuable government property, including the customs house. At Mandria, another Limassol village, the inhabitants destroyed a bridge on the main road. On 28 October the governor, under the Defence Order in Council, ordered that it should be repaired. The villagers duly complied but an old man died, perhaps from heart failure. It is contended that he was dragged from his bed by security officials, where he was lying with high fever, loaded with a heavy beam and ordered to carry it to the bridge.

At Kato Zodia, in the Nicosia district, a crowd of over 300 attempted to stop the lorries carrying soldiers and stoned them. The troops fired three rounds, killing one and wounding several others.

As the rising spread over the island it was found necessary to summon help from abroad. On 23 October two cruisers, HMS *London* and HMS *Shropshire*, and two destroyers arrived from Crete and then seven RAF troop carriers with 150 men from Egypt. On 25 October HMS *Colombo* also arrived. Their arrival, it is widely believed, caused the disturbances to recede.

There were of course outbursts of loyalty to Britain. When the revolt broke out one of the villagers of Stroumbi, in the Paphos district, hauled down the Union Jack but Savas

Papanicolaou wrapped it round himself and, marching through the village, proclaimed his total support for the British flag. He was later rewarded for his endeavours.

In the Famagusta district several forest plantations and some forest buildings were set on fire, several police stations were broken into and wrecked, one customs building was looted and destroyed by fire and a few salt stores were emptied. At Prastio over 50 villagers broke into the government warehouses and proceeded to fill their carts with salt. They were seen by the police who opened fire but there were no casualties. On 29 October a police patrol was sent to the Karpass peninsula whence the most serious damage had been reported and political leaders who were suspected of continued agitation (such as K.P. Rossides) were ordered, under the Defence Regulations, to quit the area. Two days later a small detachment of troops under the command of a sergeant was sent to supplement the police. By the beginning of November order was restored throughout the Karpass, many arrests had been made and the villagers in the area had begun to rebuild the government property which only a week earlier they had destroyed.

Within a week of the 'first outbreak of violence', order, with the exception of certain minor disturbances in a few villages, was restored. By the end of October there was no reports of disturbances and by the end of 1931 the garrison had been reduced to what should have (but never had) been its normal strength of four officers and 175 men. It was stationed in Nicosia with small detachments in the three next largest towns. A telegram from Storrs to the Secretary of State, dated 23 January 1932, confirmed that all branches of the administration were functioning smoothly, villages were quiet but in the towns there were signs of unrest; there was a common belief that the regime under the Defence Order and the deportations and new laws were purely temporary expedients.

Hence the so-called 'revolution' had been put down with a minimum expenditure of time, force, money and above all human life. The governor, referring to Nicosia, recorded: 'The sight of military patrols, the scope of the Defence restrictions, the knowledge that ringleaders had been arrested and the increasing consciousness that crime would be punished and damage paid for by those responsible sobered the turbulent and encouraged the law-abiding to exert their influence.'[2]

Meanwhile Government House lay in ruins. The archbishop in a letter to the governor on 19 November expressed the deep grief of the Greeks at what had taken place. In his encyclical of 2 November addressed to the Greek people of Cyprus he outlined 'the manner in which we understand that our national aspirations should be promoted and conducted'. Violence was excluded. The Greek members of the municipal corporation of Nicosia, headed by Them. Dervis, the mayor, expressed their regret at the burning of Government House in a letter dated 26 November addressed to the officer in command of the military forces. The burnt wooden bungalow was replaced by a stone building of outstanding beauty designed by Maurice Webb in a blend of the traditional styles of the island.

There is no evidence that the October outbreak was premeditated or prearranged. It is however probable that the outbreak would not have taken the form it did but for the enosist agitation. The ground for disturbance was prepared by the extreme leaders of the union movement in the hope that the occurrence of general demonstrations would advance the cause of union. Historical evidence also shows that a sizeable proportion of the population either kept out of the way or, in order to avoid the stigma of disloyalty, cheered for union. Moreover the movement, though strong in the towns, had less influence in the countryside, since at the slightest signs of any trouble many of the villagers descended into the towns.

Thus the people, anxious to safeguard and promote their liberties and improve their deplorable economic position, were driven to a state where direct action became inevitable. They demanded economic betterment, the ending of the British association and finally union with Greece. The revolt was a vast popular protest and not an uprising. As was shown earlier, the people demonstrated with sticks and stones since they did not plan serious trouble and did not possess arms.

Several attempts had been made to lay the blame on Greece for the disturbances. The Greek government however had nothing to do with it. From the very outset Venizelos expressed his strong disapproval, for which he was severely criticized by the Greek Press of Athens, Salonica and Alexandria. With the exception of the Royalist *Kathimerini*, which kept its attacks at a low level, the newspapers carried out a constant campaign denouncing the brutality of the troops and police and condemning Storrs as 'the tyrant Governor of martyred Cyprus'.

Venizelos informed the Press on 23 October that there was no Cypriot question between the governments of Britain and Greece, but only between the British government and the people of Cyprus. In the Greek Parliament on 18 November he was at pains to stress that force was not a Hellenic ideal and that Greece must remain on very friendly terms with Britain, Italy and Turkey. He emphasized that Cyprus was an internal problem for Britain, and Britain alone. Furthermore Venizelos, together with other politicians, had tried on several occasions to pacify and restrain the Cypriot leaders during their many visits to Athens. The attitude of the government was also transmitted to the Press on 18 November. Venizelos also stated that 'if Britain likes to regard the question as a closed one, then it cannot but be closed'.

Hence Venizelos and his government had maintained strict impartiality. In spite of the great pressure brought to bear on him by the Press and the organized supporters of the unionist movement, he had flatly refused to give any encouragement to the Cypriot politicians or their sympathizers in Greece. The Premier had clearly done his best to act with propriety and with regard to the obligations arising out of the friendship between Greece and Great Britain.

However, even the Greek government was not strong enough to check the furious agitation. A manifesto in sympathy with the Cypriot cause, signed by 45 prominent Greeks headed by Admiral Koundouriotis, was published in all the Athenian newspapers on 31 October. The Holy Synod of the Church of Greece issued a statement in the same sense and the Archbishop of Athens telegraphed to his British counterpart. Church masses were held in many districts and at Amarousion, eight miles outside Athens, 3,000 people attended. Armistice Day (11 November) was celebrated in Athens as 'Cyprus Day' and a secret committee was formed at Piraeus to equip 1,000 volunteers for Cyprus. In addition to the campaign in the Press, practically all the municipalities, chambers of commerce, leagues and local societies passed resolutions of sympathy. Student disturbances at both Athens and Salonica had to be suppressed.

Then there was Alexander Kyrou, whose father, the founder of the influential Athenian newspaper *Hestia (The Hearth)*, was born in Cyprus. As Greek consul-general in Cyprus he immediately established close relations with every branch of the ecclesiastical, legislative and national agitation. His activities for the cause of union prompted the governor to complain to the Colonial Office and to declare that Kyrou was no longer *persona grata*. Wherever Kyrou travelled he was received with enthusiasm and frequently by a band playing the Greek national anthem and the cheers of *enosis* supporters. He was so greeted even at a masonic ball held in Nicosia.

At the third time of asking, Storrs received an assurance that a protest would be lodged with the Greek government and hence Kyrou would be definitely recalled. The Foreign Office recorded on 24 October that Alexander Kyrou 'is *persona non grata* and that immediate steps are accordingly being taken for the revocation of his exequatur'. Hence the so-called 'moral force' behind the extremist views of the Bishop of Kition was finally withdrawn during the October disturbances.

The 'Koundouriotis Circular' also requires comment. Admiral Paul Koundouriotis, 'the grand old man of the Greek political world' and once Regent (18 December 1923) and first President of the Greek Republic (25 March 1924), led the prominent Greeks responsible for sending this informative circular. The circular regarding the uprising of the Cypriots and its suppression was received by British Members of Parliament and newspapers in the early spring of 1932. It contained allegations of mass killings, maltreatment of innocent civilians, the employment of brutal methods by the security forces firstly to extract the information needed and then to pacify the inhabitants, injuries amounting to thousands (mostly minor) and the confiscation of the property belonging to the deportees.

The British government dismissed it as a 'tissue of lies from start to finish' and Storrs, in his telegram to the Secretary of State on 14 March 1932, called it 'utterly false, malicious and baseless in almost every particular'. There were in fact exaggerations, but some events were certainly sidestepped or misrepresented by the authorities:

1   Storrs reported on several occasions that the total number of deaths caused by the October disturbances was six, one of the wounded dying on 29 November. He fails to say definitely however how the old man from Mandria died. The Central Committee for Cyprus (headed by Paul Koundouriotis), in its remarks on July 1932 on the governor's report (presented on 11 February 1932), is emphatic that he died of heart failure after being forced by the authorities to do heavy work on a bridge. Storrs finally admitted, in his telegram to the Secretary of State on 14 March 1932, that the death 'may have been partly due to some exertion'. In fact the sight of armed military patrols resulted in many casualties.

2   In paragraph 23 of his report, Storrs says that 'seven in all were wounded, of whom one died later' in the riots outside Government House. Yet in his despatch of 13 November 1931 he records 15 in all wounded of whom one, Onoufrios A. Clerides, died shortly afterwards. The latter figures were also given by local newspapers (under strict censorship) and were borne out by the certificates issued by the Nicosia clinics. The unrecorded casualties were in fact much greater owing to the Cypriot preference for being treated at home rather than paying (even if the money were available) for treatment in clinics. The Cypriots also feared reprisals by the police if it were found they had participated in the disturbances.

3   In paragraph 65 of his report the governor emphasized that the 'goodwill of the large Moslem population and the other minorities towards the government never wavered throughout the disturbances'. However, during the whole period of the disorders there was not the least exhibition of anti-Greek feeling, or any single instance of betrayal by Moslems to the authorities of those who had compromised themselves in the disturbances. On the contrary, one of the most prominent Moslem leaders, Nejati Bey, member of the legislative council, issued a manifesto during the disturbances calling upon his fellow Moslems to remain quiet 'because our Greek brethren are only demanding what is their right'. The good-will and co-operation between Greeks and Turks in Cyprus had of late been

strengthened by the complete reconciliation brought about in 1930 between Greece and Turkey which had convinced the Moslems of Cyprus that the union of their island with Greece would ensure the same liberal rule and the same absolute equality of political rights with the Greeks as the Moslems of Western Thrace enjoyed. An article in the Turkish newspaper *Vakkit* also expressed sympathy with the Greeks. Storrs of course informed the Secretary of State as early as 4 June 1931 that the Turkish movement 'while mischievous is in no way alarming'. The distress signals were however there.

4   The Central Committee for Cyprus, which produced a series of circulars and pamphlets, pleaded for an investigating commission, composed of impartial Britons rather than government officials, to look into the October disturbances and thus keep the union question alive. The British authorities, as in many other instances, refused.

The position of Cyprus in 1931 was that of a British possession whose inhabitants had become British subjects in law without ceasing in speech and sentiment to be Greeks and Turks. Hence the revolt was a vast popular protest and not an uprising. Outside the government service and the realm of government influence every branch of public life in the Greek Cypriot population was allied to the cause of union. The feeling for union with Greece however was stronger in the professional classes (lawyers, journalists, teachers, merchants and physicians) and the priesthood, who were the traditional Greek Orthodox leaders of nationalist movements. As Sir George Hill says: 'In all agitations only the few orators and journalists are articulate and the illiterate masses follow them only when they have been whipped into emotional excitement.'

In the four months following the uprising the number of trials and convictions were:

Persons tried	2,952
Persons convicted	2,679
Successful appeals	0
Unsuccessful appeals	22
Appeals pending	7
Persons still on remand	304

The major offence was stealing salt. Next came (in most districts) the theft of firewood from the forest. Isolated offences included the possession of firearms and entering police stations.

The official casualty figures, as already explained, are open to question. Furthermore, those slightly injured by stones and other means are not included. The civilian list prepared by the government shows the following casualties:

District	Wounded	Killed
Nicosia	19	3
Limassol	5	1
Famagusta	2	1
Larnaca	1	–
Kyrenia	2	1
Paphos	1	–
Totals	30	6

One of those wounded in Nicosia by a police bullet died on 29 November.

Altogether ten Greeks were deported. The list was later extended to include Evdoros Ioannides, N. Yerolakides and E. Nicolaides, who were living abroad but were henceforth barred from entering Cyprus. The deportation orders were issued under the Defence (Certain British Possessions) Order in Council 1928 and the Defence of Cyprus Regulations 1931. The deportees were:

Dionysios Kykkotis, chief priest of Phaneromeni church, Nicosia
Nicodemos, Bishop of Kition
Makarios, Bishop of Kyrenia (afterwards archbishop, 1947-50)
Theofanis Tsangarides, radical union leader
Theodoros Kolokasides, radical union leader
Savas Loizides, radical union leader
George Hadjipavlou, member of the legislative council
Theofanis Theodotou, member of the legislative council
Haralambos Vatiliotis, Communist party leader
Costas Skeleas, Communist party leader.

The first deportation orders, dated 23 October, applied to the bishops of Kition, Kykkotis, Hadjipavlou, Tsangarides, Kolokasides and Theodotou. The six left the island on 3 November. The deportation orders of 25 October 1931 applied to the bishops of Kyrenia, Loizides, Vatiliotis and Skeleas. They left the island on 6 November. In October 1946 the Labour government withdrew the deportation orders of the original ten (the order concerning the second group was revoked in January 1947), but only two of the ten deportees, the Bishop of Kyrenia and George Hadjipavlou, returned to the island. Theofanis Theodotou, who was dying, was allowed to return earlier. The radical unionist leaders settled in Athens and became Greek nationals. The others died in exile – the Bishop of Kition in his favourite place, Jerusalem. On 3 December 1931, the Secretary of State for the colonies rejected Storr's request of 28 November for the deportation of N.K. Lanitis and Ph. Kyriakides (members of the legislative council), A. Emiliahides and Dr. Pigasiou (respectively secretary and member of the National Organization).

By the end of October the outbreak was over. However, the causes of this mass protest remained and the British authorities were faced with three choices – to examine the question thoroughly and apply suitable remedies; to let things die a natural death; or to take the easy way out, that of repression. Britain chose repression, the measures taken being:

1   On 16 November 1931 the governor proclaimed and brought into force the Letters Patent abolishing the legislative council. Henceforth the governor was empowered to rule by decree. This was a retrogressive step even though an advisory council, consisting of the members of the executive council together with unofficial members nominated annually to represent the Christian and Moslem communities, was set up in 1933. Hence the Constitution was withdrawn. It was however contrary to the Colonial Laws Validity Act of 1865 which expressly stated that the term 'Colony' shall in this Act include all of Her Majesty's Possessions abroad in which there shall exist a legislature. Cyprus was a colony but without a legislature.

2   The Press was placed under a harsh censorship. Two laws passed in 1929 and 1930 had already encroached on the liberty

of the Press but the measure passed in 1932 (Law No. 32) caused the most irritation. No article could appear dealing with either local or international affairs without having been previously read and approved by the censor. Even the reproduction of earlier letters and articles that had already appeared in *The Times* or speeches delivered in Parliament were subjected to censorship and passages were usually omitted. Furthermore, the Press could publish nothing about local conditions except what the government handed out. Under the Seditious Publication Laws of 1921-32, 36 publications were prohibited between 1927 and 1933. Storrs informed the Secretary of State on 16 December 1931 that many letters from abroad containing expressions of sympathy with the movement had been retained.

3   Political parties were dissolved and on 15 August 1933 the Criminal Code was amended with the main object of enabling the authorities to deal effectively with the Communists and with all other unlawful associations. On the following day the KKK and eight other Communist front organizations, including the Cyprus Relief Workers Association, were proscribed.

4   Meetings of more than five persons were prohibited. Yet how would the law be applied in the case of athletic meetings, weddings, parties, civic receptions, funerals and so forth? What guarantee was there that politics would not be discussed?

5   Several other laws restricted further the liberties of the people. A law passed in 1937 empowered the government to deny entry into Cyprus of any Cypriot returning from abroad, whether he had been on business, pleasure or in search of a livelihood, 'if it is shown in evidence, which the Governor may deem sufficient, that he is likely to conduct himself so as to be dangerous to peace and good order'. By another law passed in 1939 the governor gave unlimited authority to the police 'to place under arrest or banish any person who works, or is likely to work, in such a way, or who might use his relative freedom of movement, for the propagation of ideas detrimental to the defence of the state'. Furthermore, under section 13A(1) of the Village Authorities Laws 1931-5, 115 mukhtars (government

representatives, usually in villages) were specially authorized to issue search warrants to police officers.

6   Every form of national manifestation was persecuted. The flying of the Greek flag was prohibited and the ringing of church bells except for regular services was also restricted. Education was under government control, and the teaching of Greek and Turkish history was restricted. Pictures of national heroes were not allowed in school halls or public places. The ban also extended to films, and a film of the Turkish hero Atatürk and one of a recent wedding in the Greek Royal Family were banned in 1938 on the grounds that they might furnish an occasion for the manifestation of pro-Turkish or pro-Greek sentiment.

7   Municipal elections were abolished and it was only in March 1943 that the first elections were allowed to take place. A promise that such elections would take place in 1941 was not kept.

8   Trade unions were forbidden and their members persecuted. During 1933 and 1934, after years of investigation, 28 leading trade unionists and Communists were convicted on charges of seditious conspiracy and received sentences ranging up to four years' imprisonment.

9   A meeting was held at the Colonial Office on 18 November 1931 to discuss the cost of the recent riots as far as naval, military and air force expenditure was concerned. E.R. Darnley, in the chair, pointed out that not only was it impossible for Cyprus to meet a heavy bill but it was most inexpedient to lay further financial burdens on the island when it appeared that the existing considerable weight of taxation had been a factor aggravating the troubles. The Colonial Office and the Cypriot authorities arrived at a tentative figure of £28,000 of which exactly half was to be levied on Nicosia. Government officials, certain employees of the Eastern Telegraph Company and the personal domestic servants of the governor were exempted. The Reparation Impost Law passed on 21 December 1931 implemented the decision that destroyed property estimated at £34,315 should be replaced and repaired at the cost of the responsible villages and towns. A tax imposed on land easily recouped the above amount for the authorities. The Greek Orthodox community duly paid up.

These restrictive measures, the famous 28 'illiberal laws' enacted between 1931 and 1944, did not crush but on the contrary exacerbated the feelings of the inhabitants. Political activity which was driven underground was canalized into a multitude of forms, such as professional and cultural bodies, literary and scientific societies, sports organizations, peasants' and workers' associations and producers' organizations.

Oppression not only led to underground activity but to a revival of labour unrest. In 1933, for example, 800 striking builders organized a demonstration in Nicosia and were successful in having their demands met. Two years later a disruptive general strike was organized by the workers at shoe factories in Nicosia and again its aims were achieved. Unions officially defined as 'safe' were permitted in 1932 and allowed to function freely after 1936; and from just one union and 84 members in 1932 their number rose to 62 with 3,389 members in 1940 and by 1944 there were 90 unions with 10,694 members.

7   The 1930s: Repression and Consolidation

The October 1931 outbreak coincided with the world's greatest social catastrophe of recent memory – the unmanageable economic depression which caused the ruin of millions. Economies were shattered, food prices rose, industrial depression multiplied unemployment and the masses of the urban labouring poor were deprived of their modest income at the very moment when the cost of living rocketed. The Cypriot not only faced this economic cataclysm but also had to endure martial law. This led to dissatisfaction, underground activity, a consolidation of political groupings and finally a further eruption. On the economic front it led to strikes and in the 1940s violence.

The Cypriot scene in the 1930s was dominated by five main issues:

a milder *enosis* agitation fortified by the extension of cultural, social and academic activities;
economic problems;
the archiepiscopal question;
the lack of representative institutions;
Turkish nationalism.

Open agitation for *enosis* gradually died down but it was kept alive more by persons and organizations outside the island than from within it. Following the Graeco-Turkish comprehensive settlement of 1930 the sympathies of world Hellenism were directed towards the Greeks of the Dodecanese and Cyprus. This however was in direct conflict with the Greek government's declared policy of neutralism.

In Greece the Cyprus Central Committee, formed just after the riots of 1931 with Admiral Koundouriotis at the helm, and the Cypriot Students' Brotherhood were working very hard for the enosists' cause. The former, whose motto was 'Long Live

Greek Cyprus', had most of the prominent Greek politicians and academics as members. The latter was aided by Tsangarides, Kolokasides and Hadjipavlou, the three national leaders deported for their part in the October disturbances. Early in 1934 the Society of Friends of Cyprus, with the Bishop of Kyrenia as one of the guiding spirits, was also founded. The Cyprus National Bureau, financed by the Cyprus Central Committee, was another unionist organ. After the Second World War the Students' Association for Cyprus and the Committee for Cypriot Struggle (under the presidency of the Archbishop of Athens) were also very active.

In the USA the Pan-Cypriot Brotherhood of America often protested against the suspension of the human liberties of their countrymen and demanded amongst other things the abolition of the penal code, the defence and education laws and an end to press censorship. In the course of the war the Committee for the Self-Determination of Cyprus was very active.

Of particular importance were the activities of Cypriots living in London. The London Cypriot Committee (its original name was the Cypriot Anti-Imperialist Society) was formed in 1932 and after being broadened in 1936 was renamed the Committee for Cyprus Autonomy. Another change in 1943 meant that it henceforth became known as the Cyprus Affairs Committee. The London Committee centred its activities on the labour movement and the House of Commons. But the national issue was not its only preoccupation. It dealt with economic issues and with questions concerning civil rights and liberties. The winning of democracy for the islanders however remained its main objective as opposed to outright *enosis* which it believed could come later.

After October 1931 the enosists, then, refrained from open agitation. Though relatively dormant the movement was kept alive by the several organizations in Greece, the U.S.A. and Britain. The great part of the rural population wished only to live quietly on their land. Patrick Balfour (later Baron Kinross), reflecting on his journeys in Cyprus between 1948 and 1949, explains the Greek Cypriot dilemma:

> In psychological terms, the Englishman appeals to his material interests, and to his sense of justice; but not to his heart or to his imagination. The Cypriot can respect the

Englishman, but he cannot love him. Thus he can never feel himself to be part of the British Commonwealth, as he can feel himself to be part of the Greek-speaking world. London may be his commercial capital; Athens is his spiritual, cultural and professional capital. The Cypriot feels Greek, therefore he wants, in some way, to be Greek. Such, psychologically, is the foundation for Enosis.[1]

Generally, then, the movement for *enosis* in the 1930s was based on spiritual ideals and not on material grievances. Hence the illiterate Cypriot peasant who was 'born in debt, lived in debt and died in debt' (an allegation very near the truth), and whose life, according to the 1930 *Survey of Rural Life in Cyprus*, was 'made miserable by pressures brought to bear on him by his creditors and whose moral and material progress is severely handicapped by the burden of his debts', cared much less for the national aspirations of the educated minority – the priest, physician, lawyer and schoolmaster. The unionists drew their support almost entirely from the organized urban masses and, generally speaking, from both the right and the left. Nevertheless, as Churchill stated in his memorandum of 1907, 'wherever there is economic injustice there will also be found political discontent and whenever one community uses another as if it were a milch-cow, there will inevitably be ill-feeling and estrangement'. Cyprus was no exception.

The movement for union with Greece took many forms. It also resumed its pacific phase. Hence the governor was able to report to Sir Philip Cunliffe-Lister on 30 March 1932: 'I have the honour to inform you that the 25th of March, the Anniversary of the Declaration of Independence of Greece, passed without incident. Precautionary measures for dealing with any possible disturbance had been taken and the mayors informed that any exhibition of unruly conduct would be followed by the imposition of curfew. There was no occasion to carry out the threat.'[2]

Articles appeared regularly in the Press. Professor Arnold Toynbee, writing in the *New Statesman and Nation* on 23 April 1932, emphasized three points:

1   Cyprus, he stressed, needed ventilation since it had never been properly ventilated (reformed) since 1878.

2   On internal security he complained that 'this is an unpleasant whiff of the 19th century Hapsburg police-state with an alien officialdom living in a potential state of siege'.

3   He concluded by stating that 'the choice lies between staying in Cyprus and losing face or leaving Cyprus and adding to the honours which we won for the British Empire when we left Wei-Lai-wei [in the Shantung province of China] in 1930 and the Ionian Islands in 1864'.

Toynbee's article followed practically the same lines as an earlier one in the *Economist*. Both urged the cession of Cyprus to Greece. The Colonial Office was angered by such utterings, calling them 'highly disparaging to British rule in Cyprus; tendentious, misleading, one-sided and insiduously pro-Hellene'.

Several months later the *Times Educational Supplement* of 20 August 1932 explained that the alternative to union with Greece, as a political ideal for Cyprus, was self-government within the British Commonwealth of Nations. That however should not rule out cultural communion, commerce and friendliness with the mother country of Greece, to which the majority of the sons of Cyprus felt that they belonged. It declared that what the island needed was 'a generation of creative economics based upon a renaissance in the schools'.

In 1934 Lord Strabolgi, writing in *The Nineteenth Century and After*, advocated *inter alia* the exchange of Argostoli for Cyprus. The message of this and the other three articles was that Cyprus should, and must, be handed over to Greece.

In the island itself the general lull was broken on several occasions by a variety of events and by the activities of certain individuals. Heading the list was Leontios Leontiou, Bishop of Paphos, who throughout his career, and especially as *locum tenens* during the vacancy of the archiepiscopal see, was the most 'persistent and irrepressible of agitators' and a man who threw himself 'heart and soul into his work'. He did not follow the other bishops into exile because at the time of the October rising he was a guest at Lambeth of Archbishop Lang. Nevertheless he was not allowed to land on 13 November 1931 at Limassol and proceeded instead to Constantinople. He was promised a safe return to the island if he signed an undertaking to abstain from political activities, but he refused to bind himself in such a way.

However, following the decision to treat agitation for union with Greece as sedition, it was decided by Storrs (the Colonial Office repeatedly stating 'no') that he should be allowed to return. The governor, writing to Sir Cosmo Parkinson, Assistant Under-Secretary of State at the Colonial Office, on 7 June 1932, remarked that: 'As for legislation you have indeed done us princely more especially in accepting the "parole révélatrice" that ENOSIS is an illegal and indeed a seditious doctrine.'[3]

Following the warm welcome given to Leontios on his arrival on 23 June 1932, he plunged into his self-appointed role as leader and demanded union and only union. His actions caused the authorities to retaliate. Thus he pleaded guilty to eight charges of sedition in 1932 at the Limassol assize court and was bound over for three years on his own recognizance for £250; in 1938 he was placed under police supervision for a year and confined to the municipal limits of Paphos, and in 1939 he was again found guilty (he was represented by nine advocates, led by Kriton Tornaritis and Christodoulos Galatopoulos) of certain seditious activities and a harsher punishment than that of 1938 was imposed. Leontios however renewed his activities during the war years and as *locum tenens* from 1933 to 1947 was very influential in Cypriot affairs.

Kyrillos III, Archbishop of Cyprus since 1916, died from pleurisy at the age of 74 on 16 November 1933. This occasioned a renewed outbreak of interest in Greece in the Cypriot question. It had attracted the attention of the Athens press and most of them published detailed biographical notices of the deceased prelate.

Great hopes were being placed on the Financial Commission which was appointed to investigate and report on the economic difficulties of the island. According to a British Intelligence report, reviewing Cypriot affairs up to 31 May 1934, 'if no tangible results accrue, then the pendulum may well swing back once more to Anglophobia'. A Colonial Office memorandum of September 1935 concluded that the movement for union with Greece was a basic political factor in the Cyprus situation. Hence there was no chance of it being obliterated.

It was also decided in Athens that a Pan-Hellenic flag, made of material sent from Cyprus, should be hoisted on 24 March 1935 (also on Sundays and other solemn days during the year) on the Acropolis under the auspices of the Union of Demes and Communes of Greece. The custom was that the flag should be presented for this purpose each year by a different district of Greece.

Marking the fourth anniversary of the troubles in Cyprus, the Athenian newspapers on 21 October 1935 stated that the ungenerous repression of the Cypriots since 1931 had not shaken the belief of the Greek people that the national aspirations of the island would some day be satisfied. In mid November Royalist newspapers carried big headlines declaring that King George II would return and that he 'will bring us Cyprus'. The papers contained huge portraits of the king and General Kondylis backed by a map of Cyprus. It was a fact that reports had been circulated in 1935 that Britain intended to cede Cyprus to Greece in exchange for permission to use certain Greek ports for the fleet.

A Colonial Office minute by A.J. Dawe dated 24 October 1935 stated that King (or ex-King) George of Greece had recently had an interview with Sir Samuel Hoare, the Foreign Secretary, at which he had inquired whether it would be possible to relax to any degree the rigours of the existing regime in Cyprus. The verdict of the Foreign and Colonial Offices was that it was not desirable to make it public that the king had such an interview. 'Suppress all information' was the order of the day. The king also had an interview with Anthony Eden towards the end of 1937 at which he pleaded for some of the exiled Cypriots. The king was convinced that tension would be reduced if some of them were allowed to return.

The general feeling of the 1930s was for self-government within the British Empire, pending the final settlement of the Cypriot question in accordance with the wishes of the people when normality returned to Europe. The London Cypriot Committee embraced this cause and soon became its chief advocate.

The usual British response was the touch-button phrase 'no change is contemplated'. The same answer was given in 1937 to a respectable delegation consisting of D.N. Demetriou OBE, for many years member of the executive council and mayor of Larnaca (1922-32); G.S. Vasiliades, member of the advisory council (1934-7) and deputy mayor of Larnaca; and John Clerides, a lawyer of considerable reputation in Cyprus. The governor on 18 June informed the Colonial Office that he was strongly against either Demetriou or Clerides being received at the Colonial Office, though he had no objection to Vasiliades being granted an audience. Accordingly the meeting took place on 27 July and those present were A.J. Dawe and A.R. Thomas, both senior officials at the Colonial Office, and Vasiliades. The latter attached great importance to the appointment of an independent body from Britain to investigate the whole constitutional position of the island. He was informed that the Secretary of State fully supported the policy pursued by the government of Cyprus and that there was no prospect whatever of any constitutional changes. This was also stated in the House of Commons on 29 June 1937.

The deputation, which had been supported and given promises by D.N. Pritt MP and others, returned nevertheless empty-handed and proceeded to explain their actions in the newspaper *Eleftheria*. Its issue of 19 September also included other articles on the same question. The result was that the proprietor's permit was suspended for three months.

On 1-11 March 1935 there was a military rising in Greece, which had been for some months in secret preparation. The dictatorship of General John Metaxas was inaugurated on 4 August 1936. Metaxas abolished Parliament, arrested all suspect persons and imposed a rigorous censorship of the Press; in fact he established martial law. This he called the 'third Greek civilization' – the first, to him, being ancient Greece and the second the Byzantine Empire. Hence both Cyprus and Greece suffered under the harshness of martial law.

In 1938 the situation in Cyprus was further complicated by the spread of Italian, German and Jewish propaganda. The situation was described by the governor as dangerous and potentially explosive. Sir Herbert Palmer expressed his concern to the Colonial Office in several despatches. On 16 December he informed Malcolm MacDonald, Secretary of State for the Colonies:

> There are only seventy Italian subjects in Cyprus, yet the Italian Government thinks it worth while to maintain a full complement of Consuls, and to use all means available to spread Fascist influences in Cyprus. . . . German propaganda on the other hand is more subtle and there are indications that it is greater in volume than evidence has so far been able to reveal. . . . Not long ago various priests preached against Communism in their Churches, presumably under instructions, and the Locum Tenens delivered in a Church service a panegyric on Hitler . . . it must not be forgotten that certain Zionist organizations consider Cyprus as part of the 'Land of Israel' and that they are constantly trying in various ways to get a footing in Cyprus similar to that which they have obtained in Palestine, and that this Jewish objective is well understood in Cyprus and viewed with concern and detestation by Cypriots.[4]

Such propaganda was a new phenomenon. The Germans managed to secure a fair number of converts. A broadcast from Paris on 5 January 1939 announced that a speech had been made in Berlin on the subject of Cyprus to the effect that Germany had realized that the Cypriot situation needed looking into; and that the Cypriots were a noble and ancient people who had long desired to rejoin Greece but were being kept under harsh rule by the British government. The Cypriot authorities clamped down on clear-cut adherents of the German ideology.

Meanwhile the Colonial Office received another prominent Cypriot in 1938. Dr Themistoclis Dervis OBE, mayor of Nicosia, had an interview with J.B. Williams of the Colonial Office on 19 October and discussed several matters affecting the island, of which the most important were:

1 Dervis emphasized the importance of maintaining the present constitutional position in Cyprus but with the introduction of more representative institutions.

2 He stated the Cypriots were not primitive people and deserved better treatment.

3 Some of the British officials sent to Cyprus were not of

sufficiently high standard, which resulted not only in the abuse of power but in negligent overspending.

4   He pleaded that clemency should be granted to Th. Theodotou, one of the deportees, who was 78 years of age and suffering from cerebral arterio-sclerosis. In fact Theodotou was allowed to return on 31 December 1939. At a meeting at the Colonial Office on 9 November he signed an undertaking that on his return to the island he would not engage in political activities. Theodotou was accompanied by S.C. Terezopoulos, the liaison officer for Cypriots in London. Acheson and Costley-White represented the Colonial Office.

Press articles in Britain and questions in Parliament suggested that Cyprus should have a more liberal form of government. A commission to investigate British misgovernment was also demanded by the British press, and scores of petitions praying for the restoration of constitutional liberties were received by the Cypriot authorities. Yet the British view remained static, and Malcolm MacDonald repeated on 5 July 1939 that: 'The policy of the administration is to work in the direction of more representative government; but this process cannot be hurried, and in my view it must proceed first through a gradual increase of responsibility in local government.'[5]

High taxes were still the rule, and had resulted in a serious reduction in the purchasing power of the people. Moreover the bulk of this enormous taxation fell on the poorer classes, since around four-fifths was indirect (on goods purchased) and only one-fifth direct (on income).

Their cause was taken up by the Fabian Society in London, which had repeatedly condemned such injustices. In 1941 it wrote: 'One of the inequities of Colonial administration has been the low rate of taxation of the richer elements in the Colonial populations.'[6]

Excessive taxation was also attacked by the Cypriot left in a memorandum, framed in the form of an appeal, which was sent to the United Nations in November 1949. Paragraph 8 reads:

The taxation system in Cyprus was and continues to be most unjust. Up to 1925 the principal government tax was the tithe of the cereals which was collected in kind and amounted to 10% of the annual gross produce of farmers without any allowance either for seed, rent, mortgage interest, or cultivation expenses. At the same time and up to 1941 no income tax was payable by the money-lenders, the blood-suckers of the peasants, or by the foreign mining companies, the exploiters of the workers.[7]

Agriculture was not only the backbone of the Cypriot economy but provided the base for a number of small light industries connected with food. According to the *Survey of Rural Life in Cyprus* (1930) only 18 per cent of Cypriot peasant proprietors were not in debt, compared with 17 per cent in the Punjab, and the co-operatives had not only failed to develop co-operation but had also failed to provide an alternative supply of credit. In fact the total amount of loans obtained by co-operative societies between 1927 and 1931 was £340,710 from the agricultural bank of Cyprus and £49,628 from the government. The bulk of this money was used by the peasants to pay off debts to the money-lenders.

Before the Second World War rural debts amounted to £3,000,000 and forced sales of rural property were taking place every day. On 27 May 1936 it was announced however that on loans made to farmers the interest was restricted by law to a maximum of 12 per cent per annum, and that the whole question of agricultural indebtedness would henceforth receive very careful consideration. In 1940 the government passed another law concerning the settlement of rural debts on the basis of which most of them were reduced by one-third and interest rates to 5 per cent. According to the official statistics of the Land Registration Department, during the inter-war period 18,000 mortgaged properties were sold and 19,500 judgements were given for the forced sale of property which was not mortgaged.

More than 600,000 donums (a measure of land usually less than an acre), one million trees and 8,000 houses were disposed of by forced sale, constituting one-fifth of the agricultural land, one-fifth of the fruit trees and one-tenth of all village houses. The owners remained landless and were obliged to become mineworkers at ridiculous wages, to emigrate or simply to starve.

With the world slump adding further distress, workers were forced to go on strike for long periods to defend their rights. In the first six months of 1939 a cross-section of employees ranging from blacksmiths to carpenters, tailors and bakers in the Nicosia, Limassol and Famagusta districts went on strike. Agreement was reached on some of their demands.

Legislation permitting the formation of trade unions was enacted in 1932 by which trade unions, if accepted, could register with the newly created office of the Register of Trade Unions. In 1941 three other laws were enacted – the Trade Unions and Trades Disputes Law, the Minimum Wage Law and the Trades Disputes (Conciliation, Arbitration and Inquiry) Law. These laws were based largely on British trade union legislation.

The state of the Cypriot economy was commented upon by two senior Colonial Office officials in 1938. A minute by A.R. Acheson dated 17 August included the following: 'Cyprus is the cinderella of the British Empire; though it has been under British administration for nearly 60 years it lags far behind the development of other Colonies. . . . Cyprus is the only Colony of which it can be said that the British Government has not only failed to give it any financial support, but has exacted from it heavy Tribute which has been applied to the subvention of the British taxpayer.[8]

Another minute by Sir Cosmo Parkinson on 28 October explained that 'the weakness of our position is that for some fifty or sixty years the British Government neglected Cyprus badly. Our record in Cyprus was not good. Similar remarks are found in a letter by Lord Harewood to W. Ormsby-Gore, the Colonial Secretary, on 25 March.

Two prominent Cypriots who visited the United Kingdom in 1938 and were seen by J.B. Williams of the Colonial Office emphasized in very strong terms the economic ills facing the island. Dr Dervis, mayor of Nicosia, in his interview on 19 October, stressed that interest rates for loans from the agricultural bank should be very low, and not 8 or 10 per cent as he had heard, so that the Cypriot farmer could 'regain consciousness'. P.M. Tseriotis, member of the advisory council, pleaded on 24 October that Cyprus should be included in trade agreements concluded by Britain. Its development, he believed, would thus be fostered. However, with the advent of the war nothing much was done and the 1940s were marked by economic and political unrest.

Another prominent issue of the 1930s was the archiepiscopal question. The relationship between the autocephalous Greek Orthodox Church of Cyprus and the state underwent a fundamental change as a result of the British occupation of 1878. In Ottoman times a Berat of the Sultan confirming the election of an archbishop or a bishop had to be obtained. The Berat, apart from being the formal instrument of recognition, was the charter of liberties and privileges granted to an ecclesiastic, and vested in him great ecclesiastical and temporal power.

The British at once disposed of this requirement. The activities of the Church were restricted to the spiritual field; no longer was the Church to be a tax-gatherer. It was the habit of the Turks in all their provinces to find the strongest native power and say to that power 'we want a certain tribute and what you collect over and above that sum is your business'. Their criterion of good government therefore was the efficiency of tax collection. This led to a great abuse of power; it also led, as in 1821, to large-scale massacres and interference in Church affairs.

The British stated that Church affairs would not be their concern. The Orthodox clergy were reassured by C.W. Sandford, the Bishop of Gibraltar, who emphasized in April 1886 that 'no repetition of such interference with the historic rights of their church have our Christian brethren in Cyprus to fear at the hands of English churchmen in the present day . . . as lovers of liberty we are anxious to promote, not to prejudice the independence of sister churches'. The Orthodox Church therefore continued as the leader of the Greek Cypriot nation – free from harassment and executions. The intermingling of religion, politics and personal glorification kept the Church always in the limelight.

Following the death of Archbishop Sofronios II on 22 May 1900, an undignified contest between two parties in the Church took place (see pages 83-6). The Church was once more plunged into crisis in the 1930s. The death of the peace-loving Kyrillos III on 16 November 1933 left it without an archbishop. Leontios Leontiou, the Bishop of Paphos, was unable, owing to the absence from the island of the two other bishops (exiled in 1931), to proceed to the election of a successor. The Archbishop of Canterbury suggested on 8 December 1933 that these bishops should be allowed to return for the election but they should give a guarantee that they would take no part in political activities. On 15 December the Secretary of State for the Colonies replied to the Archbishop: 'I have been definitely advised by the Government of Cyprus that the presence of the deported Bishops is not necessary for the purpose of the election; and, as you know, it is highly undesirable on political grounds that they should be permitted to return to the Colony.'[9]

Consequently Leontios, as *locum tenens*, became the *de facto* head of the Church of Cyprus. Following the death of the Bishop of Kition in Jerusalem on 13 September 1937 a renewed agitation developed in the Press about the vacant archiepiscopal see. Four laws purporting to deal with the situation were hurriedly passed. Law 25, the Churches and Monasteries of the Autocephalous Greek-Orthodox Church of Cyprus (Investigation and Audit) Law 1937, provided for the investigation of the affairs and for the auditing of the accounts of the churches and monasteries in certain cases.

On 12 November 1937 two laws (numbers 33 and 34) were enacted dealing with the election of an archbishop. The Autocephalous Greek-Orthodox Church of Cyprus (Archbishop's Disqualification) Law was an *ad hoc* law and dealt with the forthcoming election only. It made ineligible for election as archbishop the following classes of person:

persons who had been deported from Cyprus;
persons who had been convicted of sedition or of any other offence punishable with imprisonment or penal servitude for more than two years; and
persons who were not natives of Cyprus.

Ecclesiastics such as St Paul, who brought Christianity to the island in AD 45-6 but was born in Tarsus, would not have been allowed to serve the island as archbishop! An amendment to this law exempted from disqualification a native who was originally a member of the Church of Cyprus but had become a member of another branch of the Orthodox Church.

Law 34, the Autocephalous Greek-Orthodox Church of Cyprus (Governor's Approval of the Archbishop) Law, was a permanent law and reaffirmed the practice which had existed from Turkish times that the person elected as archbishop must be approved by the governor before his election was consummated. In other words, the election to an Orthodox see having been canonically made could be invalidated by the veto of a civil authority, which was generally considered to be contrary to canon law. A further piece of legislation (Law 35) defined the meaning of native of the colony more precisely.

The authorities believed that by passing these laws they would prevent the Church, which had always been the leader of the *enosis* movement, from falling under Hellenizing influences. They also stated that the government did not want to interfere in the affairs of the Church, which had been autocephalous since Byzantine times. Percy Arnold, reflecting on the state of affairs, wrote:

> This interference by an alien who was not of the Greek Orthodox faith in the affairs of a Church which had been self-governing, as its name indicates, and had fought for its survival and its independence for almost as long as the Christian era, turned the Church of Cyprus irrevocably against British rule, enabled priests to maintain with greater evidence than before that British rule was an instrument of the devil and the arrogance of Palmer's laws provoked the resentment even of those Cypriots who were normally little endeared towards their Church.[10]

The Church laws of 1937 formed part of the 27 so-called 'illiberal' laws passed between 1931 and 1937. The 28th was passed in May 1944.

A further feature of the 1930s was the emergence of the advisory council. It was set up in October 1933 on an informal basis 'to enable', it was stated, 'the government to keep itself informed of the views and feelings of the community to a greater extent than was possible in the post-1931 period'. Yet in the following March it was stated that it was not of much practical assistance to the government since the governor could not find a dozen or so honest Cypriots. During his very short tenure as governor Sir Edward Stubbs informed the Secretary of State on 16 October 1933 that he knew of no community which was so utterly unfit to take any responsible part in the government of its native country as was that of Cyprus. Yet Lord Winster, who fell in love with Cyprus, emphasized on 4 May 1949 that: 'They are people of great dignity, they have intellectual ability, extraordinary courtesy and great power of friendship, and they are very hospitable.'[11]

In fact, under the repressiveness of the post-1931 measures, no government agency whatsoever kept itself informed of the feelings and views of the community. Whether such an agency was called advisory or executive council, it existed in name only. It was neither representative nor did it possess any legislative powers. The governor was omnipotent.

The behaviour of the Turkish element also deserves some comment. Apart from isolated clashes with their Greek compatriots, relations between them had been very cordial. Even when Greece and Turkey were at loggerheads on several occasions since 1878, the two sides in Cyprus behaved well towards each other. During the First World War, when Turkey was not on the side of the Allies, and during the Asia Minor fiasco of the early 1920s, there were no outbreaks of violence. During the 1931 disturbances the Turks did not connive in any way with the authorities against the Greek demonstrators. In fact, as already observed, Nejati Bey, member of the legislative council and a prominent Turkish leader, issued a manifesto supporting the activities of the Greek agitators.

The Graeco-Turkish reconciliation of the early 1930s greatly strengthened the goodwill and co-operation between the Greeks and Turks of Cyprus. Nevertheless, the activities of extremist nationalist leaders on both sides caused some concern and on several occasions the Cypriot authorities took precautionary measures to avert possible trouble. Such fears, however, never materialized.

Yet economic discontent led to a desire to emigrate and together with the spread of 'Kemalism' nationalism was on the ascendancy. Most of the Cypriot Turks who opted for Turkish nationality and left Cyprus as a result of the Treaty of Lausanne met with conditions of such difficulty and hardship in Turkey that they returned disappointed and impoverished to the island. However, discontent amongst the Moslem population in 1936-7 fostered in them the belief that Turkey offered a better prospect of earning a livelihood than Cyprus. London was also a popular place for emigration.

Earlier, on 26 October 1934, over one hundred Turkish men, women and children left Cyprus on board the SS *Egeo* for Turkey. The majority came from the village of Galatia in the Karpass. Although the police intelligence report for December 1934 emphasized that 'most of these persons were in debt and a good many were of bad character', the fact remains that the island's deplorable economic situation and Turkish nationalist propaganda by certain individuals in Cyprus convinced some that Turkey held better prospects for them. The Turkish government and press were against such emigration. Thus Sirri Bey, a Turkish Member of Parliament who visited Cyprus in October 1934 and spoke at the Turkish (Political) Club, said that 'the Cyprus Turks should remain in Cyprus as one day they will be useful to Turkey'. These words assumed great political importance in the post-1954 period.

The spread of 'Kemalism' was directed by the Turkish consul in Cyprus and by certain other individuals such as Nejati Bey of Nicosia. The latter, in a telegram of New Year greetings to Their Majesties on 26 December 1937, concerned himself with Turkish nationalism and with opposition to the local department of Evcaf. The Evcaf was charged with the administration of Moslem charitable trusts in Cyprus and had great influence amongst the Moslem population. Delegates to that body therefore exercised considerable power. Munir Bey, a member of the executive council and the Turkish delegate to Evcaf, was incessantly attacked as being too pro-British and thus a barrier to Turkish nationalism.

Munir Bey, who served the Cyprus government for many years, was totally pro-British in both his views and actions. In 1928 he was honoured with a personal interview with HM the King and three years later he was given the OBE. Although the governors of the island often complained that there was no other Moslem to replace Munir Bey, A.J. Dawe in a Colonial Office minute of 1 May 1935 described him as an 'unsound person'.

Although people such as Munir Bey were indispensable in holding the pro-British feeling together, Turkish nationalism, especially amongst the young, was on the ascendancy in the late 1930s. Like Communism, 'Kemalism' was considered by the authorities as being mischievous but as yet not alarming. This nationalism was portrayed by the arrival of the Turkish naval training ship *Hamidiye* at Famagusta on 20 June 1938. Its arrival caused quite a stir since 5,000 people, mainly Moslems, were present. Badges of Atatürk and other souvenirs were distributed to those who boarded the ship.

This and the other problems of the 1930s receded, albeit temporarily, into the background following the war hysteria of 1939. The period up to the end of the Second World War is the concern of our next chapter.

8   1939-1945: The War Years

The state of the economy, labour relations, political confrontation and *enosis* agitation were all major problems between 1939 and 1945. Yet all were overshadowed by the Second World War. These years were crucial for the Cypriots and their aspirations.

On 1 September 1939 Germany invaded Poland and two days later Britain and France declared war on Germany. The French from the commencement of the war were anxious to use Cyprus as an advance base for aircraft on seaward patrols, especially towards the Italian Dodecanese islands, and for giving depth to the air defences of Beirut. The British on the other hand did not wish Cyprus to grow into a defensive commitment involving forces that could ill be spared. They agreed however that the airfields of Nicosia and Larnaca should be improved and that refuelling and rearming facilities should be installed and made available to the French. For attacking the Dodecanese islands sites in south-western Anatolia could be much more suitable if Turkey would consent to their use.

Even though the British garrison had been increased from one company to one battalion the French had not been satisfied and a French contingent had been sent to the island. A battalion of Cypriots was also raised. The 50th British Division worked on the defences of Cyprus and stayed until October 1941 when it was replaced by the 5th Indian Division which had been in Iraq. The British Prime Minister's private minute of 31 October 1941 expressed satisfaction with the above switch. Another minute dated 1 October 1943 showed that at that time the army personnel in the island amounted to 10,500 of which 1,500 were British, 6,000 Indian and the remaining 3,000 Cypriots.

As in 1914, the total contribution of Cyprus to the war effort of the Allies was massive. The Cypriots were the first colonial troops to take an active part in war operations against Germany and her allies. The Cypriot muleteers, doing much of their work by night, covered country impassable by wheeled vehicles. In rugged country they frequently had to climb many hundreds of feet. Five hundred Cypriots were enlisted to form pack transport companies for use in the forward areas in France and were shipped in early January 1940 to Marseilles. The Cypriot personnel stood up to discomfort and cold extremely well. The sick rate was very low and they gained a reputation for the cheerful execution of their duties under all conditions. From there some months later, by night marches, they made their way to Dunkirk. Their bearing under heavy bombing for four days in Dunkirk and during their evacuation was exemplary.

Most of those who fought risked their lives in the naïve view that Britain would reward them after the war by granting *enosis* with Greece – the eternal British ally. On the other hand, certain Turkish elements in Cyprus formed a national party and showed some signs of favouring Germany since they believed that a British victory would eventually lead to *enosis* whereas the Germans, if victorious, would consider their own and Italian interests and would also wish to placate Turkey. Yet Greek and Turkish Cypriots lived in the same quarters, fought side by side in many battlefields, and both were mentioned in despatches for their gallantry and both were duly rewarded by the granting of military medals.

The passion of the Cypriot who joined the Allies was well captured by L.A. Karaphodias, a poet of some local respectability, who wrote during the war:

Going to fight for the cause of freedom
To protect you all from our barbarian enemies
To victory against the wild beasts
To victory with Greece and Britain.

The above shows the love all Cypriots had for freedom.

The loss of three Cypriot sailors at sea as a result of enemy action during 1939 was received very badly by the islanders. Towards the end of that year the Russian attack on Finland gave rise to apprehension regarding possible Russian attacks on Turkey or the Balkans which would bring Cyprus nearer the theatre of war.

Cypriot gallantry was evident on all fronts. As already mentioned they took part in the historic Dunkirk evacuation of 29 May to 4 June 1940, where they were ordered to destroy their mules – an order which they very reluctantly carried out. The Cypriots then took part in the Abyssinian campaign where the successful conclusion of the battle for Keren was greatly helped by the ability of Cypriot pack transport companies to supply units under fire in the most inaccessible places. The presence of these companies shortened the siege by weeks and this campaign in itself more than justified the formation of the Cyprus muleteers.

At the battle for Monte Cassino, February to May 1944, the toughest spot and perhaps the most crucial in Italy, Cypriots distinguished themselves on its rugged slopes by bringing up supplies and taking down the wounded under a hail of enemy bullets and shells doubled in intensity by the splintering rock. Cypriots also served in Egypt, the Sudan and under Lord Wavell in Libya and Palestine. Above all the Cyprus Regiment fought many a bloody contest with the enemy and covered itself with glory on Greek soil. Cypriots also served in Crete, from where some of those taken prisoner managed to escape to Egypt. Of the 2,500 members of the Cyprus Regiment who were in Greece and Crete some 2,100 were lost – the vast majority becoming prisoners.

The fall of Crete sent fears around Cyprus. It was widely believed that the island was going to be the next prey of the Germans. Hitler's losses however were very high. The Cretan resistance upset the schedule of further German offensives. It meant that the opening of the Russian front had to be set back at least another week. In view of the early Russian winter of 1941 this unplanned-for delay deprived the Germans of good campaigning weather just when they needed it most. The experience in Crete made the Führer super-cautious and distrustful of all future German airborne operations. Colonel-General Kurt Student (Commander German Airborne Troops, Army Group 'H', First Parachute Army) proposed that Cyprus should follow Crete in order to provide a jumping-off ground for an air and paratroop attack on the Suez Canal. However, the plans for an attack on Cyprus were shelved. The Germans, although not yet on the defensive, were certainly losing the offensive.

Hence the Germans and their allies did not make a serious attempt to capture the island even though it served as an invaluable supply and relief station for the Allies. However, it was raided on numerous occasions by the Italians and to a much lesser extent by the Japanese. On 22 September 1940 hostile aeroplanes raided the mining port of Xero. Bombs were dropped in the sea and part of the town was machine-gunned. Three barges and a tug belonging to the Cyprus Mines Corporation were damaged.

The attacks of 1941 were more severe. On the morning of 7 July the Nicosia aerodrome was twice attacked by Italian bombers. There were five civilian and three service casualties of which one civilian and two service were fatal. One RAF aircraft was destroyed and three were damaged whilst on the ground. In the afternoon a single aircraft dropped two bombs in the sea at Famagusta but no casualties were recorded.

Early on 8 July a British ship was attacked by mistake from low altitude by French aircraft ten miles out of Famagusta, but the attack caused no damage. On the morning of 9 July seven Italian aircraft bombed Nicosia aerodrome but only minor damage was caused. During the afternoon SS *Warsawa*, carrying Greek refugees, including some escaped Cypriot soldiers, from Mersin to Haifa, was attacked by two Italian planes off Cape Greco. No casualties or damage resulted.

Italian aircraft once more bombed Nicosia aerodrome on 10 July. There were no casualties but four vehicles, a number of tents and telephone communications were severely damaged. Two days later seven aircraft attacked Famagusta. Some 30 bombs were dropped, some of which fell in the old town causing slight damage to property. The Famagusta railway was also slightly damaged. There were no casualties.

There were enemy submarines lurking around Famagusta harbour and mines were laid at its very entrance. The steamtug *Alliance* struck a mine and sank on 29 April 1942. The captain and two of the crew were killed and five were injured.

Despite the fact that by September 1941 the defences of Cyprus had been heavily reinforced, embodying the lessons taught by Crete and Tobruk, and converted into a stronghold of the RAF with good aerodromes, the fear of a possible mass attack on the island still persisted since it lay across the path of any German attempt on the Middle East, assuming that Turkey remained neutral; when reinforced, however, it was in a strong position, with its own airfields and reinforcements in Syria 150 miles away, to meet any attack by the enemy, whose nearest air base was at Kastellorizo. The latter was established as an Italian air base and is approximately 260 miles from Famagusta.

This fear was also expressed in official (secret) despatches. Hence on 15 and 29 April 1941 the British Premier very diplomatically pointed out to the Greek king and government, who wished to move on from Crete to Cyprus, that recent developments had inevitably increased the vulnerability of the island. Furthermore, operation instruction no. 114, dated 18 March 1942, stated that 'should the enemy invade Turkey and advance to and across the northern frontier of Syria, Cyprus may have to be evacuated'.

However, although an enemy reconnaissance plane was over the island on 30 May 1942, Cyprus experienced peaceful times during the last three years of the war. The desire for *enosis* or more representative government and the state of the economy caused more trouble to the British authorities.

The still proscribed KKK (Communist Party of Cyprus) at first opposed the war as imperialist-Fascist. However, following the Italian invasion of Greece in October 1940 and the German invasion of Russia on 22 June 1941, the line was altered and the war was now a fight against Fascism and for democracy. AKEL (formally founded on 14 April 1941, succeeding in effect the KKK) campaigned in earnest for the war.

Although Cypriots served with gallantry in the British army and prayed for an Allied victory, a large Greek Cypriot contingent joined the Greek army and served for much less payment. Many Cypriots just before the outbreak of war felt that instead of Cypriots being regarded as British citizens with a future in the British Empire they should be regarded as Greeks who were merely under the suzerainty of Great Britain. Administrative measures designed to repress Greek feeling and foster imperial feeling were not approved.

Sir Michael Palairet informed the Foreign Office on 4 January 1941 that the British authorities in Athens were 'embarrassed' over the numerous messages received from

Cypriots wishing to volunteer for the Greek forces. Five days later a cipher telegram from the Governor of Cyprus to the Colonial Office read: 'If facilities for enlistment in the Greek Army were available, recruiting for the Cyprus Regiment would suffer. . . . Political results of recruitment for the Greek Army likely to be most unfortunate. Post-war difficulties also likely to be considerable as demobilised soldiers who served with the Greek Army would on return here be likely to become a "Nationalist Bloc"'[1]

In Cyprus the *locum tenens* was active in enrolling volunteers for the Greek forces. The government of Greece however, after incessant pressure from the British authorities, stated in February 1941 that Leontios should abandon all such actions. This request was complied with and by the end of the month such recruitment had virtually ceased.

The Greekness of the Cypriots therefore was always in evidence. *Enosis* was an *idée fixe* and its attainment the natural aspiration of the islanders. Even though nearly 10 per cent of the island's population of approximately 420,000 in 1942 was engaged in the Allied effort, the British authorities stressed that there was a need to increase Cyprus's contribution in manpower to the war effort. Leontios, writing to the governor on 30 May 1942, pledged support on condition that an official declaration should immediately be made that Cyprus 'is an inseparable part of the Greek nation'. He demanded *enosis* immediately after the war. On the same date another letter to the governor from the AKEL central committee asked for an official assurance and a guarantee to be given by Britain that the Atlantic declaration 'will fully apply to Cyprus after the war'. The letter also requested that responsible elected representatives of the people should be given the management of the island's finances.

Such a public official statement never materialized. Yet both Leontios and AKEL continued to seek ways of helping the war effort of the Allies.

Following the resistance of Greece to Italy after October 1940, a Greater Greece movement gained ground. A memorandum sent on 24 March 1941 by the Governor of Cyprus to A.R. Acheson of the Colonial Office included the following:

The idea of a Greater Greece and of Greek Imperialism in the Mediterranean has formed the subject of speculation in Cyprus ever since Greek resistance to Italy proved successful. These speculations have recently been stimulated by an article by Mr Compton Mackenzie in 'Reynolds News'. The article itself has not reached Cyprus but according to quotations from it in Athenian newspapers which have arrived here, the author suggests that Great Britain should declare her decision to cede Cyprus to Greece; guarantee the restoration of the Dodecanese to Greece; give Greece a share in the control of the Suez Canal and ask her to undertake the mandate in Libya.[2]

A similar article appeared on 19 November entitled 'The Future of Greece'. The newspaper *Nea Hellas (Modern Greece)*, published in Greek in Johannesburg, South Africa, advocated the cession of the Dodecanese and Cyprus to mother Greece. This, the article went on, would enable Greece to become a big naval Mediterranean power and a civilizing factor in that part of Europe, retaining her integrity against all treachery. The trend was reflected in a Colonial Office minute of 22 November 1941, which recorded that the *enosis* feeling was clearly rising.

Anti-British comments by several Athenian newspapers indirectly aided the trend. Even in 1940 the circulation in the island of certain mainland newspapers (the *Proia* and the *Hestia*) containing news items of an anti-British character was condemned by the Colonial Office. MacDonald wrote to the governor stating that the banning of these papers would have an unfortunate effect on Anglo-Greek relations. His remedy was that an adequate supply of British news should be widely disseminated in the island.

The Cypriots' hopes were raised once more when in October 1941, on the anniversary of the Italian attack on Greece, Winston Churchill's message to the Greek Premier E. Tsouderos implied that when the war ended 'Pan-Hellenism will be at its peak'. Two telegrams by Leontios on 27 September to the King of the Hellenes and to Tsouderos expressed the same feelings. On 5 October Tsouderos, in a telegram to Leontios, spoke in the following manner: 'Warmest thanks for your wishes and declaration of national feelings which deeply touched me. I am looking forward to the blessed day of national resurrection when all brethren in Christ and nationality will meet in the same house of our Motherland.'[3]

In fact the *enosis* desire was clearly in the ascendancy in 1941. It was further encouraged by the 'Joint Declaration' of Roosevelt, the US President, and Churchill, the British Prime Minister, known as the Atlantic Charter, of 14 August 1941. The two world leaders announced that they desired to see no territorial changes that did not accord with the freely expressed wishes of the peoples concerned and that they respected the right of all peoples to choose the form of government under which they would live. The Cypriots demanded not only that the above principles should apply to the island but that it should also be granted freedom of speech and assembly, legalization of political parties and economic assistance.

Tsouderos was the Greek Premier from 21 April 1941 to 13 April 1944 directing affairs from places other than Athens. For some time the government functioned from abroad. Tsouderos revealed in his memoirs that in May 1941, while in Crete where his government and King George had fled after the German invasion, he informed the British ambassador that he expected an early solution to the Cyprus question in favour of Greece, and that if his government were compelled to evacuate Crete they should be allowed to establish themselves in the island where they would be 'Greeks among Greeks'. The British, according to Tsouderos, refused to consider this proposition because it might have caused the Germans to attack the island, which was unfortified.

Churchill in two instances (telegrams of 15 and 29 April 1941) stated that Cyprus was a possible location for the Greek government but there were disadvantages owing to insufficient defences. Thus by moving to Cyprus the Greek government would not escape the danger to which they were exposed in Crete. The British government suggested Kenya and Palestine. The Greeks moved to Egypt.

The British position therefore, as seen from the dates of the above telegrams, was quite explicit even before Tsouderos had made his request for such facilities in May 1941. The British wished to avoid an action which might be exploited by the people of Cyprus and by the Greek government in the solution of the Cypriot question.

Greek Cypriots were infuriated by this British refusal, but Tsouderos, in a speech to the Greek community of Pretoria on 16 July 1941, pledged that Greece would fight until victory was attained. This, he stated, 'will secure for us the restoration of the Hellenic nation by the liberation of our brothers who are in bondage, together with the return of our territories now temporarily occupied by the enemy'. The Cypriots rejoiced and, as a memorandum by the Royal Institute of International Affairs stated in 1941, 'there seems little reason to doubt that the demand for union will grow rather than diminish'.

At a luncheon given in his honour by the Greek community in London on 15 November, Tsouderos said:

> Greece, radiant with glory, is now running upon the black ridges of the mountains and walks upon the bloodstained ruins of our towns and villages. Dressed in white and with the nimbus of martyrdom round her head, she is not alone; she is followed by her beloved united daughters. One easily knows them from their costumes. Look! There is one woman of Macedonia, the woman of Crete, the woman of Cyprus, the woman of Peloponnese, the woman of the Dodecanese, the woman of Yannina, the woman of North Epirus . . . adorned with laurels they follow their mother, going forward towards victory that will unite them again in peace.[4]

Thus Tsouderos envisaged Cyprus as being part of Greece after the war. He simply echoed Churchill's message to him of the previous month stressing that after the war Pan-Hellenism would be at its peak. Tsouderos later explained that what he had said was 'a mere expression of hope, which I wish God might realize with the help of all Greeks throughout the world and the constant confidence of our great Allies'. On the afternoon of 25 November 1941 Tsouderos met Eden, the British Foreign Secretary. Tsouderos listened very carefully to accounts of the alleged considerable embarrassment caused by his statements to the British authorities in Cyprus. He explained, according to a Foreign Office record, that he had merely referred in poetic language to martyred Greece being accompanied by her daughters, among whom he had included Cyprus and Greek Macedonia. He had however no intention of raising the Cyprus question at that juncture but was content to

leave it until after the war. He observed that the terms of the
Atlantic Charter gave Greece every reason for encouragement
on that point.

That of course was not the end of the matter. The *enosis* cause
continued its customary course. The Cypriot *locum tenens* in a
letter to the governor on 20 December 1941, which he had
requested to be sent to Churchill, expressed the hope that Great
Britain would liberate this large and most Greek island of
Cyprus by ceding it to its mother Greece. Two further
references to the territorial claims of Greece were made by
Tsouderos on 5 January 1942 in broadcasts to Greece. 'We are
approaching,' he said, 'the realization of our national
ambitions, the racial and geographical completion of our
mother country.'

The question of Cyprus was also raised by Tsouderos'
predecessor Alexandros Koryzis. Eden together with Sir John
Dill (Chief of the Imperial General Staff) arrived at Athens on 2
March 1941. The purpose of this official visit was to examine
the military situation with the appropriate authorities in view
of the impending German attack upon Greece. The Greek
Premier asked whether the British would meet the Greeks on
three points. The second point concerned Cyprus. Koryzis
asked for a promise that the question of Cyprus would be settled
according to Greek desires. Eden is said to have refused to
commit himself without the previous authority of Whitehall but
asked for time to communicate with his government. On the
following day he intimated to the Greeks that Britain would be
prepared to discuss Cyprus after the war.

The future of Cyprus was also raised in the British cabinet by
the Foreign Secretary on 2 June 1941, at a time when there
seemed a grave risk that the Germans could succeed in
occupying the island. This, it was widely believed, would have
resulted in Germany handing over Cyprus to Greece.
Consequently, in paragraph 2 of his memorandum (dated 31
May 1941), Eden emphasized that 'quite apart from the
necessities of the present crisis, there is a strong prima facie case
for ceding Cyprus to Greece, subject to safeguards, after the
war'. The same conclusion on the cession of Cyprus was
reached by the foreign research department of the Royal
Institute of International Affairs in their objective

memorandum of 19 April 1941. The institute stated that Britain's interests would best be served by such a cession before the end of the war or at whatever moment promised the greatest political advantage. It further stressed that 'it is contrary to the traditions and in general to the interests of the British Empire to maintain in political subjection a people whose social and cultural level justifies the claim to self-determination'.

Two documents, one from the Foreign Secretary and the other from Lord Moyne, the Colonial Secretary, were before the war cabinet when it met on 2 June to discuss the future of Cyprus. It was decided that the Foreign Secretary should not at that stage initiate discussions with the Greek government on the future of Cyprus. If however the matter was raised he should reply that Britain was prepared to discuss the island's future after the war as part of the general peace settlement.

On 31 January 1943 Sir Winston Churchill visited Cyprus after his trip to Turkey. Addressing a gathering of leading island personalities and senior public service officers he declared: 'This is my third visit to your beautiful island. . . . Believe me, after this war is over, the name of Cyprus will be included in the list of those who have deserved well not only of the British Commonwealth of Nations, not only of the United Peoples now in arms, but as I firmly believe, of future generations of mankind.'[5]

This gave new hope to the Greeks of Cyprus, who believed that questions of territorial readjustment were to be settled after the war. At the municipal elections of 21 March 1943 all candidates freely gave undertakings to advance the cause of *enosis* and public celebrations of all kinds were taken as an excuse for demonstrations in favour of union.

On 31 March however Lord Faringdon, who knew Cyprus very well and often described it as 'so nearly approximating to an earthly paradise', expounded the theory that:

> Cyprus was not, as your Lordships will be aware, really a part of the ancient classical Greek world . . . only mismanagement could really have given strength to the movement in favour of union with the mainland of Greece which, as I say, is not truly the mother country of the Cypriots, and which is also a country from which they could obtain no possible advantages. . . . There is, in addition, the

consideration that of the population of this island roughly
four-fifths are Greek and one-fifth Turkish. This minority
would find itself, in a union with Greece, a very small
minority indeed, whereas in Cyprus, by itself, it is a very
influential section of the population. For these reasons I hope
very much that the present movement which exists in favour
of an autonomous Cyprus – a self-governing Colony within
the British Empire – will receive the encouragement it
deserves, and which I feel will be for the greatest advantage
both of Cyprus and of the British Empire.[6]

Cypriot aspirations were dented further by the Duke of
Devonshire, Parliamentary Under-Secretary of State for the
Colonies, who expounded his theory of the two pitfalls. He said:

In all political questions there are two pitfalls of which one
should beware, and this, perhaps, applies particularly to
Colonial political questions. On the one side there is the
pitfall of complacency, of accepting the view that all is for the
best in the best of all possible worlds. This is a pitfall which
particularly awaits a Government spokesman. On the other
hand there is the pitfall of too readily believing that a very
limited number of agitators, not perhaps very responsible
persons, really represent the aspirations of a nation rightly
striving to be free. That is particularly a pitfall which awaits
spokesmen from the Opposition Benches.[7]

The two speeches evoked a cascade of telegrams from Cyprus.
The American press also showed its annoyance with such
untimely declarations which were riddled with misconceptions.
On 8 April an editorial in the *Atlantis* was highly critical of such
speeches. A leading article in the *National Herald* on the
following day talked of 'an unfortunate and untimely
discussion'. Its correspondence columns of 13 April were also
filled with abuse. The Pan-American Committee on the
Cypriot National Question was set up in New York.

The Greeks stood firm by their demand for early self-
determination. The Turks, on the other hand, were opposed to
any change in the status of the island, insisting that if there were
a change Cyprus should be returned to Turkey. The Foreign
Secretary received numerous telegrams from the Moslem
councillors of Nicosia, Larnaca, Limassol, Famagusta and

Paphos and from several political clubs. The honorary secretary of the Kardashojaghi club (Turkish Brotherhood), Sukri Veysi, even protested against granting any form of self-government, which would endanger, he stressed, the existence of the loyal Turkish community.

A Foreign Office memorandum of 29 September 1943 deduced that there were three main areas in which Greece would claim territory beyond its 1939 frontiers. In order of importance they were the Dodecanese, Southern Albania (Northern Epirus) and Cyprus. The Greek claim to Cyprus rested on two arguments.

First was the offer of 1915. The Greek government argued that although this offer was not accepted at the time, since Greece did not at that date enter the war, Greece had on two subsequent occasions gone to war on Britain's side without making any conditions. In recognition of this fact alone Cyprus should be ceded to Greece. The other argument was the ethnic one that four-fifths of the population of the island was Greek. On 2 March 1943 Sir Michael Palairet wrote to Eden from Athens pleading that the eventual cession of Cyprus to Greece would be an act of generosity and wisdom.

On 31 October 1943 the Committee for Cyprus Affairs organized the Cyprus Conference at the Royal Hotel, London. Over 250 Cypriot delegates affirmed their support for the just demand of the Cypriot people to be united with Greece after the war and pledged to urge the British government to apply the principles of the Atlantic Charter to their island. On the same date an article in the *Sunday Dispatch* entitled 'Shall the Gallant Greeks Be Denied Justice?', by M.T. Aghnides, the Greek Ambassador to London, stressed that the twin poles of Greek foreign policy had always been the restoration of freedom of the unredeemed Greeks and a modicum of security against predatory neighbours.

On 11 August 1944 Sir Cosmo Parkinson, lately Permanent Under-Secretary of State for the Colonies, arrived in Cyprus as the personal representative of Colonel Oliver Stanley. He was accompanied by A.R. Thomas, a principal in the Colonial Office, as secretary. The purpose of his journey was to acquaint himself with local conditions and problems. He was flooded with telegrams expressing the Cypriots' wish for union with

Greece. At the same time the Moslems were concerned not only to assert their opposition to *enosis* and to express their desire to remain under British rule but also to voice their demand for a number of social reforms affecting their community. A deputation from the Cyprus Turkish Minorities Association (KATAK) conveyed their demands to Sir Cosmo. Common demands included the immediate abolition of illiberal laws and consequently the granting of freedom of speech, of the Press and of assembly.

The Greeks, now favouring immediate *enosis* as proposed by Dr Socratis Tornaritis as opposed to the demand for political liberties now and then union after the war, demonstrated at Nicosia and Larnaca. On 19 August 75 people, including Ploutis Servas, the mayor of Limassol, who was arrested in his hotel, Andreas Ziartides, general secretary of the Cyprus trade unions, Stelios Iakovides, secretary of the Nicosia trade unions, Georgios Christodoulides, assistant secretary of AKEL, and Kyriacos Kakoullis, a journalist, were fined or bound over for holding unauthorized processions.

The accused faced Judge Cox in Nicosia and Judge Kriton Tornaritis, later Attorney-General, in Larnaca. The latter reprimanded three people and bound them over in the sum of £20 for two years; he sent one to jail for three days and four priests were fined amounts up to £3 and were bound over in the sum of £15 for two years. Tornaritis warned the priests that leniency had its limits and prison was to be their next destination if they continued to disregard the law.

On 22 August Sir Cosmo, following his 'memorable holiday' on the Troodos mountains, held a press conference. He explained that he was on a fact-finding mission and thus was not in a position to make pronouncements of policy. But how far did his fact-finding mission really go? Percy Arnold, who was present at the conference, had this to say:

> Clearly, by keeping him in the hills, away from the hubbub, the overcrowding and ill-housing of the towns, away from frustrated businessmen who were heartily tired of civil servants trying to conduct or control business, by keeping him away from workmen who complained about the cost of living, the Government had succeeded in giving Sir Cosmo the right ideas, and he was saying all the right things, just as

if the Colonial Secretary of Cyprus had himself written the
speech for him.[8]

The official communiqué was also grossly misrepresented by
the government. It stated that the question of *enosis* had been
simply raised during the discussion that followed Sir Cosmo's
speech. It would have been more true to say that *enosis* was the
only subject constantly discussed by all. All the Greek editors,
from right and left, spoke for *enosis* and only *enosis*. The two
Turkish editors opposed *enosis* and also drew attention to
disabilities and discrimination from which they said the
Turkish community had suffered under the present British
administration.

On 23 August Sir Cosmo received two delegations at
Government House. The first delegation of KEK, the Cyprus
National Party, consisted of its general secretary, Dr Dervis,
mayor of Nicosia, and its two joint secretaries, both advocates,
Zenon Sosos of Nicosia and Zenon Rossides of Limassol. A
short memorandum presented to Sir Cosmo affirmed that the
eternal wish of the people of Cyprus was union with motherland
Greece. Sir Cosmo repeated his earlier declaration that this was
a subject he was not authorized to discuss. The second
delegation, already mentioned, was from KATAK.

Soon afterwards the parties of the left issued a manifesto
naming 28 August as the day for a general expression of the
people's national feelings. The organizers had assured Sir
Cosmo that there would be no trouble or disturbance since the
only purpose of the national day was to give the people an
opportunity to express freely their wish for union with Greece.
There were no demonstrations. There were however some
stoppages of work and several indoor meetings and the Greek
flag was freely flown. Yet the trade union paper *Anorthosis* which
published the manifesto had its licence suspended and the
government took extra precautionary measures. The Turks
held rallies in both Nicosia and Limassol and spoke against
enosis. As Percy Arnold reported, 'the crisis, if it was a crisis, was
over'.

There were other significant developments in 1944. The
third Pan-Cyprian Trade Union Conference held at Limassol
on 24-5 September expressly stated that 'union with Greece is
our invariable wish'. Yet by late autumn attempts to form a

coalition of political parties with a view to exerting pressure for
enosis broke down.

Following a suggestion by J. Parker, a British Member of
Parliament, that Cyprus should be ceded to Greece after the
war, the Kardashojaghi club sent a telegram to the Prime
Minister (received at the Foreign Office on 17 June) stating
that 'a change in the present political status quo will endanger
the existence of the 80,000 Turks'. For various reasons Prince
Mohammed Ali of Egypt provided useful support for this view.
In a letter to the Foreign Secretary in November he pleaded
against the annexation of Cyprus to Greece. He concluded by
saying that he did not wish to see any other nation acquire a
hold on the island, no matter how small, weak or friendly that
country might be. The prince's aspirations were analysed by
Lord Killearn of the British Embassy in Cairo in a letter to
Eden on 29 November: 'The Prince's representations are no
doubt partly due to the natural solidarity with the Turks in
Cyprus who have always been against union with Greece and
partly to the natural Egyptian desire that Egypt should not be
dominated by Greece.'[9]

Agitation for the furtherance of the Greek dream was
maintained in 1945. There were protests and even questions at
Westminster when in early 1945 the two municipalities of
Limassol and Famagusta, where AKEL was in office, were
prevented from subscribing £500 each to the Greek relief fund.
The reason given was that the Municipal Corporations Law
provided that all municipal revenue must be exclusively
devoted to municipal purposes within municipal limits. Yet the
British authorities admitted that in the past municipal councils
had made several small grants for charitable purposes which
had inadvertently contravened the law. In fact anything that
was believed to boost the enosists' cause was viewed with
contempt by the Cyprus government.

The Greeks however persisted and were ready to exploit
anything that came their way. Thus in December 1944, when
the British forces in Greece intervened decisively against the
Communists, Ploutis Servas denounced British imperialism as
the enemy of the people. In 1945 there was also increased
agitation for the return of the deportees. On 17 January the
locum tenens sent a telegram to London regretting and bitterly

resenting the reply of Clement Attlee, the deputy Prime Minister, concerning the status of Cyprus and stating that nothing short of union with Greece would satisfy. The Greeks explained on many occasions that they wished to live under their poor national home and not in the luxurious mansion of the British Empire.

Much excitement, recrimination and ill-feeling was caused by several incidents in 1945. The most important, the Lefkoniko incident of 25 March, attracted much attention in the House of Commons and following probing questions from Creech-Jones, T.E.N. Driberg, Thomas Fraser, D.N. Pritt and Vernon Bartlett on 18 April, Emrys-Evans, the Under-Secretary of State for Dominion Affairs, made the following statement:

> Processions and meetings took place in many parts of Cyprus on 25 March in celebration of Greek Independence Day and all applications for permits for meetings and processions were granted by the Government. At one of these meetings in Lefkoniko village, a dispute took place between opposing political parties. A procession was then formed by one of the parties for which no permit had been sought or issued. A Cypriot police sergeant, fearing a more serious clash between the parties, intervened and repeatedly called on the procession to disperse. The demonstrators failed to do so and the police sergeant eventually called on two Cypriot police constables, who had joined him, to open fire, with the result that a man and a boy were killed and fourteen other persons injured, of whom five were admitted to hospital.[10]

The dispute was not in fact between opposing political parties. The higher school of Lefkoniko applied for and was granted a permit on behalf of all parties and all were invited to meet at the church. The only dispute was over the choice of speaker following the church service. The leftists, singing national songs, left the church and very peacefully moved towards the main village club Anagnostirion E. Eleftheria (freedom reading room).

The procession was suddenly stopped at the village bridge which was directly opposite the right-wing PEK offices and only a short distance from its destination. The police, a Greek sergeant named Patsalides and two constables, Zambas a

Greek and Mukeren a Turk, both armed, ordered the procession to stop and disperse. The organizers refused to disperse, explaining that a permit had been issued and that they were only a few minutes away from their destination where the arranged celebrations were to take place. Unprovoked, the police then opened fire, killing a 28-year-old man, a boy of 11, injuring five seriously, of whom a man of around 45 died several weeks later, and slightly injuring six others.

The governor, 'in the interest of the maintenance of public order', decided to place restrictions on the publication in the Press from 26 to 28 March of reports and comments on the Lefkoniko disturbance pending the opening of a commission of enquiry appointed on the evening of 25 March. It consisted of R.A. Godwin-Austin, M.C. Melisas and M. Zekia.

Although the police action was criticized very strongly in the House of Commons, the Cyprus government never published the findings of the commission. At a Colonial Office meeting on 31 October, attended by Sir Charles Woolley, it was decided that the report should not be published and that the police sergeant should not be prosecuted.

An editorial in the *Manchester Guardian* of 27 April declared that a fresh grievance was given to a people already desperately prone to discover grievances against British rule. Percy Arnold, who evidently had considerable personal knowledge of how affairs were run in Cyprus, remarked that 'government by the clique once again got away with it but government by an alien clique with absolute powers had sunk a little deeper into contempt'. Juxon Barton of the Colonial Office recorded on 5 April that the Lefkoniko disturbances 'were disorders, but not "disorders" in the usual sense of that term'.

In fact the credibility of the administration was made even lower by this incident.

The situation in the early months of 1945 was serious. A telegram by the governor to the Colonial Secretary on 31 March was indicative of the troubled situation. Sir Charles Woolley outlined several factors which caused him great concern. Firstly, he believed that with the end of the war and the subsequent demobilization of the Cypriot troops, 'subversive agitation will enter a more serious phase'. Secondly, the governor feared the bitter reaction caused by the

Lefkoniko disturbances. He believed that Cypriot leaders would seek to make capital out of this indignation against the police by renewing their attempts to unite all the parties against the government.

In these circumstances the governor concluded that all grievances which tended to unite the parties should be eliminated. Thus all possible diversions should be created so as to concentrate the attention of the public on local affairs rather than nationalist politics.

Problems on the political front were however overshadowed by economic ones. Labour relations and the rising cost of living were thorny issues for the authorities. Cyprus suffered considerable economic disturbance on account of the war. The mines, for example, lost their principal market, Germany, and lack of shipping and the contraction of world markets affected other industries.

On 23 February 1940 a strike of electricians and mechanics employed in the public works department workshops at Nicosia began. The strike was preceded by the submission of a memorandum demanding higher wages, shorter hours and improved conditions to which a reply was requested within three days. Although the government conceded some demands the major ones were not accepted. On 7 March the government received a memorandum from the trade unions of Nicosia intimating that unless the strike was satisfactorily settled by the following day a general strike was inevitable. On 9 March around 2,000 trade unionists struck in four urban centres. However, the attempt at a general strike was limited to 24 hours.

Meanwhile, on 29 February, part of the labour force engaged on relief work in Nicosia left their employment and endeavoured, early in the morning, to demonstrate at the district commissioner's office. They were prevented by the police and 40 were arrested of whom ten were subsequently released. The remainder were brought before the courts. The charges against four were withdrawn but the others, for the sake of their jobs, pleaded guilty and after being cautioned they were discharged. 'Instead of bread – beatings and imprisonment' was the headline in the Greek London-based newspaper *Vema*.

The trade unions of Nicosia sent a telegram to Ernest Bevin, Minister of Labour and National Service, on 10 June indicating that a strike had been declared among the technical and telephone staff employed by the Cable and Wireless Company. The unions appealed for his intervention. However, on that day Italy declared war on Britain and France, and Bevin was unable to help. The workers were locked out and their demands were not met.

Protests, processions and demonstrations continued right through the 1940s. In 1942 alone there were approximately 30 industrial disputes. In December workmen employed by the government on defence and other work in Nicosia held a ten-day strike for higher pay. The workers pointed out that the cost of living index had risen to 246 from its August 1939 base of 100. Following the strike seven trade unionists were sent to prison for having threatened the life of a blackleg.

The same pattern was repeated in 1943. At a meeting organized on 22 August by the Pan-Cypriot Trade Unions Committee (PSE) (under which the union movement was finally united in 1940) it was decided to call a 24-hour general strike several days later as a protest against the failure of the government to take any effective steps to reduce the cost of living. After consultation between the union leaders and the government the strike was later called off in relation to men employed on defence work and essential services, for whom a ten-minute halt was substituted. The strike on 27 August was by no means universal and there were no disorders.

A 24-hour general strike proclaimed for 25 October as a protest once more against the rising cost of living had more success, especially in urban areas. Processions were held in Nicosia, Limassol and Larnaca. Since a permit was not granted those processions were contrary to the law of 1932, and 8 persons were arrested in Nicosia, 16 in Larnaca and 12 in Limassol; they were fined, sentenced to terms of imprisonment, cautioned or had their sentences postponed. Ploutis Servas was fined £20 in Limassol.

Towards the end of the year the government invited the trade unions to provide representatives on all advisory boards appointed to deal with the cost of living. The basic food items such as bread, beans, olives and cheese had risen (comparing

1939 and 1942) by around 150 per cent (taking a rough average of the four items), but wages had risen only by approximately 80 per cent. There was also the gnawing problem of rural indebtedness. The peasant was simply the slave of the money-lender (interest lover or *tokogliftes*), obliged to buy seeds and other essentials from him at the highest price and to sell produce to him at the lowest. (Despite this admittedly bad state of the economy, Winston Churchill reassured the House of Commons on 10 February 1943 that the Cypriots had never been so prosperous. Indeed during his third visit to Cyprus on 31 January he cautioned the islanders not to cast away their money too improvidently but to keep it for rainy days.)

The battered Cypriot economy prompted the trade unions and the municipalities of Limassol and Famagusta, where AKEL was in office, to refuse to co-operate with the government on the cost of living problem unless the government agreed in advance to accept the findings of the committees set up to deal with the cost of living. The authorities refused on the ground that it would have been inconsistent with the responsibilities of the government to the people. The same two municipalities also declined to co-operate in a scheme to regulate the marketing of perishable produce which had received the support of the producers, on the grounds that such control should have been extended to necessities which were more important and that popularly elected bodies should be given a greater say on such matters.

The year 1944 also witnessed the same pattern of strikes. On 1 March about 1,800 government labourers and craftsmen, mainly employed on military projects, struck for an increase in wages. On 13 March they were joined by 5,000 men who struck in sympathy for one day, thus bringing military and government works almost completely to a standstill. Apart from demonstrations on 19 March in the towns of Larnaca and Famagusta, where it was necessary for the police to use batons and fire-hoses to disperse the crowd, there was no disorder and there were no prosecutions. However, the so-called 'labourers' strike' ended on 24 May and the men returned to work early next morning following an assurance, given on 12 May, that the government would carry out an enquiry into the relation between wages and the cost of living, and would take into account all available evidence, including the figures which had recently been communicated to the authorities by the trade unions.

During the stoppage the government had argued that conditions and wages were fair, and that strikes against the government, especially in wartime, were 'immoral'. It was further pointed out that the strikes were 'crippling the allied war effort'. Less than 1,500 labourers prejudicing the war effort was unheard of even in worse times! The authorities asked for the strike to be called off so as to prevent the recourse to 'strike-breaking with all its unpleasant consequences'. As the strike dragged on the forces of the right sided with the government. In his reminiscences Percy Arnold recalls: 'Gradually the Right came to an appreciation that strikes in wartime were wicked, that all strikes are undesirable, and strikes against the Government, being a challenge to law and order, were especially undesirable; so, as the strike dragged on, the Right forgot the justice of the strike which had been so clear to them at the beginning and only the Left continued openly to sympathize with the strikers.'[11]

During another strike at a Limassol factory, hand grenades were thrown at the houses of some of its key employees. The government immediately decided to call up a number of special constables to assist the regular police in preserving order. These were enrolled between 5 and 8 April, but the authorities were confronted with a demand that equal numbers should be chosen from all sections of the community. When this and other requests were refused the retort was 'absenteeism', according to the Colonial Secretary who informed the House of Commons on 3 May 1944.

In August a dispute arose between the Hellenic Company of Chemical Products and Manures Ltd and the Kalavasos Miners' Union. A strike followed and it was not terminated until the following April when the conclusions of the board of inquiry were accepted by both sides. At times the conciliation measures of the government were very successful.

Riots concerning the pay of soldiers also took place in 1944. At Famagusta on 29 June and Nicosia on 3 and 24 July complaint was made regarding the allowances payable to soldiers' families and the distribution of clothing and other controlled supplies. The authorities at Nicosia accepted a committee representing soldiers' wives to discuss such matters on 28 July. The government was forced to make major concessions.

9   1945-1949: Old Problems, New Realities

There was great unrest in the immediate post-war years. Military expenditure had decreased considerably; the intensive strategic development of the island had not yet begun; the ten-year development programme was only in its initial stages and competitors were returning to markets which during the war had provided easy outlets for Cypriot produce, such as tobacco, vincs and carobs. During the war, owing to inflation and to shortages of many essentials required by the peasants, rural debts were reduced to £1,000,000. After 1946 however such debts had increased rapidly and by 1949 they had reached the pre-war level of £3,000,000. Yet the government made only half-hearted attempts, through the Debt Settlement Board, to review these debts and always hesitated to control supplies and prices and to combat profiteering and the black market. On the whole the British record in the 20 years following the disturbances of 1931 was one of short-sightedness and utter neglect.

Measures to alleviate poverty were introduced in the 1940s. From 1941 to March 1946 Cyprus received free grants under the Colonial Development and Welfare Act of May 1940 totalling £720,000, to be spent mainly on agriculture and irrigation, medical and education services.

On 23 October 1946 Arthur Creech Jones, the Colonial Secretary, promised, amongst other things, that the government would press on with the programme of economic development and social welfare initiated during the last few years. Up to the end of 1948 a sum of £1,178,036 had been spent on development projects, notably – in a period marked by acute shortages of essential imported materials and frequent lack of skilled labour – on irrigation. Expenditure was restricted to projects classified in the published programme as of first priority. The ten-year programme of development was estimated to cost £6,000,000 while the cost of a separate scheme to provide the whole island with electric light was estimated at £3,350,000. It was hoped to raise revenue from local loans, since bank deposits amounted to £11,500,000.

However, it was not enough. The end of the war not only brought the soldiers home but put a halt to military employment. Thousands became unemployed and there were no unemployment benefits, old age pensions or other welfare benefits. If no work was available only private charity could save them from starvation. Furthermore, taxation was high and unjust and the cost of living soared. Above all, as Sir Charles Woolley, the governor, wrote in 1945, 'chronic indebtedness and the stranglehold of the moneylender were a millstone round the farmer's neck', and agriculture was neglected.

Education suffered the same fate. The figures below show the gravity of the situation:

		Attending
Number of children of elementary school age –	77,000	46,926
Number of children of secondary school age –	60,000	4,784

The low attendances, 61 per cent and 8 per cent respectively, show that the Cypriot young, as in the England of Dickens's *Oliver Twist*, had to find work and receive next to nothing or toil in the fields for ten to fifteen hours a day to supplement the meagre family income. The alternative was starvation for most peasant families. The figures above relate to 1938 and 1939; for several years during and after the war they were even worse, though the trend was reversed in the 1950s and 1960s. Understandably therefore the 1940s were marked by strikes, demonstrations, imprisonments and fines, and the eruption of right- and left-wing emnity resulted in violence.

The chief nationalist organizations were the Ethnarchic Council and the Cyprus National Party (KEK), formed in 1931. The Pan-Agrarian Union of Cyprus (PEK), though a professional association, was intensely political and on the side of the right-wing forces. It advocated a rural development programme, crop insurance and an expanded medical and educational programme for farmers. The Confederation of Cypriot Workers (the formal organization of the 'new' trade unions – SEK) was founded in 1943. On the other hand,

AKEL, by far the best organized party and the only one with a constructive programme, and PEO (Pan-Cyprian Federation of Labour representing the 'old' trade unions) belonged to the forces of the left. Towards the end of the 1940s there were 34 Greek political parties of which 20 were right-wing, 12 left-wing and two combined; there were also three Turkish parties, making 37 political parties in an island whose population in 1949 was only 475,886.

The relatively young KKK (Communist Party of Cyprus) was declared unlawful and went underground on 16 August 1933. The progressive party of the working people, AKEL, was formally founded on 14 April 1941 at a private meeting in a taverna at Skarinou, a village half-way between Nicosia and Limassol, by the remaining hard-core Communists and a group of leftist intellectuals. Among those who attended were some intellectual idealists and a few politicians previously associated with outlawed nationalist movements, who hoped to win supporters in the forthcoming municipal elections by espousing the workers' cause. Two of them, George Vasiliades, an advocate and later chief justice of the Cypriot supreme court, and Zenon Rossides, also a lawyer and later Ambassador to the UN and the USA, were elected to a small central committee.

The formation of AKEL was ridiculed in newspapers unsympathetic to the labour cause and was completely overshadowed by the war and the invasion and subsequent occupation of Greece. Several months later Akelists sought permission for a second meeting to exchange views concerning their position in view of the new circumstances created by the war and also to discuss questions of national policy.

The Pan-Cyprian meeting on 5 October at the Rialto Theatre, Limassol, was to be AKEL's first party congress. The gathering was a representative one. The delegates were trade unionists, representatives of the rural communities and organizations, peasants, representatives of the professions – lawyers, doctors, journalists – and members of cultural associations. The first disciplined political party in ten years was thus born. Ploutis Servas became its general secretary and immediately defined the aims of the party.

AKEL's programme was support of the war, the granting of

political and civic freedom, satisfaction of the immediate and pressing economic demands, the abrogation of the restrictive decrees, the lifting of the ban on meetings and public demonstrations, the restoration of the right to teach Greek and Turkish history in schools, free education of the people according to their religion and nationality, and compulsory education up to the age of 14 which would include two years of secondary schooling, the settlement of the tribute issue, the abolition of monopolies and, finally, national rehabilitation after the war.

The party disseminated political propaganda all over the island and its central committee had a decisive influence on the trade union movement. There was considerable overlapping of membership between AKEL and the trade unions as there is in the membership of the British Labour party and trade unions; but in Cyprus this interlocking was regarded by the island's rulers as sinful and as a seditious conspiracy.

Cyprus had been without an archbishop since the death of Kyrillos III on 16 November 1933. The first elections since 1916 were held in 1947. A new archbishop was elected and the Church question thus finally settled.

The laws passed in 1937 dealt a heavy blow to the autocephalous Church of the island. These illiberal laws were denounced as degrading to the whole Hellenic world. By February 1939 however a draft bill was ready, designed to ensure that an election should take place. The bill was drawn up by N. Paschalis, the Solicitor-General, an expert on Orthodox ecclesiastical law. It was designed to force the *locum tenens* to form a synod and hold an election, or failing this to enable the governor to initiate action for the purpose on receipt of petitions from the people. The Church replied that under such conditions it was unable to elect an archbishop. In fact the *locum tenens* had earlier threatened that if such legislation were passed against his will he would create a 'terrible schism' and 'horrible tempest' in Cyprus which would throw all ecclesiastical affairs into complete confusion.

The outbreak of the war caused the whole question to be shelved. Nevertheless, some pressure on the government to repeal the laws still persisted. In 1943 the Pan-Cyprian Organization of Religious Orthodox Institutions demanded that the laws of 1937 should be repealed. In London P. Emrys-Evans, the Under-Secretary of State for Dominion Affairs, declared on 16 February 1944 that the time had not yet come to review them.

The advent of the Labour government in Britain in 1945 was received with great enthusiasm. The announcement of Creech Jones on 23 October 1946 provided a ray of hope. He stated that 'there seems little doubt that the three local laws enacted in 1937 with the object of controlling certain aspects of the election of a new Archbishop had impeded the settlement of this problem'. The repeal was effected by Law No. 20 of late October 1946.

Elections in Cyprus followed in 1947. The obvious winner was Leontios Leontiou, but he repeatedly declared to his supporters that he would not accept nomination as archbishop. On 27 April he resigned all his offices and announced his intention of retiring to a monastery on Mount Athos. Yet on the following day he yielded to the persuasion of the representative of the Oecumenical Patriarchate of Constantinople, Ioakim, Bishop of Derkon, who had come to complete the quorum of bishops, and withdrew his resignation. By now the left was solidly behind Leontios.

At the primary election on 4 May his supporters won an overwhelming victory and the electoral college so chosen duly gave him, on 20 June, 58 votes. Porphirios, Archbishop of Sinai, received 17 and Gregorios, abbot of Maheras, one. Leontios again refused to accept election but again yielded to the urgent appeal of the patriarchal representative. The aged Bishop of Kyrenia, always considered 'a pillar of the right wing', thereupon shouted 'I will not enthrone you and I will not recognize you'. But he also was eventually persuaded to withdraw his opposition, so that the electoral synod was able to announce that Bishop Leontios of Paphos had been unanimously elected archbishop.

The Bishop of Kyrenia officiated at his enthronement and Leontios became archbishop on 20 June. However, being a chronic diabetic he died of typhus on 26 July. Although it is true that he had unusual influence over AKEL, Lord Winster's description of him, in the journal *United Empire*, as 'a man of the extreme left' is grossly misleading. He was a leader of great tolerance, a sincere priest and a true Christian, and was always ready to listen to different points of view; but he had always been a right-wing enosist and died as such.

Thus despite the support he had received from the left, the new archbishop immediately signalized his appointment by rejecting an invitation from the Patriarch of Moscow for him or his delegate to represent the Church of Cyprus at a forthcoming conference of all the Orthodox Churches in the Russian capital. It was, he said, the prerogative of the Oecumenical Patriarch of Constantinople to convene such a conference.

Furthermore, following the governor's proclamation on 9 July 1947 that nominations were being invited for a consultative assembly, His Beatitude immediately issued a statement that the governor's proclamation was 'hostile to the people of Cyprus, and we shall do everything in our power to thwart its objectives'. The Ethnarchic Council boycotted the assembly and, as Lord Winster wrote, 'there was no cooperation whatsoever'. He was at pains to explain both before his arrival in Cyprus and after his departure that the elections for an archbishop should have waited until a consultative assembly was in existence, since 'agreeing to bring a powerful opponent into the field before we proceeded with our plans was dangerous and contrary to the British spirit'.

The archbishop in a widely circulated counter-proclamation declared that Britain was offering the Cypriots a knife with which to cut in pieces their own national rights since they were asked to endorse the perpetuation of their enslavement. The composition of the proposed assembly, he said, 'was based on anti-democratic and fascist prototypes and thus dealt a mortal blow to democratic conceptions'. He emphasized that the people would be united in continuing their lawful struggle and would thus seal their ears to the governor's proclamation.

This was his last political act. A second election followed in October. AKEL decided to oppose the aged Bishop of Kyrenia and to support an outsider, the Bishop of Derkon, who had earlier been the patriarchal representative at the election of Leontios. The veteran nationalist campaigner however defeated the latter by 40 votes to 26 and thus became Makarios II, Myriantheus.

With the help of some energetic disciples, among whom the

best known was Xenophon Koumparides, he took sole command of the nationalist forces. The plebiscite of January 1950 represented the culminating achievement of his career. He died on 28 June 1950 and was succeeded by the 37-year-old Makarios III, Moskou, Bishop of Kition since 13 June 1948.

Although the Church question was finally settled the post-war years witnessed not only the normal demands but new ones. On 30 May 1945 Petros Voulgaris, the Greek Premier, in an introductory address to the committee of foreign affairs, expounded the theory that the minimum Hellenic claims after the war came under the headings of 'justice and security' and that justice required that the territories inhabited by Greeks should be handed over to Greece. He repeated that all Greek islands, no matter how far away, should return to the embrace of their motherland. Greek Cypriots who rejoiced when the declaration was made known were further elated when it was learnt that the USA Congressional Record for Thursday 21 June included an appeal (No 4 out of 13) from the Hellenic Right Claims Association of America to all Allied representatives at the San Francisco Conference requesting that Cyprus should be ceded to Greece in exchange for any naval base· on the island which was required for the preservation of peace.

As soon as the war ended Anthony Eden, the British Foreign Secretary, was flooded with telegrams. In May Galatopoulos, the mayor of Paphos, said that the promises of the victors of a free and just world should also be applied to the Cypriots. On 18 July Andreas Fantis, the AKEL general secretary, expressed the belief that Cyprus would be nationally rehabilitated and ceded to mother Greece. In the same month a resolution passed by the Cypriot Brotherhood of Athens also pleaded for such a union.

Ernest Bevin, who succeeded Eden (Labour took over on 26 July 1945), received similar requests. A telegram from the *locum tenens* on 7 September, on the occasion of the meeting of Allied foreign ministers, asked that Britain should cede the island to Greece. On 11 September the Foreign Office informed the Chiefs of Staff that Cyprus might be ceded to Greece on condition that the Greek government granted Britain military rights and bases in Cyprus and also a base and other rights on the Greek mainland or in the islands.

The meeting at Sir Orme Garton Sargent's room on 14 June 1945 to discuss Greek territorial claims, attended by himself as Deputy Under-Secretary of State for Foreign Affairs and Sir Reginald Leeper (British ambassador to a great variety of Greek 'governments' in the Middle East, Italy, and Athens from March 1943 to March 1946), was highly important. Leeper expressed the hope that if the British government intended taking any action to meet Greek desires it should do so instantly and not wait until it had the appearance of giving in to agitation. In fact he strongly recommended the cession of Cyprus at that time and was very disappointed at the outcome.

On 5 September a draft memorandum by Sargent gave in detail the arguments in favour of such a cession. In brief these were: we ought to; it would strengthen our position in Greece, and we stand to lose nothing.

The reply from the Chiefs of Staff to the Foreign Office initiative contained two main points. Firstly, the military advantages of maintaining the status quo considerably outweighed the advantages of accepting the suggestions contained in the letter; and secondly, Britain should therefore retain her sovereignty over Cyprus even at the risk of increased agitation in the island and of unfavourable reaction in Greece.

'Good. We are not without friends,' was the Colonial Office remark on 17 September. On the same day Archbishop Damaskinos, the Regent of Greece, discussed this problem with Bevin. His Beatitude felt that the matter was bound to be settled sooner or later and urged that an early settlement would give added prestige to the British government. Bevin replied that 'the possibility of change is a strong one although the full consequences of such a cession must be worked out and a hurried decision should not be taken'.

Damaskinos made it clear that he would have to make some reference to this subject on his return to Greece, and it was subsequently agreed that he would confine himself to a declaration authorized by the Foreign Office stating that although the question of Cyprus was mentioned no conclusion was reached owing to the short time at the regent's disposal; but that the problem would be further examined in due course. (At his interview with Sir O.G. Sargent on 8 September the regent stated that if Cyprus were ceded to Greece Britain would be granted bases not merely in Cyprus but wherever was needed on Greek territory in order to strengthen its position in the eastern Mediterranean.)

It can be deduced that the Foreign Office was willing to reconsider its position over Cyprus, but the Colonial Office officials were adamant that such a move should not materialize. An exchange of letters between the Colonial and Foreign Secretaries throws further light on the divergence of opinion between the two departments. G.H. Hall writing on 18 September 1945 pleaded against the contemplated cession of Cyprus to Greece. Replying on 21 September, Bevin explained that he was not persuaded that the arguments in favour of the retention of Cyprus were sound, nor did he find the paper produced by the Chiefs of Staff convincing. Although he was not in favour of making any declaration at that moment in favour of either cession or retention, he expressed the belief that when several other problems, such as the future of the Dodecanese, were cleared up, the whole question would have to be considered by the Cabinet.

Lightning strikes at the hospitals of Nicosia, Limassol and Famagusta in June 1945 led to a temporary curtailment of hospital services. There were also demonstrations against further service overseas and for the expedition of demobilization. The strength of the Cyprus forces at the end of the war (31 May 1945) was as follows:

	Cyprus Regiment	Cyprus Volunteer Force
Abroad	6,846	430
In Cyprus	1,967	844
	8,813	1,274

In addition there were Cypriots, both men and women, in the British Army and RAF, and a few in the Royal Navy.

On 8 October 1945 Indian troops were called to the Famagusta transit camp to get two reluctant Cypriot companies (due to be taken to either Syria or Palestine) aboard a transporter. (Four days earlier, under the same conditions, embarkation had been completed without incident.) During the chaos shots were fired, killing one Cypriot sergeant and wounding six privates and one Indian soldier.

The authorities explained that the first shots came from 'soft-nosed pistol bullets fired by certain persons in the crowd and not by the Indian troops who were not armed with such pistols nor with ammunition of that type'. In fact the officer in charge ordered the Indian detachment to fix their bayonets and advance to disperse the crowd. The death of sergeant Takis Kythreotis produced quite a stir in the island. Protests flowed into the governor from all quarters and many organizations held special meetings to consider the incident and register their disapproval. A military court later convicted the soldiers of refusing to obey orders. The local press and other commentators repudiated the official view that 'soft-nosed pistol bullets' were fired from the crowd. The findings of the enquiry into the incident were not published.

The Cypriots, already smarting over the Lefkoniko affair of 25 March (see page 189) and the balking of their national dreams, were rightly aggrieved over the Famagusta shooting. Such occurrences continued unabated and were slowly undermining the people's confidence in British justice.

The rift between the government and the governed was widened even further by the PSE (Pan-Cyprian Trade Unions Committee) trial of 1945-6. With a total membership of around 15,000 PSE and its leader Andreas Ziartides had considerable influence in Cypriot affairs. The presiding judge himself stated that it was the 'highest directive body and was entrusted with the leadership and coordination of the activities of all the trade unions throughout Cyprus'. By 1944 there were 122 registered trade unions and at the Pan-Cyprian conference of trade unionists held in September 1944 435 delegates representing 13,500 members attended. The government certainly knew of its existence since in January 1945 it afforded every facility to Ziartides and Servas to leave the island and represent Cyprus at the London conference of world trade unions.

L.J. Solley, a lawyer and Labour MP for Thurrock, told the House of Commons on 5 March 1946 that the trial was 'unjust and political' and that 'the true facts will shock the conscience of every true democrat'. He went on:

> The war being over, apparently the Colonial Office thought the time was ripe to clamp down on these trade union and labour activities and go back to their despotism of 1931. They raided the offices of this Greek T.U.C. and obtained a

certain amount of literature, which was no more lurid or dull than that which can be bought in England in any Socialist bookshop. They then began this prosecution. . . . It is a fantastic state of affairs when Labour rules at Westminster, and Socialism is a crime, according to the law of Cyprus.[1]

The case was listed as Rex v Ziartides *et al*, Nicosia assize court, 17 December 1945; in other words the government versus the entire Cyprus TUC composed of 18 persons. The court was formed by three appointed judges sitting alone, since there was no provision of trial by jury. A Colonial Office minute dated 13 March 1946 stated that 'this is the Ottoman form of judicial procedure'; but this was Cyprus, 67 years after its occupation by Great Britain.

Some of the offences against PSE were as follows:

unlawfully conspiring to overthrow the island's constitution; conspiring to overthrow by violence the established government;
attempting to bring into hatred the lawful government; and attempting to excite disaffection against the government.

The substance of the 17 counts, under various sections of the Cyprus Criminal Code law 1928 to 1944, was that the accused were engaged in publicizing the classic works of socialism: that they were carrying out a class struggle. Stelios Pavlides (Attorney-General), Kriton Tornaritis (Solicitor-General), G.N. Chryssafinis and C. Myrianthi appeared for the Crown. The defence was composed of John Clerides, P. Ioannides, Potamitis and Saveriades. The defence claimed that much of the propaganda to which the prosecution took exception was quotations from Marxist classics. An extract from an exchange of questions and answers between Mr Cox, the president of the court, and the Solicitor-General will suffice to illustrate the offence:

President: Is Marxist theory a crime?
Solicitor-General: According to Cyprus law, yes.
President: Is the possession of Marxist books a crime?
Solicitor-General: Yes.

The defence denied all charges. The trial began on 17 December 1945 and ended on 21 January 1946. These shameful days brought out into the open once more the naked despotism that had prevailed in Cyprus since 1931. Twelve of the accused were sentenced to 18 months' imprisonment and the other six to 12 months. PSE was found to be an illegal organization, not because it was a trade union body but because it was a conspiracy advocating the overthrow of the government. It was dissolved but was succeeded by PEO (Pan-Cyprian Federation of Labour) in 1946. Another Colonial Office minute dated 11 March 1946 explained that 'by English standards the sentences seem severe'.

And so they were. The government was denounced as Fascist and anti-working class and progressive forces in both Cyprus and Britain vowed to fight for the release of the trade union leaders. Thanks to their activities, especially those of the British trade union movement, the colonial government was forced to release all of them within nine months of their imprisonment. The sentencing of the accused was followed by a strike on 22 January as a protest against 'unlawful brutality'. During a so-called 'week of protest' (September 1946) over 700 meetings were held demanding the annulment of the harsh laws and the release of the prisoners.

The 18 PSE leaders were originally charged in police stations on 15 June 1945 with conspiring to overthrow the government of Cyprus by revolution, but were released on bail of £1,000 each. They were again charged, and released, by the Nicosia court in August. The court committed them to be tried at the Nicosia assizes. The assize court granted leave of appeal which was subsequently refused by Sir Edward Jackson, the Chief Justice.

General feelings of unrest in Cyprus were shared by British trade unionists and even by senior government officials. Thus at a meeting in the Secretary of State's room on 23 November 1945 the Secretary of State said that there was much feeling in the UK that actions taken so far against PSE were unnecessarily harsh. The meeting took place several weeks before the PSE trial. Sir Charles Woolley, the governor, replied that the PSE was the nucleus of Communism and *enosis* and sought to use the trade unions for seditious aims. He also explained that if action had not been taken against them he had little doubt that something in the nature of 'a minor revolution would have taken place'. Woolley had already informed Whitehall by telegram on 31 March that everything possible should be done not only to eliminate the authentic grievances which tended to unite the parties but to create diversions to concentrate the attention of the public on local affairs rather than on nationalist politics. Arthur Creech Jones, the Colonial Secretary, stated on 23 October 1946 that the government had reviewed its policy on Cyprus. He promised four 'constructive' policies:

1 A more liberal and progressive regime would be established in the internal affairs of the island.

2 The government would press on vigorously the economic programme of development and social welfare which had already been 'successfully initiated'. The ten-year development plan was the government's 'promised messiah'.

3 The three local laws of 1937 concerning the election of a new archbishop would be repealed (see page 199).

4 Those exiled following the disturbances of 1931 would be allowed to return.

The minister also expressed the hope that these measures 'would inaugurate a new and happier era' in the relations between Britain and the island's inhabitants. On the following day the Ethnarchic Council cabled to Whitehall rejecting categorically any solution of the Cyprus problem which did not provide union with Greece.

The Greek parties of the island urged the formation of a united front to continue the struggle for *enosis*. On 1 December, at a mass meeting of over 20,000 Cypriots, a resolution demanding *enosis* was passed in connection with the proposal to raise the Cyprus question at the United Nations. The meeting was organized by the left and was not attended by right-wing parties.

Some excitement was provided by the municipal elections. Those of 21 March 1943 returned a middle-class enosist mayor in Nicosia whilst AKEL had won the mayor's seat and a majority in the municipal councils in the two leading ports of the island, Limassol and Famagusta. Many observers felt that this was an electoral freak which could never be repeated. These polls were also significant since undertakings were freely given by candidates to advance the cause of *enosis*.

The following elections were on 26 May 1946. They were contested by the right-wing National Front and by the left-wing National Co-operation (or National Unity) Front, whose nucleus was AKEL. The swing to the left continued. AKEL not only retained its hold on Limassol and Famagusta but won Nicosia and all but two of the principal towns.

A series of protests was soon evoked by the uprooting of the Jews following the war. On 15 May it was stated in the House of Commons that Cyprus might take around 13,000 of the 100,000 Jewish refugees to settle in holdings. The famous Palestine Report was greeted with great dismay by the Cypriots. In August it was decided to transfer to a detention camp near Famagusta the Jewish refugees from Europe who were then arriving illegally in Palestine in considerable numbers.

This inspired an immediate declaration from the town's mayor that the people were being led to suspect an attempt 'to weaken the Greek majority by an influx of foreigners'. Following an official statement that the refugees would not be allowed to become residents of Cyprus, the Limassol mayor nevertheless submitted a demand to the governor that their transfer to the island should be stopped, since it was widely believed that their provisioning was leading to a shortage of supplies and an increase in prices, causing a considerable hardening of Cypriot opinion. In fact 51,000 Jewish immigrants passed through the Cyprus detention camps of Karaolos and Xylotymbou during their two and a half years' existence.

During the discussions on the Burma constitution in the Commons on 20 December, Clement Attlee, the Prime Minister, said 'we do not desire to retain within the Commonwealth and Empire any unwilling peoples'. What about us? the Cypriots claimed. In the same debate Winston Churchill, a politician much revered in Cyprus, complained that: 'The British Empire seems to be running off almost as fast as the American Loan. The steady and remorseless process of divesting ourselves of what has been gained by so many generations of toil, administration and sacrifice continues.'[2]

Yet as Prime Minister during the war Churchill repeatedly paid tribute to the gallant Cypriots and in the course of his early parliamentary career he did more than most in pinpointing the Cypriot grievances caused by the tribute and British maladministration. 'Cyprus has played its part so well,' he told the Commons on 11 February 1943.

It was against this background that a national delegation led by Leontios Leontiou and consisting of Zenon Rossides representing the Ethnarchic Council, J. Clerides, mayor of Nicosia, representing the left-wing National Co-operation Front, and D.N. Demetriou, chairman of the chamber of commerce, representing the right-wing National Front, arrived in London at the end of December to put their case for union with Greece. The delegation travelled by way of Athens, arriving there on 16 November 1946 and receiving expressions of deep sympathy from the public and total support from the mass media. They met the most important Greek political leaders and were received by the king on 4 December. However, when Kouloumvakis, a populist Member of Parliament, proposed a reading of the delegation's resolution (for the union of Cyprus to Greece) to Parliament on 28 November the proposal was rejected by the president. Furthermore, the government refused permission to the Cypriot organizations of Athens to hold a rally on 1 December. Later the delegation cabled a request to Tsaldaris, the Greek Prime Minister, in New York to submit their claim officially to the British Foreign Secretary.

While British sympathizers expressed doubts as to whether union was desirable at that particular moment when Greece's internal politics were in such turmoil (the civil war of 1946-9, which followed the German occupation, brought further devastation to the country), the delegation nevertheless submitted a memorandum at its interview with Creech Jones on 7 February 1947, stating that the island and its people were in religion, language, tradition and national conscience staunchly and immutably Greek, and therefore rejecting the constitutional reforms and economic proposals announced the previous October. It was also emphasized that the rights of the Turkish minority would be fully safeguarded and arrangements would no doubt be made with the Greek government to ensure British defence interests in the eastern Mediterranean.

The minister replied that no change in the status of the island was contemplated. He then asked them to co-operate with the authorities in implementing his earlier proposals. He also urged them to ask for self-government, which would be sympathetically considered by the British government, instead of union. The national delegation refused to discuss anything other than union.

The Moslem position was made clear by KATAK – the Association of the Turkish Minority in Cyprus. It not only opposed the cession of Cyprus to Greece but demanded that if Britain decided to relinquish sovereignty the island should go back to Turkey, its previous suzerain and nearest neighbour, which was therefore in a much better position to defend it. KATAK also disapproved of the existing British administration because the island's Turks were not only suffering under the illiberal laws passed after 1931 but were discriminated against in ecclesiastical and educational affairs.

At a meeting of the major parties presided over by the Bishop of Kyrenia on 16 January 1947, it was decided that the ultimate purpose was still *enosis* and therefore the collection of money for the national struggle should be continued. Even though the national delegation failed, the unity of action was seen as a step forward. A demonstration followed. On 16 February the Bishop of Kyrenia (now in Cyprus following his exile) addressed a very large crowd in the capital. There was no disorder but the offer of constitutional liberties was rejected and resolutions were passed protesting against the refusal of the British government to cede the island to Greece and against the 'trampling of the weak by the strong'.

Moreover the Ethnarchic Council and the political parties gave instructions for the boycotting of the new governor on his arrival. However, most of the Turkish organizations arranged to welcome him on his way from the airport to Government House and also telegraphed to the Prime Minister and Colonial Secretary protesting against the claim of the Ethnarchic Council to speak for all the people of Cyprus.

The threatened boycott of Lord Winster was actually carried out. When the new governor arrived on 27 March the island's

Christian inhabitants kept their Hellenic flags at full mast (25 March is celebrated as Greek Independence Day), and on the following day the Greek notables invited to a reception to meet him absented themselves on the instructions of the Ethnarchic Council, which had already sent to Lord Winster a memorandum which spoke of 'an enslaved people struggling for self-determination'. He was thus welcomed only by the British officials and by the Turks.

Of the Greeks only government officials attended the reception. Among the absentees were the Bishop of Kyrenia, J. Clerides and four members of the advisory council. Two days later the four members were bluntly informed that their services were no longer required and that they would not be received at the forthcoming meeting of the council to which they had accepted invitations. The new governor saw their absence not only as a personal snub but more so as an insult to the king. Lord Winster explained his actions to the Secretary of State for the Colonies in a secret telegram dated 1 April 1947.

The so-called 'removal of the four' was interpreted by many commentators as an 'unhappy event'. The *Times* correspondent wrote that instead of improving the prospects of co-operation between the government and the irreconcilable leaders of the movement for union with Greece, they were worsened.

After this sad beginning Lord Winster, in a message to the people of Cyprus on 6 April, reaffirmed the statement made on 11 December 1946 by the Colonial Secretary that there would be no change in the status of the island. The inhabitants were promised not only economic prosperity but the establishment of a liberal and progressive regime in internal affairs.

As expected the reaction of the Press was hostile, especially since great hope had been entertained of a sympathetic attitude on the part of the Labour government which was swept to power in 1945. The authorities in Cyprus reacted sharply and on 26 April warned newspaper editors that while the right of commenting on current political affairs would be maintained and respected, they could no longer tolerate the use of the Press for propaganda campaigns and extensive attacks on the government. The editors were further informed that the press laws would be used without hesitation to suspend or suppress any publication.

Following much pressure from several directions, notably the Fabian Colonial Bureau which sent a memorandum on the position of Cyprus to the Colonial Office in June 1946, Creech Jones, as already seen, announced on 23 October that a more liberal and progressive regime would be established. The Cypriots realized that the Constitution would be offered as an irrevocable alternative to *enosis* and therefore its acceptance implied a tacit renunciation of national aims.

On 9 July 1947 Lord Winster sent invitations to various persons and organizations to take part in a consultative assembly which would make recommendations on the form of constitution to be established in order to secure participation by the people of Cyprus in the direction of the internal affairs of the island, due regard being paid to the interests of minorities. The right, headed by the newly elected archbishop, turned down the invitation. The left, after some hesitation and a good deal of deliberation, decided to accept it. In fact the Turkish representatives, the mayors of Nicosia, Limassol, Famagusta and Larnaca, PEO and one Greek member of the Committee of the Co-operative Central Bank accepted the governor's invitation. The other 14 Greeks explained that since their sole political aim was union with Greece they had to decline all such offers and accused the left of assisting towards the national enslavement of the island.

The left replied that through self-government Cyprus could more easily march towards *enosis*. This however was not a particularly convincing reply. In its report of July 1948 the AKEL central committee stated that 'our participation in the consultative assembly was a fundamental mistake'. It went on to give two reasons for its participation: it was so advised by the Communist Party of Great Britain and it failed to realize fully the intentions of Anglo-American imperialism.

The situation was complicated further by the death of Archbishop Leontios Leontiou on 26 July. However, the short intermission was soon over. His successor, Makarios Myriantheus, followed his predecessor's stand by denouncing the government's initiative and calling for a strict abstention from the proposed constituent assembly.

The assembly was finally convoked under the chairmanship of Sir Edward Jackson, but from its first meeting on 1

November there were disagreements as to the interpretation of the terms of reference. The Greeks assumed that they were given the power to submit proposals for a constitution which they would consider to be the best for Cyprus. But as soon as they began to put forward their recommendations they found that the terms of reference were highly restrictive. Jackson ruled out of order any reference to self-government or any attempt to give the elected representatives real executive authority. The deliberations of the assembly were then suspended pending referral of the demands to the Colonial Secretary in London.

The left, aggrieved by such absurd technicalities, explained that they wanted only to be allowed to submit their views on a constitution providing for self-government. They submitted a memorandum on 24 November to the Colonial Secretary requesting a constitution similar to those of Malta or Ceylon providing for:

> a parliament consisting entirely of elected members without appointed or *ex-officio* members;
> elections to be held on the basis of a universal franchise;
> the establishment of a cabinet to act as a central directing body;
> the reservation of certain powers in the hands of the governor; and
> the retention by Whitehall of responsibility for defence and external affairs.

The memorandum contained an undertaking that the cabinet would include a minister for Turkish affairs, to be appointed from among the Turkish Members of Parliament. No reply was received and hence a leftist deputation was despatched to London in February 1948.

Athens also took its stand on *enosis* in 1947. Greek interest in *enosis* had grown since the war. Damaskinos discussed the problem with Ernest Bevin in 1945, as did Sofianopoulos, the Greek Foreign Minister, and King George II in 1946. The king had a conversation with Bevin on 14 September about his plans and fears for the future, and argued that a favourable hint by Britain on the Cypriot problem would have a stabilizing effect on the situation in Greece. Bevin was not particularly encouraging at any of the meetings.

At first the Greeks believed that their sufferings for the cause of freedom would be rewarded by the fulfilment of their territorial claims. The forces of the left, notably the KKE (CPG) and EAM (National Liberation Front), openly agitated for the Cypriots and sent several telegrams to the delegates at the Paris Peace Conference requesting the cession of Cyprus to Greece. On 26-7 May 1945 Zachariades, the KKE leader, insisted in statements to the Paris press that Cyprus and the Dodecanese should decide their own futures. On 5 June the KKE newspaper *Rizospastis* demanded that Cyprus should be ceded to Greece. This prompted all centre or right parties to follow suit. During his interview with the British Foreign Secretary in New York on 12 December 1946 Constantine Tsaldaris, the Greek Prime Minister, emphasized that Communist agitation in Cyprus was on the increase and that patriotic Greeks also had to urge the return of Cyprus in order not to be accused of being traitors.

Eventually all the main political parties came to echo the Communists and on 28 February 1947 the Greek Vouli adopted a historic resolution stating that the moment had arrived for a happy settlement of the sacred national demand for the union of Cyprus with its motherland Greece. Even King Paul asserted, during his interview in the *New York Times* on 28 July 1948, that Greece certainly desired the union of Cyprus with the rest of Greece. He intimated that if it could be arranged under the UN Greece would be prepared to offer, in exchange for Cyprus, further base facilities to Britain or the USA in Crete or elsewhere. In Cyprus the left protested strongly against this suggestion. However, nothing came of the king's offer and it did not provide any basis for future negotiations. Nevertheless the interview caused a great uproar within the Colonial and Foreign Offices.

The miners' strike at Mavrovouni-Xero, in the Solea Valley district, proved to be the most bitter of the three major strikes of 1948. In September 1947 the workers of the Cyprus Mines Corporation decided to demand their basic rights. (The sporadic stoppages of 1943-4, which interfered briefly with the shipping of copper concentrate, resulted in the appointment of a board of enquiry which recommended slightly higher daily rates.)

On 16 December 1947 the demands of the unions were

presented to the CMC management. The six proposals were:

shorter working hours, especially for underground workers;
an increase in daily wage rates;
some changes where work was given to contractors;
some alterations in overtime pay;
public holidays to be increased to thirteen days per year of which five were to be paid for by the employers;
welfare improvements to be speeded up.

The CMC tried to get out of the first meeting by questioning the status of the union. After a further meeting on 7 January 1948 the union leaders were not only ignored but were insulted by R.J. Hendricks, the company's resident director and manager. Four days later, following a meeting of unionists at Mavrovouni, a five-day strike was declared to commence on 13 January.

The company retaliated by sacking around 150 union members, suspending the free milk it had hitherto given to some children and removing from its hospital all those who could walk. On the following day (15 January) the children of Lefka (which was predominantly Turkish) and of Xero missed classes and on the 18th worker demonstrations at both these places unanimously approved the extension of the strike. Hence from a temporary five-day strike it developed into a prolonged one.

The strike developed into a great test of character and strength on both sides. The company used all the available legal and illegal means at its disposal, e.g.:

1   It issued bulletins pleading for the miners to return;

2   It claimed in thousands of leaflets that 'scores of miners' were ready to return to work;

3   It used agents to 'invade' the Solea district to enlist new workers;

4   Hendricks met the rightist newspapers on 12 February and equated the strike with Communism, announcing plans to smash 'this new menace'. The editors gave full coverage to his views.

These new tactics were faced with even greater resistance by the workers. On 3 February the electricians and night-watchmen joined the strike and four days later PEO called a general strike for 10 February. It was to be a protest against the continued government silence, the one-sided stance of the police and the degrading attitude of the CMC.

From 12 February to 3 March the struggle became 'hard and indefinite'. Following two meetings and demonstrations at Lefka and Xero on 15 and 16 February, the workers resolved to fight until final victory was achieved. On 19 February the company sent out notices to quit to most of the leaders and four days later it enlisted 21 strike-breakers or backlegs. On the same day 14 innocent miners were fined for suspicious movement and on 2 March 23 workers were accused of unlawful assembly.

Between 3 March and 9 April there were severe clashes, starting with the so-called 'bloody events of 3 March'. On 10 March Rees-Williams, the Under-Secretary of State for the Colonies, explained the events in this way:

I understand that the events of 3rd March were as follows: At 10.30 a.m. when 12 prospective employees of the Cyprus Mines Corporation were attending the clinic at Mavizovouni mine for a medical examination, a crowd of about 1,000 persons, understood to be strikers, assembled outside the clinic equipped with sticks and stones. One police sergeant and five constables, all unarmed, warned the crowd to disperse but they refused. Two police inspectors and additional men were sent for and the final reinforcement brought two rifles. The inspectors again ordered the crowd to disperse, without effect. When the 12 prospective employees left the clinic the crowd assaulted them and the police with stones. An inspector gave a further warning, telling the crowd that unless they dispersed he would open fire. The crowd succeeded in knocking down the unarmed police sergeant and were kicking and beating him. Upon this, fire was opened and 15 rounds were fired, not into the main body of rioters, but mainly directed against those who were attacking the sergeant, who was later admitted to hospital with a broken arm and head injuries. Four members of the crowd were wounded by the police, three being minor casualties and only one serious, and two of the prospective employees of the CMC were injured by the crowd. My information goes to show that the police behaved with restraint in a difficult situation.[3]

The above statement contains gross misrepresentations and inaccuracies:

1   The so-called '12 prospective employees' were in fact strike-breakers or, as they were locally known, *kalikantziari* (demons), brought from the remotest parts of the island. Their number was much greater than 12, and they arrived in lorries and cars escorted by a strong police unit. Most of them, moreover, could neither read nor write, and consequently any wage offered seemed extremely attractive.

2   The clinic was at Mavrovouni not Mavizovouni and only around 25 per cent of the crowd that assembled were strikers, of whom only a few carried sticks.

3   The police were said to have requested the crowd to disperse, but it was rather the strike-breakers who pleaded unsuccessfully with the police to meet the strike committee 'to discuss the whole thing'.

4   The unarmed police sergeant was in fact armed, but did not fire himself and received only very minor cuts during the scuffle which lasted for over one hour.

5   Over 20 were injured, five (not one) seriously.

The clinic incident was followed in the evening by very large demonstrations in Mavrovouni itself and Xero. Three days later a general strike followed and on 8 March the bloody events of Mavrovouni were repeated at Xero, where six were injured and the wives of the strikers seized the guns of the police officers who were contemplating opening fire.

   The trial of the 25 strikers who took part in the events of 3 March commenced on 12 March. Four days later came the famous 'train battle'. The celebrated 'ten heroines of Xero' stopped the train which usually carried copper and mine workers and after stoning the strike-breakers beat up two of them and injured the British driver.

   By mid March strikers and other demonstrators were

imprisoned indiscriminately and without pretext. Police harassment and collaboration was at its peak. Yet a Colonial Office minute dated 16 March 1948 recorded:

> the comparative reasonableness of the Communist mayors, who agreed when they saw the Colonial Secretary to call off the projected general strike on the grounds that violence would prejudice any chance of negotiation;
> the stiffnecked attitude of the Corporation, which henceforth refused to deal with the existing trade union leaders on the grounds that they were responsible for the past acts of violence.

The miners were further hit by a circular, issued on 20 March by Archbishop Makarios II, calling for an unconditional return to work and promising to use his good offices to mediate between the two sides. Three days later, after a silence of 70 days, the government issued a leaflet setting itself firmly on the side of the CMC. The workers were not only stunned but angry, crying 'shame, shame'. A new plan by Hendricks and Makarios II issued on 9 April set out the government's terms for involvement.

A Colonial Office minute dated 19 March recorded that 'the CMC must be persuaded to take a rather more accommodating attitude'. Another minute dated 3 June repeated that 'the American company's attitude has been high-handed and unconciliatory'.

Harvey Mudd, the CMC president, arrived in April and had two meetings with the strikers on 29 April and 1 May. Even so the miners held a large meeting on 4 May and on 7 May sent a petition of protest to the CMC and the government, asking the latter to intervene. The petition was signed by nearly all the miners – 1,323 Greek and 428 Turkish. The Colonial Office (as shown by a minute dated 21 May) was alarmed at this combination. In fact the Pan-Cyprian Labour Federation and the Pan-Cyprian Committee of Turkish Trade Unions fought the CMC jointly.

After further meetings and demonstrations the strike, which lasted for four months and four days (124 days in all), ended on 16 May. It was *inter alia* a demand for trade union recognition which the CMC had refused. On their return to work the miners found 200 blacklegs, of whom around 150 had departed within ten days.

This strike, together with the others of 1948, revealed the Cypriot working class, led by AKEL, as a well-organized and militant force. Hence the popular belief that they also had a political aim – to assist the fight for self-government and as a first step to demand the abolition of illiberal laws. Harvey Mudd in a letter to his friend Lewis Douglas, US Ambassador to Great Britain, remarked on 8 May 1948 that he was convinced that 'AKEL will so weaken the hold of GB upon the island that its security will be imperiled'.

The next major strike of 1948 was by 1,500 employees of the Anglo-American asbestos mines at Amiandos in the Troodos mountains. The miners proclaimed a general strike on 2 August to enforce their wage and other claims. They occupied the underground and surface workings from which police baton charges failed to dislodge them. When the news reached Nicosia many demonstrators marched through the streets demanding self-government and protesting against anti-working class legislation. The usual police prosecutions followed. Twenty-seven people, including ten trade union and AKEL leaders, were charged with taking part in an unauthorized demonstration.

The builders' strike was the third major strike of 1948. On 26 August around 1,000 workers struck for higher wages and better conditions. A leading British journal commenting on the strike recorded:

> There was nothing illegal in this, but the Right-wing Greeks took the strike as a challenge and did their utmost to encourage Right-wing black-leg labour to continue work on the buildings. Right-wing contractors agreed in this course, and Left-wing resentment brought deepset Right and Left emnity into open conflict. Strikers used violence against black-legs and perpetrated a number of dynamite outrages on buildings where black-leg labour went on and on houses of black-legs. No outrage was meant or directed against authority, and only one did much damage. Throughout the strike's course no danger threatened the country's general security, and incidents were unduly magnified into

'considerable trouble and sedition'. The exaggeration probably originated from Rightists who, being less well organised than Leftists, urged the authorities to do to Leftists what they themselves would have done if they had had the means.[4]

During the strike (which formally ended on 18 December) the police arrested 78 people between 31 August and 11 November, and after detaining them for a period ranging from three to twenty days released them without bringing any charge. However, the police also arrested 14 others and having detained them for eight days charged them for assault and other offences and sent them before the district court. The court, unable to find anything against them, dismissed their cases.

In the end victory belonged neither to the employers, who were backed by the right and the government, nor the strikers, who were supported by the left. Like the much more bitter CMC strike, it was a revelation to the Cypriot political and labour leaders. A regrouping of forces and tactical policy changes followed on both sides.

The 'breaches of law and order' perpetuated during industrial disputes were explained to the Commons by Rees-Williams on 17 November 1948:

> There are two groups of Greek trade unions in Cyprus; the 'old' trade unions under the leadership of the Pan-Cyprian Labour Federation, which is dominated by the Left-Wing Akel party, and the 'new' trade unions, a comparatively recent growth sponsored by Right-Wing parties. Rivalry between the two groups is taking the form of a political struggle between them, which has in recent months assumed an increasingly violent character. Since 1st June there have been 29 incidents in which dynamite has been used and 74 cases of assault, malicious injuries and arson, credibly related to conflicts between rival trade unions.[5]

Rivalry continued and there were charges and counter-charges from both sides. In 1948 violence erupted again when 'Olympiacos', the official headquarters of 'X' (the Greek letter khi, describing the extreme right-wing bands which operated in Greece after the war), was burnt down. The government reacted by imposing fines and imprisonment even when sufficient evidence was lacking. The left, which combined union rivalry with anti-American demonstrations, especially over the transfer of the American radio station (a listening device) from Egypt, was by far the harder hit.

On 10 November 1948 Adamantos (the 'adamant one'), mayor of Famagusta, was fined £100 (£50 for deviating from the authorized subject and £50 for using loudspeakers contrary to the terms of the permit) for making a political speech at Kythrea on 10 October, when he had been authorized to speak only on the builders' strike. He was sentenced under section 12 of the Assemblies, Meetings and Processions Law No. 54 of 1932. Other labour leaders were fined up to £50 for putting up loudspeakers to relay the offending speech without authorization.

Ploutis Servas, his Limassol counterpart, was sentenced to three months' imprisonment on 26 November (his eighth similar conviction since 1943 and his third in 1948) for taking part in an illegal procession in Limassol to demand a general election. Thirty-one other members of AKEL were also sentenced for periods of up to two months.

Failure by the Colonial Office to answer the memorandum of November 1947 prompted a leftist deputation, which included Ploutis Servas, to visit London in February 1948 to press the claim for self-government. Creech Jones, on the advice of Lord Winster and senior departmental officials, is said to have refused to receive the deputation officially but accepted the suggestion of a number of Labour MPs to meet it informally. The Colonial Secretary was sympathetic – at least unofficially – and took note of what had been discussed. Although the delegation returned empty-handed it also discussed the constitutional deadlock with members of the influential Fabian Colonial Bureau, which incessantly attacked the inequities of the British colonial administration.

In an attempt to break the deadlock Whitehall issued a statement in the form of a despatch to Lord Winster on 7 May 1948 making proposals for constitutional reform on the basis of the scheme already outlined to the assembly on 7 November 1947. These were:

1   These would be a legislature composed of 18 Greeks, four

Turkish elected members and four English official members. Its chairman was not to be the governor but some other person of distinction, not a member of the legislature but appointed by him. He would not have an original vote but whether he should have a casting vote was a question left open for discussion.

2   The introduction of bills on finance, external affairs, special minority rights and the constitution itself would require the governor's prior approval. Nothing was *ipso facto* excluded from the scope of the legislature except the status of Cyprus within the British Commonwealth.

3   An executive council should be set up to assist the governor. It was to consist of three Greek and one Turkish members drawn from the assembly together with the four official members of the legislative assembly. The governor however was not bound to take its advice but was bound to report to the Secretary of State for the Colonies when he acted contrary to its recommendations.

It was made clear at the time that it was open to the constituent assembly to recommend variations in these and other details of the proposed constitution. These proposals were published on 12 May 1948.

On the following day the Holy Synod, in a message to the people of Cyprus, rejected these proposals as being inconsistent with *enosis*. The limitations imposed and the powers reserved for the governor were sufficient to wreck the chance of acceptance by most Cypriot politicians. Thomas Anthem (a well-known political writer) explained on several occasions that 'the Cypriots after 70 years of economic neglect and mild misrule, and now suffering from an inglorious period of despotic misrule, were not very enthusiastic about the new policy of Britain'.

A wholly unrepresentative chamber was reconvened on 20 May and on the following day a motion that 'it would be in the best interests of the people of Cyprus that a constitution in the form offered by HMG should be established with the least possible delay' was carried by eleven votes to seven. Of the majority six were Turks, one a Maronite and four independent Greeks. The minority was composed of five Greek mayors of the

left and two Greek trade union representatives who then
announced their intention to withdraw from the constituent
assembly.

Although it was suggested that the proposed constitution
was an advance on that which had existed before 1931, the
chairman of the assembly in his speech on 20 May made it clear
that 'there will be restrictions in the powers of the new
legislative assembly which did not exist before, but these will be
counter-balanced by the greater powers which the assembly
will have resulting from its composition'.

Following the withdrawal of the seven members, the
assembly, as officially stated, lost its representative character.
The chairman adjourned it *sine die* and the governor formally
dissolved it on 12 August, stating that these or comparable
constitutional proposals would be re-examined and
implemented if at any time this was requested by representative
leaders of the people. This offer was to remain open for the next
six years until Britain announced on 28 July 1954 that a
modified constitution was to be introduced.

Thus the governor's action of 12 August created an impasse.
The government insisted on its own plans and perpetuated the
existing illiberal regime which the chairman of the assembly
himself condemned as 'autocratic'.

The campaign for self-government was continued with even
greater vigour during the following months and found
expression in some powerful demonstrations held in many
parts of the island under the slogan 'self-government-union'.
Strikes and protests abounded in 1948. A peak was reached in
October when AKEL sponsored a demonstration in Nicosia
which attracted a crowd of over 25,000. This rally however was
not concerned primarily with economic and constitutional
issues but was a protest against King Paul's offer to allow
British and/or US bases to be built in Crete or elsewhere in
exchange for the union of Cyprus with Greece. This hardened
AKEL's line in support of self-government, which remained
firm up to at least the municipal elections of May 1949 which
proved more rewarding to the forces of the right.

On 21 March 1949 a district court sentenced Minos Perdios,
editor of the AKEL newspaper *Neos Democratis*, to three months'

imprisonment, with a fine of £50, for alleging a government conspiracy to prepare false electoral lists. On 29 March the Cyprus government gazette published an amendment to the criminal code, raising from six months' to five years' imprisonment the maximum penalty for the publication of words or documents with seditious intent.

On 12 April Servas and one of his Limassol councillors were struck off the electoral list because they served three months' imprisonment and the judge ruled that this interrupted their legal residence and hence the requirement of two years' consecutive residence. Servas was again in trouble in the following month. A Nicosia court sentenced him on 12 May to pay £1,000 libel damages for publishing an article calling an executive councillor a 'malicious collaborationist with the government'.

Meanwhile, by the time the constitutional wrangle was over, the relationship of the political forces in the island, as well as the international position of Cyprus, had undergone a change. The forces of the right, with the Church, the Cyprus National Party (KEM) and the Pan-Agrarian Union of Cyprus (PEK) at the forefront, were not only strengthened by their non-participation in the assembly but by the municipal elections of 1949. They began to orientate their policy towards Greece and to appeal to the government of Athens to use its good offices to promote a solution of the Cypriot question. They also demanded a referendum, but the British stated on several occasions that it would serve no practical purpose. On 8 December 1949 the archbishop called upon the people to take part in a national plebiscite on the question of *enosis*. The referendum, as we shall see in the next chapter, resulted in a unanimous 'yes'.

Towards the end of the year everyone was clamouring loudly for 'union and only union'. AKEL had by now shifted from its lukewarm campaign for self-government and initiated an uncompromising enosist policy.

The 'cold war' reached the island in 1948. Britain was constructing air bases equipped with radar and was transferring to Cyprus from Palestine (where its mandate was due to expire on 15 May 1948) a considerable number of troops, the Middle East radio monitoring service and the Arabic

broadcasting station ash-Sharq al-Adna. Thus in October the
RAF station in Cyprus was raised to the status of Air
Headquarters Middle East and rumours were also current that
Military Headquarters Middle East would be established in
Cyprus – as it was in 1954. The Cyprus problem assumed
henceforth a new dimension. A strong movement for peace and
against the bases developed in the island and in 1952, for
instance, over 100,000 signatures were collected demanding the
dismantling of all bases.

With the island gaining such strategic importance, the
Cypriots, who were now united on the national issue, appealed
to the world at large to support their cause. On 9 August 1949
the London Cypriot Committee submitted a highly informative
memorandum to the Special Assembly Committee of UNO for
the Non-Self-Governing Territories. Although it had no power
to deal with questions concerning non-trust territories, a
summary of the memorandum's contents was circulated by the
UNO Secretariat to all the representatives of the member
states.

News of the memorandum spread and by October many
individuals and organizations sent telegrams to Lake Success
USA in support of the London Cypriot Committee. Thus a
memorandum by the left entitled 'The People of Cyprus Accuse
GB' was sent in November reiterating the Greek Cypriot wish
for *enosis* and pointing out that if any doubt existed about it a
free plebiscite under the supervision of the UN should be
carried out. This, it was believed, would dispel all doubts and
prove that a genuine all-embracing movement for *enosis* existed
in the island.

As was shown by the governor's telegram to the Secretary of
State for the Colonies on 1 February 1949, the Cypriots in 1949
made the following demands:

> union with Greece;
> abolition of the illiberal laws;
> release of all the political prisoners; and
> the island should not be turned into a war base.

During the last two years of the 1940s the authorities continued
their old policy of repression, using vague statements to thwart
self-government and self-determination. The people of Cyprus

were to endure more drastic and suppressive measures and the denial of most of the fundamental human rights. The basic freedoms of speech, thought and association were still beyond the reach of the inhabitants. Hundreds had been sent to jail, including a mayor, a deputy mayor and two municipal councillors, and several thousand pounds in fines had been imposed for spontaneous peaceful assemblies or demonstrations against the national, political and economic oppression of the islanders.

The free use of loudspeakers was forbidden. Even the substitution of one street name for another in Limassol was prohibited. The town council decided in June 1950 to alter the name of a street from Sir Richard Palmer Street (it was during his governorship that most of the illiberal laws were passed in the 1930s) to 28th October Street, its original name for some time, possibly from 1945 to 1949. Six of the eight councillors present were accordingly punished for contempt.

Nevertheless the press laws had been relaxed, trade unions and political parties were freer to function, the ten-year economic development programme had begun and the deportation orders of 1931 were removed.

The government also made a modest advance in representative government in the rural areas. A law was enacted in 1949 providing for the establishment of 'improvement boards' where elected local authorities did not exist. The governor was empowered to declare a village an improvement area whose inhabitants were invited to elect a number of representatives to join certain official members on the improvement board under the chairmanship of the district commissioner. These boards were vested with many of the duties and powers of elected municipalities.

This law came under the most severe criticism from the Church, the nationalists and the left, who denounced it as a trap and an attempt by the government to distract the public from the national cause. A vociferous and sustained campaign was launched against the boards with the result that only around 50 villages (less than 10 per cent) were subsequently designated improvement areas. On 24 June 1951 the archbishop told the villagers of Lyssi that Cypriots did not want improvement boards but desired only *enosis*.

Where the law applied, improvements were evident. If these improvement boards had been set up 70 or even 50 years earlier, together with other reforms, the *enosis* outcry might have been muted.

The troubles in Cyprus caused the departure of its governor. The resignation of Lord Winster, who was on leave from 9 February to 29 March 1949, was accepted with effect from 30 March. He was the first governor of the island to resign. He had had several differences with Whitehall before his arrival and during his stay in Cyprus, and stated on many occasions that Whitehall should announce its purpose unequivocally and execute it without delay.

Lord Winster's resignation came after repeated visits to London for discussions on the form of constitution to be granted to the island. The Democratic Organizations of Cyprus, in a memorandum addressed to the Colonial Secretary, emphasized that this act was conclusive proof that the policy pursued by the British government had failed. Likewise the archbishop, in a new year's message to all Greeks, stated that the expected governor's resignation was the outcome of the *enosis* campaign during 1948 and asserted that 'the campaign will be intensified during 1949'.

Sir Andrew Barkworth Wright, a senior civil servant who had seen many years' service in Cyprus in the 1920s and 1930s, succeeded Lord Winster as governor. He was appointed on 16 May. The left, especially, compared him with Sir Herbert Richmond (often known in Cyprus as 'Richard') Palmer and regarded his appointment as 'an indication of the disposition of imperialism to clamp a new dictatorship on the people of Cyprus and complete the work of turning the island into an imperialist war base'. On 11 July 1949 the Holy Synod stated: 'The arrival of the new Governor will mark the beginning of the second stage in our struggle. With the same, and still stronger, steadfastness with which we opposed the Consultative Assembly let us now reject also any legislative council or other body, whether imposed or elected. Let our motto be again "Union and only Union. Away from the constitution, away from the ballot boxes".[6]

Municipal elections were held in different municipalities on four successive Sundays between 8 and 29 May 1949. Before they were held the forces of the left alleged that the Municipal Corporations (Amendment) Law of 1948 was detrimental to their interests. The law was attacked on two grounds: firstly, it restricted the municipal vote to those who had lived at least two years in the same town; and secondly, it conferred the responsibility for preparing the electoral lists on right-wing headmen – mainly mukhtars. The authorities explained that the purpose of the two years' residence rule was to exclude from such electoral registers casual labourers and villagers who came into towns for work over short periods and had therefore no permanent interest in municipal affairs. The rule inflicted some harm on the left, which expected only a six-month residential qualification and relied considerably on the excluded workers.

On the first Sunday AKEL won seven out of the eight seats at Morphou (the largest rural municipality), but the returns of the following three Sundays showed a swing in favour of right-wing candidates. AKEL retained control of its strongholds (the ports of Limassol, Famagusta and Larnaca) by narrow majorities, but Nicosia was lost. Dervis triumphed over Clerides amid outbreaks of violence between the two rival groups as a result of which one man was killed, several were injured and nearly 200 arrested.

The nationalist groups, which polled around 60 per cent of the votes cast, were now in control of 11 out of the 15 municipalities. The left, though not routed, was decisively beaten. AKEL's shifting line between self-government and *enosis* resulted in a loss of popular support while the Ethnarchy, consistently for *enosis*, had increased its influence. After the 6th party congress of August 1949, when Ezekias Papaioannou, who had been active in Cypriot affairs in Britain during the war, replaced Fifis Ioannou, the official line once more changed to the *enosis* and only *enosis* position. A message sent to the UN on 21 November 1949 reiterated that 'the entire Greek population of Cyprus is unanimous in its ardent desire for union with Greece'.

It is evident therefore that the movement for *enosis* was gaining fresh momentum. Several factors were responsible for this upsurge:

1   The Dodecanese were ceded by Italy to Greece in 1946. The

islands nearly went to Greece in 1919 but the Italians changed their minds and under Fascist rule Hellenism was being extinguished. The victory of the Allies and Turkey's attitude (by 1944 it had renounced its claims) secured the islands for the Greeks. 'We must be next in line to join the motherland,' remarked the Cypriots.

2   The Greek government had for the first time formally associated itself with the movement for union, though in terms courteous to Britain. Greece had depended economically and militarily on the UK. The Labour government however, finding the financial strain too heavy, asked the USA to take over, and Greece became virtually an American protectorate after 1947. The historic resolution of 28 February 1947, by which the Greek government was openly committed to demand the national restoration of Cyprus, has already been mentioned.

3   By 1948 many parts of the British Empire were being granted independence – Transjordan in 1946, India and Pakistan in 1947, Burma and Ceylon (now Sri Lanka) in 1948. 'That the Senusi should be free and the descendants of Socrates remain slaves' rankled with every Greek patriot. Asked if he still stood by his statement of 1 March 1936 that 'it is fundamental to socialism that we should liquidate the British Empire as soon as we can', Sir Stafford Cripps, Chancellor of the Exchequer, replied on 31 October 1948: 'Certainly, that is what we have done in the case of India, Pakistan, Burma and Ceylon.' Yet the more Britain's imperial position crumbled elsewhere, the more doggedly it clung to Cyprus.

4   The growth of nationalism in the Middle East had slowly eroded the Anglo-French position there, and new sovereign states were springing up.

5   The Ethnarchic Council was expanded in 1945 to include laymen. Its total membership, regular and deputies, including the *locum tenens*, was 21. Cyprus moreover had an elected archbishop after 1947 and the council devoted itself with renewed vigour to the cause of *enosis*.

6   Apart from relying on emotional factors the Cypriot politicians concentrated on the economic problems, pointing

out to the people that they had nothing to lose materially by ending the British connection.

7   After 1949 the forces of the left joined in earnest the right-wing chorus for *enosis* and for a time took the initiative. AKEL's losses in the 1949 municipal elections and probably the defeat of the Communists in the Greek civil war prompted this change of tactics. (AKEL of course had always demanded the abolition of colonialism.) The left rationalized its support for union with 'monarcho-Fascist' Greece by stating that this was the first step towards the liberation of the Greek people from Anglo-American imperialism. In furtherance of its objective a memorandum was sent to the Security Council and General Assembly of the UN on 21 November 1949 requesting that a plebiscite should be held in Cyprus, under UN supervision, if there was the slightest doubt of the entire Greek population's desire for *enosis*. The mayors of Limassol, Larnaca, Famagusta and Morfou and seven other leftist leaders signed the memorandum. This document followed the pattern of the one sent to Creech Jones on 26 November 1948 which emphasized that Cypriots would never abandon the basic demand of national restoration.

8   The Atlantic Charter of 14 August 1941 declared the right of all peoples to choose the form of government under which they will live. The Universal Declaration of Human Rights approved by the General Assembly of the UN on 10 December 1948 proclaimed as the highest aspiration of the common people that 'human beings shall enjoy freedom of speech and belief and freedom from fear and want'. These and similar declarations caused the Cypriots to believe that their case was also 'just' according to the canons of international law. Cypriots constantly quoted them to justify their struggle for ultimate union.

9   After the war the Cyprus movement was supported by the Greeks scattered around the globe. Thomas Anthem in an article entitled 'The Cyprus Farce' wrote in 1947:

The million Greeks in America are just as anxious to see Cyprus restored to the motherland as are the Greeks in Europe or the Greek Cypriots themselves. Under the race-conscious and powerful Greek-American society, the

A.H.E.P.A., they have used their influence in keeping the subject constantly in the minds of the American public, and in fact the matter has long been on the files of the State Department. When the secret documents of this department relating to the plan to give aid to Greece and Turkey were circulated in confidence to the Foreign Affairs Committee of the House of Representatives a short time ago, they contained a recommendation that Britain should cede Cyprus to Greece, 'provided due provision is made for the security of British lines of communication'. On the urgent representations of the British Government, all reference to Cyprus was subsequently deleted from the papers.[7]

Hence the Cypriots had sizeable pressure groups not only in Britain and Greece but also in America to help them achieve their declared goal. Cypriot leaders understood from American documents and papers that there was no joint Anglo-American strategic plan for the defence of the eastern Mediterranean which would perhaps have justified Britain's desire to retain the island. They also emphasized that Britain was promised bases on Greek sovereign territory if *enosis* were finally conceded. It was widely argued that as long as the USA remained in Greece and kept her fleet in the Mediterranean the British retention of Cyprus against the will of the great majority of the people was indefensible.

10   'Political immaturity', 'a weak island unity', 'power is concentrated in a few hands' – all the powerful arguments put forward by the authorities against national self-determination were not present in the late 1940s to the same extent as in earlier years. Patrick Balfour, a well-known writer on the area, describing the village of Lapithos (in the Kyrenia district), pointed out that 'politics, like picnics and backgammon, is the national sport of the Cypriots, as of the Greeks'. Power was more fairly shared – the enlargement of the Ethnarchic Council to include laymen was well received, and the fact that by 1948 there were 37 political parties of various sizes showed not only the divisions that could exist but also the sharing of power and responsibility. Involvement was at its peak around this time. In spite of the press laws, daily and weekly newspapers in Greek, Turkish and English abounded and literary magazines also

made their appearance, the most important of which was the monthly *Kypriaka Grammata (Cypriot Letters)*.

Also of great significance was the formation of the Society of Cypriot Studies in 1936 by the leading intellectual figures of the island who vowed to collect, study, preserve and publish historical material; collect, preserve and study linguistic material concerning the history and development of the Cypriot popular language; and study popular art in all its aspects and establish a museum of popular art. Its annual publication *Kypriakai Spoudai (Cypriot Studies)* has proved invaluable to students of Cypriot history. Elementary and secondary education had also shown great strides. According to the 1911 census only one Cypriot in four could read and write. By 1950 illiteracy was rare even in the remotest villages.

Consequently the British arguments that 'they know not what they are asking' and 'if Cypriots possessed common sense they would thank God that they were ruled by us' can easily be refuted. As early as 1939 Achilleas K. Emilianides, a leading advocate, writing on the theme of Cypriot political immaturity, stated that the accusation was 'untenable, incorrect, frivolous and slanderous'. Moreover, he wrote that during the 60 years of British administration Cypriots were not given the opportunity to try their political merits and faculties. Lord Winster explained in 1949 that 'the Cypriots, above all, had great intellectual ability'. Steven Runciman, representative of the British Council in Greece from 1945 to 1947, said after Lord Winster's speech on the administrative problems of Cyprus:

> The feeling in Cyprus in favour of union with Greece was deep, and even the moderate Cypriots who lacked the moral courage to criticize politicians, when one talked to them, particularly in their own language, confessed that their ultimate hope was union with Greece. They admitted that probably this was in the material interests of Cyprus, but although the Cypriots were materialists in short-term policy, in long-term policy they were very romantic and very much swayed by ideas.[8]

Hence the Cypriots appeared to be fully equipped to run their own affairs and decide their own future. They continued to pressurize the authorities at every possible opportunity. Thus the arrival of the new governor in August 1949 was made an occasion for renewed expressions of political demands. The Greek nationalist newspapers came out with the Greek flag printed across their front pages and repeated demands for union with Greece. Meetings were also held in the island's towns and villages, organized by AKEL, where the *enosis* slogan was reiterated. Claims for *enosis* by both left and right were continued by means of press and pulpit.

Neither the government of Cyprus nor the Colonial Office wanted to admit that a genuine *enosis* movement existed. A memorandum by the foreign research department of the Royal Institute of International Affairs recorded in 1941: 'The nationalist aspirations of modern Greece have been shared, since 1821 at least, by an increasing number of Greek-speaking Cypriots. At the present time, the desire for the union with Greece is felt by the great majority of Greek priests, school-teachers and lawyers, and by the larger part of the Greek population of the towns, while it is probably making headway in the rural districts.'[9] The conclusion drawn by this very objective exposition was that Britain's interests would best be served by the cession of the island to Greece before the end of the war or at whatever moment promised the greatest political advantage.

The Cypriots therefore, who felt quite capable of deciding their destiny for themselves, resented Britain's evasiveness. Percy Arnold, in his most lucid account of Cypriot affairs in the 1940s, explains:

Here then is the Cyprus dilemma. Britain retains the island as a defence against Russia, or any other power which might threaten the Near East. Most Cypriots know this perfectly well, most of them understand this perfectly well, but they do not think this is a good enough reason for Britain to remain in Cyprus, nor a good enough reason for denying them union with Greece. Britain therefore thinks up every other reason to convince Cypriots – and to some extent also to allay the liberal conscience lurking within most Englishmen – that Cyprus should not throw in its lot with the Greek state. In quiet times and in troubled times Britain has sent Governors to play with pomp and dignity this two-faced role, aided by their conscientious officers who dutifully recited that Britain was in Cyprus to build roads, eliminate malaria and plant forests. For over three quarters of a century Britain maintained this false, make-believe relationship with the Cypriots, each Governor hoping he would make the greatest possible success of the farce and praying that it would not fall to him to have to end it. But the Greek-Cypriots grew increasingly exasperated. As colonial government in the modern world becomes increasingly an anachronism, the two-faced system of government becomes more and more difficult to maintain in the last of the subject territories in the Eastern Mediterranean, where other peoples, one by one, have acquired independence.[10]

A letter by Sir C.J. Norton (appointed Ambassador to Greece on 17 March 1946) to C.H. Bateman of the Foreign Office on 8 December 1949 also voiced the same concern. It emphasized the following: 'What specially worries me is the fear that no one Department of State in England is in a position to consider the whole problem of Cyprus objectively, and that one day we may wake up to find we are in for a spot of bother as in 1931, at which point our prestige will be involved, as well as our friendship with Greece.'[11]

The military bases on the island were said to be essential for the protection of western oil interests in the increasingly turbulent and anti-British Arab world, as well as to support the eastern flank of NATO. This view was to be challenged in the years that followed.

The situation was complicated further by the Turkish Cypriot position, which showed a marked change in the last two years of the 1940s. Following a large Greek demonstration in Nicosia in favour of *enosis* and autonomy on 3 October 1948, the National Popular Party of Turkish Cypriots (the predecessor of the Cyprus is Turkish Party – Kibris Turktür Parti) protested and sent telegrams to Turkey expressing its annoyance. In the following year Turkish agitation against *enosis* grew more intense and J. Sadak, the Turkish Minister for Foreign Affairs, at a press conference in February 1949, declared that Britain would 'never' cede Cyprus to Greece. The archbishop, in a cable to the Greek Premier, requested that his government should take steps to curb the Turkish statesman's 'unwarranted and tactless interference' in a matter which concerned only Greece and Cyprus.

The Turkish Cypriot efforts to counter the Greek Cypriot demands of October 1948 had echoes in both Ankara and Athens. A widely attended students' meeting in Ankara demanded that Cyprus should be returned to Turkey if and when Britain relinquished her rule over the island. It was argued that cession to Greece would push the island towards a Communist takeover. While the Turkish government kept silent, the Turkish press warmly supported the cause of their Cypriot brethren. On the other hand Athenian newspapers deplored the Turkish attitude and pointed out that a Greek Cyprus would by no means imply a deterioration of Turco-Greek friendship. Turkey shifted from its role as observer and, with British prompting, became (especially after 1955) the third interested party when the Cypriot question was discussed.

10 1950–1955: From Plebiscite to Open Revolt

By 1949 both the nationalists and the Communists were wholly committed to *enosis*. The Church organized a plebiscite, the prime mover being the young Bishop of Kition enthroned on 13 June 1948 who as Makarios III was to become the island's first president in 1960.

A month after Makarios' enthronement the Ethnarchic Council was reconstructed. Soon afterwards the council set up the Ethnarchy Bureau, later known as the 'Ministry of Enlightenment', with Makarios at its head. One of its main tasks, begun in 1949, was the publication of an illustrated monthly magazine *Greek Cyprus*.

The plebiscite, intended to give free expression to the people's wishes for the island's future, was held on 15 and 22 January 1950. Out of the 224,757 Greek Cypriots eligible to vote, 215,108 or 95.7 per cent signed the petition for *enosis*, and many Turkish Cypriot names could be seen alongside the Greek signatures; civil servants and government employees did not take part.

The result of the plebiscite had no effect on the British government. It accused the Church of putting pressure on the people to vote for *enosis*, pointing out that the archbishop on 8 December 1949 pleaded for a unanimous affirmative vote. The Church countered by stating that on 12 December it had challenged the British authorities to conduct the plebiscite themselves.

The archbishop officially reported the results of the plebiscite to the governor on 4 February 1950. Sir Andrew Barkworth Wright replied on 22 February that the information had been transmitted to London and that the Colonial Secretary had endorsed all previous statements that as far as the British were concerned the question of *enosis* was closed. The British were not prepared to go further than the 1948 Winster constitutional proposals which had led to the plebiscite in the first place. The government's decision was reaffirmed in a reply in the House of Commons to Tom Driberg MP from John Dugdale, Minister of State for the Colonies, on 21 June.

Following the plebiscite, delegations were sent abroad to enlighten both governments and people on the Cypriot question. The first one, from the Ethnarchic Council, consisted of Kyprianos (Bishop of Kyrenia), N.K. Lanitis and Savvas Loizides, representative of the Ethnarchy in Athens; the other, from the AKEL-dominated National Liberation Coalition, consisted of A. Adamantos, E. Papaioannou and Evdoros Ioannides, secretary of the London Cypriot Committee for Cyprus Affairs.

The first delegation visited Greece, France and Britain and then went on to Lake Success where it established contacts with delegates to the fifth UNO Assembly. Alexis Kyrou, the Greek permanent representative at the UN, gave them valuable assistance. The second delegation visited Britain and France and published a pamphlet called *Cyprus Presents Its Case To the World* in English and French, which it distributed to Members of Parliament, private individuals and organizations in both countries. Several other countries were subsequently visited.

The two acknowledged Greek Cypriot protagonists of *enosis* were Grivas and Makarios. George Grivas, born in the Nicosia hospital on 23 May 1898, comes from the village of Trikomo, about 12 miles north of Famagusta. As a youngster he won both academic and athletic awards at the Pan-Cyprian Gymnasium. In 1916 he was admitted into the so-called 'school of the promising ones' – the military academy of Athens – and after graduating in 1919 he took part in the ill-fated Greek campaign of Asia Minor. At the age of 26 he was promoted to captain.

When the Italians invaded Greece in 1940 the Greek masses fought bravely and repelled the enemy. Grivas became Chief of Staff to the second Athens Division on the Epirus front and for his services on the Albanian front was promoted to lieutenant-colonel. There the outnumbered Greek forces under the command of General Papagos, backed by small Allied air contingents, defeated the Italians.

Then came the German occupation of Greece and in 1943 Grivas formed his own secret organization of Royalist officers under the name of the Greek letter X (khi). Its twin aims were the return of the king and the neutralization and liquidation of the Communists who controlled the chief resistance movement. The story of the occupation and the civil war which followed is well narrated by leading historians of the period. Grivas was retired in 1945 but returned shortly afterwards to side with Papagos against the left-wing resistance forces.

Following a short period of inactivity, the career of Grivas entered a new phase in 1951, when he failed twice to be elected as leader of his own political organization which was founded upon 'X'. He then stood for parliament as a populist candidate, but though the populist party and its supporters won the election with a large majority, Grivas failed miserably. The western powers, whose purpose he had served during the resistance, showed no willingness to help him in his chosen career. Angry and bitter, he then swore that he would give up politics for ever.

Meanwhile his attention was also focused on Cyprus and during the late 1940s he held regular discussions with people who shared his enosist aspirations. On his first post-war visit in 1951 Grivas made a thorough inspection of the entire island. Two meetings chaired by Makarios were held in Athens on 2 and 21 July 1952. Makarios had no confidence in guerrilla tactics but the opposing view eventually prevailed and at a meeting of Grivas, S. Loizides and Archbishop Spyridon of Athens on 11 September, the last declared that 'freedom is never won without bloodshed'.

In October 1952 Grivas was back in Cyprus and when he returned to Greece on 25 February 1953 he devoted much of his time to drawing up a comprehensive guerrilla plan which he said, 'with minor modifications, acted as a general guide to my operations from start to finish of the struggle'. In March came a fateful meeting in Athens of the political and military leaders of the Cyprus struggle. Makarios, who had just returned from New York, presided and all 12 present took an oath of secrecy and dedicated themselves to the cause of *enosis*.

Makarios subsequently informed Grivas that he did not want any guns in Cyprus, only mines and hand grenades. His attitude concerning which tactics should be adopted was explained by Grivas in this way: 'Archbishop Makarios in actual fact did not desire the use of force, but yielding to my pressure, consented to doing something which would be limited to sabotage over a period of three to four months, at the end of which he hoped that our demands would be met by the British government. In addition to the above, in explaining the stand of the Archbishop, I think that his fear of being deported if an armed struggle commenced was also important.'[1]

Grivas recounts that for the rest of 1953 and during the early months of 1954 he faced opposition not only from Makarios but from the Greek government. However, in March 1954 the first caique (light sailing vessel) arrived from the mainland with arms and ammunition and it was followed by another in October. Grivas also recalls his meeting with Makarios on 15 February 1954, in which he detected that the young archbishop was then very nearly ready to comply with his plans, which the secret liberation committee had decided on 28 January should be put in practice as soon as possible.

Yet the final decision as to what should be done and when was not at all clear, as was shown by the October meetings in Athens between Grivas and Makarios. The former, in his so-called 'historic mission', resolved to return to Cyprus, but he had no visa. Consequently he left his house on 26 October 1954 and with Socrates Loizides set sail for Rhodes. Only seven people knew of their departure. His diary for the day reads: 'God help us . . . I depart with faith and courage . . . I shall succeed.'

They reached Rhodes at three o'clock the following afternoon but the weather delayed their departure for Cyprus. Grivas however made full use of their 12-day delay by organizing a centre in the island from which arms could be shipped and made arrangements for the next delivery to Cyprus. After dark on 7 November the two men boarded a small craft at Gallithea Bay and finally set sail at 15 minutes past midnight. Another storm on 9 November left Grivas, a poor sailor, in a state of dizziness. According to Loizides, he 'lay in the boat with his eyes closed, as white as a sheet, and seemed to be unconscious'. 'Mal de mer, mon ami' (sea sickness, my friend), Grivas explained later.

At around 8 p.m. on 10 November the small craft arrived off the west coast of Cyprus at the quiet bay of Khloraka, a small village, and the home of Azinas was to be his temporary headquarters. He moved to Nicosia towards the end of the month. At that juncture Grivas not only lacked a proper set-up but also the unqualified support of Makarios. He set about his task of forming an organization to fulfil his purpose. From his memoirs we find that he concentrated on:

the distribution of arms according to his original master plan;

the formation and training of groups for armed combat and sabotage;

the formation of secondary groups in the villages to undertake the essential minor functions of an armed struggle – to keep the villagers informed of the movement's activities and to serve as a reserve for the armed groups;

the formation and setting up of an intelligence network to find out, above all, the current strength of the police and armed forces and to serve as an anti-spy organization; and

the establishment of associations which 'would cater for our needs during the preparatory stage of our armed struggle'.

The decisive date was 11 January 1955. Makarios, who had arrived on the previous day from America, summoned Grivas to the house of the Bishop at Larnaca, and there informed him that he had secured the support of Papagos, the Greek Premier, for their aims, which were still to be sabotage. It was at this meeting, and at Grivas's suggestion, that the new secret organization was christened EOKA (Ethniki Organosis Kyprion Agoniston – National Organization of Cypriot Fighters). It replaced EMAK – the Cyprus National Liberation Front. Grivas also declared that he would not lay down his arms until Makarios told him to do so. Several days later Grivas was extremely fortunate to meet Gregorios Afxentiou, who soon became his trusted second-in-command. In the opinion of many Afxentiou, noted for his honesty and bravery, was to become the most revered hero of the Cypriot struggle.

Grivas believed that the 'rising' should commence by the middle of March whereas Makarios preferred 25 March – the day celebrated as the beginning of the 1821 Greek Revolution. However, it was delayed by the capture of the *Ayios Georgios* bringing the third shipload of explosives into the island. During the night of 25-6 January HMS *Comet*, a British destroyer, intercepted it and a shore party closed in, catching Socrates Loizides and 11 other men unloading small arms and ammunition. Loizides was later sentenced to 12 years' imprisonment and remained in a British jail until 1959.

The failure to land the explosives at Khloraka hampered Grivas's initial operations. Moreover, a document found on Loizides revealed not only the existence of EMAK, which aimed at *enosis*, but also the liquidation of traitors and the non-acceptance of Communists. Nevertheless on 29 March Makarios gave Grivas permission to start his sabotage. Grivas added 'God is with us'.

During the early hours of 1 April 1955 a series of bomb explosions wrecked government offices, police stations and military premises throughout the island. The radio transmitter in Nicosia was blown up by a four-man group under Markos Drakos; the unguarded secretariat was also damaged as well as the wireless installations at the Wolseley barracks. On the same day EOKA proclaimed its existence in leaflets signed 'Digenes'. This was Grivas's *nom de guerre* in his capacity as leader of EOKA. Digenes was a tenth-century epic hero of Byzantine Asia Minor whose full name was Basil Digenes Akrites. Digenes and Akrites were the surnames: Digenes may be translated as 'born of two peoples' and originated because his father was a Mohammedan Arab and his mother a Christian Greek.

Makarios was born Michael Christodoulos Mouskos in the Paphos village of Panayia near the monastery of Chrysorroyiatissa. The date was 13 August 1913 and, while disclaiming any tendency towards superstition, he had always regarded 13 as his lucky number.

In 1926 he entered Kykko monastery as a novice and took the name of Kykkotis. He stayed there for twelve years and also from the age of 20 attended the three top classes of the Pan-Cyprian Gymnasium. At the age of 26 he was ordained deacon and sent to the University of Athens on a scholarship to study theology and some law. He graduated in 1942 and entered the church of St Irene where he was ordained as a priest on 13 January 1946. Some months later one of the ten scholarships offered by the World Council of Churches was granted to him and in September he departed for the Methodist Theological College at the University of Boston.

On 13 June 1948 he was consecrated Bishop of Kition and following the death of Makarios II on 28 June 1950 he was elected, on 18 October, as Archbishop Makarios III. He was destined to become internationally known for his leadership of the *enosis* movement, being appointed archbishop at a time when the *enosis* movement was at its peak. In a sermon preached at Nicosia on 4 December 1949 he discarded the belief that *enosis* would be realized within the framework of Anglo-Hellenic friendship and asserted that if it could not be granted it could be won only by 'continuous struggle'. On 20 October 1950, the day he was enthroned, he told large cheering crowds in Nicosia that Cypriots would always reject Britain's plans for constitutional progress in the island. He pledged that he would not rest for a moment in his efforts to achieve union with Greece.

The *enosis* campaign was turned by Makarios into a personal crusade. His total involvement was channelled into three main avenues:

1 *Extensive travel abroad*. His aim was to win support from as many countries as possible. As bishop he went to Greece in 1949 and as archbishop he returned in 1951. This marked the beginning of a long series of trips that took him half-way round the world. He always spoke of the need for world peace and supported the ideals of Greek civilization. In 1952 he went to the USA to watch the UN at work. In the USA several Justice for Cyprus Committees had been set up and the Cyprus Federation of America was very active in aiding the Cypriot struggle. Also in 1952 he visited Egypt, Syria and the Lebanon. His political thinking, still in the formative stage, must have been influenced by his visits to the middle east and later the far east.

During the early months of 1954 he was back in Athens and in the autumn once more at the UN – this time with higher hopes because he had at last prevailed upon Papagos, the Greek Premier, to raise the question of Cyprus there. In the spring of 1955 he travelled to the far east to look for further support among the largely anti-colonial Afro-Asian powers then meeting in Bandung, Java. In Cyprus tensions were heightened by the Baghdad Pact of early 1955 (signed by Britain, Turkey, Pakistan, Iran and Iraq), since the withdrawal from the Suez base and Iraq forced Britain to make the island its chief fortress for the conduct of operations in fulfilment of the pact's obligations. On his return from Indonesia Makarios expressed the attitude of all middle east neutralists when he declared that 'the British government by its international machinations is undermining and endangering the peace of the eastern Mediterranean'.

2 *Systematic preparations at home.* The archbishop's main target was to grasp the national liberation struggle initiative from the leftist forces of the island. In order to do so several organizations needed to be set up. In 1952, with the help of Grivas, he founded PEON (Pan-Cyprian National Youth Organization), which with its special initiation ceremonies later became a recruiting centre for EOKA. Stavros Poskottis was appointed to head PEON. There was a slightly more religious background about OHEN (Organization of Orthodox Christian Youth), which came directly under the control of Makarios and the bishops. Its president was the senior priest of Phaneromeni church in Nicosia, the stout and jolly Papastavros Papagathangelou ('Father Good Angel'), who was nominated for the post by Makarios. He became the spiritual and physical link between OHEN and EOKA and was later to be deported with the archbishop to the Seychelles.

In his *enosis* referendum anniversary speech on 13 January 1952, Makarios declared that the struggle, both at home and abroad, for the achievement of national liberation would be intensified. Indicative of this struggle was the involvement of PEON in the Paphos riots of 1952 on the occasion of Queen Elizabeth's succession to the British throne. In the following year the government refused to renew the registration of PEON clubs. However, most of their members were absorbed into OHEN.

In the autumn of 1954 the archbishop set about reorganizing such right-wing associations as PEK (Pan-Agrarian Union of Cyprus), and Andreas Azinas, whom Grivas met during his second reconnaissance visit to Cyprus, succeeded Loizides in 1950 as its secretary and became the main liaison officer between Makarios and Grivas. PEK was particularly active in procuring arms and explosives in preparation for the armed struggle. In order to cover the towns as well, Makarios and his associates also reorganized SEK – the Cyprus Workers' Confederation.

3   *Conciliation*. Like a true Aristotelian, Makarios believed in striking a happy medium. Basing his claim on the resolution of the UN General Assembly of 16 December 1952 on the right of all peoples to self-determination, he wrote to the governor on 27 April 1953 requesting that the result of the 1950 plebiscite should be accepted or a new one held.

Unlike some of his predecessors, Makarios did not neglect to engage the sympathies of the left, although in the first two years of the 1950s he failed to come to grips with the realities of the Cypriot class system. Thus the composition of the Ethnarchic Council, though widened on several occasions to include laymen, was not at all a cross-section of Cypriot society; it simply represented the Church and the higher echelons of the Greek Cypriot community. Moreover, attempts by the left to form a unified pan-liberation front were sneered at by the right. The Akelist EAS (Ethnikos Apeleftheroticos Senaspismos – National Liberation Coalition) played a major role in the fight for *enosis*, especially in 1951, when it demanded that the Cyprus issue should be placed before the UN. In a booklet published in 1952 (*The Path Towards Freedom*) AKEL advocated a joint front for action and demanded the union of Cyprus with Greece.

Makarios came to understand that the forces of the left, on both the domestic and the international scene, should not be alienated. Makarios reputedly told a journalist, before he left to attend the October 1952 session of the UN General Assembly, that 'if the Soviet Union raises the Cypriot question we shall not be displeased'. On 22 March 1953 he declared before a church congregation that 'we shall seek the support of every nation and we shall accept support from every hand'. On 28 June 1953, a day when an important statement of policy was to be announced, a large crowd at the Phaneromeni church in Nicosia heard the archbishop say that 'in our efforts to gain our desired freedom we shall stretch out both our right hand and our left hand to receive any help offered from the east or from the west'. Yet the policy of the 'national centre' (Athens) was to seek aid only from western powers.

In the summer of 1954, 12 days before the Cypriot appeal to the UN was lodged by the Greek government, the first open and official contact took place between Makarios and AKEL. The leftist newspaper *Neos Democratis (New Democrat)* reported on 10 August that a delegation consisting of Ezekias Papaioannou, the secretary-general of AKEL, and Pavlos Georgiou, its organizing secretary, had called on the archbishop and 'exchanged views on the best way of facing the situation', adding that 'on many points there was agreement'. Perhaps the main result of the meeting was the general protest strike called by all trade unions, both left and right.

The young ethnarch however, still a novice in the art of diplomacy, committed several mistakes which contradicted his earlier statements. For example, in an interview with the diplomatic correspondent of *The Times* given whilst passing through London, he was reported in the issue of 15 October 1954 as saying: 'I have many times read in the papers that the church co-operates with the communists. This is not true. The church can never compromise with communist doctrine. I do not take into consideration the existence of the communist party.' Perhaps Makarios was speaking about general situations and not about the existing state of affairs in Cyprus during the early 1950s. Certainly the archbishop could not ignore such a sizeable proportion of the island's population. (AKEL and its affiliated organizations had the solid support of around 40 per cent of the entire Greek and Turkish Cypriot electorate.)

When EOKA's campaign opened on 1 April 1955 AKEL was quick to condemn violence. Though it desired *enosis* AKEL preferred full independence without conditions such as the granting of bases to Britain or to any other country. It desired to achieve its goals by political means, not by an armed struggle which it believed would create more problems than it would solve. Although AKEL did not support EOKA's violent tactics it never betrayed its armed struggle for self-determination. Nevertheless the British colonial administration proscribed the party in 1955.

Hence the agreed strategy of the early 1950s was as follows:

1   The rejection of constitutional proposals put forward by Britain.

2   The intensification of the campaign to inform the Greek people.

3   Co-ordination with liberation organizations in Greece and the preparation for an armed struggle. Makarios in 1952 became chairman of the revolutionary committee set up by Grivas and his associates in Athens. The plans for guerrilla activity in the island were prepared by army officers such as Grivas, P. Xentaris and E. Alexopoullos, university academics such as D. Vezanis, G. Konidas and G. Stratos and by Cypriots living in Greece such as N. Kranidiotis, Savvas and Socrates Loizides. The plans were backed by the Greek Church, and the Archbishop of Athens was also president of the Panhellenic Committee for the Union of Cyprus with Greece.

4   The solution of the problem by the UN with Greek government initiative and help. It was here that Cypriot expectations, as we shall see below, foundered.

After the turbulent experiences of the 1940s Greece had no choice but to steer a peaceful course. Hence the problem of the late 1940s and early 1950s was that if the government came out openly in favour of *enosis* it would be accused by its western allies of seeking territorial gains regardless of the defence requirements of the middle east. Thus the official Greek policy had been to express sympathy with the desire for *enosis* but, in pressing for a solution, to demand only the human rights of the UN Charter including the right of self-determination. Therefore the statement of Premier Tsaldaris in 1946 that 'the question of Cyprus is not a demand and it should not therefore be posed in a vindictive manner because it only concerns Greece and her friend Great Britain' was supported, at least up to 1954, by successive Greek governments.

   Hence in 1950 Plastiras refused to receive the results (in volume form) of the 1950 plebiscite in Cyprus in case Britain was offended. D. Gondikos, the President of the Greek Vouli, accepted them unofficially. However, the Cypriot delegation was welcomed at the palace by King Paul and a massive meeting was held at the Panathinaikos football ground. Even so a conversation between Themistocles Dervis, mayor of Nicosia, and George Papandreou, Minister of Public Safety, went like this:

Dervis: Does the Greek government officially recognize the Cyprus demand for *enosis*?
Papandreou: Greece today breathes with two lungs, one British, the other American; it cannot for the sake of Cyprus let itself suffocate.

American economic and military aid to Greece from 1947 to 1951 amounted to around 1,672 million dollars. A government that depends upon such foreign bounty necessarily surrenders its freedom of action.

In 1951 a Cypriot delegation once more failed to pressurize Greece into taking the Cyprus case to the UN. Makarios then threatened that he would ask Syria to do so. The Greeks pointed out that such a move would result in failure and a consequent loss of prestige for the archbishop. Plastiras told Makarios to 'sit down' and that he would not 'destroy Greece' without doing anything for Cyprus. During the UN debates on the Cyprus issue the Syrian representative stated quite emphatically that 'Cyprus has always been a part of Syria'.

Sophoclis Venizelos, who succeeded Plastiras, also rebuked the pleading archbishop, who demanded in 1952 that Greece should sponsor the Cyprus cause, by saying 'you will not direct the foreign policy of Greece'. He also emphasized that one of the reasons for his attitude was the fact that the USA, at that time fairly sympathetic to the Cypriot cause, had stated that it was not in a position to help. Venizelos admitted to the Greek Vouli on 12 December 1958 that it was the USA which prevented Greece in 1951 and 1952 from talking the Cypriot question to the UN. The 'reign' of John Peurifoy, American Ambassador in Athens, was virtually unchallengeable.

And there was Field-Marshall Papagos, a pillar of strength in the Greek armed forces, government and royal circles. A Foreign Office minute, dated 12 August 1952, recorded that, 'We have Papagos to thank for the Archbishop's lack of success. He has consistently advised Venizelos that any active move by the Greek Government would be misguided and foolhardy.'

When on 14 February 1951 Kenneth Younger, Minister of State at the Foreign Office, told the House of Commons that no Greek government had asked officially for the union of Cyprus with Greece, Venizelos pointed out that every Greek administration since 1912 had in a sense made this request. On

15 February he declared in the Greek Vouli that 'the union of Cyprus with mother Greece constitutes an ardent desire on the part of the people of Cyprus and the people of Greece'. No Greek government could ignore the Cypriot demand for *enosis*. This demand however was not pressed, since the Greek attitude at the time was to settle the question within the framework of Anglo-Hellenic friendship.

Nevertheless Cypriots continued to pressurize Greek Members of Parliament and government officials. Following the plebiscite of 1950 a debate in the Greek Vouli resulted in 205 members (out of 250) signing a petition expressing their support for *enosis*. Political activity was intensified, with the Panhellenic Committee for the Union of Cyprus with Greece always playing a leading role. However, the post-war Greek was unlucky in that no Greek government was there long enough to pursue a consistent policy. The formation of the Greek Rally (Ellinikos Sinagermos) was to play a decisive role in Cypriot affairs. The architect of this party was Spyros Markezinis.

At the elections of March 1950 the Greek Rally obtained one seat, but after four unstable governments fresh elections were set for September 1951. Five weeks before polling Papagos, the man favoured and sponsored by the Americans, entered the political arena and the Greek Rally secured 114 seats. On 16 November 1952 it received 239 out of 300 seats under the American sponsored so-called 'straight ballot' voting system. Although the Greek Rally won with less than 50 per cent of the popular vote it claimed 80 per cent of the total number of seats. Reading his government's programme to Parliament on 17 December, Papagos emphasized that a realistic treatment of the Cyprus issue was considered basic to the lives of all Greeks. He had earlier promised Makarios that should the Greek Rally win the election he would use his position to take up the Cyprus question.

Papagos was to remain Prime Minister until his death in October 1955. Markezinis became Minister of Economic Co-ordination and in December 1952 successfully launched a realistic economic programme. Markezinis, who ranked the Cyprus problem sixth on his list of priorities, withdrew from active politics in April 1954 and Alexis Kyrou became thereafter Papagos's right-hand man in foreign affairs. The Kyrou family, natives of Cyprus who ran the influential Athenian newspaper *Hestia*, belonged politically to the old Venizelos wing of liberals and had always been, at least in private, Anglophile; but being Cypriots by origin they were passionately for *enosis*. Hence they influenced the Premier greatly in believing that there existed sufficient international support for the union of Cyprus with Greece. This strengthened Papagos's growing anti-British sentiments (dating from 1941 when he was described as a 'defeatist' by the British) and caused him to remark in 1954 that 'Cyprus is Greece herself' – an assertion which later laid him open to Turkish and British accusations that he was pursuing a policy of annexation.

Eventually Papagos took the Cyprus question to the UN. The annual pilgrimage had begun. Yet it was not the first time that the Cyprus problem had been mentioned at UN deliberations. On 25 October 1950 Gregory Kassimatis MP, contrary to the advice of Kyrou, the Greek permanent representative at the UN, obliquely cited the issue at the Assembly's fifth session. It was necessary, he told the Political Committee, to proclaim the principle of the right of peoples to self-determination, regardless of the national interests of great powers. 'Foreign domination, whether by friends or enemies, is always an evil,' Kassimatis continued.

At the Assembly's 1951 sixth session, Jean Politis, the Greek representative, again without mentioning the island by name, referred to the question in the general debate as an instance of discrimination that was not consonant with the spirit of the UN Charter. He added that it ought to be remedied either by an official interpretation of the Charter or through measures taken by the administrative power on its own initiative. The question was also referred to in the Human Rights, Trusteeship and Non-Self-Governing Territories Committees. In the Trusteeship Committee it was pointed out that while Libya had become an independent state Cyprus, though more advanced in every way, was still a British colony.

However, the British, through Anthony Eden, the Foreign Secretary in the newly elected Churchill government (October 1951), and Lennox Boyd, the Minister of State at the Colonial Office, pleaded with the Greek delegation not to continue with their chosen policy. The plea was accepted in Greece by the combination of Averoff, Kartalis and Rallis.

Nevertheless the above discussions triggered off a meeting between Averoff, the Greek Under-Secretary of Foreign Affairs, and Eden during a NATO meeting in Rome in the same month. The meeting was hastily arranged by Sir Charles Peake, the British Ambassador in Athens, who had been disturbed by the effect on Greek opinion of the Cyprus plebiscite of January 1950 and the subsequent vote in favour of *enosis* in the Greek Vouli. From the Greek archives we now learn that in return for the union of Cyprus with Greece Averoff offered Britain what bases she needed in the island and four bases on a 99 years' lease in Greece itself, including Caphalonia in the Ionian islands and Suda Bay in Crete. Eden, a sick man with a bad temper, replied that 'the British Empire is not for sale and the Cyprus question does not exist'.

Gradually however the belief that emerging nations had the right, guaranteed by the UN Charter, to self-determination was gaining momentum. Kyrou believed that a legal right would be established for the Cypriot people to ask the UN to supervise a repetition of the 1950 plebiscite. Kyrou also believed that this would constitute a very important psychological weapon in carrying out direct Anglo-Hellenic negotiations concerning the island, with the participation, if possible, of the USA because of common NATO interests in the Mediterranean.

In 1953 Papagos informed Sir Charles Peake (the British Ambassador to Athens, 1951-7) that as a solution to the Cyprus problem he proposed the granting of a liberal constitution to the island, with a plebiscite to follow within two years so as to give the people an opportunity to decide their own future. He repeated the offer of bases on Greek territory; but he advised Makarios that Greece would try to solve the Cyprus problem 'within the framework of current realities'. This meant that the government's Cyprus policy was one of firmness and compromise best calculated to serve eastern Mediterranean security and Anglo-Greek ties.

On 21 September 1953 Kyrou raised the quesiton in the general debate at the 8th Assembly, cautiously warning about the possibility of a recourse to the international organization if no bipartite negotiations with the British government were forthcoming. At the British Embassy in Athens the next day Papagos met Eden, Churchill's heir-apparent, who was on a convalescent cruise in the Mediterranean following a serious illness. Much to the dismay of Peake, Eden refused to discuss *enosis* then or ever. 'Britain,' he said, 'will never give up the island.' A violent quarrel followed.

At the UN resolution 742 (VIII) was adopted on 27 November 1953. Clause 6 provided that the self-government of non-self-governing territories would be primarily attained through independence but could also be achieved by association with another state if done freely and on the basis of absolute equality. Eden remained unmoved: in December 1953 he told V. Mostras, the Greek ambassador, that his government had the means to repulse a recourse to the UN and the British delegation would walk out of any committee meeting that might discuss the question.

In February 1954 Makarios had another meeting with Papagos in Athens. The first point on the agenda was 'Cyprus at the UN'. At a conference on 15 April, attended by Stephanopoulos, the Foreign Minister, Kyrou, Mostras and another high ranking diplomat, Papagos decided to go ahead with the recourse to the UN unless bipartite discussions took place. On 3 May Papagos committed himself publicly to his decision of 15 April. On 14 May the UK through diplomatic channels again said 'no' and on 28 July Henry Hopkinson's (a junior CO minister) statement of 'never' emphatically confirmed it in public.

The Greek appeal to the UN, signed by Papagos on 16 August 1954, was transmitted four days later to Dag Hammarskjold, the UN Secretary-General, by Christian X. Palamas, the Greek permanent representative. Secret talks between officials of the British Embassy in Athens and K. Maniadakis, a Greek MP, failed to discourage Papagos. The item requested was as follows: 'Application, under the auspices of the UN, of the principle of equal rights and self-determination of peoples in the case of the population of the island of Cyprus.'

Sir Pierson Dixon, Britain's UN delegate, opposed placing the Greek request on the Assembly agenda on the grounds that Cyprus was a territory in whose affairs the UN could not intervene because it was entirely within the domestic and exclusive jurisdiction of the UK. Article 2 (VII) of the Charter states that 'the UN is not authorised to intervene in matters which are essentially within the domestic jurisdiction of any state'.

The General Committee examined the Cyprus item on 23 September. For Greece Kyrou requested that the principle of equal rights and self-determination, as defined in Article 1 (2) of the Charter, should be applied to Cyprus. He declared that his government would abide by the decision taken by the population of the island.

Selwyn Lloyd, British Minister of State at the Foreign Office, accused Greece of seeking to annex British sovereign territory. He went on to warn of the danger of communal strife arising out of such action since such moves were opposed by the Turkish community. Cyprus, moreover, was vital to the discharge of Britain's responsibilities in the middle east and under the Atlantic Treaty: 'Leases expire, treaties are whittled away, Greek governments change, hence full administrative control is necessary,' he argued.

However, by nine votes to three, with three abstentions, the General Committee recommended the inclusion of the Cyprus item in the Assembly's agenda. The USA was among the abstainers. On 24 September 1954 the Assembly adopted the General Committee's recommendation. The voting was as follows:

Bloc	Yes	No	Abstentions
Afro-Asian	12	–	5
Eastern European	6	–	–
Latin America	10	5	5
Western European	2	14	1
	30	19	11

The Cyprus item was discussed at the very end of the Assembly's session in four meetings of the Political Committee on 14 and 15 December. On 17 December the General Assembly adopted resolution 814 (IX) by 50 votes to none with eight abstentions. The adopted resolution read: 'The General Assembly, considering that, for the time being, it does not appear appropriate to adopt a resolution on the question of

Cyprus, decides not to consider further the item entitled . . . '[2]

Of vital importance were the words 'for the time being'. The way was now open for the Cyprus question to be submitted in 1955. At a meeting of the Greek Parliament on 7 February 1955 Papagos and Foreign Minister Stephanopoulos expressed their satisfaction with resolution 814 (IX) and stressed that the Cyprus problem was no longer the internal affair of Britain. It was now an international issue and both believed that the UN could deal with it.

However, all opposition leaders, in the course of the debate, accused the government of gross misconduct. It was pointed out that preparations for the recourse had been inadequate and that either Papagos or Stephanopoulos or both should have led the delegation. Moreover, Greece should have insisted on a strong draft resolution of its own and should have refrained from voting in favour of the adopted resolution. Events had proved that the Greek delegation had been over-optimistic about the eventual outcome.

During the UN deliberations there were riots in Greece. As early as March 1953 a student demonstration in Athens urged that the government should take the Cyprus issue to the UN. In April 1954 there were demonstrations in favour of *enosis* in Athens, and it was these, with pressure from members of the Greek Rally and Archbishop Makarios, which forced Papagos to take a firmer line on Cyprus. There were further demonstrations on 20 August – on the very day when the Greek appeal was transmitted to the UN Secretary-General. In Athens and Salonica the demonstrators clashed with the police. Many were injured and scores were arrested.

Following the USA's stand in the UN debate a large crowd in Athens on 14 December denounced that country as a 'treacherous friend'. Around 5,000 demonstrators surrounded buildings housing American officers and attempted to march on the US Embassy. At least 59 people were injured. On the following day Papagos declared that Greece had been 'betrayed' by its allies, including the USA, on the Cyprus issue; but he apologized to Cavendish Cannon, the US ambassador, for the anti-American riots. However, on 16 December similar riots occurred in Salonica where a US information agency centre was damaged. King Paul, in a broadcast four days later, appealed to all Greeks to abstain from violent demonstrations against the USA and Britain over the issue. He predicted Cyprus's eventual 'reunion' with Greece through favourable UN action on self-determination for the islanders.

In the early 1940s the USA was generally disposed to an early cession of Cyprus to Greece and as late as 1951 it viewed the Cypriot cause with sympathy; but it did not regard as timely the raising of the issue by Greece at the UN. In January 1954 Kyrou met Dulles, the US Secretary of State, and informed him that the Greek government was likely to resort to the UN. Dulles did not raise any objections of substance, yet in a note to the Greeks on 28 July he stressed:

1   The government of the USA was opposed to the planned recourse to the UN.

2   Talks between the Cypriots and the British government to arrive at a 'step-by-step' solution of the problem were essential.

3   Turkey must now be seen as a party primarily concerned in the future of Cyprus.

4   The policy of friendship and co-operation between Greece and Turkey, inaugurated by the Balkan Pact of 1953-4, should be continued.

5   It was essential that the unity of the western alliance should remain intact.

The American stance caused the resignation of Alexis Kyrou, who as Director-General of the Ministry for Foreign Affairs had played a leading role in the handling of the Cyprus problem.

The British indicated on several occasions that any sort of plebiscite in Cyprus would serve no useful purpose. As early as 7 July 1948 Rees-Williams, the Under-Secretary of State for the Colonies, stated so explicitly. An answer by John Dugdale, Minister of State for the Colonies, to Tom Driberg MP on 21 June 1950 repeated that no change in the sovereignty of the island was contemplated. On 14 February 1951 Kenneth Younger, Minister of State at the Foreign Office, informed Thomas Reid MP that he had not received any communication from the Greek government over the Cypriot *enosis* demand. The November meeting between Averoff and Eden also proved abortive. On 15 June 1952 Anthony Nutting, Under-Secretary of State at the Foreign Office, in an interview with a journalist, stated that Cyprus was a British island of the highest strategic value, and since Greece and Britain faced common problems and common dangers the time was 'inappropriate' for the cession of the island to Greece. The interview was published in the Greek newspaper *Kathimerini* on 18 June.

On 23 February 1954 the House of Lords debated the island's future: Lord Winster, a former Governor of Cyprus, stated that 'there is no widespread demand for enosis', which contradicted some of his earlier statements, and Lord Killearn hoped that the traditional Anglo-Greek friendship would not be marred by the Cypriot question.

On 15 March Eden informed Lena Jeger MP that the government could not agree to discuss the status of Cyprus nor could there be any bilateral discussions between Britain and Greece. On 12 May Selwyn Lloyd, Minister of State for Foreign Affairs, informed E.L. Mallalieu MP that the government was not prepared to discuss the status of Cyprus with the Greek government. Mallalieu, very angry, replied: 'Does the reply of the right honourable and learned Gentleman mean that in spite of the fact that 80 per cent of the population of Cyprus is Greek and wishes to go to Greece, and that we derive no military or economic advantage from a dog-in-the-manger attitude, Her Majesty's Government are going to sit on their ample backside until there is violence in Cyprus or until NATO is shaken by quarrels with our old friends the Greeks?'[3]

On 29 June 1954 the Potomac Charter, embodying the common principles of Anglo-American policy, was signed by President Eisenhower and Churchill, the British Premier. Of particular interest was Clause III which applied to emerging nations. Part of it reads as follows: 'We uphold the principle of self-government and will earnestly strive by every peaceful means to secure the independence of all countries whose peoples desire and are capable of sustaining an independent existence. We welcome the processes of development, where still needed, that lead towards that goal.'[4]

However, when Oliver Lyttelton, Secretary of State for the Colonies, was asked by Emrys Hughes MP on 20 July whether Clause III would be applied to Cyprus, he replied that it reflected what had been for many years the policy of British governments of all parties in regard to the political advance of all colonial territories, including Cyprus. Consequently on 28 July it was announced in the House of Commons that it was proposed to introduce a modified constitution, based on the 1948 proposals, in the island. The proposals were intended to:

appease but not please;
combat the emergence of Communism;
preserve Britain's strategic interests in the area; and
emphasize once more that no change in the status of the island was contemplated.

Part of the speech, delivered by Henry Hopkinson, was as follows:

Her Majesty's Government have decided that the time has come to take a fresh initiative in the development of self-governing institutions in Cyprus. They are convinced that, given good will, an early start can be made in associating the people of Cyprus in the fuller management of their own affairs. They wish to make it clear once again that they cannot contemplate a change of sovereignty in Cyprus. . . . It has always been understood and agreed that there are certain territories in the Commonwealth which, owing to their particular circumstances, can never expect to be fully independent. . . . I have made it clear that this is a first step towards self-government . . . of course, there is a Communist Party in Cyprus and it is probably the biggest and the best organised. While we want to establish a legislature, it certainly would not be in the interests of anybody to do so in a form in which it would be Communist-dominated. As we made it clear in British Guiana, we are not prepared to tolerate the establishment of Communist regimes in British Colonies.[5]

Hopkinson had used the highly undiplomatic word 'never'. Oliver Lyttelton was more diplomatic when, during the same debate, he said 'I can imagine no more disastrous policy for Cyprus than to hand it over to an unstable though friendly Power'. On 19 October Churchill, in two answers to Tom Driberg's probing questions, stated that Hopkinson, who was speaking impromptu, was not aware at the time that he had used the word 'never'. But, he added, 'wiping out the word "never" does not mean that you substitute any other date'.

The restraint formerly shown by Athens was now replaced by increasing antagonism. An editor and a journalist who criticized Papago's policy were severely reprimanded and sentenced to imprisonment. A postage stamp showing an inkblot on the column from Hansard that contained Hopkinson's 'never' statement was hurriedly printed. Hostile broadcasts (described as 'most objectionable' by the British) over the state radio were condoned, if not encouraged. One such broadcast on 16 November called on all Greek Cypriots to reject the British constitutional proposals and to stigmatize relentlessly all the renegades who co-operated with the authorities. The same broadcast attacked as 'sheer hyprocrisy' the British argument that if Cyprus were given to Greece she would run the risk of falling into the hands of Communists.

On 19 August the British government issued a terse statement:

1   Cyprus belonged to Greece only for a brief period in the fourth century.

2   The Russian danger which had brought Britain to Cyprus in 1878 still existed.

3   Strategic considerations required continued British sovereignty over the island.

4   The internal political development of the island had been retarded by the Greek Cypriot rejection in 1948 of the proposed constitution.

5   The Communist party in Cyprus constituted a real menace to the island's democratic development.

6   The Cyprus question was entirely within the domestic jurisdiction of Britain and the UN intervention would therefore be contrary to article 2 (VII) of the Charter.

7   Debate in the General Assembly would exacerbate feelings at such a delicate stage, thus delaying indefinitely the political progress of Cyprus which was the responsibility of Britain to promote.

8 Debate in the UN would thus benefit only those who sought to disrupt western unity.

The July announcement of Britain's proposals was swiftly followed by the decision to enforce the island's anti-sedition laws. The *Cyprus Gazette* of 2 August recorded that 'in future, criticism of government policy must not stray into the sphere of sedition.' The British press was highly critical of such laws. The *Manchester Guardian* of 3 August called them 'monstrous restrictions on the liberty of the press'. In Cyprus 13 Greek newspapers went on strike for a week and in 1954 180 cases of sedition were reported. Yet when Archbishop Makarios defied the laws at Trooditissa monastery on 12 August they were left in abeyance.

As expected the constitutional proposals were promptly discredited as an obstacle to *enosis*. On 29 July Makarios rejected them out of hand and in a message to the people warned that no one should co-operate with the authorities in this 'constitutional conspiracy' which aimed at prolonging the enslavement of the Cypriot people. In his historic speech of 22 August, delivered at the Phaneromeni church, a crowd of around 50,000 heard Makarios demand self-determination for the Cypriot people.

Athens radio called for a flat rejection of the proposed constitution. Stephanopoulos, the Greek Foreign Minister, also rejected it and explained that his government would take the issue of 'self-determination for the Cypriots' to the UN.

Opposition was also registered by various non-Greek bodies and organizations. A number of British Labour MPs, seeing that the constitution would provide a legislature made up of an elected minority and a majority composed of colonial officials and appointees, criticized the scheme because it did not allow Cyprus to leave the British Commonwealth if its inhabitants wished it to do so. The Labour Party Conference in October adopted a resolution deploring the policy of the Conservative government and urged its MPs to oppose its Cyprus policy on all occasions. A resolution passed by the Liberal Party Council in December also demanded the granting of a more democratic constitution.

Mayors and councillors voted at a meeting in Nicosia on 11 August to reject all British offers of a constitution that did not provide for the island's eventual union with Greece. This meeting followed closely the Pan-Cyprian National Conference of 23 July held at St John-the-Theologian church in Nicosia, which defined such a union as being the first aim and desire of all Greek Cypriots. Makarios spoke of a 'peaceful struggle', but he pointed out that recent events in Egypt showed quite clearly that only through the use of force could the British be made to understand.

On 12 August most shops and offices were closed throughout Cyprus in a 24-hour general strike against the decision to enforce the island's anti-sedition laws and for the union of Cyprus with Greece. On 20 August there were demonstrations throughout Greece to back the *enosis* demand. However, apart from a few noisy demonstrations and minor acts of violence, Cyprus remained quiet pending the outcome of the appeal to the UN. The island's government reorganized and strengthened its intelligence services and by a series of local broadcasts, pamphlets and press communiqués tried to counter the *enosis* agitation.

It appears that strategic considerations were always at the centre of policy declarations. On 27 July, the day before the Hopkinson revelations, the British and Egyptian governments, after long and frequently interrupted negotiations, had signed the 'Heads of Agreement' that were to lead to the conclusion of a final agreement on 19 October 1954 under which the British undertook to withdraw their troops from Egypt within 20 months. Britain consequently decided to implement the decision, taken in principle in December 1952, to transfer its Middle East Command to Cyprus. The already mentioned British announcement of 19 August outlined the following strategic considerations necessitating continued sovereignty over the island:

1   Control of Cyprus was essential for the fulfilment of British strategic obligations in the middle east and to NATO.

2   A Cyprus base leased from Greece could not afford the necessary security of tenure.

3   Britain would no more consider relinquishing sovereignty over Cyprus than over Gibraltar and its experience in Egypt

showed that bases without sovereignty could not always be relied upon.

In fact the withdrawal from Suez was not only a blow to British military power but an even more serious setback to British self-esteem. The British could see themselves becoming a second- or even third-rate power. The domestic impact was therefore alarming. The Tory government was punctured from within and was seemingly beyond repair. Assurances were therefore freely given that the Middle East Command Headquarters in Cyprus would 'never' be given up. In his celebrated speech at Norwich on 1 June 1956 Eden repeated: 'No Cyprus, no certain facilities to protect our supply of oil. No oil, unemployment and hunger in Britain. It is as simple as that.'

Diplomats therefore saw Cyprus as the last stable foothold in the middle east, which with Malta and Bahrain formed a vital link in the chain of airfields to India and beyond. The island's strategic value was increased because of its proximity to the oilfields and pipelines of the surrounding sea.

Cyprus however was not a base in the same sense as the Canal zone. It was not intended, as the Canal base was, to support by itself a major theatre in a global war, but rather to provide a forward post (serving this purpose on several occasions both before and after 1954) from which British interests and commitments in the middle east could be safeguarded in the event of local upheaval or conflict within the middle eastern area. Thus Lennox Boyd, who succeeded Oliver Lyttelton as Secretary of State for the Colonies on 28 July 1954, repeated on 28 October that 'in the present troubled state of the world we cannot foresee a time when a relinquishment of our sovereignty over Cyprus would be compatible with our responsibilities for security in the middle east'.

The decision by Greece to bring the Cyprus question before the UN meant that the problem of *enosis* had entered the most critical phase of its long history. Political ideology and military expediency came into sharp conflict. Even those who viewed the prospect of Greek rule with deep misgivings felt that they could not let the cause down. Thomas Anthem, a distinguished commentator of the time, pointed out in 1954 that 'rightly or wrongly, whether the Cypriots are misguided and foolish in desiring to exchange a rich stepfather for a poor mother of their own blood, the fact remains that Greeks everywhere, at home and abroad, including the Greeks of the US, are solidly behind the enosis movement'. Sir Harold Nicolson, another prominent writer, in a letter to *The Times* on 15 July 1954 explained that 'even though there are several arguments against the union of Cyprus with Greece, if tied tightly together they make a sorry little bundle and if taken separately they snap at once'.

On 17 December 1954 the long-awaited resolution 814 (IX) was adopted by the UN. It was decided not to consider the Cyprus question further for the time being. Almost at once there was a general strike in Cyprus and demonstrations by students culminated in rioting in Limassol and elsewhere on 18 December. There was also rioting in Greece – particularly in Salonica. In Limassol British troops fired and three youths were wounded, of whom one was later treated in Britain. These were perhaps the worst disturbances since October 1931. Once more unarmed demonstrators, mainly schoolchildren, were fired at. Was this to be the beginning of armed struggle in Cyprus? Although there were several demonstrations after December, it was not until 1 April 1955 that the Cypriot 'revolution' was initiated.

Turkish separatist leaders, annoyed by the persistent Greek demands for union, demonstrated in Nicosia on 28 November 1948 and sent telegrams of protest to the President and Premier of Turkey. Similar protests were registered after the plebiscite of 1950. The vast majority of the Turkish Cypriot population however accepted the fact that they were a minority and showed no strong reaction to the moves of their Greek counterparts. Even as late as 5 December 1955 Ian Mikardo MP informed the House of Commons that during his visit to Cyprus 'the Turks put forward the same sort of views and arguments as are put forward by minority communities living in the midst of people more numerous than themselves'. Ten days after the Turkish national elections of 2 May 1954 a delegation of seven Cypriot Turks flew to Ankara to discuss the problems of the Turkish community in Cyprus with the new Turkish government before going on to London for a similar purpose. Before the establishment of the Turkish Republic in 1923 no Cypriot Turks under British rule would have dreamed of sending a deputation to Turkey to discuss their communal affairs with the Porte.

In 1951 Venizelos went to Ankara as an official guest of the Turkish government. He enquired, in a private conversation with Menderes, his Turkish counterpart, as to what would be the government's attitude to the question of Cyprus. Menderes answered: 'Don't worry. This will be solved within the framework of Greek-Turkish friendship.' Nevertheless the Greek demand for bilateral talks with Britain continued, and the comment was soon made by many observers that if the island's future were discussed the existence of a Turkish minority in Cyprus would give Turkey the right to have a say in the matter. One of the enlightened few to acknowledge the Turkish factor was Mostras, the Greek Ambassador in London. Since January 1954 he had drawn his government's attention to it and had predicted the likelihood of tripartite rather than bipartite negotiations.

In 1952 both Turkey and Greece became members of NATO. The 1953 treaty of friendship and co-operation and the 1954 treaty of alliance bound the two countries more firmly together. Two Turkish statements, of 19 February and 2 April 1954, informed all that Turkey was of the opinion that there was no Cyprus question and that no modification of the island's status was necessary. This was also made clear in early April 1954 by the Turkish ambassador in Athens, who also informed the Greek authorities that any future negotiations over the status of the island should be tripartite.

British unwillingness to discuss the Cyprus question with the Greek government and the eventual Greek decision to seek justice at the UN hardened Turkish opinion. The tone of the Turkish press became hostile and the dangers posed to NATO's eastern flank were widely discussed. In his memoirs Eden recalled that it was 'right' that it should speak out in that way, 'because it was the truth that the Turks would never let the Greeks have Cyprus'. Eden was convinced that 'the Cyprus problem would only be resolved between the three governments of Britain, Greece and Turkey'. He suggested therefore that 'the Turkish press should play up the problem a bit more and thus denounce all Greek moves'.

Hence when Menderes, at the invitation of Papagos, stopped

briefly in Athens on his flight back to Ankara on 7 June 1954, the Turkish ambassador implored Kyrou to make sure that his Premier would not mention the Cyprus question. Such a conversation, he said, would have extremely undesirable consequences for the Greek-Turkish alliance. Moreover, when the Balkan Treaty of Alliance was signed at Bled in Yugoslavia on 9 August 1954, Stephanopoulos sought to raise the question with his Turkish opposite number, but the latter curtly replied 'there is no Cyprus question'.

Lastly, after the Greek recourse to the UN Papagos sent George Bakalbasis, a Turkish-speaking MP, to Ankara to probe the Turkish government's attitude. On his return Bakalbasis reported that the Turkish Premier had asked him to convey to Papagos the courteously ambiguous assurance that Greek-Turkish friendship was far more important than the Cyprus question. Menderes was more explicit on 31 August when he publicly declared that Cyprus would 'never' be annexed to Greece. The Ismet Inönü remark of 1923 that Turkey would never accept a Greek Aegean or a Greek Cyprus was at the forefront of Anglo-Greek-Turkish relations in the post-Second World War period.

At the same time, both in 1954 and 1955 Stephanopoulos, the Greek Foreign Minister, received cables from Fuat Köprülü, his Turkish counterpart, as well as from Menderes himself, assuring him that the Cyprus question would never affect Greek-Turkish relations and that this friendship was above the 'small dispute' over Cyprus. Köprülü even said that the Cyprus issue was just another of the 'internal problems' facing the government of Athens. Was the Turkish attitude so amicable because the British were taking an unyielding stance? Or was it because the Turks had British assurances that Cyprus would never be ceded to Greece?

11 1955–1959: The National Liberation Struggle

Diplomacy therefore failed miserably. On 1 April 1955 leaflets were distributed all over the island declaring that a secret association calling itself EOKA had embarked on an armed struggle to throw off the British yoke. Its leader was the egregious General Grivas. Its name was derived from a similar organization set up in the early 1940s in Crete called Ethniki Organosis Kritikon Andarton – National Organization of Cretan Guerrillas.

Like the IRA, EOKA soon became a household name for many Britishers. The oath taken was as follows:

I swear in the name of the Holy Trinity that:

1   I shall work with all my power for the liberation of Cyprus from British rule, sacrificing for this even my life.

2   I shall perform without objection all the instructions which may be entrusted to me and I shall not raise any objection, however difficult and dangerous these may be.

3   I shall not abandon the struggle unless I receive instructions from the leader of the organization or until our aim has been accomplished.

4   I shall never reveal to anyone any secret of our organization, neither the names of my superiors nor those of the other members even if I am caught and tortured.

5   I shall not reveal any instructions or orders which may be given to me, even to my fellow combatants.

If I disobey my oath, I shall be worthy of every punishment as a traitor and may eternal contempt cover me.

EOKA made its first appearance on the Cypriot scene with acts of sabotage in the districts of Nicosia, Larnaca and Limassol.

Damage to government property for the first night's incidents (31 March to 1 April) was estimated to be around £56,000, most of which was to broadcasting equipment. Twenty-one people were arrested. For over three years a fierce battle raged between EOKA and nearly 30,000 British soldiers for the control of the island.

Militarily, EOKA was a success, but both sides were guilty of various forms of unorthodox behaviour: the island was ravaged by a guerrilla war unprecedented in its recent history.

EOKA was able to wage a fierce armed struggle against overwhelming odds only because of the mass support it received from the Greek Cypriot people. The British forces (unlike the Germans in Greece) were under the continuous restraint of public opinion. Professor Crouzet has aptly remarked that 'the British were unable to crush EOKA because they were British'.

The guerrilla movement was seen as a chance to fight not only for national freedom but for social justice. Thus although EOKA was almost entirely a right-wing nationalist-led movement it had a proletarian base because it was seen to be carrying on an anti-imperialist struggle. Hence under the banner of national freedom EOKA was able to weld together vast sections of the working peasantry with the higher strata of Greek Cypriot society and the Orthodox Church in a struggle for national self-determination.

Despite his fanatical mistrust of the left Grivas tolerated left-wingers but not hard-line Communists in his organization. Hence such left-dominated organizations as EAEM (United Unbroken National Front) and PEO (Pan-Cyprian Federation of Labour) provided massive support in the struggle to liberate Cyprus.

Turkish nationalism however was neglected. Many Greeks were under the illusion that it was not so genuine, passionate or long-standing as theirs but was expressed in the extreme policies of Dr Fazil Kutchuk, Rauf Denktash and a few other diehards. Turkish nationalism existed but was neither so active nor so well controlled as its Greek counterpart. Kutchuk was chairman of the Kibris Türktür Parti (Cyprus is Turkish Party), which propagated the theory that self-determination for Cyprus would result in the annihiliation of all Turks, civil war and ultimately total unrest in the middle east.

EOKA had no reason to attack and antagonize the Moslem inhabitants, and in July 1955 issued a Turkish leaflet assuring the island's Turks that it was struggling not against them but against British colonialism, that EOKA's feelings towards them were friendly and that it was expecting them to be its allies. Its fighters had specific written instructions not to alienate them. Yet it was short-sighted to ignore the possibility that Britain would encourage such a reaction from Turkey.

Such were the new realities facing Cyprus in 1955. Alas there were no statesmen to make the proper appraisal and act accordingly. The British continued to make half-hearted attempts to reach a political settlement while still pursuing their so-called primary task of restoring law and order. On 15 July 1955 a Detention of Persons Law, similar to the British Defence Regulation 18B, was decreed. Britain invited the Greek and Turkish governments to a tripartite conference in London to discuss political and defence questions affecting the eastern Mediterranean, including Cyprus. She was aspiring, using the Cyprus issue as bait, to bind together her strategic plans with those of Greece and Turkey, and thus attempting to bolster her ailing international prestige. The Suez débâcle made things even worse.

The British invitation of 30 June was accepted by the Turks on 2 July and by the Greeks six days later. Harold Macmillan recorded in his memoirs (*Tides of Fortune*) that to his astonishment Stephanopoulos accepted the invitation without any conditions or reservations, even saying that the Greeks would be glad to meet their Turkish friends. The pressure exerted by King Paul I on Papagos, the ailing Greek Premier, ensured acceptance.

Hearing that Greece had accepted, Makarios, who earlier in the year had attended the Bandung Conference and visited Cairo and Athens to pave the way for the new Greek appeal to the UN, returned to Athens. His views on the London Conference were quite explicit. 'It is a trap,' he pronounced, 'aimed at torpedoing recourse to the UN. The people of Cyprus will never accept any decisions of the conference which do not accord with their rights and aspirations even if those decisions are endorsed by the Greek government.'

However, Britain, Greece and Turkey, represented by their Foreign Secretaries (Harold Macmillan, Stephanos

Stephanopoulos and Fatin Zorlu), attended the conference which opened at Lancaster House on 29 August. Immediately the widely differing views of the three countries were brought sharply into focus. Before the conference the Greek government had already made its application to the UN Secretary-General for the inclusion of the Cyprus question on the agenda of the General Assembly.

The Greeks expounded the view that since most of the island's inhabitants were Greek they ought to have the absolute right of joining their chosen country. They appealed to the principle of national self-determination. At the third plenary session on 31 August Stephanopoulos repeated his country's pledge to Britain over bases in Cyprus, saying: 'In sponsoring the Cypriot people's demand for their right of self-determination, Greece has never (and I emphasize never) for a single moment entertained the idea of a withdrawal from Cyprus of the British Forces.'[1]

Macmillan had earlier dismissed the idea that Britain could manage with a base in Cyprus, stating that the island was a headquarters as well as a base, and what the British needed there was a 'whole complex of inter-related facilities'. He added that his government did not accept the principle of self-determination as one of universal application since exceptions had to be made in view of geographical, traditional, historical and other considerations.

At the fourth plenary meeting on 1 September, Zorlu insisted that Turkey looked upon the Cyprus question as a British domestic issue, and the status quo should be maintained. The Turkish position rested on two arguments: firstly, the theoretical or juridical thesis that Cyprus was given to Britain by Turkey in 1878 and if she wished to relinquish sovereignty the island should revert to Turkey; secondly, the practical argument of proximity, Ankara's view being that Cyprus was in fact an extension of the Anatolian peninsula. Thus its long thin promontory which stretches to the north-east is often romantically described as 'the dagger which points at the heart of Turkey'. The Turks borrowed a Churchillian phrase in saying that Cyprus faced their 'soft underbelly'.

The conference brought out the two problems of internal affairs and of international status. Some measure of agreement had been reached on the first but on the second it was felt that the status of the island should be left open, each side fully reserving its position. On 6 September Macmillan put forward specific proposals which sought to take advantage of such common ground as existed. These were:

1 The constitution would provide for an assembly with an elected majority and a proportionate quota of seats reserved for the Turkish community.

2 All departments of the Cyprus government would be progressively transferred to local ministers responsible to the assembly, with the exception of foreign affairs, defence and public security which would be reserved for the governor. Proper safeguards for the integrity and independence of the public service would be provided.

3 As part of the safeguards to be provided for the Turkish Cypriots, a proportion of the ministerial portfolios would be reserved for that community.

4 A Cypriot chief minister to head the new administration would be chosen by the assembly with the governor's approval.

5 The conference should set up a special tripartite committee in London which would be responsible for examining the detailed proposals drawn up by the British government, and should consider a suitable system of guarantees to safeguard the interests of all communities and the appropriate method of their implementation.

6 When the new constitution was in good working order, a similar special conference should be called and if sufficient progress were made in the meantime elected representatives of the Cypriot people should be invited to attend.

In his diaries Macmillan explained that the Cyprus problem was both 'delicate and painful'. The Turks were 'confident, assertive and tough'. In contrast the Greeks were 'torn by internal difficulties and rivalries within the government' and Papagos was seriously ill. Finally he called the conference 'abortive but by no means useless', and speaking to the Commons on 5 December 1955 he diagnosed another issue. 'The inhabitants of Cyprus were civilised when the inhabitants of Britain were primitive. . . . Here, therefore, is a problem which is very different from the more normal problem of colonial development.'[2]

Perhaps this admission should have made a lasting solution much easier. Instead the policies of the Conservatives, generally backed by the Americans, ensured a prolongation of this 'tangled, difficult and delicate issue'. In fact the conference underlined the potential Greek-Turkish antagonism over the problem – a side effect which Eden had deliberately planned when calling it in an effort to disprove the thesis that the Cyprus troubles were due to old-fashioned British colonialism. Britain, the sovereign over the island, was thus placed in the position of 'mediator' in a 'dispute' between Greece and Turkey over the future status of an island that belonged to neither of these states. The novelist Lawrence Durrell reflected in 1957 that 'the key was finally turned upon Cyprus'.

The British proposals for self-government in Cyprus were rejected by both Athens and Ankara. The Greek reply of 17 September noted that even though Whitehall had departed, to a certain extent, from its original inflexible attitude, it was still impossible to reach agreement on two points, namely the right of self-determination (the word 'never' was changed to 'maybe' and 'some time') and the right of self-government. Even the constitution offered could not be regarded as adequate for so highly developed and civilized a people as the Cypriots. George V.Melas, the Greek Ambassador in Washington, described the conference as 'a tragic intermezzo bound to fail even before it began'. Of the proposed Macmillan proposals, 'they are,' he said, 'a negation of democracy'.

Meanwhile news of an explosion on 6 September in the grounds of the Turkish consulate at Salonica (formerly Atatürk's house) precipitated murderous anti-Greek riots in Smyrna and Istanbul. Hasan Ucar (a former employee of the consulate) and Oktay Engin (a student) were convicted by a Greek court of causing the explosion. During a night of terror in Istanbul on 6-7 September an estimated 76 Byzantine churches were burnt or destroyed, 862 shops wrecked and many others looted, and over 7,000 houses damaged. The Greek quarter of Peran was described by the *Daily Mail* correspondent on 14 September as being similar to the bombed parts of London during the Second World War. Another reporter remarked that Istanbul on the night was 'turned into the site of the Apocalypse'. Capital goods valued at $150 million were destroyed.

The police simply stood by and watched. Shortly before the demonstrations President Bayar and Premier Menderes were on a train *en route* to Ankara, leaving their rioting compatriots behind them. After travelling about 100 kilometres (60 miles) Menderes returned and ordered the army to step in; but it was too late. The 'crucifixion of Christendom' was complete. In fact the incidents were sufficient excuse for the leader of the nationalist action party, Colonel Alparslan Turkes, to build a swimming pool in the shape of Cyprus at his Ankara headquarters. Turkes's party still believes in 'Pan Turanism', that all races which can in any way be linked to the Turks, including the Finns, the Hungarians and even the Irish, should unite and build up a new empire.

The official Turkish view was that the riots were simply a Communist plot aimed against western interests and Greco-Turkish friendship. Yet the Communist party in Turkey was proscribed. The incidents in fact were undoubtedly connived at, if not directly inspired, by the Turkish government and were aimed at putting pressure on the USA to oppose the inclusion of the Cyprus item on the agenda of the tenth General Assembly. The incidents also provided useful ammunition for Zorlu in his negotiations with his British and Greek counterparts in London.

At the trials at Yassiada (an island in the sea of Marmara), which opened on 14 October 1960, case number two was listed as 'September 6-7 incidents'. Ten former government officials were tried with inciting riots against the Greek population of Istanbul as a means of pressing the Turkish viewpoint on the Cyprus dispute. Evidence was given by defence witnesses that the government had been put up to staging a Cyprus demonstration by Harold Macmillan but that the rally, badly mismanaged by Menderes, had degenerated into an uncontrollable riot.

The court, applying the harsh Article 146, announced its verdicts on 15 September 1961 – eleven months and one day after the trials opened. They were:

15   were condemned to death; the death sentences of all
     except Menderes, Zorlu and Hasan Polatkan
     (Finance Minister) were commuted to life
     imprisonment by the National Unity Committee;
31   were sentenced to life imprisonment;
418 received prison terms ranging from 2 to 15 years;
123 were acquitted, most of them minor figures against
     whom no individual wrongdoing could be proved;
5   cases were dropped because of insufficient evidence.

The trial of the fallen regime had ended. Zorlu and Polatkan
were hanged on 16 September in the prison island of Imrali and
Menderes also at Imrali on the following day. Messages from
world leaders pleading for mercy failed to save Menderes.

In 1955 even the staunchest supporters of the Greek
government were shocked by the recent events. 'Greece,' said
the normally pro-western and conservative newspaper
Kathimerini on 25 September, 'has been betrayed.' Ominously it
added that Greece should withdraw from NATO. Athens was
the scene of massive demonstrations and following the receipt
of the highly undiplomatic and terse Dulles note mentioned
below, anti-US, anti-western and anti-NATO sentiment
reached a very high peak.

The Greek government recalled its unit sent to fight in Korea
with the UN forces as well as its officers serving under NATO
command at Izmir (Smyrna). Its NATO allies were also
informed that its future position might become problematic if
they did not show a better understanding of the Greek
viewpoint and if Turkey failed to give moral and material
satisfaction for the September vandalism.

Turkey consequently organized a ceremony in Izmir during
which its troops saluted the flags of all NATO countries. It also
passed a law granting reparation to the Greeks whose property
had been damaged or destroyed during the riots. Moreover,
Greece obtained the abolition of a measure adopted in 1948
under which US nationals serving with American non-
diplomatic missions in Greece were exempted from the
jurisdiction of local courts.

The USA was naturally alarmed by the recent
developments. On 18 September 1955 John Foster Dulles, the
Secretary of State, sent identical notes to Athens and Ankara: 'I

have followed with concern the dangerous deterioration of Greek-Turkish relations caused by the Cyprus question. Regardless of the causes of this disagreement, which are complex and numerous, I believe that the unity of the North Atlantic community, which is the basis of our common security, must be restored without delay.'[3]

The USA urged that 'quiet diplomacy' amongst friends was the most constructive approach. In similar vein the Greek ambassadors in London and Washington henceforth advanced the thesis that if NATO were not careful Moscow might take advantage of such rifts between western allies. With Egypt turning to the eastern bloc for arms and other supplies the middle east and eastern Mediterranean were transformed into a massive theatre of possible confrontation. The US, Britain and to a lesser extent France found a powerful competitor in the Soviet Union.

In November 1955 Whitehall presented its 'Formula for Cyprus' to the Greek and Turkish governments and to Archbishop Makarios. The formula stressed that it was not Britain's position that 'the principle of self-determination can never be applied to Cyprus' but that account should be taken of the 'strategic position of the island'. As for self-government, 'it is the intention of Britain to work for a solution which will satisfy the wishes of the people of Cyprus'. Britain was assured of the USA's active help over its constitutional plans and was also confident of the support of Constantine Karamanlis and Spyros Theotokis, the new Premier and Foreign Minister, over the self-determination formula.

Chosen over the vastly more popular Stephanos Stephanopoulos, Karamanlis had been favoured by the Greek palace and by the USA because he had agreed in principle to work towards a solution of the Cyprus question in accordance with the wishes of his western allies. The ex-Minister of Public Works succeeded Papagos (who had died) in 1955 and until June 1963 remained continuously in office, longer than any other Prime Minister in the history of modern Greece.

Karamanlis therefore played the Cyprus issue too soft for the taste of many Greeks. Secret conversations were arranged with British officials and an emissary was sent to confer with Makarios and Harding, the governor. His guiding principle, known as the 'policy of the national centre', soon became an irritant in Greco-Cypriot relations. At the root of this British-American concept lay the view that the alliance interests of Greece must prevail over her interests in Cyprus. The conflict between the national desire for absolute sovereignty and the pragmatic necessity of retaining powerful friends was at the root of the long-standing Greek dilemma over *enosis*.

Field-Marshal Sir John Harding was appointed Governor of Cyprus on 25 September 1955. He was on the eve of retirement after serving as Chief of the Imperial General Staff since 1952. For a government to choose a top-ranking soldier to fight EOKA was certainly a big tribute to Grivas and his combatants. On 3 October he arrived in Cyprus and Makarios readily expressed his willingness to meet him, hinting that a compromise was possible. Discussions between the governor and the archbishop proceeded intermittently throughout the following few months. A final meeting was held in Nicosia on 29 February 1956 which was also attended by Alan Lennox-Boyd, the Secretary of State for the Colonies.

In the course of these discussions (based on the recent Macmillan proposals) the archbishop was informed that Britain formally recognized the principle of self-determination but considered its application not to be a practical proposition at the time on account of the situation in the eastern Mediterranean. Makarios was also told that Britain was prepared to offer the people of Cyprus a wide measure of self-government at once, only reserving to the governor defence, external affairs and, for so long as the governor thought necessary, internal security. A constitutional commissioner would be appointed to make recommendations for the implementation of these proposals.

The discussions eventually broke down and Harding, who was given wider powers than his predecessors in relation to security, was prompt in building up an intelligence network. After EOKA had captured a large consignment of arms transferred from Suez to Famagusta he became personally responsible for the direction of all security operations. He requested troop reinforcements and had them trained in riot-breaking by police methods, and outlying police posts were given military protection.

Road-blocks and house-to-house searches were intensified. Travelling through the night without lights along narrow mountain roads, troops usually surrounded suspect villages at dawn. All males over the age of 12 were taken outside for questioning while the houses were searched in the presence of women and children. After many fruitless ventures vast quantities of arms, ammunition and army uniforms were eventually discovered and, with the help of police dogs, commandos found a network of caves in the Troodos mountains.

Yet intensified security operations brought no early results and the last week in October saw one of the worst outbreaks of disorder since the commencement of hostilities. At the beginning of November the Special Court Law came into force, providing an extra civil court to try offences prejudicial to internal security. Tension mounted during the trial of Karaolis, who was sentenced to death under normal criminal law for the murder of Michael Poullis, a Greek policeman, following a rally. The Cyprus supreme court's dismissal of his appeal on 12 November was followed by a campaign against British servicemen. Five were killed in one week alone. However, the sentencing of Karaolis, a mild-mannered youth who worked in the government's income tax department, provided the Greeks with the first of their *enosis* martyrs.

Harding's announcement on 16 November, following discussions in London, that Britain had approved a £38 million development programme for Cyprus was largely eclipsed by the political situation. Ten days later a state of emergency was declared, which in the view of the authorities had now become necessary owing to the 'increase in terrorist outrages and widespread disorders leading to serious injuries to life and property. . . '. Under the new regulations the unauthorized possession of firearms and explosives carried a maximum penalty of death. Provision was also made for deportation, censorship, the placing of large sums of money on the heads of wanted men and collective punishment. A collective fine of £2,000 was levied on the villagers of Lefkoniko for the destruction of the local post office by fire; its inhabitants were personally informed by the governor on 4 December.

Measures taken on the night of 13-14 December were also

very drastic. After countless visits security forces arrested 129 leading AKEL and PEO members and removed them to a detention camp near Larnaca. AKEL and AON, its youth organization, were banned under the emergency regulations as dangerous associations whose real objects were 'to prolong dissension and turbulence on the island'. The offices of the Communist paper *Neos Demokratis* were closed. But PEO and other Communist-orientated organizations affiliated to AKEL were not proscribed, apparently because the British authorities in Cyprus wished to interfere as little as possible with the trade unions and the labour movement.

Most of the AKEL leaders were set free a few months later and permission was given for the publication of a new daily newspaper giving expression to AKEL policy. International pressure, especially from British Members of Parliament and trade unions, was successful in securing their early release. There were several probable explanations for these Draconian measures:

1   Britain responded to the pressure of rightist newspapers in Greece which complained that the authorities were clamping down hard on the Cypriot nationalists but were allowing the Communists full freedom of action.

2   Britain desired to create a better atmosphere for negotiations with Archbishop Makarios by making sure that he would not be criticized by the left.

3   It was necessary to stifle the progress of AKEL, at the time Cyprus's largest political party.

4   It was part of Britain's two-faced policy. Kenneth Robinson MP (St Pancras North), who together with Lena Jeger MP (Holborn and St Pancras South) represented the overwhelming majority of Cypriots in England, had this to say on 5 May 1955 during a four-hour debate on Cyprus:

> 'This demand for Enosis has been there all the time, sometimes fairly quiescent, at other times flaring up, and in recent years the demand has become constant and clamant. What is the attitude of Her Majesty's Government? It is the attitude of the ostrich. They pretend that it is not a popular demand, that it is merely a noisy agitation on the part of a

small minority led by Communists, now described in terms of the favourite Foreign Office cliché as 'Communist terrorists', and by a few leaders of the Greek Orthodox Church.'[4]

5   Britain wanted to demonstrate to Washington and to Athens that Cyprus was first its child and then that of the west, so that it was desirable for the problem to be solved under British initiative but within the compounds of western interests.

6   It was alleged by Grivas that this was a device to promote popular sympathy for AKEL.

After a second Greek recourse to the UN over Cyprus, it was decided on 21 September 1955 not to include the question on the General Assembly's agenda. Four countries voted in favour, seven against and four abstained. The Greek delegation challenged this recommendation in the plenary meeting of the General Assembly on 23 September, but the exclusion of this item from the agenda was agreed by 28 votes to 22 with 10 members abstaining.

This setback, coming after the experiences of late August and early September (the tripartite conference and the anti-Greek riots in Smyrna and Istanbul), caused great bitterness in Greece. Even the pro-western newspaper *Kathimerini* complained that Greece had been deserted by its allies (amongst the countries voting against being the USA, Britain, France, Canada and the Netherlands) and proclaimed that 'Greece must have the courage to stand alone'. The government hinted that it might even withdraw entirely from NATO. However, the years that followed showed that these were hollow threats since the country was still in the vice-like grip of American capital.

The Harding-Makarios talks continued into the first two months of 1956. The British assurances based on the Macmillan proposals were vague and ambiguous, although indirectly the principle of self-determination was recognized. On 2 February 1956 Makarios made his reservations clear and 12 days later Harding's reply expressed satisfaction at the archbishop's readiness to assist in the pacification of the island and at his willingness to co-operate in the framing of the constitution. In fact Makarios put forward five general

principles for the proper functioning of self-government and
Harding put forward six points which should serve as the basis
for discussion.

A solution seemed near, but differences arose apparently
over amnesty, public security and the elected majority
provisions. Terrorists convicted of violence against the person
and of illegal possession of arms, ammunition and explosives
were excluded from the amnesty and the British were not
willing to fix a date for the relinquishment of control over
internal security or to guarantee in advance that the elected
majority in the assembly would be Greek. The British argued
that the needs of security could not be anticipated.

It is widely believed, and was often argued by Makarios
himself, that the intervention of Lennox-Boyd, who arrived in
Cyprus on 29 February, prevented a possible solution. In fact
there were at least seven other possible reasons for the eventual
collapse:

1   The British refused to commit themselves as to the
approximate date for granting self-determination. They were in
fact insisting that the archbishop should have faith and trust
them; but on 9 March he was to be exiled.

2   Britain's position in the middle east was crumbling, and it
was concerned about internal security.

3   The activities of the Turkish clubs and associations such as
the National Committee for the Protection of Cyprus (based in
Ankara) and the Kibris Türktür Parti (based in Nicosia)
embarrassed the British into promising that no binding
constitutional commitments would be undertaken before they
had been consulted. The Turkish government had long ago
been brought into the dispute by British diplomacy. As C.M.
Woodhouse reflected in his book *The Story of Greece*, 'the British
seemed to argue the Turkish case before the Turks even
thought of it'.

4   There was a general Greek commitment to immediate *enosis*
or as a second best to the granting of self-determination.

5   During February 1956 the Greek government was trying to
force on the Cypriot leadership the acceptance of a 'conciliatory
solution' which it was ready to accept itself. In a telegram to

Makarios on 17 February the Greeks explained that he could use the British proposals in any way he liked – that is accept, amend or reject them. Athens therefore abdicated from the final decision and future consequences. Sir Charles Peake spoke of the 'moral paralysis' on the part of the Greek authorities which was in fact due mainly to the political situation. At the elections of 19 February the democratic union (DE) received 49.8 per cent of the votes, the national radical union (ERE) 45.7 per cent and the remaining candidates 4.5 per cent. However, the complex electoral system promulgated before the Greek Vouli was dissolved on 10 January transformed the majority of votes into a minority of seats and Karamanlis was returned to power with 155 seats against 145 for the opposition.

6 Grivas quite unexpectedly declared from his secret headquarters that he would not accept the settlement which Makarios appeared to be negotiating. On that very evening when agreement seemed to be forthcoming bombs exploded in certain parts of the island.

7 The British claimed that they did not believe in the archbishop's good faith and proceeded to deport him. Even though Eden informed the House of Commons on 14 March 1956 that 'every concession on the part of the British government is accompanied at once by new demands on the part of the Cypriots', the truth is that nearly all the yielding had been done by Makarios, who had shifted decisively from his original demand of 'nothing less than enosis'.

Whitehall's policy in the first 11 months of EOKA's struggle passed through several distinct and contradictory stages. It had begun with a categorical denial that the problem existed at all, or at least that it involved anyone except Great Britain. The Greeks were warned by Anthony Nutting in December 1954 to 'stop playing with fire'. The next stage was the attempt to enlarge the issue by drawing in Greece and Turkey. The British 'domestic' issue had now become an 'international' issue. When this policy failed it was restricted to Britain and Makarios and direct negotiations followed. When these looked like being successful they were broken off because it was felt that the whole structure of middle eastern security would be jeopardized. Eden informed the Commons on 14 March that these commitments could not be 'speedily and effectively carried out unless Britain had the assured and unfettered use of bases in Cyprus'. In his memoirs Eden recorded that he regarded the alliance with Turkey as 'the first consideration in our policy in that part of the world'.

The linking of Cyprus with Turkish territorial security was a direct invitation to Turkey to enter the dispute. Another complication was added to existing difficulties, out of which grew the demand 'ya taksim ya ölüm' (partition or death), and hence more tension and bloodshed. By the second half of 1956 the USA had quietly endorsed the principle of partition, reminding everyone of other 'successful' partitions such as Trieste.

Finally, Britain became the arbiter in what was portrayed as a Greek-Turkish dispute and the protector of the west's interests in the middle east. These shifts and turns were constantly attacked by the British press. The *Daily Telegraph* demanded on 7 June 'a genuine and positive action'. The *Spectator* of the same date described the Conservative policy as 'silly, chaotic and barbaric'.

Following the breakdown of the Harding-Makarios talks the next policy shift was to banish Makarios who was henceforth seen as an obstacle to a settlement (a decision taken while the negotiations were still going on). The archbishop, who was on the point of leaving Nicosia airport for further talks in Athens on 9 March 1956, was instead ordered to enter an RAF plane. He was deported to the Seychelles where he was to stay for 13 months. With him went Papastavros Papagathanelou, chief priest of Phaneromeni church in Nicosia, Bishop Kyprianos of Kyrenia and Polycarpos Ioannides, a journalist and secretary of the latter's see. There was however to be another notable deportee. Father Kallinikos Macheriotis, Archimandrite of the Greek Orthodox Church in Camden Town, London, was served with a deportation order by police officers on 11 June. His crime was that of being chairman of a committee which collected funds in England for the Cypriot national struggle.

Politically the banishment of Makarios was a serious miscalculation; he was the one true representative of the island's Greek population, who could not easily be replaced, and the only person who could curb acts of violence. The news of his arrest was followed by a week-long general strike. Army units cordoned off the archbishop's palace and soldiers were posted to guard all government buildings and all the approaches to the capital. Riots also broke out in Greece and on 10 March the government recalled Vasilis Mostras, its ambassador, from London.

Deportation was criticized as being 'insane' and 'unreasonable'. In fact it was also contrary to Article 9 of the UN Charter which states that 'no one shall be subjected to arbitrary arrest, detention or exile'. However, the four deportees were lodged comfortably in the San Souci villa at Mahé, Seychelles, in the middle of the Indian Ocean. Being the summer residence of the local governor, it had a sitting room, three bedrooms and a verandah and was looked after by four servants. A police guard of non-commissioned officers and constables commanded by two assistant superintendents was responsible for their security. Makarios is often quoted as referring to his exile as 'a great experience and an unforgettable event'.

In Cyprus meanwhile violence grew and in April Harding undertook large-scale operations against EOKA in the Troodos mountains. Between April 1955 and 27 July 1956 the following deaths were recorded:

	Killed	Wounded
Armed forces and police from the UK	43	235
Cypriot civilians:		
(a) men	76	152
(b) women	5	13
(c) children	2	6
British civilians from the UK	7	34
	133	440

Casualties were far greater in the months following Makarios' banishment. The seven deaths of British civilians all took place between April and July 1956.

In London politicians of all parties criticized both the failure of the discussions and the deportation of Makarios. Lord Hailsham, an eminent Tory, described the British policy as 'ham-handed in the highest degree'. Lord Winster blamed the administration for their 'pomposity of evasion' after they had yielded on the principle of self-determination. On 14 March 1956 Aneurin Bevan MP tabled a motion regretting the British government's failure 'to reach a settlement in Cyprus and in particular their action in discontinuing negotiations about the points now outstanding after the major issue of self-determination had been resolved'. Eden, who successfully proposed an amendment to Bevan's motion, justified the power of deportation which, he said, 'as in the case of India was an effective policy in the primary task of restoring law and order and then effecting a settlement'. The man of a thousand paradoxes had blundered yet again.

A suggestion by James Griffiths MP on 14 May that the archbishop should be brought back to London for discussions was derided by the government. Another request by A. Lewis MP that Makarios should be allowed to visit Britain and address an all-party meeting of both Houses of Parliament on the Cyprus question was also rejected. On the same day (27 June) he followed up with an oral request that the UN should hold a referendum in Cyprus to ascertain the views of the islanders on their future. Lennox-Boyd replied that 'it would not be a means of bringing peace and tranquillity to Cyprus'.

On 10 May 1956 Michael Karaolis and Andreas Demetriou were hanged (the latter for wounding a British intelligence agent) after the Judicial Committee of the Privy Council had rejected an appeal by Karaolis in the previous month. Shortly afterwards two British soldiers who had been held for some months as hostages were executed by EOKA as a reprisal.

The two impending hangings caused a mass uproar in Athens. On 9 May the Panhellenic Committee for Enosis requested permission from the police to hold a rally at 1 p.m. Although it was rescheduled by the police to the off-peak hour of 3 p.m. an estimated crowd of 10,000 assembled earlier at Omonia Square where they were addressed by Archbishop Dorotheos. The Greek government, Britain, America and NATO were condemned by the demonstrators who, after burning a Union Jack, moved in force towards the British Embassy. At that juncture the police, with guns at the ready, suddenly appeared from everywhere and indiscriminately fired shots at the crowd. Seven people were killed and over 200 injured. It has since been established that the police acted on the direct orders of the government.

More hangings followed. On 8 August Andreas Zakos, Harilaos Michail and Iakovos Patatsos were executed in the Nicosia central prison. The first two were captured by Major Brian Coombe, following a clash which is popularly known as the 'famous battle of Soli'. It was also here that Makarios's cousin Haralambos Mouskos died in combat on 15 December 1955. Patatsos, on the other hand, was an extremely religious youth who paid the penalty for shooting at a Turkish policeman.

The people of Nicosia immediately staged noisy demonstrations, but more executions followed. On 21 September Michael Koutsoftas and Andreas Panayides were hanged for killing British airmen and Stelios Mavrommatis for firing at them. Consequently, during the so-called 'Black November', there were 416 acts of violence and 34 people died – a record. However, after the collapse of the Suez operation (the British presence in the island greatly facilitated the attack on Egypt) Harding had more troops available and inflicted severe blows at EOKA. In November the death penalty was extended and became mandatory in a number of cases where previously the courts had the power to impose an alternative sentence. Furthermore, a new Emergency Law enabled the governor to prohibit the sale and distribution of publications prejudicial to security.

Around this time Anglo-Greek relations were at a very low ebb. In Britain there was much distress at the strained relations with a country that had been its ally and friend. By permitting Harding to set up what was tantamount to a military dictatorship (reminiscent of Palmer's in the 1930s), and indulge in the jailing and whipping of schoolboys (a practice more associated with Hitler and General Franco and one not approved by the British public), to impose collective fines on villages (after the manner of Nazi collective punishments), to carry out mass detentions and round up villagers behind barbed wire as though they were prisoners of war or criminals, the British had so deeply offended and embittered the kindly Greek Cypriots that the most indispensable condition for any military base, the goodwill of the local inhabitants, had been practically destroyed.

During that crucial summer of 1956 the Cyprus problem was temporarily overshadowed by an even more disturbing one for the British: Gamal Abdul Nasser had nationalized the Suez Canal. During the summer Grivas created PEKA (Politiki Epitropi Kiprion Agoniston – the Political Committee of the Cyprus Struggle), which amongst other things organized demonstrations and arranged hiding places for EOKA. It was also realized around this time that in order to achieve the original aims the use of force must be fortified by propaganda. There was also a youth movement, ANE (Alkimos Neolea tis EOKA), which was particularly active in riots and demonstrations.

Tension had arisen between the Greeks and Turks of Cyprus. Racial strife which started mildly in January 1956 reached a climax in May when the murder of several Turks set off serious riots and the Turks then killed two Greeks. Pitched battles were fought between them and a barrier was set up in Nicosia to separate the two sides. The creation of an auxiliary police force manned entirely by Turks but under British officers, whose task was to control Greek riots and help the armed forces fight EOKA, served further to polarize the two communities. By February 1957, the mobile reserve of the Cyprus police consisted of 32 officers and 551 men of whom none was Greek but 560 were Turkish Cypriots.

The Secretary of State for the Colonies announced on 12 July 1956 that he had appointed as constitutional commissioner the distinguished jurist Lord Radcliffe, who was charged with the preparation of proposals for a liberal measure of self-government for Cyprus under British sovereignty, giving the people a wide measure of control over their own affairs while at the same time safeguarding both the interests of the Turkish minority and British strategic requirements. Lord Radcliffe was remembered by some Cypriots because in 1947 he took charge of the commission that defined the frontiers between India and Pakistan in both Bengal and the Punjab. Partition there led to a devastating war between the two newly independent states. Lord Radcliffe visited Cyprus twice in the course of his mission to hear the views of all sections of opinion before completing the new constitution. However, no Greek Cypriot of major political standing came forward. All demanded that any meaningful discussions should include Makarios, their acknowledged leader.

His suggestions were published as a White Paper in the UK and Cyprus on 19 December 1956. Lennox-Boyd visited both Athens and Ankara before the proposals were announced in order to explain them to the Greek and Turkish governments and to invite their support. The report, which Lennox-Boyd described as a 'statesmanlike document', was in two parts:

(a) the recommendations for a constitution, and

(b) a covering note which explained why Lord Radcliffe preferred his conclusions to other possible arrangements; he emphasized that the people of Cyprus 'were an adult people enjoying long cultural traditions and an established educational system, fully capable of furnishing qualified administrators, lawyers, doctors and men of business'.

The key proposals were:

1 There would be a legislative assembly consisting of a speaker, a deputy speaker and 36 other members of which 6 would be elected by members on a Turkish Cypriot communal roll, 24 on a general roll and 6 would be nominated by the Governor.

2 A chief minister must act as the head of government in self-governing matters. He would be appointed by the governor according to his discretion, but it would be the governor's duty to select for this purpose the person who appeared to him to command the largest measure of general support among the members of the legislative assembly.

3 A minister for Turkish Cypriot affairs would deal with the special affairs of his community including education. Laws affecting these affairs would require the consent of two-thirds of the assembly's Turkish elected members.

4 No bill passed by the legislative assembly should become law unless and until the governor had signified assent to it.

Simultaneously with their publication, Whitehall announced that it had accepted Radcliffe's proposals. Lennox-Boyd however referred to another possible solution, that of partition. He informed the Commons on 19 December 1956 that it was simply another option: 'As regards the eventual status of the island, HMG have already affirmed their recognition of the principle of self-determination. When the international and strategic situation permits, and provided that self-government is working satisfactorily, HMG will be ready to review the question of the application of self-determination. . . . HMG recognise that the exercise of self-determination in such a mixed population must include partition among the eventual options.'[5]

He also disclosed that partition was discussed with the Greek and Turkish governments. In 1961 and on other occasions both Grivas and George Melas, Greek Ambassador to the USA up to 1958, asserted that Averoff himself talked of partition as being another possible solution to the Cyprus problem. Both gave as their example the Averoff-Iksel talks of 6 October 1956.

What were the results of Britain's attempt to maintain sovereignty over Cyprus?

1   It involved immense military expenditure. This prompted many to remark that the government was betraying the true economic interests of the British nation.

2   A disproportionate amount of Britain's slender military strength was diverted to the island.

3   The loyalty and friendship of the islanders was lost.

4   It involved the use of a repressive policy which met some criticism in the rest of the world. The emergency regulations in the island amounted to an almost total denial of civil liberties and even *The Times* in December 1956 accused the government of amending the rules to the point of severity 'which is nothing but ruthless'.

5   Perhaps the most serious effect was that prolonged strife in the island weakened NATO's eastern flank.

The UK therefore was faced with several possibilities:

1   Cyprus could in theory be handed over to Greece, since most of the island's inhabitants were Greek in every sense of the word.

2   Britain could attempt to operate some kind of a constitution which would grant self-government and prepare for further resolution of the problem at a later date.

3   Cyprus could in some way be internationalized.

4   British colonial rule could continue.

5   The island could, as a last resort, be partitioned between Greeks and Turks, with a voluntary exchange of populations which would presumably have to be financed by the British or American exchequers. However, the two peoples were neither geographically isolated nor economically divisible. Hence this policy was both impracticable and dangerous.

British diplomats were always aware of the above possibilities and of the threat of partition which, through their policy of divide and rule, they were bringing closer to actual fulfilment. Plans for the island's partition are believed to have been thought of first by the Americans in the mid 1950s. Partition, they believed, would satisfy both Greece and Turkey.

The proposals of Lord Radcliffe were accepted in principle by the Turkish government and by the Turkish Cypriot community almost immediately after they were published. The Greek government, on the other hand, rejected them, giving three reasons:

1   They were neither democratic nor liberal since the elected majority principle was strangled by the almost unlimited powers of the governor.

2   They did not envisage the right of self-determination for the Cypriot people and were not therefore in accord with the fundamental principles of the UN Charter.

3   These and other deficiencies precluded therefore the solution of the Cyprus problem.

The proposals were also rejected by the island's Greek inhabitants. Their feelings were voiced by the newspaper *Ethnos* (*Nation*) which stated on 27 December 1956 that, 'the Greeks are not so foolish as to swallow the pill which was prepared in the laboratory of constitutional alchemy by Lord Radcliffe'. The legislative assembly was described as not an assembly 'but in essence a body without heart and with borrowed legs'.

The proposals and the statement by Lennox-Boyd were also shown to Archbishop Makarios on 19 December 1956 and D.L. Pearson (Lord Radcliffe's secretary) and C.G. Tornaritis (a senior Greek-speaking officer of the Cyprus government) arrived in the Seychelles on 21 December to explain any parts of the proposals to him on which further elucidation was required. However, as Hector Hughes MP asked on 23 January 1957, 'would it not be more logical and constitutional for the government and Lord Radcliffe to hold direct conversations with the Archbishop in London instead of sending Lord Radcliffe on a wild goose chase, on a mission of apology to the United States?'

Meanwhile on 19 July 1956 (seven days after Lord Radcliffe's appointment) Aneurin Bevan MP (a prominent member of the Labour party) pleaded with the Cypriots to stop forthwith all acts of violence, 'not only because it is the proper thing to do but because it would, at present, be the most ingenious thing to do'. Bevan argued that if violence were terminated the government 'would be stripped stark naked of any further excuse for not proceeding' with their proposed plans. His plea followed an increase in tension and commencement of racial strife in January which reached its climax in May.

On 16 August Grivas ordered suspension of operations, the truce coinciding with the far more crucial British, French and Israeli military preparations for an all-out attack on Nasser's Egypt. Grivas declared that the object of the truce was to test the sincerity of the British, who claimed that his operations stood in the way of a settlement. The government responded on 22 August with surrender terms which were to remain open for three weeks:

1   Arms were to be laid down.

2   Terrorists could either go to Greece, provided that country accepted them, or remain in Cyprus.

3   British subjects who went to Greece would lose British citizenship and the right to re-enter Cyprus.

4   Terrorists remaining in Cyprus would be brought to trial only for crimes involving violence against the person.

5   When peace returned an amnesty would be declared for those already convicted of certain offences.

Digenes dismissed these terms and declared that if the authorities did not show a change of heart his units would go over to the offensive on the morning of 28 August. All over Cyprus the British conditions were described as 'uncompromising and tactless'. Even in London Harding's attitude was criticized. Some Members of Parliament even described him as a 'liability to Britain's cause in the island'.

However, the Colonial Office announced on 27 August that documents seized by the security forces, including extracts from Grivas's own diaries, had established beyond all doubt that Makarios had taken a leading part in the foundation and operational planning of EOKA. The Colonial Office, which interpreted Grivas's truce as a sign of weakness and as an attempt to gain himself some breathing space during regroupment, still believed that there was no hope of any real peace so long as EOKA was undefeated. With the Suez crisis receding temporarily to the background, the authorities decided to make a stand against EOKA. A bomb explosion at Larnaca on 28 August opened a new campaign of violence. The Bishop of Kition and Nicos Kranidiotis, secretary-general of the ethnarchy, who had been mentioned in the captured documents, were placed under house arrest.

On 22 October 1956 Averoff, the Greek Foreign Minister, told 35 foreign journalists that Greece believed that Cypriots should soon be given the right to govern themselves 'within the framework of the British Commonwealth'. He also stated that his government did not ask for a radical solution because it accepted that international complications did not admit a quick solution. By some observers this statement was rightly regarded as a step forward. Yet the British response, as set out by Lennox-Boyd on 19 December 1956, talked of partition as another possible solution.

Also on 22 October 1956 Karamanlis announced that he would be leading the Greek delegation to the UN in the following month and that representatives from all opposition parties would be welcome. He attended the Assembly's early meetings in November specifically to promote the Cyprus question in the UN as well as in the USA. Going to the UN however involved, according to Karamanlis, 'the public airing of the most difficult problem of foreign policy Greece has ever had to face'. Consequently the Greek Premier heeded American advice that the UN was not the proper forum for settling the Cyprus question but that 'quiet diplomacy' was the most constructive approach. He went on to confer in private with high ranking members of the US Administration on the security problems of eastern Europe and of the middle east.

Nevertheless on 22 February 1957 a draft resolution on Cyprus was introduced before the UN Political Committee by Krishna Menon, the powerful head of the Indian delegation. As an apostle of self-determination and non-alignment he longed to see an independent Cypriot state. It replaced a draft 'that never was' which had been favoured by the US delegation and circulated, but never tabled, by the delegation of Thailand. It also replaced four other draft resolutions – two by the Greek delegation, one by the British and another by the delegation of Panama.

The Political Committee recommended Menon's resolution for adoption by a show of hands vote with 76 members voting in its favour, none opposing it and only 2 abstaining – Panama and Afghanistan. On 26 February it was adopted by the General Assembly as resolution 1013 (XI), which stated that the solution of the Cyprus problem required 'an atmosphere of peace and freedom of expression' and that 'a peaceful, democratic and just solution' would be found 'in accordance with the purposes and principles of the Charter of the UN, and that negotiations will be resumed and continued to the end'. The vote was 57 in favour, none against and one abstention.

It was widely interpreted that such negotiations would take place between the Cypriot people and the British government. The British replied that other and wider interests had a right to be consulted. Bilateral talks between Makarios and the British government were out of the question.

When Makarios asked for bilateral talks he meant talks between the Cypriot people – both Greek and Turk – and the British authorities. He made this clear both in the Seychelles in interviews with colonial officials and later when he was allowed to return to Athens. The British Foreign Office misled British and world opinion by pretending the archbishop wanted to exclude the Turkish element.

The first few months of 1957 were marked by British intelligence successes in the island and by intense diplomatic activity abroad. Harding made several claims that the days of EOKA were numbered and on 25 February had thousands of leaflets making his assertions scattered abroad. It was true that a few top ranking EOKA men were killed. Markos Drakos on 18 January, Gregorios Afxentiou and Avgoustis Efstathiou on 3 March, were notable losses. It appeared that the new General Officer Commanding, Major-General D.A. Kendrew, was highly successful in hunting down these men.

Averoff put forward a scheme in February for a customs union linking Greece, Turkey and Cyprus in the event of *enosis*. Under this plan Cypriot Turks were to have dual nationality and exemption from conscription. The Turks, who did not accept this proposal, were further infuriated when Averoff, speaking to the Greek Vouli on 11 March, declared that 'if in order to reach enosis one were obliged to make the manoeuvre of a temporary independence, would he who had done this deserve criticism?' Averoff, knowingly or unknowingly, played straight into the hands of the British and the Turks. It was a fatal blunder.

Also of great significance was the announcement on 15 March that Lord Ismay, the NATO Secretary-General, had offered his good offices for promoting a conciliation in the dispute in accordance with the resolution on the peaceful settlement of disputes which was adopted by NATO the previous December. Lennox-Boyd announced on 28 March that Britain was glad to take advantage of the NATO conciliation machinery. The Turks were also in favour but Greece, after considering the offer for five hours at cabinet level, rejected it and insisted with Archbishop Makarios that the question was outside the competence of NATO and a matter only for the UN. The Greeks also feared that such mediation might lead to partition.

For reasons outlined below Britain declared in March that Makarios and the other deportees could leave the Seychelles but should not return to Cyprus at such an auspicious hour. This announcement caused a great uproar within the Conservative party. To Lord Salisbury, the keeper of the Tory conscience, the decision to free the wily priest was a sign of 'scuttle policy' and he resigned from the Cabinet and the leadership of the House of Lords on 29 March.

Makarios and his co-exiles left Sans Souci on 6 April 1957

and boarded the Greek ship *Olympic Thunder* bound for
Madagascar. They arrived in Athens at 10 a.m. on 17 April,
where they were given a hero's welcome. The Greek capital
became the archbishop's new base. He gathered men of real
calibre around him and commenced once more his difficult task
of keeping world opinion informed of the continuing tragedy of
Cyprus.

The deportees were released because:

1   Following the recent Radcliffe proposals, Whitehall was
pledged to changes in the status of Cyprus.

2   Britain's middle eastern policy had failed, especially after
the Suez 'misadventure' of late 1956 and early 1957. Perhaps of
even greater significance for the Cyprus problem was the 1958
crisis created by events in Iraq, Jordan and the Lebanon.
Generally speaking, therefore, British military commitments in
the Middle East had by the end of the 1950s shrunk to cover
only those remaining areas of direct and indirect economic and
political interest. Strategists had 'requested' that Cyprus
should not be abandoned, while the Turks believed a British or
partly Turkish Cyprus was essential for their own security.

3   The British believed that only Makarios could stem the
escalation of violence in the island. Grivas in fact announced a
truce on 14 March 1957 to facilitate negotiations as soon as the
Cypriot ethnarch was released. Furthermore, the archbishop
repeated on 22 March that he would appeal to EOKA to
declare a cessation of all operations if the UK would show a
spirit of understanding by simultaneously abolishing the state
of emergency. Other conditions laid down by him included that
talks should be resumed between the government and the
Cypriot people and that he should be allowed to return to the
island. James Callaghan MP remarked, in a celebrated
Commons debate on 15 July 1957, 'the Archbishop threw the
ball back into the government's court'.

4   British policy had collapsed and by 1957 there was no
positive plan whatsoever. British troops and personnel in the
island were becoming exasperated.

5   Britain was bitterly criticized at home and abroad.
Parliamentarians at home pleaded for the release of Makarios
and for the resumption of meaningful negotiations. Even

though the deportees were released the government put up a rock-like resistance to any other concessions. In the debate mentioned above Callaghan stated: 'The Government are guilty not only of a great waste of public money, not only of straining our relations with our allies unnecessarily, but are guilty, so far as the people of Cyprus are concerned, of sacrificing their hopes as free men to choose their own Government for the sake of an apparently non-vital British strategic base. That seems to me to be the height of folly and madness.'[6]

Callaghan was referring to the visit of Duncan Sandys, Minister of Defence, to Cyprus and to the minister's recent report which emphasized that in the face of new realities Britain did not need the island as a base but just a couple of airstrips so that atomic bombers might fly off in pursuance of the west's defence obligations.

6 Official and unofficial pressure had been exerted by the United States. The major Greek-American associations demanded a just and peaceful solution to the Cyprus problem. However, at the Bermuda Conference which opened at Nassau on 21 March 1957 Britain and the USA agreed on the future course of the Cyprus issue. President Eisenhower suggested to Harold Macmillan, Prime Minister since 10 January, that there was no point in keeping Makarios a prisoner in the Seychelles any longer. From Eisenhower's account of the conference it is clear that Macmillan, who was so 'obsessed with the possibilities of getting rid of Nasser', was impressed with the suggestion. Eisenhower had earlier received a letter from King Paul of Greece, dated 10 March, pleading that his release would be a definite step towards a possible solution of 'this thorny problem'. On 28 March Macmillan took that step.

7 Makarios was proving an embarrassment to Britain, which wished to improve its image on the Cyprus question abroad, because there was no recognized leader but himself to conduct any meaningful negotiations.

With his release a new wave of diplomatic activity began. On 28 May 1957 Makarios wrote to Macmillan recalling the wording of resolution 1013 (XI) of the UN adopted on 26 February 1957 and the truce as from 14 March and said that Britain had not

taken any corresponding action. He also stated that the
emergency measures ruling the island must be terminated. He
talked of solving the question in a spirit of goodwill and mutual
understanding and concluded that he was 'ready and willing to
take part on behalf of the people of Cyprus in bilateral talks on
the basis of the application of self-determination in accordance
with the Charter of the UN'. The British, replying on 30 May,
stated that 'other and wider interests have a right to be
consulted'. According to Kenneth Robinson MP the British
reply was 'a smack in the mouth'.

Towards the end of May Macmillan recorded in his diary
that 'we still have no clear or positive plan'. He wrote that even
though he disliked the idea of dividing so small an area into two
separate nations, with the usual frontier troubles and with the
obvious economic disadvantages, he had begun 'reluctantly' to
feel that perhaps 'partition will be the only way out'.
Government advisers were sceptical and warned that wherever
tried partition was a total failure. Moreover, they stressed that
in Cyprus, owing to its size and past history, the two
communities were neither geographically isolated nor
economically divisible.

However, at a series of meetings during the first week of July
between ministers and top-ranking armed forces personnel a
new scheme was worked out. Its main provisions were:

1   Military enclaves would be delineated where full British
sovereignty would remain.

2   The rest of the island would be ruled by a 'condominium' of
the UK, Greece and Turkey with sovereignty held in
'partnership'.

3   The three powers were to be jointly responsible, through the
appointed governor, for external affairs and for certain reserved
subjects.

4   For internal affairs responsible government would be
created upon the general lines of that proposed by Lord
Radcliffe, adapted to the concept of 'triple sovereignty' or 'tri-
dominium'.

5   There would be two communal assemblies but matters of
common interest would be under the governor, assisted by a

council of six (four Greek and two Turkish) chosen from their respective assemblies.

On 16 July the Cabinet discussed Cyprus once more and there was wide agreement on the 'tri-dominium' concept; but, as Macmillan himself noted on that day, 'it would be most difficult to work out, to present and to achieve'. However, during the summer of 1957 private discussions were initiated by the government with the Greek and Turkish authorities. On 3 August Sir Roger Allen (since 6 May the new British Ambassador in Athens) suggested to Averoff that there should be a round-table conference, held in private and with no fixed agenda, to find a solution to the international aspects of the problem, thus paving the way for the settlement of the island's internal problems.

Since strained relations between Greece and Turkey created complications within NATO, the USA was prepared to take a close interest in such a conference, and Spaak, the Secretary-General of NATO, had been invited to attend as an observer.

The Turkish government after some deliberation accepted the British proposal. The Greeks, although not rejecting the idea of a conference, insisted that the basic outlines of a solution must first be agreed between the parties concerned through the normal diplomatic channels. They also pointed out that the intransigent stand of Turkey, which insisted on partition, rendered any conference nugatory and could only cause further harm to allied relations. The Greek *aide-mémoire* of 7 August assured the British government that Greece earnestly desired to see Greek-Turkish relations restored and Anglo-Greek friendship resume its former cordiality. However, the Cypriot people's claim to self-determination had to be supported.

Whitehall presented further notes to the Greeks on 12 and 14 August. The response from Greece on 27 August said that it was well known that its basic position on the Cyprus question was:

1   The issue lay between the British government and the people of Cyprus as set down in resolution 1013 (XI) of the UN.

2   Other states had indirect interests of greater or lesser importance which should undoubtedly be considered in any agreed solution. In no case should one of the aforementioned

states have the power of a quasi-veto.

3 No solution that would disregard the fundamental principles of the UN Charter should be adopted.

Another British note on 4 September and the Greek reply two days later also proved abortive. The original British note of 3 August was explained to Makarios on 5 August by Averoff and two top Foreign Office officials. Meanwhile, from late July, the archbishop was orientating himself towards a solution that envisaged independence. Grivas however was greatly disturbed and urged continued insistence on self-determination.

Averoff, at a press conference on 28 August, presented the Greek views on how Turkish anxieties about security, minority rights and economic matters might be allayed. Averoff later repeated the same views before the UN General Assembly. At another press conference on 5 September Karamanlis said that he would not reject a solution providing for an independent Cyprus if this was acceptable to the Cypriot people. He added that his government would take no part in any conference on the future of the island unless there were preliminary assurances that self-determination would be granted to the inhabitants within a fixed period. The Premier also pledged Greece's continued adherence to the western bloc and suggested that, since Greece was not a colonial power, it might play a pacifying role between the west and the Arab states.

Before leaving for the USA at the end of August to inform public opinion about the Cyprus problem and to follow the debates on the question in the UN, Makarios made his position clear:

1 He would be inclined to accept self-government as a stepping-stone to self-determination.

2 He was willing to take part in a conference in which each side would be represented in accordance with its numerical strength.

3 He expressed the hope that the USA would abandon its policy of non-involvement on the Cyprus question.

4 His object before the UN was to obtain the right of self-

determination for the island as the only solution consistent with democratic principles.

5 He alleged that Britain was trying to present the Cyprus problem as though it were a Greek-Turkish dispute in order to play the role of mediator in the matter.

6 He expressed approval of the Greek government's attitude towards the proposed tripartite conference.

Other possible solutions were put forward in the mid 1950s. Some had argued that the island should be put directly under NATO administration. However, at a news conference on 17 April 1956 the US Secretary of State stated that it would not be feasible because 'NATO is not, I might say, a corporate entity'. Some believed that Cyprus should be either placed under UN suzerainty or internationalized. Others thought there should be a Turkish millet, similar to the Greek millet when Cyprus was under Turkey before 1878, with very wide powers over the Turkish population. One protagonist of this view was John Parker, a British MP. The NATO Secretary-General held that a solution envisaging dominion status for the island for 15-20 years at the most had a great chance of success. Spaak however was less optimistic about a solution that would grant full and guaranteed independence to Cyprus for a fixed number of years. If the provisions of some of the world's greatest peace treaties could be regarded as mere 'scraps of paper' under new circumstances, who could say that a treaty covering Cyprus would not be so regarded?

Meanwhile in Cyprus the armed struggle for self-determination was entering its third year. The British had not managed to crush EOKA or the patriotic zeal of the Cypriot population. Influential sections of the population were constantly putting forward proposals. The mayors' proposals of 2 March 1957 asked for the release of all the deportees and for their return to Cyprus; the abolition of all emergency regulations; and the resumption of negotiations between Britain and Cypriot representatives. In the same year leaflets by AKEL in Greek and Turkish called for national and brotherly co-operation and not division and for a just and democratic solution for all Cypriots. AKEL also asked for the abolition of all emergency regulations; the return of the exiled leaders; the dismantling of the concentration camps; amnesty for all political prisoners; and the free functioning of all suspended newspapers and organizations.

In November Harding retired on completion of the two-year tour of service previously agreed. He was replaced by Sir Hugh Foot, a liberal colonial civil servant, who arrived on 3 December. Foot was previously Governor of Jamaica, and as Colonial Secretary of Cyprus from 1943 to 1945 often acted as governor in the absence of Sir Charles Woolley. Foot's appointment was a clear indication that Britain wished to initiate a milder policy. The Turks however felt that he would give in too easily to the Greeks, and there was consequently rioting and arson in Nicosia on 9 December. Foot wrote that throughout 1958 he was 'an unpopular figure in Turkey'.

Towards the end of 1957 the fourth Greek appeal to the UN was being considered. Greece had her draft resolution accepted by the Political Committee on 12 December by 33 votes to 20 with 25 abstentions, but it failed to gain the required two-thirds majority in the General Assembly. Yet the fact that the Cyprus question was discussed at the UN was considered a success and a springboard for even greater achievements. There was much lobbying behind the scenes and pressure was exerted on key representatives. The USA was convinced however that the UN was not the place to arrive at a solution of the Cyprus problem. An eventual settlement could come only by agreement between those parties directly concerned.

Sir Hugh Foot appeared to have two major objectives, to relax tensions in the island and to work out some plan for settling the Cyprus problem. He visited detention camps, walked through the streets of Nicosia, spoke to leading local personalities, rode through villages and argued in the coffee shops. The famous 'honeymoon period' was in full swing. In his Christmas Eve broadcast he announced three gestures of goodwill (one being the release of 100 detainees) and gave explicit assurances to the Turkish community that its interests would be well looked after.

Foot was back in London within a month with his recommendations. He was very pleased because he had 'a positive policy' to take to his superiors in Whitehall. He left the island on 1 January 1958 and recorded: 'Within ten days all was agreed. My recommendations were accepted in full. The time-table was worked out. I would go first to Ankara to talk to the Turkish Government, then to Athens to explain the new policy to the Greek Government and to Archbishop Makarios, then back to Cyprus to announce the policy and the end of the Emergency.'[7]

Turkey immediately rejected the British initiative. As Foot recalls, 'Turkish intransigence was such that no conceivable proposal we put to them would be acceptable – short of partition'. Nevertheless, on 26 January Foot, accompanied by Selwyn Lloyd, the British Foreign Secretary, arrived in Ankara for a four-day conference, ostensibly in connection with the Baghdad Pact. Whilst he was there pro-partitionist Turks rioted again in Cyprus and seven of them were killed by security forces in Nicosia and Famagusta. Foot and Selwyn Lloyd achieved nothing in Ankara and flew to Athens to consult the Greek leaders. The governor had a half an hour's conversation with Makarios. Foot recollects that they had 'established that morning a personal understanding which was invaluable later'.

Although for the moment fruitless, the two visits were to signal the beginning of intense diplomatic activity between the three countries. A new idea was started and Whitehall believed that Britain, being the sovereign power with ultimate responsibility for Cyprus, should take a firmer stand to ensure that future negotiations succeeded. The failure to find common ground for a settlement induced Britain to introduce its own policy.

The new constitutional programme was in the first instance worked out by Foot and Macmillan on 15 February after an hour's conversation at Nicosia airport. At a Chequers meeting on 11 May agreement was reached on the relevant details. The draft prepared embodied Foot's plans for internal self-government and the earlier British proposals for the external solution of 'Tri-Dominium'.

The full text was communicated to the Turkish and Greek governments on 10 June. Ahnan Menderes declared that nothing short of partition, itself a great sacrifice on the part of his countrymen, could assuage Turkish fears. The Greek reply on 21 June pointed out that Turkey had no direct interest in the Cyprus question since by the 1923 Treaty of Lausanne it had surrendered all its rights. On 16 June NATO welcomed the British initiatives.

The 'Foot-Macmillan Partnership Plan' was presented to the Commons on 19 June 1958. Macmillan made it clear that Cyprus was now not a 'colonial problem' but an 'international' one – a drastic switch from his attitude as Foreign Secretary three years before when he had said at the Tripartite Conference that 'the internal affairs of Her Majesty's possessions cannot be discussed with foreign powers'.

He now suggested an 'adventure in partnership' between the island's two communities and between the British, Greek and Turkish governments. For seven years the international status of Cyprus would be unchanged. The administration of the island as a whole would be directed by a council composed of the British governor, representatives of the Greek and Turkish governments and six Cypriot ministers, four elected from the Greek assembly and two from the Turkish. External affairs, defence and internal security would be matters specifically reserved to the governor acting after consultation with the Greek and Turkish government representatives. The government said that it would welcome any arrangement which would give Cypriots Greek or Turkish nationality while enabling them to retain their Britain nationality.

According to Macmillan the Greek and Turkish response was 'disappointing'. However, in a letter to Diefenbaker, the Canadian Premier, he confided on 1 July that he hoped gradually 'to wear them down to a kind of acquiescence'.

In a message to Macmillan on 31 July Karamanlis reiterated that the participation of the three governments in the administration of the island, the separate assemblies for each segment of the population and dual nationality would divide rather than unite the island. The Greeks stressed that if applied the proposals would lead to an intense antagonism both between the majority and the minority of the population and between the governments of the countries involved in the island's administration. Thus the plan prejudged the future by preparing the ground for the island's partition. Makarios also voiced his dissent. He described the idea of partnership as 'the imposition of a triple condominium'. Denktash on the other hand branded the plan as a 'stepping-stone to enosis'.

Zorlu however continued to maintain in a statement on 19 June that 'the best possible solution is partition' and suggested that the principles of partnership and partition be fused in a perfected plan at a tripartite conference that would determine the final international status of Cyprus. At such a conference, he said, 'the Macmillan Plan would be acceptable as a conference paper'.

In the House of Commons the opposition declared that such a plan would divide rather than unite the island. The Labour party's position was clear. Its third policy statement, on 7 June 1957 (in all nine were published on various policies between June 1956 and September 1957), declared that 'Cyprus should have the right of self-determination, after which she might opt for union with Greece or decide to stay in the Commonwealth'. At its annual conference Mrs Barbara Castle explained that the next Labour government would confer self-government on Cyprus and would not 'include partition in their definition of democratic self-determination'.

In Cyprus the reaction was an increase in violence. On 7 June 1958 Turkish Cypriots started fires in Nicosia. The result was two months of bitter communal strife in which 56 Greeks and 53 Turks were killed. Most of the casualties however were caused by isolated shootings, often of old people and lonely shepherds. Nevertheless more British troops and police were sent to the island. The killing of Mrs Cutliffe whilst shopping in Varosha (the Greek area of Famagusta) on 3 October caused her husband's regiment, the Royal Artillery, together with others from the Royal Ulster Rifles, to break discipline and seek reprisals. There were mass arrests, curfews and three deaths, including that of a ten-year-old girl.

Pro-partitionist Turks who joined Dr Kutchuk's Turkish Cypriot Popular party gave form and expression to growing nationalist sentiment. The party was reorganized under the amazing name of Cyprus is Turkish Party by Hikmet Bil, who arrived in 1955 from Turkey for this purpose, and encouraged by the Turkish and British governments he expressed through the media the Turkish opposition to *enosis*. In *Greek Atrocities against the Turks* in 1956 it was alleged that the Greek aim was to annihilate the Turkish community the moment the principle of self-determination was applied to Cyprus or the Greeks were given full control of the government.

However, charges of Greek ill-treatment of Turkish minorities were utterly baseless. Between 1948 and 1955 12,910 Turks left Greece, especially western Thrace, because of intensified Turkish propoganda about improved political and economic conditions in Turkey; but within the same period 9,690 of those Turks had returned to Greece and many of them told reporters that they were glad to return to their homes, land and friends. Those that came back (around 80 per cent) preferred symbiosis with the Greek majority to alienation.

The original Turkish position was that the status quo should not be disturbed, but if it was and Britain left the island should be handed back to Turkey. Later however this position was redefined as a demand for the partitioning of the island.

The failure of Britain's Cyprus policy in the 1950s was incessantly criticized. Lena Jeger MP, speaking in the celebrated Commons debate on 15 July 1957, explained why: 'Since the emergency and since the present Government have been in power there has been a deterioration of racial relationships inside Cyprus which is quite unnecessary, and is not borne out by historical experience. The Government have created some kind of Frankenstein about the Turks, and now do not know what to do about it.'[8]

From Cyprus Harding explained on 30 August 1957 that in the villages and districts he had visited he had ascertained that Greek and Turkish Cypriots were living in harmony and that their relations were friendly. Yet British policy in the island served to further the polarization of the two communities. As EOKA hit harder at British military personnel and installations, more British jobs were taken away from Greeks and given to Turks. Separate police units were formed, manned mainly by Turks under British officers, whose task it was to control Greek disturbances and help the army fight EOKA. From an oral question in the Commons from Desmond Donnelly to Lennox-Boyd we learn that the strength of these police units on 17 June 1958 was as follows:

	Mobile reserve	Auxiliary police
Turkish Cypriots	536	1,281
Greek Cypriots	0	56

In 1956 and 1957 racial strife was not serious. However, on 11

January 1956 Abdullah Ali Riza, a Turkish police sergeant who had given evidence at the trial of EOKA members, was shot dead. This precipitated Turkish Cypriot attacks against Greek stores in Nicosia. The Turkish underground organization Volkan (The Volcano), modelled on EOKA and simply anti-Greek, issued leaflets on that occasion threatening reprisals – five Greek lives for every Turk killed. Kutchuk protested to Harding and in a message to Makarios demanded that the Greek community should condemn the murder.

At the village of Vassilia fighting broke out between Greeks and Turks on 19 March 1956 and about 20 people were hurt. On the following day some 500 Turks smashed the windows of Greek-owned shops and offices in the Turkish quarter of Nicosia. On 23 April fighting again broke out after a Turkish policeman had been shot dead. Communal fighting continued for two days. On 25 May crowds of Turkish Cypriots attacked Greek stores and premises in Nicosia, Limassol, Larnaca and Paphos. The Turkish Cypriot leader, in cables to the US, UN, Britain and Turkey, denounced the terrorists and declared that all Turks were determined never to live under Greek rule.

Similar disturbances took place in January and February of 1957. The Turkish government was determined to achieve its object of *taksim* (partition). In Cyprus Volkan, whose leader was Rauf Denktash, an admirer of Menderes, was ready to do its bidding. It was to be officially proscribed in November 1957 but in fact survived into the independence period. The fighting arm of Volkan, and its successor late in 1957, was called the Türk Müdafaa (or Mukavemet) Teskilati – Turkish Defence or Resistance Organization, known as the TMT for short.

A TMT leaflet distributed in Larnaca on 6 June 1958 included the following:

> O Turkish Youth!
> The day is near when you will be called upon to sacrifice your life and blood in the PARTITION struggle – to the struggle for freedom.
> You are a brave Turk. You are faithful to your country and nation and are entrusted with the task of demonstrating Turkish might. Be ready to break the chains of slavery with your determination and will-power and with your love of freedom.

All Turkdom, right and justice and God are with you.
PARTITION OR DEATH

The TMT, though cruder, smaller and less well organized, modelled itself on EOKA. Hence the boycott of British goods which EOKA had ordered on 6 March 1958 was now applied by the Turks to Greek produce. Turks caught smoking Greek cigarettes or using Greek shops were beaten up by gangs of youths. Any Turk who deviated from the national line that coexistence with the Greeks was impossible was liable to be denounced as a traitor. In the spring of 1958 two Turkish Cypriot democrats who belonged to a Greek and predominantly left-wing trade union were murdered by TMT not primarily for their ideological beliefs but mainly because such membership involved co-operation with the Greeks. Much of the intimidation which took place at the time was carried out by self-appointed exponents of the cause.

By mid 1958 Turkish Cypriots were absolutely sure that soon the tide would turn their way. This confidence stemmed from several related factors:

1   As in 1955, Ankara was determined to show the world the strength of its feelings on the Cyprus issue. Huge demonstrations in favour of partition were held in many parts of Turkey. On 8 June a wax effigy of Makarios was burnt in front of a vast crowd in Istanbul. The Oecumenical Patriarch and the Greek minority were subjected to persistent attacks by the local press. But elaborate precautions were taken by the authorities to ensure that the anti-Greek riots of September 1955 were not repeated, so despite the massive scale of the rallies and the enthusiasm they generated no incidents of note were recorded. However, these events were regularly broadcast to Cyprus by Ankara radio and their effect on the Turkish Cypriot community in whipping up agitation was disastrous. Broadcasts from Athens, especially in 1955 and 1956, had a similar effect in building up anti-British resentment in the Greek Cypriot population.

2   Loss of confidence in Britain's ability to settle the problem without detriment to Turkish interests encouraged the Turkish Cypriots to step up their agitation for *taksim*. As a minority they were dependent on the support of the Turkish government and

their recourse to violence reflected simultaneously their own fears and the attitude in Ankara.

3   Tension was exacerbated by the government's prolonged delay in publishing its new plan for Cyprus. Fearing that the plan (announced on 19 June) would not provide for partition, the Turks, as we shall see below, intensified their activities and serious communal strife broke out on the night of 7 June 1958.

4   Such over-confidence was fostered by the firm belief that Turkey would if necessary send troops to their assistance. Behind the scenes Turkey certainly made such threats. Thus the fact that in the island the Greeks outnumbered then by four to one was no deterrent. In a fair number of Turkish houses posters were displayed showing Cyprus partitioned across the figure of a helmeted Turkish soldier.

In January 1958, as already mentioned, seven Turkish Cypriots were killed by security forces during anti-British demonstrations. Turkish hostility towards the British reached its peak after an incident in which an army truck driving through a crowd of demonstrators knocked down and killed two Turks, including a woman. The British authorities had hitherto been able to count on the restraint of the Turkish community and its vital co-operation in the struggle against EOKA, but from then onwards were faced with the possibility of armed opposition on two fronts.

The Turks were insisting on partition. A telegram sent to the governor on 4 May stated that they intended to hold their own local elections and to refuse to pay local taxes to the legally elected councils. In the previous month Refik Köraltan, President of the Grand Turkish National Assembly, had said in London that a settlement which precluded partition would result in a Turkish invasion of Cyprus. Menderes and Zorlu, as already noted, were also adopting the partition slogan.

In June and July violent clashes broke out between the two communities. A bomb explosion outside Turkey's press office in Nicosia on the night on 7 June marked the beginning of the most acute phase of racial tension the island had seen. Following disturbances at Omorphita, a Nicosia suburb, on 3 July, Greek families were forcibly driven out. Most Greek dwellings in Lefka and some in Paphos were burnt down. In

Nicosia the Olympiacos club and other places suffered the same fate. Passions reached a climax on 12 June 1958 when eight Greeks were massacred by the Turks during a clash near the Turkish village of Guenyeli. A report by the commission of inquiry published in Nicosia on 9 December 1958 found that the Greeks had been rounded up by British security forces and surprisingly released on the same day near Guenyeli, seven miles from where they were arrested and some distance from the nearest Greek villages. This incident has gone down in Cypriot history as the 'Guenyeli Massacre' – organized by the British and executed by the Turks.

Arson, murder and destruction continued for two months. In the end 56 Greeks and 53 Turks had died. Claims by Dr Kutchuk that thousands of Turks had been killed in the disturbances were described in the House of Commons on 24 June as 'ludicrous.'

It was widely believed that the bomb which exploded outside the Turkish press office in Nicosia was of Turkish origin. The Yassiada trial of the Menderes government in 1960-1 confirmed it. Aydin Konuralp of the Turkish Cypriot weekly *Nacak* testified that news of a coming massacre by the Greeks was fabricated in order to incite the Cypriot Turks into action. This testimony was fortified by the evidence of Emin Dirvana, who was to become Turkish Ambassador to Cyprus after independence. He explained that the bomb was planted by Turkish terrorists.

The Turks, with a view to partition, began to withdraw their minorities from predominantly Greek areas and evicted Greeks from areas where Turks formed the majority. In one week over 600 families left their homes of which two-thirds were Greek. Many of the Turks who left the Greek areas at this stage did so largely under the pressure of Turkish agitators. Nevertheless, despite the tension, Dr Dervis, the Greek mayor of Nicosia, and Denktash, the acting Turkish leader, co-operated with the governor in issuing a statement on 12 July calling on everyone to stop the violence. A few days later this appeal was endorsed by the archbishop from Athens.

Violence however continued to gather momentum. Sir Hugh Foot ordered an island-wide standstill for 48 hours on 22 July. Civilian movements and communications were completely restricted. The TMT was proscribed. Sixty Turks and around 2,000 Greeks were arrested.

Towards the end of the month Macmillan made an appeal for the end of violence. This was backed up by similar pleas from his Greek and Turkish counterparts. On 4 August Grivas issued a cryptic leaflet declaring a five-day cease-fire against the British and Turks but reserving the right to future action in the event of provocation. The TMT responded two days later with orders that all armed groups should stop their activities until further notice, that no Greek property should be touched unless Turkish property was touched and that no pressure should be brought to bear on Greeks in the minority.

Although communal strife did not break out again the August cease-fire soon broke down because the authorities continued to hunt EOKA men. Digenes, who had by now become more of a legendary figure and was described as 'Apiastos' (which translated literally means the one who cannot be taken), ordered his execution squads back to work. Resentment in the British army increased once more, and in mid 1958 a secret society calling itself Cromwell emerged among the security forces and in several of its leaflets threatened indiscriminate reprisals against the Greek population. The British Resistance Party and AKOE (EOKA spelt backwards) were similar organizations.

When EOKA's campaign opened in April 1955 AKEL was quick to condemn violence, pointing out that armed conflict would lead only to greater complications. AKEL also expressed its misgivings when it was learnt that Grivas, a fanatical anti-Communist, would lead the Cypriot struggle. This uneasy alliance endured many strains. Thus when Grivas proclaimed a truce in March 1957 it was soon clear that it did not extend to Greek Cypriots. Masked and armed men began to appear more and more frequently in the villages seeking out 'undesirables'. The victims tended to be members of left-wing families, which often meant that the workers in them belonged to the 'old' trade unions dominated by AKEL.

The shooting of left-wingers in Lyssi and Komi tou Yialou by masked men on 21 January 1958 heightened tension. On 22 January PEO called a 48-hour strike to be observed throughout the island and there were demonstrations in most of the big towns. A cable to the archbishop in Athens begged him to use his influence to stop such incidents. Makarios's answer, given 48 hours after the murders, was surprisingly a call for unity and not a condemnation of the murders. Karamanlis made a similar call for unity. A few weeks later news leaked out that EOKA had formed a special section to deal with the Communists. AKEL had by now come out openly in favour of independence and Grivas's pamphlet *The Communist Leadership Against the Cyprus Struggle* helped to widen the breach between them.

Perhaps the worst flare-up between the two factions was in August 1958 after clashes between Greeks and Turks had already brought the island to the verge of civil war. At Milia, near Famagusta, a so-called left-wing home guard formed to protect the village against possible Turkish Cypriot attacks was instead ambushed by EOKA. Two people were killed and around 20 injured – nearly all left-wingers. (An urgent appeal to Makarios to intervene resulted in another belated call for unity.) Similarly, TMT was responsible for the killing of several Turkish Cypriot progressives who spoke out for full co-operation between the island's two communities. Not surprisingly, the British seized on this rift between right and left as an excuse for not putting forward final proposals for the solution of the Cyprus problem.

12   Early 1959: The Zürich-London Accords

In the previous chapter it was noted that the Foot-Macmillan proposals were unfavourably received. Macmillan however was prepared to persist and made arrangements to visit both Athens and Ankara. For various reasons Britain surmised that both Greece and Turkey were becoming increasingly anxious and more ready to consider some accommodation:

1   The Soviet Union was putting pressure on the western powers in Berlin and elsewhere. Cyprus in the meantime was drifting into a civil war which threatened to involve Britain, Greece and Turkey in deepening conflict. The USA called for a closing of the ranks in NATO to meet the new Soviet threat. Hence all the interested parties had reasons for considering a compromise. Relations between Greece and Turkey resembling those between the Arab states and Israel must, it was stated, 'be prevented at all costs'. NATO directed that 'an impasse should not be allowed to set in'.

2   The British government had come to the conclusion (following a visit by Duncan Sandys to Cyprus in 1957 and careful reviews by its Chiefs of Staff) that it no longer needed the whole island as a base since part of it under its sovereign control would be enough. Moreover it was concerned at the great cost – in men and money – of dealing with the EOKA rebellion. At one stage there was one British serviceman for every five adult Cypriot civilians.

3   The USA sided with Britain over the Macmillan initiatives since such a policy offered 'multiple advantages'. John Foster Dulles, the Secretary of State, speaking before the Senate Committee on Foreign Affairs, declared on 6 June 1958 that 'the foreign policy of the US is designed to protect and promote the interests of the US in the international field.' Over Cyprus it meant that Britain, Greece and Turkey had to settle their

differences within the western alliance and preferably under the aegis of NATO.

4   Both the Greek government and Makarios feared that the island was in serious danger of being partitioned. In fact the archbishop was visited in Athens by an increasing number of Cypriots who urged him to exert his influence in favour of a compromise settlement before final catastrophe overtook the island. The message was that the islanders had had enough and now desired a more peaceful life. Moreover it was widely believed that the Cyprus question was approaching a dead-end at the UN. Its decision of December 1958 (see pages 318-19) confirmed this belief. Makarios was henceforth prepared to accept self-government. In fact from the summer of 1957 he appeared quite ready to accept independence for Cyprus and a moratorium on *enosis* at least as a basis for discussion, and he was willing to grant base facilities to Britain.

According to Averoff, Athens believed that the British were seriously thinking of partitioning the island from north to south along the 33° parallel, with Turkey taking the west of the island. The Turks however favoured partition along the 35° lateral, west to east, with them taking the northern part. In his memoirs Eden recorded that he regarded partition as 'the last refuge of baffled statesmanship', but he went on to issue the warning that 'if there is no cooperation between Britain, Greece and Turkey in finding an acceptable solution, then the island will be partitioned'. The Conservatives were finally converted by the thesis presented by Walter Elliot MP on 17 July 1956 that the ultimate solution would be the establishment of a Greek sector, a Turkish sector and a British base sector.

5   In the early months of 1958 Greece was going through a crisis of its own. The defection of two key ministers (George Rallis and Panayiotis Papaligouras) and 13 parliamentary supporters caused the Karamanlis government to resign on 2 March. The crisis, precipitated by a dispute over the new electoral bill, left Greece unable to take any step forward towards a settlement of the Cyprus problem at a most critical period. Michael Pesmazoglou, the Foreign Minister of the interim government (headed by Constantine Georgakopoulos, President of the Greek Red Cross), was not the equal of Averoff,

who returned when the Karamanlis-led National Radical Union (ERE) received 173 seats out of 300 in the elections of 11 May. The government also had its hands full carrying through its schemes of industrial development and the reorganization of the country's administration and education which they necessitated. Even more important was the fact that his so-called 'policy of the national centre' meant that Greece's alliance interests had to prevail over her interests in Cyprus. This became a constant irritant in Greco-Cypriot relations.

6   Turkish reaction to the British plan had mellowed considerably. The Turks were now saying that 'partition and partnership are not irreconcilable'. Macmillan's record of a private meeting between himself, Menderes, Zorlu and Nuri Bergi, the Turkish Ambassador in London, on 29 July shows that Turkey accepted in full the British plan which it regarded as 'fair, honourable, statesmanlike and well-balanced'. It can be assumed that the Iraqi *coup d'état* in July 1958, following the Turco-Syrian crisis of May 1957, with its potential dangers to Turkey, had led to a more accommodating approach at diplomatic level. The new Iraqi regime spurned the Baghdad Pact, which shifted its headquarters to Ankara and renamed itself CENTO. Soon Turkey became the linch-pin of NATO and CENTO and the bugbear of the non-aligned. Turkey moreover was in serious financial difficulties through overspending on imports for her development programme. She counted on the USA and her European creditors to keep her afloat. In fact both Turkey and Greece benefited from the new programme of economic and military assistance announced to the US Congress by the President on 5 January 1957. It became known as the 'Eisenhower Doctrine'. Such economic dependence meant in the end political compliance.

In the face of the above realities, Whitehall began studying new initiatives. In the meantime however it was confronted by the 'Spaak Plan'. On 4 August 1958 the NATO Secretary-General informed the permanent representatives of the three countries of his propositions, which were temporary, to last for seven years until a more fair and permanent solution could be worked out. *Enosis*, partition and the triple partnership idea proposed by Macmillan were excluded.

Needless to say, Macmillan was resolved to push his modified plan forward and thus show the world that Britain was determined to solve the Cyprus problem. Accompanied by Foot, Macmillan arrived in Athens on 7 August and on the following day the first meeting was held. Macmillan pleaded for peace and for a seven-year period with provisional solutions but without prejudice to any final settlement. He claimed that both were necessary because of the state of world politics particularly in the Middle East. He repeated that 'partnership is a fine and noble ideal'. Karamanlis surprised Macmillan by stressing that 'the Cyprus problem is a simple one' but had become complicated because of the British refusal to satisfy the just and undeniable rights of the Cypriot people. According to the Greek Premier, four main points were totally unacceptable:

1   The ministerial ratio of four to two on the council was unfair; four to one would be more equitable.

2   There was no provision for a joint assembly.

3   The proposals for dual nationality were in direct conflict with international law and together with the other propositions would divide rather than unite the island.

4   The provision for two government representatives (one each from Greece and Turkey) was out of the quesiton. Macmillan was warned by Spaak on 31 July that this proposal would be strongly resisted by the Greeks.

The Greeks also disliked partnership as a principle, since that would have been equivalent to admitting *de jure* a Turkish presence on the island. The two sides met again on the following day and Macmillan promised that he would keep Karamanlis informed of his talks in Ankara and that he would meet him again either in London or in Athens. Macmillan failed to honour either of his promises. On the same evening Robert Murphy, American Under-Secretary of State for Foreign Affairs, visited Karamanlis at his private residence in Kifisia where he heard a résumé of the Greek position. He listened very carefully but said nothing because Macmillan had already secured American support for the British proposals.

During his flight to Ankara on 9 August Macmillan recorded that since the Greek government was 'frightened' of Makarios, of Parliament and of the rising Communist vote (24.3 per cent in May), the politicians were in serious difficulties when considering his proposals. Meetings took place in Ankara on the evening of 9 August and on the following morning. No progress was made because the Turks, according to Macmillan, 'continued to praise the perfect symmetry and beauty of the plan as it stood and refused even to consider amendments'. Although he secured no concessions from them he was positive that the British position was well understood by them. He admitted that 'the Turks like Englishmen, do not easily reveal their feelings' and added that 'the primitive way of thinking which the Turks followed meant that everything is black or white – there is no such colour as grey'.

At 1 p.m. on the following day Macmillan arrived at Nicosia airport. After a short helicopter tour he met Dervis and Demetriades, the mayors of Nicosia and Kyrenia. Then he met Kutchuk and Denktash. The British plan was attacked by the Turkish leaders as pro-Greek and thus very dangerous. 'Clearly,' Macmillan wrote, 'the word to support it has not yet come from Ankara.'

At that juncture Whitehall concluded that certain modifications of its general policy, announced in June, were necessary. These were:

1   Greek and Turkish government representatives should not have seats in the central council although they would be consulted by the governor as envisaged in the original proposals.

2   The question of dual nationality was shelved in view of the complexities of international law.

3   Reference was made to the establishment of a common legislature as a possible later development.

Spaak and Dulles were immediately informed of the changes – the latter by Selwyn Lloyd who was at the time in Washington. The Greeks were informed on 14 August and the Press on the following day. On the evening of 19 August the Greeks rejected the changes and a week later the Turks voiced their approval. Greece now believed that NATO would help their cause. Whitehall also surmised that NATO and the Americans would soon be very helpful. The British planned to put their policy into operation and authorized the setting up of separate municipal councils, thereby increasing Greek fears of a *de jure* and *de facto* partition. Turkey announced that it would soon appoint its representative in Nicosia.

September 1958 was the month of 'shifts and turns'. On the 7th Makarios told the Greek government privately that he was now willing to accept independence for Cyprus under UN auspices after a period of self-government. Nine days later the archbishop made his views known to Barbara Castle MP, a senior member of the British Labour party. She, in common with many others, believed that parts of the Macmillan plan would have regrettable consequences.

On 22 September he authorized Mrs Castle to give the news to the press. The date coincided with the decision of the UN General Assembly to include the Cyprus question in its agenda. Six days later Makarios wrote a letter to Grivas explaining the reasons for his decision:

1 It was imperative to crush the Macmillan initiatives.

2 British public opinion and the Labour party were now looking for compromises.

3 American support for Britain was now more noticeable.

4 Of all the possible solutions, the UN was only willing to consider that of independence.

Grivas answered that Makarios should stick to the original demand for self-determination. Bishop Kyprianos was also irritated by the archbishop's change of line.

Makarios' new plan for an independent Cyprus was rejected by the Conservative government, which refused to commit itself to any final solution, but was supported, even before September 1958, by the Labour opposition. This support cheered the Greeks but dismayed the Turks, who stiffened their determination to insist on a quick solution by partition.

The Greek foreign policy-makers, whom Makarios had not consulted before making this particular public announcement, were also annoyed. They were keeping in reserve their independence proposal and intended to spring it upon the UN Assembly at an appropriate moment. In an attempt to scotch the Macmillan plan Greece also intended to suggest that the whole Cyprus question be put 'in a freeze' for at least three years with EOKA halting its operations. Thus the Makarios-Castle interview had left its mark on the history of Cyprus.

Under constant pressure from Britain and the USA, Greece decided to seek NATO mediation. On 20 September Karamanlis wrote to Spaak that 'Britain's insistence in applying the plan unilaterally will be so shocking to public sentiment in Greece that it will render our position within the Alliance as problematical'. The Greek NATO force at Izmir had been withdrawn on 13 June, at the height of the intercommunal disturbances. There were also reports of large Turkish army concentrations on the Evros river (the Greek-Turkish frontier) and on the shores to the north of Cyprus. The Greek contingent returned to Izmir on 25 and 28 February 1959.

On 23 September Spaak arrived in Athens determined to reach a solution acceptable to all. It was agreed that he should submit the following 'personal proposals' at the NATO council meeting which was to take place within the next few days:

1   The Macmillan plan should be neutralized.

2   A seven-point plan would be adopted which included provisions for a single legislative chamber and the future of the island remaining open.

3   A conference should be held under the aegis of NATO with all interested parties present.

Makarios agreed to the NATO initiative. Selim Sarper, the Turkish delegate at NATO headquarters, described it as being 'a dagger at the back of Turkey'. The British representative said that he had no instructions to do anything. Their Greek counterpart accepted.

The impasse continued and the date for the application of the Macmillan plan – 1 October – was approaching. Makarios' worries were increasing very rapidly. The Greek government had made no public declaration in favour of a solution embracing independence; he was convinced that the NATO initiative would in the end not be enough because Britain would drop its plan only if there were a real danger of Greece leaving the western alliance; and the arrival in Cyprus of the Turkish government representative, scheduled for 1 October, was only a few days away.

From 2 to 5 October a series of top level discussions took place at the private residence of the Greek Premier which included the archbishop and M. Melas, the Greek representative at NATO. The conclusion reached was that both Makarios and Greece would come out 'bruised' from the projected conference where they would be opposed by Britain, Turkey, the USA and by the Turkish Cypriots. On 3 October Christian Herter, Under-Secretary of State for Foreign Affairs and later US Foreign Secretary, promised Karamanlis, in a private letter, that his government would support a Cypriot single legislative chamber and urged Greece to participate in the proposed conference. On the following day the Greek government stated that the discussion of a final solution should also appear on the agenda of the conference; and, still suspecting that such a meeting would frustrate the forthcoming appeal to the UN, suggested that it should also include delegates from France and Italy.

Such a forum never materialized. Shortly afterwards Greece, for the fifth time, took the Cyprus question to the UN. Macmillan resolved on 25 October that, 'it's Makarios who has bullied poor Karamanlis, Averoff and co into their absurd position'. Makarios however had no control over them. Their only fear was Greek public opinion which was inflamed by the British, USA and Turkish attitudes. The Greek government had come to realize that the Cyprus controversy had reached a complete deadlock and decided that the threat of war by Turkey and the danger of estrangement from Britain and the USA could best be met by strategic retreat.

On 4 October Macmillan explained that 'it was quite impossible for us to have postponed the operation of the plan because Britain would have lost Turkish goodwill and civil war would have begun'. Selwyn Lloyd also informed his Greek counterpart, who had proposed the suspension of the plan's application in exchange for the withdrawal of the Cyprus item on the General Assembly's agenda, that his government had officially committed itself to the Macmillan plan and 'if dropped, Turkish terrorism would be multiplied'.

Yet within weeks, as will be seen below, the scene was transformed and by February 1959 the Zürich-London Agreements (which finally set up the Cyprus Republic) were signed. On 19 February the Labour party leader said of the Conservatives 'they deserve particular credit for eating so many of their words'.

Between 25 November and 2 December seven draft resolutions were put forward in the UN Political Committee. Britain attempted in effect to get the Assembly to endorse its efforts to impose its proposals for self-government originally announced on 19 June. Greece endeavoured to get the Assembly to approve in principle the establishment of an independent Cyprus instead of urging it to call for national self-determination as it had done on previous occasions since 1954. It was Turkey now that was calling for self-determination, but for the Greeks and the Turks separately, in a way which would lead to the partition of the island.

The remaining four draft resolutions were introduced by Iran, India (co-sponsored by nine other countries), Colombia and Belgium. The Indian resolution was definitely anti-partitionist and the UK's rejection of it heightened Greek fears that the British plan would lead to partition. The Iranian one, eventually adopted with amendments, urged something more than the tripartite conference which the British had suggested to the Greek and Turkish governments in August 1957. It called for something closer to the procedure which Spaak had first mentioned in September 1957 during his exploratory talks with Averoff. On that occasion he had suggested Cypriot participation in the tripartite conference the British were trying to convene. Whitehall judicial experts explained that it was difficult to organize such a conference since the Cypriots were British subjects and it was not easy to find a formula that would permit British representatives, Cypriot leaders and foreign envoys (Greeks, Turks and Americans) to sit together at a joint international diplomatic conference.

James W. Barco, counsellor of the USA delegation to the General Assembly, explained the American position on 28 November 1958:

The US regrets, Mr. Chairman, that we must once more take

up the complex and difficult problem of Cyprus in the General Assembly. As we have made plain on the previous occasions when this problem was under consideration here, this is not the place to arrive at a solution of the Cyprus problem. I must emphasise the conviction of the US that the parties to this dispute must work out a solution themselves. In the course of our discussion here, we cannot expect to solve the problem of Cyprus. . . . The US supported the very real efforts which took place under the aegis of NATO to arrange a conference where 'quiet diplomacy' could have an opportunity to permit all concerned to come to an agreement. We were disappointed when these efforts collapsed, since we were convinced that they offered real promise of substantial progress.[1]

Barco expressed his delegation's gratification that 'the three governments directly concerned' had recognized that only negotiation and conciliation could provide a solution acceptable to all.

On 4 December the Political Committee accepted the Iranian resolution by 31 votes to 22 with 28 abstentions. The USA, Britain, Turkey and most of the other NATO countries voted in favour while Greece was amongst the opponents. The Greeks at once charged the USA government with failing to keep its promise to remain neutral.

On that same evening however an event took place which ultimately led to the Accords of 1959. At the entrance of the Political Committee hall where the vote was taken, Zorlu approached Averoff and congratulated him on the splendid fight he put up in the debate. After a brief exchange of views, especially on the countries' common defence interests, Zorlu said 'would you like us to meet?' Averoff replied in the affirmative although he wanted to see what would happen in the General Assembly the following day. When it met on 5 December Señor Rafael de la Colina, the Mexican delegate, presented a compromise declaration drafted after private discussions with the British, Greek and Turkish delegations.

Dr Charles Habib Malik, the Lebanese President of the General Assembly, upheld the Mexican's motion that it should be put to the vote in the plenary session. Resolution 1287 (XIII) was adopted by 57 votes to nil with one abstention. It recalled resolution 1013 (XI) of 26 February 1957 and expressed confidence that 'continued efforts will be made by the parties to reach a peaceful, democratic and just solution in accordance with the Charter of the UN'. None of the other resolutions was put to the vote in the plenary session.

In the delegates' lounge of the UN building on the morning of 6 December, Zorlu and Averoff talked for two hours. It was agreed that further discussions should take place. The *rapprochement* between Greece and Turkey led to the Paris talks of 18 December when the two ministers, together with Selwyn Lloyd, their British counterpart, had informal discussions on Cyprus during a NATO meeting. The talks, officially described as 'useful', followed the easing of tension in Cyprus itself as a result of an eleventh-hour reprieve granted to two convicted men by the governor (at the request of Averoff and Zorlu) and the release of a further 50 detainees.

On the following day the two sides met again. The Turks were now willing to drop outright partition but insisted on the maximum separation of communal affairs and a guarantee of Turkish Cypriot participation in the island's administration on the basis of equality rather than proportional representation. They also insisted that the security of the Turkish mainland *vis-à-vis* Cyprus could be achieved only by stationing Turkish troops on the island. Thus Ankara's minimum demands were for an independent and jointly administered state in which the two communities would share power equally and for a Turkish military presence on the island to guarantee the security of her southern border.

These demands and proposals which Greece had accepted in principle were communicated to Makarios in New York by Xanthopoullos Palamas, the Greek permanent representative at the UN. The Greeks were now talking of a 'binding independence', and Karamanlis on 13-14 December described the Cyprus question in the Greek Vouli as being his country's 'national gangrene'. Others described it as being a 'typical case of a collective Oedipus complex'.

Averoff and Zorlu had further private talks in Paris between 18 and 20 January 1959 during an OEEC (Organization for European Economic Co-operation) meeting convened to discuss problems connected with the European Common

Market. According to Greek ministerial accounts Makarios was kept informed and approved.

The Turks insisted that at the next top level meeting the Premiers of both countries should be present. Zürich was chosen as the next venue. The Greeks arrived first at the Dolder Grand Hotel on 4 February. On 11 February a declaration was initialled by the two countries confirming that Cyprus would become an independent state with a Greek Cypriot president and a Turkish Cypriot vice-president and detailing the 'Basic Structure of the Republic of Cyprus'. This caused the London *Daily Express* to complain rather naïvely on the following day that 'Great Britain is leaving the island without having its voice heard'. It was also agreed that the proposed constitution would not be subject to a plebiscite and that the Cypriots would not be permitted to bargain for changes in the constitution that would in any way alter the political rights granted to the Turkish minority.

The joint communiqué stated that the two governments had reached a 'compromise solution' subject to agreement with Britain. With the Zürich concordat under their belts, Zorlu and Averoff flew to London and conferred on the same evening with Selwyn Lloyd. Similarly Karamanlis left for Athens and immediately informed Makarios of the agreements initialled at 2.45 p.m. The archbishop nodded his approval but after carefully reading the documents expressed certain doubts. Following a series of meetings, which also involved the Bishop of Kition and the abbot of Kykko monastery, Makarios asked on 14 February that nothing should be said about the bases because he wanted to negotiate with the British himself. Likewise the Turkish government had called on the advice of Denktash, an able lawyer, chief political adviser and heir-apparent to Dr Kutchuk.

The London Conference of 17 February 1959 was widened to include two separate delegations headed by Makarios and Kutchuk. The purpose of the three governments, which had agreed beforehand on the plan to be implemented, was to present the Cypriots with a *fait accompli* which they would be forced to accept. Pressure to sign was exerted on the archbishop, particularly from Greece and Britain, and he, preferring perhaps some kind of independence to further bloodshed and partition, accepted. A personal message from King Paul to the archbishop acknowledged that Makarios' responsibility was a heavy one but stressed that the sufferings of the Cypriot people, whom he regarded as no less Greek than the inhabitants of Greece itself, could not be prolonged indefinitely, nor could the Cyprus problem be allowed to continue poisoning relations between Greece and her western allies.

Early next morning Makarios announced that 'after a night of prayer and meditation' he had decided to accept the Zürich Agreements. The archbishop reflected later that he was never in his life confronted by a greater dilemma. On 19 February the London Agreements were finally initialled at Lancaster House.

The Zürich-London Agreements, characterized by all opposition parties as a 'betrayal', were ratified by the Greek Vouli on 28 February after a four-day debate, by 170 votes to 118, and by the Turkish Grand National Assembly on 4 March by 347 votes to 138. The British Parliament followed suit on 19 March. A Labour motion however, proposed by Bevan, reiterated that 'the policies of HMG since 1954 have been a major factor in preventing an earlier settlement'. From across the Atlantic the Department of State stated on 19 February that with this achievement 'the leaders of the three governments concerned and the Greek and Turkish Cypriot communities have earned the thanks of the entire free world'. On the same day Eisenhower addressed messages of congratulation to the Premiers of Britain, Greece and Turkey upon the successful conclusion of the Accords.

The settlement that evolved had two main parts: a draft constitution for Cyprus and three treaties. British rule in the island was to end not later than one year after 19 February 1959. The republic finally came into being on 16 August 1960. Before it could be established the constitution and the final texts of the three treaties had to be drafted and administrative arrangements to be made for the transfer of power and for the holding of presidential, parliamentary and communal elections.

Three *ad hoc* committees were immediately set up. The Transitional Committee in Nicosia, composed of the governor and Cypriot members, was responsible for the adaptation of government machinery in preparation for independence. The

London Joint Committee, composed of representatives from Britain, Greece and Turkey and from the two Cypriot communities, was charged with drafting the final treaties. The Joint Constitutional Commission, composed of representatives of the two communities and of the Greek and Turkish governments with legal advisers, had the task of drafting the republic's constitution. It was however bound by the 27 articles laid down at Zürich. The commission met for the first time on 13 April 1959 under the leadership of Marcel Bridel, a professor of law and one-time Rector of the University of Lausanne.

The sovereignty of the island was safeguarded by Britain, Greece and Turkey under the Treaty of Guarantee which precluded under Article I either the union of Cyprus with any other state or its partition. The Treaty of Alliance provided for co-operation between Greece, Turkey and the republic in common defence, for the stationing of Greek and Turkish military contingents (950 and 650 respectively) on the island and for the training of a Cypriot army. The Treaty of Establishment concerned the retention of British sovereign bases and ancillary facilities on republican territory and problems of finance and nationality arising out of the end of colonial rule.

The texts of the first two treaties were presented at the Zürich and London Conferences and required little alteration. Work on the Treaty of Establishment, with its complex administrative and legal problems, did not begin until after the Agreements were signed. Macmillan described the signing of the Agreements as 'a memorable occasion'. On the same evening he informed the House of Commons of the above events and said:

> I believe that we have closed a chapter of bitterness and strife in the history of Cyprus and that we are now embarking, with our Greek and Turkish Allies and the people of Cyprus themselves, on a new approach where partnership and cooperation take the place of strife and dissension. . . . I regard this Agreement as a victory for reason and cooperation. No party to it has suffered defeat. It is a victory for all. . . . It is a sacrifice all round.[2]

At Lancaster House Karamanlis explained that 'at the present moment we have to rejoice as godfathers at the birth of a new state'. In a statement to the Press he praised the high level of diplomacy used to solve the Cyprus problem and added that such methods should be employed to resolve much bigger international issues. In the absence of Menderes, Zorlu confirmed that 'the agreed solution represents an equitable and fair settlement of the Cyprus question'. Following Zorlu, Makarios expressed his satisfaction and explicitly announced that: 'This is a great day . . . a new era, I firmly believe, opens up today for the people of Cyprus, an era of peace, freedom and prosperity.'[3]

In a broadcast to the people of Cyprus on the same day he said that 'at long last, after centuries of foreign subjugation Cyprus is free to pursue its own future'. Dr Kutchuk also emphasized that all Turkish Cypriots joined 'in this atmosphere of good relations and happiness'. What remained now was for the work of the three committees and negotiations for the British facilities (size of bases and number of sites for training and other purposes) to be completed before Britain actually relinquished sovereignty to the new state.

Hence the turbulent years of 1955-8 were at an end. Peace was preserved in the south-eastern flank of NATO. In real terms the total British military and internal security expenditure between 1 December 1954 and 31 December 1959 was estimated at £90 million. In human terms lives lost since 28 July 1954 owing to armed action and civil disturbances were 142 British and 492 Cypriot. Would the Cypriots be allowed to live in peace? Only the passage of time can answer such questions.

13 August 1960: On and Off to Final Independence

Under the Zürich-London Agreements Great Britain relinquished sovereignty over the whole island except for two base areas (Akrotiri and Dhekelia) and other facilities; Greece sacrificed *enosis* and Turkey partition. The archbishop, though expressing many reservations in private (forming perhaps the basis of his 13 constitutional amendments proposed in 1963), was reasonably happy. Kutchuk was also pleased because the constitution offered the Turkish minority the lion's share of almost everything. Yet many commentators took a critical view.

After an absence of almost three years Makarios returned to Cyprus, where vast crowds of Greek Cypriots gave him an overwhelming welcome, though open hostility to the ethnarch came from Grivas and his staunch unionist supporters, who attacked him for having 'betrayed' *enosis* and the national cause. However, on 9 March the EOKA leader issued a leaflet calling on his followers to lay down their arms and accept the settlement. Grivas proclaimed the need for 'harmony, unity and love' instead of the 'paean of war'. Eight days later he returned to Athens – the city he had left more than four years earlier. At the airport he was greeted by the Archbishop of Athens and Averoff in a state reception during which vast crowds welcomed him back as a national hero. Almost immediately the Greek Vouli gave him the highest honour it could bestow, proclaiming him 'Worthy of the Nation'. King Paul conferred on him the Order of Valour and the Grand Cross of the Order of George I. He also received the freedom of the city of Athens and the gold medal of the capital's Academy.

The archbishop had the unenviable task of persuading the diverse segments of the Greek community to accept the spirit of the Agreements and of convincing the Turkish community that its future on the island could best be served by emphasizing the unifying rather than the divisive elements of the compromise settlement. The left criticized the provisions which allowed British bases and the stationing of Greek and Turkish troops on the island.

The 18 months prior to 16 August 1960 (independence day) were nearly as troubled as the months before the Agreements were signed. The early preparations for independence took place against a background of lawlessness. In a 16-day period after 22 February 1959 the remaining three detention camps were closed, the principal emergency regulations were revoked and an amnesty for all members of EOKA, including a safe conduct to Greece for Grivas and anyone who might wish to accompany him, was provided. The release of EOKA prisoners and suspects was, in the opinion of many, premature in the interests of security even if politically expedient. Many kept their arms after the voluntary surrender called for by Makarios and the British authorities. Incidents were reported between Greeks and British soldiers and amongst the Greeks themselves.

Even so by 27 March agreement had been reached between the archbishop and Kutchuk on the allocation of portfolios in the first Cypriot provisional government, which was to hold office until the island officially became self-governing. The list was approved by the governor on 5 April and announced the same day:

Name	Portfolio	Greek/Turkish Cypriot
Tasos Papadopoulos	Interior	Greek Cypriot
Glafkos Clerides	Justice	"
Righinos Theocharous	Finance	"
Antonios Georghiades	Communications and Works	"
Paschalis Paschalides	Commerce and Industry	"
Polycarpos Georghadgis	Labour and Social Services	"
Andreas Azinas	Deputy Minister of Agriculture	"
Osman Orek	Defence	Turkish Cypriot
Fazil Plümer	Agriculture	"
Niyazi Manyera	Health	"
Mehmet Nazim	Deputy Minister of Finance	"

Together with Makarios – who provisionally took over the post of foreign affairs – Kutchuk and Foot, the above-named constituted the Transitional Committee referred to in the Agreements. It was an EOKA-controlled government composed of extremely young men.

Nevertheless the Cypriot political scene was dominated during the summer months by a prolonged controversy between Grivas and Makarios arising out of a number of allegations by the former in connection with the Agreements. Grivas asserted, *inter alia*, that the Agreements contained 'verbal commitments' of which he had been unaware at the time and on which he had not been consulted beforehand, and that they embodied far-reaching concessions to the British and Turkish viewpoints. On 30 July Makarios, Kutchuk, Karamanlis and Averoff issued statements denying such accusations as 'absolutely unfounded'.

In an attempt to resolve the differences between Grivas and Makarios, six former prominent members of EOKA, among them A. Georghiades and P. Georghadjis (both members of the provisional government), visited Greece between 16 and 19 July for talks with their former leader. On 20 July Grivas explained that he was 'ready to struggle with all his might' and that he had fought 'toughly for the island's liberation while others watched the struggle from afar in safety'. Six days later at Ayios Nicolaos church Makarios called on his hearers, a crowd of some 10,000 which included most Greek Cypriot ministers and many former EOKA men, to 'turn away their faces with contempt from demagogues who seek to exploit our struggle for their own personal ends and to sow dissension among Cypriots'.

This oblique warning to Grivas was reinforced on the following day by Kutchuk, who said that the archbishop's timely statement would help the two communities to collaborate more closely and to live together in harmony. Grivas hit back on 29 July, declaring that he would 'fight with all his might to frustrate the nationally harmful endeavours to enslave the Cypriot people'. In a further attempt to bring about a reconciliation between the two leaders Georghiades again visited Greece during the first fortnight of August. Makarios then sent Anthimos, Bishop of Kition, to confer with the general. Grivas however avoided meeting him and the bishop returned to Cyprus on 6 September after waiting in vain for nearly a month.

Meanwhile the situation in Cyprus was obscured further by three factors:

1   Kyprianos, Bishop of Kyrenia, made a number of speeches and sermons calling for *enosis*, expressing full support for Grivas and denouncing the Zürich-London Agreements.

2   An underground organization appeared in May called K.E.M. (Kypriakon Enodikon Metopo – Cyprus Enosis Front), which distributed leaflets attacking the archbishop and the Greek government and denounced all opponents of *enosis* and of Digenes as 'traitors'.

3   An alleged conspiracy to overthrow Makarios and the provisional government was attributed to KEM and resulted in the expulsion from the EDMA party (Eniaion Democraticon Metopon Agoniston – United Democratic Front of Fighters) of one of its leading members, Photis Papaphotis, in August. The editor of *Ethniki*, who criticized the dismissal, was beaten up by armed gangs.

Grivas made further statements between 12 and 14 September, and invited the ethnarch to enter into discussions with him in order to restore 'peace and normal conditions in Cyprus', but he qualified his invitation by insisting on three conditions before such a meeting materialized. On 15 September Makarios issued a press statement in which, for the first time during the controversy, he rebuked Grivas openly and by name. Two days later the general repeated his offer to meet the archbishop in 'open debate'. He also dismissed the reputed plot to overthrow Makarios as a 'fairy-tale'.

However, a reconciliation soon followed. On 11 September Georghiades left Nicosia for Athens to confer with the general. Consequently Grivas and Makarios met in Rhodes from 6 to 9 October, the archbishop finally persuading the general that only the Communists and the Turks would gain if their forces were divided.

Despite his pledge, at the time of his return to Athens, to take no part in partisan affairs, Grivas soon made a number of declarations criticizing the government and expressing his readiness to 'serve the nation' if he were asked to do so by a majority of the people. During a tour of Epirus he announced that he visualized 'a powerful Greece which will include within its borders all the enslaved territories such as Epirus and Cyprus'.

Suddenly, Grivas stated on 20 September that he had been informed by a foreign source that the Greek leaders were planning to exterminate him on the pretext of a fictitious military conspiracy organized by himself to overthrow the government. A government reply said that 'if Grivas is not deliberately lying, he is evidently suffering from persecution mania'. That was the end of Grivas's political dreams. His attempts then and later to mobilize Greek public opinion proved futile.

Apart from the rivalries which divided the right, which were, albeit temporarily, pushed below the surface by the Makarios-Grivas *rapprochement*, tension was further aggravated by renewed political activity by the other Greek Cypriot political elements. In April 1959 EDMA, the political successor to EOKA, was formed out of ex-fighters in support of Makarios and the settlement. During a three-day rally held at the end of May the short-lived EDMA publicized its first policy statement, promising wealth for the farmer and opportunity for youth. But the occasion was chiefly significant for the militant Hellenism preached by some of the former EOKA leaders and the provocative effect this was bound to have on the Turkish minority.

Also in April the leftist forces formed EDON (Eniaia Democratiki Organosis Neoleas – United Democratic Organization of Youth) to give 'expression to the worries and problems of the workers, peasants, employees and intellectuals'. EDON was a counterblast to the EOKA-inspired EDMA.

Left-wing speakers at a mass meeting in Nicosia on 28 June attacked the settlement and the efforts of the right to monopolize the island's political life. Political cleavages grew wider. In the previous month both nationalist and Communist mayors came into open conflict with the archbishop over Article 20 of the Zürich-London Agreements which provided for separate Greek and Turkish municipalities. Dr Dervis, the nationalist mayor of Nicosia and a former supporter of Makarios, publicly denied reports in an Athens newspaper that he had approved the article when it was discussed in London. The mayors demanded that this article should be modified and severely criticized preliminary proposals made by Makarios for its implementation on the ground that they would have transferred certain functions hitherto exercised by the municipalities to the central government. The mayors, as the only important elected representatives in Cyprus, constituted a formidable body in united opposition. However, the archbishop reasserted his determination to stand by the Agreements, and the trouble with the mayors subsided temporarily.

Shortly after his return from Rhodes, the Greek mayors of the six main towns resumed their offensive and submitted a memorandum to the archbishop calling for the replacement of his advisory council by a Pan-Cyprian Congress representative of the people, and for the revision of the Agreements. On 30 October Dervis announced that the mayors had decided to boycott the advisory council, which he claimed represented no one but Makarios himself. Dervis was to say more than once that 'Fascist rule by black-robed clergy is far worse and more dangerous than even British colonialism'.

Criticism of Makarios was steadily mounting. His transitional cabinet excluded older men of influence and of all shades of political opinion, but with the approach of the presidential elections the main targets for attack were the archbishop's reputed authoritarian methods. The appearance in November of a new weekly newspaper *Epalxis (Rampart)* reflecting the views of the Bishop of Kyrenia marked the start of a campaign for the overthrow of the Agreements and for the removal of Makarios as the island's undisputed leader.

Opposition to the archbishop was further consolidated when on 15 November John Clerides QC, a distinguished citizen of moderate views, and his former political rival Dr Dervis organized a large meeting in Nicosia at which it was unanimously decided to form a new party, the Democratic Union (D.U.), to oppose Makarios at the forthcoming presidential elections.

Dervis launched an attack on both Athens and Washington for their part in the Cyprus settlement and on the archbishop for failing to use the *Deniz* incident (see page 331) as an argument against the clauses relating to the stationing of Greek and Turkish troops in Cyprus. Clerides denounced the settlement as worse than the Macmillan proposals of 1958 and emphasized that the policy of the Democratic Union would be to support a presidential candidate who would avoid authoritarian actions and appoint ministers solely on the recommendations of the elected representatives, and parliamentary candidates who would oppose expenditure on a Cypriot army. On 26 November Clerides was nominated as the Democratic Union's candidate for the presidency.

The state of emergency which had been in force since 1955 was formally ended by Foot on 4 December 1959; AKEL and its affiliated organizations were once more legalized. However, the party had for some time functioned almost openly. Its position in the forthcoming presidential elections was uncertain. On 25 November it issued a statement revealing the failure of negotiations with Makarios. It was subsequently disclosed that the latter had offered to support AKEL candidates for seven seats in the future House of Representatives in return for support in the presidential elections. AKEL rejected the offer. It appeared to have asked for equal representation for all three Greek parties – EDMA, the Democratic Union and AKEL – and for a coalition cabinet with an agreed programme.

AKEL announced on 27 November that it would back the candidate of the Democratic Union in the forthcoming elections. Thus the DU had rallied to its side right-wing extremists determined to overthrow the settlement or at least to modify it radically; leftists sufficiently realistic to accept it as an interim necessity; and many men of ability and moderation. Clerides himself described the Agreements as a 'political disaster' but advised against repudiating them in their entirety because that would have 'incalculable consequences'.

As a concession to its numerous critics EDMA had reappeared as the Patriotic Front (being a loosely organized coalition of nationalists it lacked a social base and a corresponding ideology, and eventually split into different blocs that formed the basis of political parties); its members resorted to a smear campaign of extreme viciousness, especially over allegations of Clerides's past co-operation with the British colonial administration. Mass meetings were held by both groups and fighting broke out between the opposing factions in several districts. Both the archbishop and Clerides appealed for order, and polling day on 13 December 1959 went off peacefully.

In a 90.53 per cent poll, the archbishop received 144,501 votes against 71,753 cast for his opponent. The electorate totalled 238,879 and women were eligible to vote for the first time. Whether Makarios owed his election to the 'housewife vote' or not, his 66.82 per cent share was due less to approval of the Zürich-London Agreements than to the belief of a majority of Greek Cypriots that in any situation the archbishop was the best man to handle their affairs. Makarios, now president-elect of Cyprus, also had control of the foreign affairs portfolio, and since the resignation of A. Georghiades on 19 November, on the pretext that he would continue studies in Athens, that of communications and works.

On 14 December the archbishop called for unity and for co-operation between Greek and Turkish Cypriots. Kutchuk, returned unopposed on 3 December as vice-President-elect, welcomed the result of the Greek election and expressed his confidence in effective future collaboration between Makarios and himself.

Another domestic irritant was the friction between Greek and Turkish Cypriots. Attempts were made by both sides to eradicate major sources of tension. A joint committee was set up to investigate incidents in villages with mixed populations. Makarios and Kutchuk made several joint appeals to their respective communities to avoid clashes. One such appeal on 4 July went to the local press (a perennial source of mischief-making between the two communities), urging them to co-operate in restoring friendly relations. However, between 27 August and 28 September unidentified gunmen murdered a Turkish special branch sergeant in Nicosia, a Turkish night-watchman on the Limassol-Nicosia road, a third Turkish Cypriot in the village of Mansoura and a Greek Cypriot in the village of Kilani. Makarios and Kutchuk jointly requested the public to collaborate in fighting the current wave of violence. AKEL called on all armed groups to surrender their weapons.

On 18 October the *Deniz* (a Turkish motor-boat registered at Izmir) was spotted off the north-east coast of the island by the minesweeper HMS *Burmaston* which was on a routine patrol. A search party was put on board, whereupon its three-man crew (all Turkish nationals) scuttled their vessel and threw two cases of ammunition overboard before they were arrested. The men appeared at a Famagusta court on the following day and were remanded in custody on a charge of attempting to import munitions into Cyprus without a permit. Objecting to bail, the police said that the quantity of ammunition involved was 'not a few rounds but thousands' and that '73 boxes were still missing'.

The crisis intensified suspicions in Cyprus that TMT was still active and that the Turks were stockpiling arms and ammunition not only to defend themselves but to attack their Greek compatriots. On 21 October Makarios informed Kutchuk that he was suspending the constitutional negotiations since the arms-running attempt seemed to imply insincerity and lack of goodwill on the Turkish side and had deeply perturbed all Greek Cypriots. In reply Kutchuk stated that Turkish Cypriots could not accept responsibility for the acts of 'some irresponsible persons', called for peace and tranquillity between the two communities and offered to sign a joint appeal with the archbishop calling for the surrender of all illegal arms. Denktash criticised Makarios for breaking off the constitutional discussions and dismissed the incident as no worse than the gun-running activities of the Greek extremists. The Turkish foreign ministry declared on 23 October that 'Turkey has never encouraged arms smuggling to Cyprus and will not do so', and Ankara radio claimed that the *Deniz* was 'hunting dolphins'.

Public confidence was severely shaken. Nevertheless, on 28-9 October the two leaders issued press and radio appeals to the two communities calling for the handing in of all illegal arms and explosives by 15 November, failing which the police would carry out searches and apply 'the full rigour of the law' to all persons who had not complied. At the same time Makarios announced that the constitutional negotiations would be resumed during the following week. On 11 November the *Deniz* crew were found guilty of the illegal possession of ammunition in Cyprus's territorial waters and sentenced to one year's imprisonment. However, in view of the wider interests involved the governor commuted the sentences and the three men were immediately deported.

Despite the disturbed political scene, preparations for independence went ahead. However, a number of immediate practical problems which did not depend on the operation of the constitution were of major importance in the year prior to the establishment of the Cyprus Republic. Some of these were:

the island's relationship with the rest of the international community – with NATO and the UN for example;
its relationship with the British Commonwealth of Nations;
its wider economic future – should it remain in the sterling area and how much aid was it to receive;
the attitude of Greece and Turkey now that both countries guaranteed the island's independence and had troops legally on Cypriot soil;
the size of the British sovereign bases and training areas (i.e. ancillary facilities) outside these areas;
the nationality of Cypriots living in other countries;
the goodwill and co-operation to be shown by the two communities and by the three protecting powers.

There were also several constitutional problems:

the allocation of jobs in the public service;
the creation of separate municipalities;
the composition of the Cypriot army;
the powers of the president and vice-president – especially the final veto power of the latter.

In fact the workload of the Constitutional Commission, which met for the first time on 13 April 1959, was unenviable. Nevertheless, on 11 February 1960 the draft constitution was completed in Lausanne. After a gruelling period of complicated negotiations the commission's assignment was fulfilled and a ceremony was held in Nicosia on 6 April to make a formal announcement of the event. The constitution, consisting of 199 articles and six annexes, embodied the Zürich-London Agreements and formed the fundamental law of the new state. The form of government created combined a central administration having a 70:30 proportional representation and a division of power between the Greek and Turkish communities with a system of separate community governments to deal with purely communal and local affairs.

The Transitional Committee, which held its first meeting on

4 March 1959, made rapid progress. Foot emphasized that 'by the end of 1959, as far as internal government was concerned, we were ready to hand over'.

Despite the many problems the achievement of independence, though postponed several times, was not far away. Hence on 28 October 1959 the Treaty of Alliance between Greece, Turkey and Cyprus was initialled in Athens. On 10 November Makarios and Kutchuk announced agreement on the respective powers of the president and vice-president. On 3 December Kutchuk was returned unopposed as vice-president-elect and on 14 December the archbishop was also proclaimed president-elect of Cyprus. On 4 December the Governor ended the state of emergency and on the 31st the controversial electoral law (based on the recommendations of the Constitutional Commission) was formally enacted.

Under this law the island was divided into six multi-member constituencies, the Nicosia district being the largest with 12 Greek and 5 Turkish members. The two communities would vote separately and the individual elector would vote for several candidates according to the number of vacancies in his constituency. For example, the Greek voter in Nicosia would have 12 votes which he could either give *en bloc* to one party or have them dispersed in any ratio he pleased. As specified by the Zürich-London Agreements, the House of Representatives was to be composed of 35 Greek and 15 Turkish Cypriots.

The electoral law was the subject of acute controversy because of its complexity and because the size of the constituencies made a victory for the Patriotic Front (the Archbishop's 'party') a certainty and the election of opposition candidates virtually impossible. Clerides criticized it as being 'unfair and undemocratic' and his Democratic Union subsequently refused to contest the elections. Both the DU and AKEL urged a system of proportional representation, or alternatively the British system of single-member constituencies and simple majority vote. AKEL however agreed to co-operate with the Patriotic Front in exchange for five seats in the House of Representatives.

Elections scheduled for 7 February 1960 were held on 31 July. The abstention rate was high – 36 per cent of the Greek and 26 per cent of the Turkish Cypriot electors did not vote.

There were several explanations for the Greek apathy:

1 Voters were convinced that a victory for the PF was inevitable.

2 Many right-wing electors may have abstained in opposition to the co-option pact between the PF and AKEL.

3 In constituencies where AKEL was not represented abstentions rose. Thus 59 per cent of the Larnaca electors failed to turn up on polling day.

4 Prior to the poll a new party was formed in mid July by former EOKA members under the name of the Pan-Cyprian Union of Fighters, in opposition to the archbishop and with the avowed aim of overthrowing the settlement and the treaties arising therefrom. The new party strongly condemned the electoral deal between the PF and AKEL, pledged its full support to Grivas and announced that it would launch a campaign to enlighten the people of the island on the consequences of the Agreements. On 22 July Grivas issued a statement in Athens expressing his desire to stay out of the electoral strife. Consequently the new party decided not to contest the elections but only to put up eight candidates as independents in token resistance to the Agreements.

5 Some voters were simply disenchanted with everything going on around them.

The elections resulted in the return of 30 PF supporters and 5 AKEL members for the 35 Greek Cypriot seats and of 15 National Front Party supporters (Kutchuk's party) for the 15 Turkish Cypriot seats. The eight Greek independents fared very badly; their seven Turkish counterparts did slightly better.

Shortly after the elections the formation of a new Turkish Cypriot party, in opposition to the NFP, was announced by two lawyers, Ahmet Gurkan and Ayhan Hikmet. At a press conference in Nicosia on 4 August Gurkan explained that the new party (its name was not announced) fully supported the external agreements reached so far and the foreign policy of Kutchuk, but differed from the latter in internal policy, particularly in its opposition to the 'dictatorial and one-party tendencies' of the NFP. Gurkan denied Kutchuk's allegations of a plot against himself and other National Front leaders. He also claimed that the principle of a Turkish Cypriot opposition party was viewed favourably by Ankara.

The final stage of the elections took place on 7 August with the formation of the two Communal Chambers which, under the Zürich-London provisions, would legislate on such communal matters as education, social welfare and religious affairs. Of the 26 seats in the Greek Chamber, 20 were won by the PF and 3 by AKEL candidates standing on PF lists under the electoral pact, while the remaining 3 seats were filled by one representative each of the minority religious groups – Armenians, Maronites and Roman Catholics. All seats in the Turkish Chamber were won by the NFP.

Although the preparations for independence were virtually completed, Anglo-Cypriot negotiations over the size and administration of the two bases and other facilities took longer than originally anticipated. A round-table conference in London on 16-18 January 1960 attended by the Foreign Ministers of Britain, Greece and Turkey, Foot, Makarios, Kutchuk and Julian Amery (Under-Secretary of State at the Colonial Office) failed to end the deadlock. It was however decided that self-rule should be postponed by one month. On 13 February Macmillan wrote: 'Cyprus goes "on" and "off" – like a dish at a cheap restaurant. Julian Amery was sent out to see the Governor and the Archbishop. No progress. A complete deadlock. . . . I think Makarios will bargain up to the last point.'[1]

Makarios on the other hand, speaking on the occasion of the fifth anniversary of EOKA, accused Britain of sinister designs in delaying independence and asserted that the Cypriots would, if need be, establish the republic by themselves. He also stated that 'the epic grandeur and glory of EOKA's liberation struggle had laid the foundation-stone of national freedom . . . the realisation of our hopes and aspirations are not complete under the Zürich-London Agreements'. This speech however brought a strong and immediate reaction from Kutchuk, who warned that his compatriots could not co-operate with those who looked upon the settlement as 'a bastion for new campaigns'.

Britain asked for 170 square miles in April 1959 but on the

advice of its Chiefs of Staff, who reassessed the whole situation, it was successively reduced to 152 and then 120 square miles, which constitutes around 3 per cent of the island's area. The archbishop on the other hand consecutively announced areas of 36, 70 and 80 square miles. Agreement was finally reached on 99 square miles, i.e. 2.5 per cent of Cypriot territory.

The size and location of the training areas outside the two base areas were also very much in dispute. In the end Britain was allowed 11 such areas which included the Lefkoniko artillery range, a high-level bombing range in the vicinity of Akrotiri and an instrument flying area which covered the district from Dhavlos and Ayios Elias almost to St Andreas monastery. The UK was also allowed to control 31 sites and installations scattered around the island and including the radar complexes on mount Troodos. It was therefore only restricted independence that the Cypriots won in 1960.

It was also agreed that over the next five years Britain should provide aid to the sum of £12 million. Provision was made for the amount of assistance in future five-year periods to be determined after full consultation with the Cypriot authorities. In addition there were payments and commitments for particular purposes, including a special grant of £1.5 million to the Turkish community.

On 1 July 1960 the British and Cypriot delegations announced that agreement had been reached on all outstanding issues. Nine days later it was proclaimed in London that the transfer of power would take place on 16 August. On that day Makarios was invested as President of Cyprus and Kutchuk as vice-president. Two days earlier the archbishop announced a reconstitution of the cabinet. The foreign minister designate, Nicos Kranidiotis, declined to take office and on 22 August Makarios accordingly appointed another person and also a new Minister of Justice. The recomposed cabinet was as follows:

Name	Portfolio	Greek/Turkish Cypriot
Spyros Kyprianou	Foreign Affairs	Greek Cypriot
Polycarpos Georghadgis	Interior	"
Andreas Araouzos	Commerce and Industry	"
Stella Souliotou (Mrs)	Justice	"
Andreas Papadopoulos	Communications and Works	"
Tasos Papadopoulos	Labour and Social Services	"

Righinos Theocharous	Finance	Greek Cypriot
Andreas Azinas	Deputy Minister of Agriculture	"
Osman Orek	Defence	Turkish Cypriot
Fazil Plümer	Agriculture	"
Niyazi Manyera	Health	"
Mehmet Nazim	Deputy Minister of Health	"

Thus the new Republic of Cyprus came into being on 16 August 1960 – 18 months after the signing of the Zürich-London Agreements. On 24 August the Security Council unanimously recommended its admission to membership of the UN and on 20 September the Cypriot application sponsored by Sri Lanka (Ceylon) and the UK and supported by Greece and Turkey was accepted by the General Assembly. Through resolution 1489 (XV) Cyprus became the 99th member state of the UN. On 16 February 1961 it was admitted to the Commonwealth and on 24 May Cyprus became the 16th member-state of the Council of Europe.

In practical terms was the settlement a 'victory for all' or simply 'the death of a people'? The island's Greeks and Turks, already polarized (especially since 1954-5), now found themselves grouped against each other in order to guard their respective communal interests within the framework of the so-called 'unique arrangements'. The constitution offered was likened to the mythical multi-headed hydra. It was a constitutional monster because it not only gave to the Turkish minority, constituting 18.4 per cent of the total population, disproportionate power but it encouraged resentment and separation instead of coexistence and co-operation. In an article entitled 'A Respite for Cyprus' W.M. Dobell wrote: 'Its architects were interested outsiders, and Cypriots were allowed to choose the wall-paper and the furnishings. Of its 199 articles, its 48 major articles were in substance pre-determined . . . clause after clause bears the imprint of open conflict. To wend one's way through this complex labyrinth is to stumble from pebble to bed-rock and back to pebble again.'[2]

There are several examples of the 'imprint of open conflict':

1   The Turkish Vice-President representing around 20 per cent of the population and elected solely by that electorate held veto powers on foreign affairs, defence, security and some

financial issues. The Turkish stance on this problem was perfectly summarized by Harry J. Psomiades in an article 'The Cyprus Dispute'. He wrote: 'They visualized the vice-president as a co-president. The president would control the steering wheel but the vice-president would control the gears and the brakes.'[3]

2   The two executives were empowered to appoint their own ministers – seven Greeks and three Turks. The ratio of seven to three was to be applied to positions in the public service, the police and gendarmerie and in the House of Representatives. The proportion in the Cypriot army was to be 60:40.

3   Each community was to have its own communal chamber with the right to impose taxes and levies on members of its community and to exercise authority on religious, charitable, education and personal status questions. In the event of a conflict of authority between the House of Representatives and the communal chambers, such a clash was to be decided by the supreme constitutional court composed of one Greek, one Turk and a neutral judge appointed jointly by the president and vice-president.

4   Article 173 provided that separate municipalities should be created in the five largest towns – Nicosia, Limassol, Famagusta, Larnaca and Paphos – by their Turkish inhabitants. In fact the separate Turkish municipal councils set up during the last years of colonial rule were not only continued and strengthened but were now given legal existence.

In reality Cyprus was given a solution of convenience and presented with the most bizarre and complicated of constitutions. The will of 80 per cent of the population was equated with the will of 20 per cent; instead of majority rule and minority check the Cypriots were given dualism in government, and instead of co-operation and coexistence the constitution encouraged resentment and separation. The chief architects were the Conservatives, who by their policies after 1954 (of which conclusive evidence can be found in the Eden and Macmillan memoirs) firmly implanted separatism and finally partition on the Turkish inhabitants. James Callaghan, speaking of Eden's government during the second reading of the Cyprus Bill on 14 July 1960, emphasized: 'The British PM went out of his way to foment the troubles which he knew existed and did it because he wanted reinforcement from the Turks in order to preserve our position in the base. . . . It was a shabby and discreditable period. . . . They have done that of which Britain has always been accused – divide and rule.'[4]

During the same debate H.A. Marquand refuted the thesis that Greeks and Turks never did and never could live in peace in Cyprus: 'There were few differences between Turkish and Greek Cypriots. Although there may occasionally have been some tension between them, as there is tension in the City of Glasgow from time to time, especially when Celtic play Rangers, between Protestants and Catholics, on the whole people lived together very well.'[5]

Thus before 1954 it cannot be denied that the island's Greeks and Turks had lived amicably together. Even during the two world wars there were no incidents of great importance. Since the mid 1950s however the state of tranquillity was transformed into one of conflict and antagonism. Even since 1960 Cyprus has been subjected to the influences and pressures of the respective governments of Greece and Turkey, and the political instability in both these nations, the two 'mother' countries, has been allowed to spill over and create tenseness within the republic and between its people.

Nevertheless Cyprus in 1960 had its own flag, its own elected government and was no longer embarrassed by the stigma of colonial status. Autonomy however did not entail an independent economy, nor did it allow the formation of a sovereign state free from all foreign troops. This in turn implied the impossibility of an independent political line being pursued by the infant state. The Zürich-London Agreements made sure of that. In itself the British presence on the island had no major significance but within the context of NATO the bases were of paramount importance. They formed a link in the south-eastern flank of NATO and during the 1967 Arab-Israeli confrontation were used as such by USA planes supplying arms to Israel. The bases were also used by the British as a staging-post for intervention in Suez and Jordan in 1956 and 1958. After the farcical débâcles in Iran, Iraq and Egypt in the 1950s it became clear that Britain's pathetic attempts to control the area were endangering western interests, particularly oil.

Britain in fact had become an embarrassing liability and the USA had to seize authority from its senile ex-master. This factor does much to explain the strong American involvement in Cyprus, mediated through Greece and Turkey.

Another integral part of the settlement which prompted widespread criticism was the Treaty of Alliance. This allowed the permanent basing of 650 Turkish and 950 Greek troops on the island. Thus America could rest assured that her interests were being looked after by the military presence of three NATO members. However, perhaps the greatest objections voiced by Makarios, the great majority of Greek Cypriots and the opposition in Greece were that the new Accords gave Turkey legal rights on the island which she had earlier surrendered by Article 16 of the Treaty of Lausanne 1923, and that the Greek Cypriots were being sacrificed for the most general interests of western security.

Greek Cypriots also disapproved of the Treaty of Guarantee which gave the three protecting powers the right to take joint or individual action in Cyprus with the sole aim of re-establishing its independence, territorial integrity and security, as well as respect for its constitution. The constitution imposed on the Cypriot people invited such intervention; it was completely unworkable and required only a few flash points to destroy the island's unity completely. The pot was to be kept simmering by the appropriate agencies and it was just a matter of time before America would achieve complete domination of the island through its junior partners in NATO.

In the first years of independence Cyprus was to pay dearly for the precarious settlement granted her by the allied western powers. The folly of the 'peacemakers' and 'godfathers' personified by Macmillan and his Tory entourage, Karamanlis and Averoff, Menderes and Zorlu, was to have unprecedented consequences. It was in fact a rogues' deal – nothing more and nothing less.

Part III

THE CYPRUS REPUBLIC

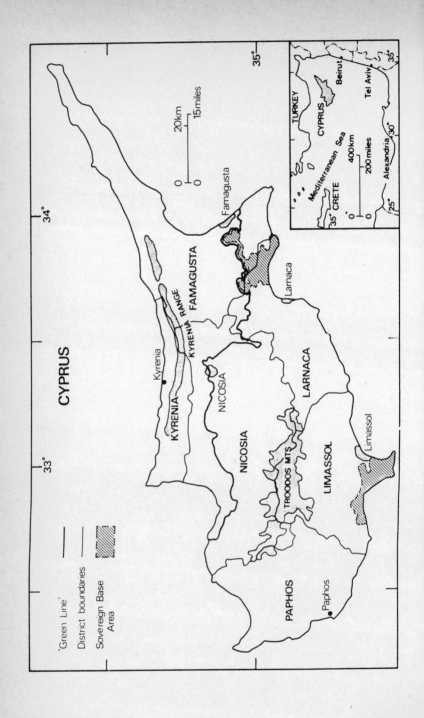

CYPRUS

'Green Line'
District boundaries
Sovereign Base Area

KYRENIA
FAMAGUSTA
KYRENIA RANGE
Kyrenia
NICOSIA
NICOSIA
Famagusta
Larnaca
LARNACA
TROODOS MTS.
LIMASSOL
Limassol
PAPHOS
Paphos

34°
33°
35°

20km
15miles
0
0

TURKEY
Beirut
Tel Aviv
CYPRUS
Mediterranean Sea
CRETE
Alexandria
35°
30°
25°
35°
400km
200miles
0
0

14 Cyprus Since 1960

The setting up of the Cyprus Republic meant, in theory at least, that a number of Greeks who had earlier led the struggle for *enosis* and a number of Turks who had successfully led the resistance to it would come together to collaborate in running the new state. Such co-operation was not easy in view of:

the recent enmity between EOKA and TMT;
the complexities created by the settlement;
the imposed rifts within the two communities which were not conducive to creating harmony or promoting the Cypriot consciousness;
more generally, the relationship between the two opposing nationalisms; Cypriots were conscious of their Greekness or Turkishness (their national leaders never stopped reminding them of that), and their first loyalties were to their own communities and leaderships.

Thus in order to appease a dissatisfied section of the community (the enosists or ethnikofrons), the archbishop declared on 1 April 1960 that 'the task we began five years ago will soon be completed and bear fruit'. On 16 August he declared that 'new bastions have been conquered and from these bastions we will march on to complete the final victory'. At the 1961 Belgrade Conference of Non-Aligned Nations, Makarios called for an all-German plebiscite on the German reunification issue. In Cyprus however no one doubted that such a course would produce an overwhelming vote for *enosis* with Greece – a concept subversive to the Cypriot constitution.

Kutchuk on the other hand reminded everyone that the Turkish army was not far away. An editorial in *Halkin Sesi* on 29 January 1963 expressed the firm conviction that 'Cyprus can in no way be different from Mersina, Alexandretta or Adana'. In April 1963 Denktash told a group of Boy Scouts that 'our flag owes its colour to the blood of 80,000 martyrs' and he took an oath before it that 'the Turkish community will never become a minority, nor will the island ever become Greek'.

It appears therefore that the immediate objective of the Turkish Cypriot leadership was to accept the new constitutional order but their long term objective was to find ways of proving it unworkable and thus to argue that partition was the best solution. In Ankara such an arrangement was seen as the best setting for its declared partitionist policy and even for its 'future' annexation of the island. To the Greeks the many weaknesses of the constitution produced imbalance. Governmental dualism and ethnic separatism between Greek and Turkish Cypriots were institutionalized. The constitution had brought into being a state but not a nation.

Conflict, inevitable given the peculiarities of the constitution, intensified as the Greeks tried to show that only a unitary system of government would work in Cyprus, while the Turks took every opportunity to block government business whenever they felt that their rights were infringed or their needs unmet. Soon they were deadlocked on a host of issues including civil service staffing, the army, separation of municipalities and the use of the Turkish veto on central government taxation.

Hence the complex and rigid settlement imposed on the Cypriots by British, Greek and Turkish diplomats, who rejoiced over the triumph of goodwill and international understanding, soon broke down. On paper the constitution was incomprehensible. In application it was a legal monster. Cyprus in fact was given two governments – a majority one and a minority one – functioning together and overlapping. As pointed out by constitutional and legal experts, Cyprus was the first country in the world to be denied majority rule by its own constitution.

Inevitably the new state was arrested in infancy. The devisive municipalities provision (Article 173) was probably the greatest source of trouble in the 1960 constitution. The focal point of friction regarding the municipalities was in the headlines of the Greek Cypriot press even before the declaration of independence. The Cypriots failed to produce any agreed criteria for the division of the municipalities. The Turkish Cypriots answered the refusal of their compatriots to accept their recommendation for the geographical division of the municipalities by voting down the customs law in March 1961 and the income tax law in December.

On 19 March 1962 another bid to end the deadlock was made at a meeting between Makarios and Kutchuk. The archbishop expressed the view that geographical separation would jeopardize the interests of both communities and suggested a unified municipal authority with representation of Greek and Turkish councillors based on the proportion of the respective communities in each town. He then offered a three-point formula to safeguard the interests and rights of the Turkish residents under such an authority. On the following day Makarios' proposals were described as 'unrealistic' by Denktash, the President of the Turkish Communal Chamber.

The last attempt to reach a mutually acceptable solution to the so-called 'battle of the five towns' was made in December 1962. On Christmas Eve, after negotiations lasting late into the night, it looked as if a compromise had miraculously been achieved. A joint communiqué drafted by Clerides and Denktash was issued announcing an agreement 'in principle', but within 24 hours Kutchuk had repudiated it. Did the Turks have second thoughts or did they receive instructions from Ankara?

Separation, which became an end in itself, bred tension and afforded the opportunity to extremists to plunge the country into strife. Such extremism was shown earlier in the year when two London-educated barristers were murdered by TMT gunmen on 24 April. Ahmet Gurkan aged 38 and Ayhan Hikmet aged 33 were leaders of the Turkish Cypriot People's Party which was in opposition to the majority NFP led by Kutchuk and Denktash. Hikmet was the editor of the weekly newspaper *Cumhuriyet*, founded by Gurkan, which advocated closer association between the two communties.

Hirber Hikmet declared that the assassinations were 'a political murder by Turkish extremists' because the two lawyers 'stood for the idea of brotherly co-operation between the two communities'. Makarios also spoke of a 'political motive — the intimidation and neutralization of Turks who favoured co-operation between the island's inhabitants'. Influential Turks also denounced the assassinations. Emil

Dirvana, the Turkish Ambassador in Nicosia and a prominent supporter of intercommunal co-operation, unreservedly condemned the murders. Ali Dana, the Turkish Cypriot Mufti, expressed his disgust for them. However, following Denktash's protests Dirvana was shortly afterwards recalled to Ankara. Thus all the obstacles were now removed to the Turkish Cypriot insurgence and gradual separation long prepared by Turkish extreme chauvinists both in Cyprus and in Turkey.

The precedents for such terrorism were certainly there. In 1958 progressive Turkish Cypriots were the targets of TMT. The ethnocentric elements who were determined to divide and rule attacked their leading compatriots who were members of AKEL and the united trade unions in order to force around 3,500 Turkish Cypriot workers, organized in the joint Greek and Turkish Cypriot trade unions known as PEO, to leave such all-Cypriot unions and form exclusively Turkish ones. In 1958 the membership of such unions consequently increased from 1,137 to 4,829. Furthermore, prominent Turkish Cypriot members of AKEL and other democratic Turkish Cypriots were attacked and a number of them murdered in cold blood because they fought for friendship and co-operation between the two communities against colonialism and imperialism and for independence.

Even though acts of violence, arson and destruction of property were a regular occurrence, the British administration reacted by arresting Turkish democrats, political and labour leaders instead of the reactionary Turkish Cypriot leaders and their diehard supporters who were responsible for such civil and criminal disobedience. Thus when Francis Noel-Baker MP asked Lennox-Boyd, Secretary of State for the Colonies, on 17 June 1958 what action the authorities of Cyprus intended to take against Kutchuk and Denktash in view of their repeated violations of the emergency regulations, the curt reply was 'no proceedings have been taken'.

During the first months of 1958 relations between the two communities were strained even further. Ankara radio spoke daily in very strong terms of the impossibility of the Turks and Greeks living together in peace. It emphasized that since they had completely different political, religious and cultural backgrounds they could not coexist under a single political system. The Turkish ruling élite therefore demanded that the island should be partitioned, with Turkey fully controlling financially, politically and militarily 'its' sector. In such an atmosphere it was easy for their supporters to brand as traitors all those who disagreed with its crazy pro-imperialist policy.

Even so hundreds of Turks joined with their Greek compatriots in the 1958 May Day celebrations, as they had done in previous years. The marchers, shouting anti-imperialist slogans and protesting against the divisions being enforced by the western powers, paraded through the streets of Nicosia with their national flags and vowed to fight for the common ideals of the working class.

The reaction of the extreme right-wing Turkish leadership was vicious. On that very night hordes of wild Turkish Cypriots looted the Turkish sport and cultural club of Nicosia, set fire to it and then accused its members of having been sold to the Greeks. The crime took place under the noses of the security forces, yet no one was arrested. The burning of the club gave the signal for a general attack to exterminate the progressive and peace-loving Turks. The first murder attempt was made on 22 May 1958 against Ahmet Sadi, a trade unionist in charge of the PEO Turkish office. He was shot by three Turkish terrorists on his doorstep and seriously wounded. Two days later Fazil Ondur was shot dead. On 27 May TMT admitted in leaflets that the murder of Ondur was its work. Other exponents of peaceful coexistence such as Ahmet Vahya and Ahmet Imbraim were also brutally murdered. The assassins however continued their work unpunished.

In December 1962 the Greek majority in the House of Representatives rejected a Turkish proposal to extend the existing municipal laws for one year from 1 January 1963. On 2 January the council of ministers brought the town councils under the direct control of the central government by setting up developments boards to run the main towns. The Greek municipalities surrendered their powers to these boards but the Turkish ones refused to do so, the Turkish communal chamber declaring that the separate municipalities were still legal.

The Turkish Cypriot leaders consulted Ankara and referred the dispute to the Cyprus Constitutional Court, whose neutral president, Dr Ernest Forsthoff (a West German Professor from the University of Heidelberg who later resigned), ruled on 25 April that both moves were illegal. Since the same court had already decided on 8 February that the Turkish veto on the tax laws in 1961 meant that the government had no authority to collect customs duties and income tax, both central and local government were henceforth threatened with paralysis.

On 9 April 1963 Makarios explained that the blocking of the taxation laws had caused 'great difficulties'; that the insistence on separate municipalities in the five main towns was 'unreasonable and wastefully expensive'; and that 'the real damage' had been caused by the Turkish obstruction of proposed legislation for setting up a development bank. Nevertheless the first five-year plan (1962-6) concentrated on developing the economic potential of the island by mobilizing all unemployed resources, thus providing the necessary infrastructure for the diversification of the economy with a view to removing the causes of pre-1960 economic instability. Despite the internal problems of the island the plan succeeded in getting the productive resources moving and restored internal and foreign confidence in the economy.

Yet in 1963 Cyprus was without an income tax law, a customs law and a municipalities law, and the two communities seemed headed for a major confrontation. Convinced by now that the Turks would not consider any change in the constitution by agreement and that their ultimate aim was to partition the island, the Greek Cypriots began to talk of removing the divisive and negative elements of the constitution. At the same time the Turkish Cypriots threatened that any Greek effort to amend the constitution without their approval would meet with Turkish might and would result in 'partition or death'. A strong Greek Cypriot lobby had even suggested that the government should use the good offices of the UN to carry through the proposed amendments.

On 4 August 1963 Makarios said that he had finally made up his mind that the constitution was in dire need of a change. He would seek this revision since certain provisions of inapplicable character threatened to 'paralyse the state machinery'. In reply Kutchuk declared on 22 August that the Turks might resort to civil disobedience if the Greeks attempted a unilateral revision of the constitution which would 'not be binding on the Turkish community'.

The president however, in his desire to facilitate the smooth functioning of the infant state and remove the causes of intercommunal friction, submitted on 30 November concrete proposals (glossed over by Mr Clark, the British High Commissioner in Cyprus) for amending the constitution. These were transmitted to Kutchuk and copies were sent to the governments of Britain, Greece and Turkey for 'information purposes only'. These proposals, as set out below, were intended to establish a more unified state and were in logic undeniable:

1   The right of veto of the president and the vice-president was to be abandoned.

2   The vice-president was to deputize for the president in case of temporary absence or incapacity to perform his duties.

3   The Greek president of the House of Representatives and the Turkish vice-president were to be elected by the House as a whole and not, as before, by separate Greek and Turkish majorities within the House.

4   The vice-president of the House of Representatives was to deputize for the president of the House in case of his temporary absence or incapacity to perform his duties.

5   The constitutional provisions regarding separate majorities for the enactment of certain laws by the House of Representatives were to be abolished.

6   Unified municipalities were to be established.

7   The administration of justice was to be unified.

8   The division of the security forces into police and gendarmerie was to be abolished.

9   The numerical strength of the security forces and of the defence forces was to be determined by law.

10   The proportion of participation of Greek Cypriots and Turkish Cypriots in the composition of the public services

(70:30) and the forces of the republic (60:40) was to be modified in proportion to the ratio of the population of Greek to Turkish Cypriots.

11 The number of members of the public service commission was to be reduced from ten to five.

12 All decisions of the public service commission were to be taken by simple majority.

13 The communal chambers would be abolished and a new system devised. Should the Turkish community however desire to retain its chamber in the new system, such a course would be open to it.

Proposals one and nine were designed to amend those constitutional provisions which led to the army deadlock; number five was intended to amend the constitutional provision which caused the tax legislation deadlock; proposals ten, eleven and twelve were devised to amend those provisions which led to the friction in the public service. Thus it was intended to remove the obstacles which hindered the smooth functioning of the state and to establish a more unified state, abolishing the so-called 'separatist constitutional provisions'.

Meanwhile the two 'mother countries' were going through a political crisis. Just before Christmas both were left simultaneously with unrepresentative governments. In Greece the eight-year reign of Karamanlis came to an abrupt end and on 11 June 1963 he resigned (or perhaps was sacked) following the decision of King Paul and Queen Frederika to disregard his advice of not proceeding with the royal visit to London.

In Turkey the situation was even worse. In May 1960 the Menderes regime was overthrown by an army revolt led by Lt-General Jemal Gürsel, but in 1962 and 1963 attempted coups against the new civilian regime were suppressed. Finally, on 2 December 1963, Inönü's government resigned.

It was in the middle of this crisis, and when Greece, after inconclusive elections on 3 November, was also struggling to form a government, that Makarios chose to make his first formal bid to change the 'Cyprus constitutional oddity'. Kutchuk, to whom the proposals were addressed, failed to reply, although at press interviews he reiterated that the constitution could not be changed. However, on 7 December F.K. Erkin, the Turkish Foreign Minister, announced that Ankara had rejected them and on 16 December Ozkol, the Turkish ambassador, handed to Makarios Turkey's written rejection. Makarios however refused to accept the rejection, pointing out that the proposals had been sent to the Turkish Cypriot vice-president for reply and not to any foreign government.

On 20 December the Foreign Ministers of Cyprus, Greece and Turkey had a meeting in Paris to discuss the situation. Within a few hours of their first encounter shooting broke out in Nicosia. An initial attempt to bring intercommunal tension to boiling point was averted on 3 December. The government managed to cool tempers after a bomb exploded at the base of the newly erected statue of Markos Drakos, a Greek Cypriot hero during the EOKA campaign.

However, in the early hours of 21 December a police patrol car with Greek Cypriot policemen driving down Hermes Street in the old city of Nicosia (the same area which had been the scene of arson and looting by Turkish extremists in 1958) stopped a car for a routine check. Shots were fired and one of the policemen was wounded. The policemen returned the fire. A young Turk was killed and a Turkish woman wounded, dying on her way to hospital. Within minutes shooting broke out in various quarters of the city. By 5 a.m. an angry Turkish crowd started moving into the Greek quarter and by 6 a.m. one Greek and one Turk had been brought to hospital with gunshot wounds.

There were further attacks on Greeks in the early morning of 22 December on the Nicosia-Kyrenia road, in the Omorphita area, Louroudjina, Chatoz and Ayios Sozomenos. A Turk was shot at passing through the village of Deftera and later both Makarios and Kutchuk arrived in the village to investigate and make statements calling for calm.

By midday all Turkish Cypriot government employees and policemen had left their posts. The Turks fortified themselves in their own areas, the fortifications proving to have been well prepared in advance. In order to further their partitioning aims they forced several thousand innocent and contented Turkish peasants to abandon their farms and animals and move into their overcrowded quarter of Nicosia. Thus the aim of partition, camouflaged by Turkish propaganda as 'federation', was relentlessly pursued regardless of loss of human life and the human misery created. However, this so-called 'first phase' of the invasion of Cyprus by Turkey only partly succeeded, since well over half of its brethen refused to obey instructions to abandon their homes for the predetermined enclaves.

The clashes had caught the leadership of the two communities completely unprepared. There is no evidence to suggest that the outbreak of violence had official sanction. In fact Makarios and Kutchuk met Greek and Turkish Cypriot ministers at the Paphos Gate police station and there was another call to the public for calm and for the shooting to stop. On 23 December the acting British High Commissioner and the USA ambassador called on the president and expressed the grave concern of their governments at the turn of events in Cyprus. They appealed for moderation from both communities. Athens also urged Makarios to use his influence to end the intercommunal bloodshed, and Ankara appealed to the Turkish Cypriots to assist responsible administrators with calm and dignity; but such pleas were too late.

At 2.25 p.m. on 23 December Turkish Cypriot extremists moved into the Armenian quarter of Nicosia and forced the inhabitants to leave their houses, shops, church, school and clubs. Shortly afterwards British servicemen and civilians were shot at in Larnaca and Lefka by TMT gunmen. A ceasefire was hastily arranged on 24 December. It failed because of clashes on the outskirts of Nicosia, but a new accord was concluded on Christmas Day.

At the discussions on 27 December between Major-General Peter Young (GOC Cyprus) and the Greek and Turkish army commanders on the island, agreement was reached on the establishment of a headquarters for the joint peace-keeping force. British troops began patrolling Nicosia and Larnaca on the same day and a 'green line' (reminiscent of EOKA days and regularly likened to the more famous Berlin Wall) was subsequently established on 30 December in Nicosia to separate the Greek from the Turkish Cypriot quarters. The line, guarded by British troops, cut straight across the mixed suburbs of Omorphita and Neapolis and put the entire

Armenian quarter as well as the Greek areas of Kermia, Ayios Kasianos and Ayios Iakovos behind Turkish lines.

The renewal of the Cyprus conflict brought Greece and Turkey once again to the brink of war. The joint plea for peace issued by the protecting powers on 23 December was followed the next day by rumours of a Turkish invasion. Late on 24 December the Turkish army contingent in Cyprus marched out of its appointed camp and took positions on the northern outskirts of Nicosia and along the Nicosia-Kyrenia road which leads to the northern coast. On the following day Turkish jets screamed low over the rooftops of Nicosia and Turkish naval units were spotted manoeuvring off the island's coast. Following suit the Greek army contingent also left its barracks and took positions to counter a possible Turkish invasion. Cypus had become 'the new apple of discord' between the two countries. In the circumstances the peace-keeping force was composed only of British troops.

For the reasons mentioned below NATO became an interested party and tried to forestall, albeit unsuccessfully, international initiatives:

1   The island's three guarantor powers were integral members of this organization. The western alliance could not simply disregard this dispute as it had already done other colonial conflicts.

2   There was a real fear at the beginning of the crisis that the Soviet Union might exploit the position of the Cypriot left to acquire a foothold in Cyprus.

3   It was widely believed that if the conflict continued the island might eventually become a 'Mediterranean Cuba'. Makarios followed a non-aligned policy. Thus, he retained close links with Britain and other western countries (he carried out state visits to West Germany and the USA in 1961), and he made openings towards the USSR and Warsaw Pact countries. This has been Cypriot policy since 1960. The US Pentagon, sensing the coming tensions in the middle east, considered Makarios too vague and uncertain a quantity and saw that ultimate stability for the bases could be achieved only if the island were brought under NATO control. Alternatively, Makarios and all other opposition should be removed.

While the Cyprus government relied on non-alignment for the removal of its constitutional shackles, the Turkish Cypriot leadership relied on anti-Communist orientation to preserve its rights. There was little internal opposition to this since the Turkish left, as we have already seen, had been suppressed. Thus between 1960 and 1963 Kutchuk was particularly opposed to the expansion of trade with the socialist countries and the government's association with the Afro-Asians. After the outbreak of fighting in 1963 he appealed to President Johnson of the USA to prevent Cyprus from being turned into another Cuba by 'Communist armed infiltration'.

4   Cyprus was of direct strategic interest to NATO. The organization was concerned with the security of the British bases on the island. These were primarily needed to maintain the mobility of the British strategic reserve and to function as a reserve of strategic power for CENTO and therefore for NATO itself. The sites on the island provide the British V-bomber force and the Canberra light bombers with a base from which to vary their angle of attack on the Soviet Union. Thus until the V-bombers and other sophisticated types are assigned to an interdiction role, the bases will continue to be an element in the strategic force of the western alliance.

The NATO philosophy therefore was that serious inter-member disputes should be avoided and that if such disputes occurred they should be settled quickly and peacefully. In fact the threat of war between NATO partners was averted by the swift action of the British who arranged, as already noted, a cease-fire. The British desire to safeguard the status quo was instrumental in saving Cyprus from further catastrophe.

Meanwhile on 26 December the Cyprus government requested the intervention of the Security Council. It called for an urgent meeting to consider charges that Turkey had committed aggression and intervened in the internal affairs of Cyprus by violating the island's air space and territorial waters. Turkey denied the charges and the Council adjourned the debate without taking any action. At all times of course the Cyprus government insisted that the UN was the only international forum at which the crisis could be resolved.

Kemal Gürsel, the Turkish president, also cabled a plea to various foreign capitals to 'prevent further acts of genocide' on the island, and for the second time jet fighters were sent to buzz Nicosia. Although the government had withdrawn its earlier request for UN invervention, the second threat of a Turkish invasion prompted Foreign Minister Spyros Kyprianou to telephone foreign envoys in Nicosia to apprise them of the situation. In the last days of December the Soviet Union consequently denounced any attempt at foreign intervention in Cyprus and President Johnson sent cablegrams to Makarios and Kutchuk calling for a peaceful settlement of the dispute.

On 28 December Duncan Sandys, Secretary of State for the Colonies and Commonwealth Relations, arrived in Cyprus and suggested a conference to discuss the island's future government. The conference, with Sandys in the chair, opened at Marlborough House on 15 January 1964. The Greek and Turkish delegations were led by their respective foreign ministers, Palamas and Erkin, and the two Cypriot delegations by Clerides and Denktash. The conference could not suggest a settlement since those who attended it had completely different views on the Cyprus problem. On 10 February it ended in complete failure. Demetris Bitsios, a young Greek diplomat, recalled: 'The existing circumstances evidently favoured Turkey. The British, and with them the Americans, wanted above all to prevent the internationalization of the problem. They were disturbed also by the support given to the Archbishop by the Soviet Union. Besides, they wished to buy out the Turkish desire to use military force against Cyprus with the promise that no solution would be granted which did not satisfy their views.'[1]

Makarios now sought the assistance of the UN. Simultaneously however the USA, pulling strings to make the UN take its time, proposed a NATO solution. An Anglo-American scheme (later termed the Sandys-Ball Plan) for a NATO force was formally submitted to the parties concerned on 31 January. The scheme involved the landing of 1,200 US combat troops and a NATO mixed force of 10,000 men to be used for peace-keeping duties and a neutral mediator to search for a political solution. Security considerations would then make its permanent presence necessary and the island would thus become a NATO base; Makarios' neutralist tendencies would be discouraged and a *de facto* condominium of Greece, Turkey and NATO would perpetuate Allied military influence.

The British Labour party voiced its opposition to such a scheme. During question time in the Common on 30 January Harold Wilson declared that 'the sooner it is possible to give that force a UN status, the better it will be for peacekeeping and the reputation of the UN'. However, Turkey and Greece were persuaded to back the Anglo-American initiative. Paraskevopoulos, the Greek caretaker Prime Minister, made some objections which were immediately overruled after a lightning visit to Athens by the NATO Commander in Europe, General Lyman Lemnitzer. Makarios proved adamant. Yet he stated that he would accept an international force under the Security Council. The plan America had in mind was in fact double *enosis* through partition – the whole island thus becoming a NATO base with Britain removed.

George Ball (acting as US Secretary of State in Dean Rusk's absence) was despatched to Cyprus, but even he could not 'bully' Makarios (they met twice on 12 February) into accepting the plan. Ball visited London, Athens, Ankara and Nicosia between 9 and 14 February. The governments of Britain and of the USA drew up a revised version of their plan which was accepted by Greece on 8 February and by Turkey on the following day. Makarios did not yield an inch. (Ball never forgave the archbishop for this and during a Brookings Institution Conference in 1969 repeatedly said 'that son of a bitch will have to be killed before anything happens in Cyprus'.) Makarios thus succeeded in sidetracking a trap laid for him to recognize the American position, which was to make Cyprus a NATO responsibility. In this he had the support of the USSR. On 7 February Khrushchev strongly protested in a letter to the heads of government of Britain, Greece, Turkey, France and the USA against the proposals for a NATO force which he described as 'a case of crude encroachment on the sovereignty, independence and freedom of the Republic of Cyprus'.

Meanwhile Lemnitzer is said to have tried to impose *de facto* partition. He sent telegrams to the governments of Greece and

Turkey urging them to disembark troops on the island which would have led to the landing of a NATO mixed force to interpose itself between the two communities and confront Makarios with a *fait accompli*. In the end Makarios' determination prevailed. He was also backed by the strong administration of George Papandreou, who was sworn into office on 19 February after a decisive victory at the polls; as far as he could Papandreou resisted American pressure. Hence he sent a message to the archbishop on 25 February assuring him of the solidarity of the Greek nation and government. On 13 April, after a meeting with Makarios in Athens, it was announced that complete agreement had been reached on the handling of the Cyprus problem. At that meeting a critical decision had been made. Papandreou proposed, and Makarios accepted, that troops and arms should be sent to Cyprus to prevent a future Turkish invasion. By midsummer an estimated 10,000 officers and men, fully equipped, were in the island. The bargaining strength of the Greeks and of the Greek Cypriots was greatly reinforced.

Makarios was now assured of the support not only of the USSR and the neutralist world but also of a leading member of the western alliance. Behind Greece, ready to profit from the dissensions of western polycentrism, stood France (the Gaullist notion being that Europe's destiny was not America's concern), unwilling to see the Cyprus crisis taken up by NATO and willing to back Greece in its dispute with the other member (Turkey) of the western alliance.

The archbishop had several motives in seeking refuge at the UN:

to secure a guarantee against a possible Turkish invasion;
to gather enough support to nullify in due course the treaties of Alliance and Guarantee; on 27 February 1964 Spyros Kyprianou informed the Security Council that the Cypriot government intended to take all appropriate steps in accordance with international law and practice to rectify the intolerable and unacceptable situation caused by the two treaties;
to make the UN directly responsible for the solution of the Cyprus problem and thus escape from the straitjacket of new negotiations with the three guarantor powers alone or with

NATO; since 1955 Makarios feared all American-backed
Anglo-Turkish combinations against Greece and himself;
to isolate, as far as possible, the Turks who had evidently
fewer friends at the UN than at NATO headquarters;
Turkish pressure on NATO was intensified but a UN
involvement made it all the more difficult for NATO to
mediate usefully in the dispute;
to rule out partition;
to pave the way for a unitary state with majority rule –
Makarios, though paying lip-service to *enosis*, desired Cyprus
to remain a neutral state.

On 15 February, one hour before Zenon Rossides, the Cypriot
ambassador, was to make his appeal to the UN, Britain asked
for an early meeting of the Security Council to deal with the
'dangerous situation' in Cyprus. Two days later U Thant, the
UN Secretary-General, submitted certain proposals to the
Greek Cypriot delegation led by Kyprianou and Clerides. The
Cypriots, though pleased with U Thant's initiative, gave him
no encouragement to proceed further. During the Security
Council meeting Kyprianou asked on 25 February whether the
Treaty of Guarantee gave the three guarantor powers the right
to invade Cyprus. Denktash, on the other hand, three days later
expounded the theory that symbiosis between Greeks and
Turks was impossible.

However, on 4 March the Security Council through
resolution no. 186 unanimously recommended the
establishment of a UN peace-keeping force and the
appointment of a mediator 'for the purpose of promoting a
peaceful solution and an agreed settlement of the problem
confronting Cyprus, in accordance with the Charter of the UN,
bearing in mind the well-being of the people of Cyprus as a
whole, and the preservation of international peace and
security'. The force was to be stationed in Cyprus for three
months and all costs were to be met by the states providing
contingents, by the government of the island and by voluntary
contributions. In effect the Cypriot authorities accepted an
international force funded and manned largely by NATO
members but controlled by the Security Council.

On 12 March Turkey rejected Rolz-Bennet of Guatemala as
mediator on Cyprus and on 25 March Sakari Tuomioja of

Finland was appointed instead. Following the death of Tuomioja, Señor Galo Lasso Plaza, ex-President of Ecuador, succeeded him on 16 September. On 27 March the UN force became operational and was placed under the command of Lt-General P.S. Gyani of India. By 8 June its strength was 6,411, composed as follows:

Military (UNFICYP)		Police (UNCIVPOL)	
Austria	55	Australia	40
Canada	1,122	Austria	33
Denmark	676	Denmark	40
Finland	1,000	New Zealand	20
Sweden	954	Sweden	40
Ireland	639		173
UK	1,792		
	6,238		

The resolution of 4 March however failed to reduce tension in the island. On the following day Turkish armed bands fired the first shots around the Saint Hilarion fortress and on 6 March a bomb exploded in the building of the Turkish Cypriot communal chamber. The aim, as in 1958, was to put the blame on the Greeks and thus provide an excuse for further strife. Outbursts of shooting and killing continued unabated.

On 13 March Turkey threatened once more to invade Cyprus and demanded that Makarios should put an end to the fighting, release Turkish hostages and restore freedom of movement. Stavros Costopoulos, the Greek Foreign Minister, replied that if Turkey used military force against Cyprus his country would also fight. At 6 p.m. on 13 March the Security Council met and adopted resolution no. 187, calling upon all members to comply with its resolution of 4 March and to refrain from any action which might worsen the situation.

Events now moved very fast in Cyprus. On 4 April Makarios denounced the Treaty of Alliance with Greece and Turkey. On 11 and 26 April heavy fighting was centred around the Saint Hilarion fortress. On the following day U Thant explained that in spite of the presence of UN forces there had been 126 outbursts of shooting in the past month. On 29 April he reported that the UN mission had no hope of succeeding until all the irregulars in the island were disarmed. Nevertheless, in a memorandum to Tuomioja on 14 May, Makarios set out his proposals for a Cypriot unitary state containing wide guarantees for the Turkish minority. Turkish plans on the other hand had previously recommended partition into two cantonal states with a federal government responsible for foreign affairs, finance and defence.

The month of June was particularly critical. On the first day conscription was introduced and three days later the first recruits were called up. Almost immediately Turkey threatened another invasion. The US again intervened and George Ball undertook his second mission to Athens and Ankara, inviting both Premiers to visit Washington. On 5 June Johnson sent a secret letter to Ismet Inönü that, in the latter's words, 'included all the juridical thunderbolts that could be assembled'. The president argued that:

1 The Turkish decision to intervene by military force to occupy a portion of Cyprus was unwise and fraught with far-reaching consequences.

2 The purpose of such intervention would be to effect a form of partition and thus produce a solution which was specifically excluded by the Treaty of Guarantee.

3 Such an invasion would violate a number of international commitments: first, a commitment to complete consultation with the US before any such action was taken; second, a commitment to consult with the other two Guarantor Powers, which had by no means been exhausted; third, a commitment to NATO not to undermine the strength of that organization or to run the risk of involving the Soviet Union; and fourth, a commitment to the UN to act in a manner consistent with its efforts to bring peace to the island.

4 Under the US-Turkey Agreement of 12 July 1947, American consent was required for the use of military assistance for purposes other than those for which assistance was furnished. 'I must tell you in all candour that the US cannot agree to the use of any US supplied military equipment for a Turkish intervention in Cyprus under present circumstances,' the president continued.

Replying on 14 June, the Turkish Premier stated that 'the necessity of a military intervention in Cyprus has been felt four times since the closing days of 1963'. Inönü also expressed great concern that the pending report of the Secretary-General to be submitted to the UN on 15 June would result in another defeat for Turkey 'similar to the one we all suffered on 4 March 1964'.

The Cyprus crisis of 1963-4 marked a watershed in US-Turkish relations. The specific event which triggered the reaction, after a long-simmering discontent, was Johnson's letter. Numerous anti-American demonstrations were staged in Ankara throughout the summer of 1964 and there was strong opposition in the Turkish press to US efforts to restrain Turkey from military intervention. In fact, as in the 1950s, there were guaranteed demonstrations in Greece or Turkey whenever it was seen that American policy was tilting against either country. Thus the US-Turkey honeymoon which had lasted since 1947 was at least temporarily interrupted. This incident in particular disabused the Turks of the belief that their interests were in every respect identical and that they could count on American support in every eventuality.

On 20 June UNFICYP was extended by resolution no. 192 for a further three months. General Kodendera S. Thimayya, also of India, succeeded Gyani as commander of the force. Towards the end of the month the USA made mediation moves via its seasoned diplomat Dean Acheson, Secretary of State from 1949 to 1953 and then adviser to both Kennedy and Johnson. He went to Geneva where Tuomioja was to be stationed. Before the month was out Tuomioja informed D. Bitsios, the Greek permanent representative at the UN, that the differences between the two sides were virtually unbridgeable, that war between Greece and Turkey was a distinct possibility and that he needed Acheson's help in Geneva to enable him to carry out his task. The Americans had of course stated on several occasions that they viewed with pessimism the role and functions of the UN mediator. June also witnessed the return of Grivas to Cyprus. By 15 August he had succeeded General Karayiannis as supreme commander of the Cypriot national guard.

In that climacteric month both Inönü and Papandreou visited the USA. The latter met Johnson at the White House on 24 June and his son Andreas, present at that fateful meeting, recorded:

It was clear that he had been briefed and that he was
unwilling to depart one iota from his briefing. I could sense
my father's desperation. His logic, his carefully prepared
arguments were useless. Johnson had a line: that he,
Papandreou should meet with Inönü, that summit-level
negotiations should take place. Nothing Papandreou would
say could change Johnson's mind. It had not been a
discussion. It had been a monologue. But it eventually
turned out to be more than that. It became a brainwashing
operation. We were staying at Blair House. Next day Dean
Rusk came. I had imagined him to be a flexible, intelligent
conversationalist. He was not. He hammered out his phrases
unsmilingly. His purpose in visiting us was to convince us
that unless we followed President Johnson's prescription,
Turkey would attack Cyprus and/or Greece, and America
would be unwilling to lift a finger.[2]

US pressure on the Greek government was intensified in July.
As early as May Senator Fulbright, Chairman of the Senate
Foreign Affairs Committee, was despatched to Greece and
Turkey to convey the sense of urgency felt in the US regarding
the restoration of order on the island. On 2 July Johnson sent a
letter to Papandreou urging him to come to terms with Turkey.
Specifically he appeared to have suggested an exchange of
territories under which Cyprus could be united with Greece.
But Johnson warned that in the event of war, which Turkey was
bound to win, the USA would be obliged to stand aside.

Meanwhile further fighting in Cyprus was used as an excuse
for the expulsion of Greeks from Istanbul. On 17 July U Thant
warned the Greek, Turkish and Cypriot governments that
military preparations in Cyprus were leading to greater risks of
a showdown. On the previous day Turkey had gone through
the motions of preparing for a landing on the island. Top level
Greco-British talks in London on 20 July proved abortive since
Whitehall was presenting only a more polished version of the
Washington formula. While these talks were under way
President Gursel was threatening to bomb Cyprus. In Athens
Makarios agreed with the Greek government on 27 July to take
the Cyprus issue to the General Assembly of the UN instead of
merely to the Security Council.

In the meantime Acheson was in Geneva where he was in

almost daily contact with Tuomioja and the Greek and Turkish representatives. These discussions (in which Ball insisted that no Cypriot should participate) were aimed at the final settlement of the Cyprus problem and were held in the greatest secrecy. The now famous Acheson Plan was taking shape. Cyprus as an independent state was to be eliminated. The key provisions were:

1 Cyprus was to be united with Greece, in return for a 30- to 50-year lease of a military base to Turkey. The Turks would have sovereignty over the base, whose size was to be approximately equal to one-fifth of the island, i.e. 'to engulf most of the Turkish Cypriot population'. Castellorizon, a small island on the Aegean, was also to be ceded to Turkey.

2 Cyprus would be cantonized, creating two parallel governmental structures, one for each of the ethnic groups.

3 A joint military command for Greece and Turkey would be set up.

4 Compensation would be paid to all Turkish Cypriots who wished to leave the island.

The USA's direct and active interest in the dispute was intended to safeguard the south-eastern flank of NATO and to curb Soviet infiltration of the area. In fact Greece was to eliminate AKEL's influence and neutralize Makarios' capability for political action. The return of Grivas in June 1964 was intended to serve as a countervailing force to Makarios.

The Turkish government accepted the above proposals only as a basis for negotiations. It saw the plan as another variant of partition or double *enosis*, the bargaining being centred on the size of the Turkish area. For exactly the same reason it was rejected by both Athens and Nicosia. Moreover the Greek Cypriot leadership was increasingly identifying itself with a policy favouring independence with neutrality but without *enosis*. It was also believed that greater reliance should be placed on the UN, both for peace-keeping functions and as a guarantor of the independence and territorial integrity of Cyprus. Thus the Acheson proposals of 28 July were found to be inconsistent with existing realities and therefore unacceptable.

In August 1964 the supply of arms by sea from Turkey into the Mansoura-Kokkina Turkish stronghold had reached large proportions and it was felt that an attempt to link up with either Lefka or Polis would be made by the Turks, thus effectively cutting off the western road from Xero to Paphos. A strong national guard contingent directed by Grivas was moved in to cut off any intended armed attack. As the Greeks pushed forward, four Turkish air force jets appeared and fired warning shots out to sea off Polis. By the early hours of 8 August the Turks had been pushed out of Mansoura and Ayios Theodoros and retreated into Kokkina. In the afternoon however 30 Turkish jets appeared and on the following day 64 similar jets machine-gunned everything in sight. Peaceful Cypriot villages and other targets were indiscriminately bombed with napalm bombs. Hospitals were hit and scores of women and children, as well as doctors and nurses, were either killed or wounded. Reports from UN representatives in the field concluded that 'these raids on defenceless people killed and maimed many innocent civilians and destroyed much property'.

The irony of this ghastly episode was that the planes and napalm bombs were supplied by the Americans for NATO defensive purposes but were used instead to attack a smaller state, a member of the UN and British Commonwealth. Furthermore, the US Sixth Fleet ('the grey ghost of the Mediterranean'), which had been in the vicinity for some time, did nothing to prevent the outrage.

At the Security Council the Turkish representatives explained on 8 August that Cyprus was being bombed on a 'limited and restricted basis only'. He told everyone to sleep well since there would be no further action. Yet shortly afterwards napalm bombs were used.

Athens retaliated by warning that if the bombings did not stop 'intervention' would be the only answer. The Greek telegram, resembling an ultimatum, was delivered at the Security Council. P. Morozov of the Soviet Union supported the Greek demands. Both Johnson and Khruschev, the Soviet leader, once again made it clear to Turkey that they would not approve an invasion. The Turks complied and the Security Council, after denouncing the Turkish action, passed yet another resolution (no. 193) on 9 August calling for a cease-fire. Two days later it noted with satisfaction that 'the cease-fire is being observed throughout Cyprus'.

On 9 August it was also announced in Nicosia that the Cyprus government had appealed to the USSR and Egypt for military aid to protect the sovereignty and independence of the island. In reply to this appeal the Kremlin emphasized on 15 August that 'if a foreign armed invasion of the island takes place, the Soviet Union will help Cyprus to defend her freedom and independence . . . and is prepared to begin negotiations on this matter'. Consequently a joint communiqué was issued in Moscow on 1 October stating that agreement had been reached between the two countries on 'practical measures of assistance' to be given by the Soviet Union to Cyprus for 'safeguarding the freedom and territorial integrity' of the latter. The Cypriot Foreign Minister remarked that the Soviet Union's aid was being provided with 'no strings attached and no conditions whatsoever'.

The Acheson proposals were abortive, but the talks were resumed in August and Acheson on the 20th suggested a revised (final) version of his plan. He proposed *enosis* in return for a NATO base on Cyprus under Turkish command. The base would be leased to Turkey for a 'reasonable' number of years. Both the Turks and Makarios answered 'no' but a sizeable proportion of the higher Greek establishment believed that the plan should be accepted. Professor Andreas Papandreou, a leading proponent of Cypriot independence, explained: 'The King, in his eagerness to maintain positive relations with the US, took the initiative in promoting this plan, and pressure was put on our government by the Americans to denounce Makarios' policies as a prelude to the execution of the plan.'[3]

At the UN resolution no. 198 was adopted on 18 December. The Security Council recalled its earlier resolutions and asked members to abide by them; informed members of a marked improvement in the internal condition of the island; and extended UNFICYP for another three months.

The search for a solution was now centred on the UN mediator. On 26 March 1965 the Secretary-General transmitted a report by Galo Plaza to members of the Security

Council. The report, composed of 173 paragraphs, was a full background investigation into the entire Cyprus problem. After a careful examination of the internal aspects of the Cyprus puzzle and the positions of the parties concerned (Britain, Greece and Turkey), Plaza made specific observations on the prospects of dealing with the situation. In fact the report was intended to serve as the basis for a new solution. Its main points were:

1 Cyprus should remain an independent state, renouncing its right to unite with Greece. The report stressed that 'if Cyprus should become fully independent by being freed from the 1960 treaty obligations, it would automatically acquire at the same time the right of self-determination.'

2 The island should be 'demilitarized'. The question of the British bases was set aside for later consideration.

3 There should be 'no partition or physical separation of the two communities'. Turkish Cypriots 'wished' to be physically separated from the Greek community, but this separation was utterly unacceptable to the majority community and could not be imposed except by force. Nevertheless, Turkish Cypriot rights should be guaranteed by the UN and supervised by a UN commissioner in Cyprus.

4 'A settlement should depend in the first place on agreement between the people of Cyprus themselves and talks should take place between Greek and Turkish Cypriots.'

Plaza concluded by reiterating his conviction that 'every endeavour must continue to be made to bring about a peaceful solution and an agreed settlement of the Cyprus problem consistent with the provisions of the UN Charter'.

The Plaza Report was in general sympathetically received by Greece and the Greek Cypriots. Turkey and the Turkish Cypriots rejected it as 'unacceptable'. In fact the government of Suat Hayri Urguplu, which had taken over from Inönü, was a caretaker administration formed to fill the gap until the national elections of October 1965. A weak government, conscious of the army in the background, it felt obliged to take a strong line in public over Cyprus. It not only rejected the plan outright but also rejected Plaza himself as a future mediator, proposing instead direct talks between Greece and Turkey. As Plaza himself stated (paragraph 107), the Turks continued to insist that any settlement must contain two elements, the prohibition of *enosis* and the geographical separation of the two communities under a federal system of government.

The proposal for a Greco-Turkish dialogue, strongly opposed by Makarios, was taken up, following American pressure, by the two countries. When Suleyman Demirel, leading the Justice party, came to power in October 1965, he too demanded such talks. However, the political instability in Greece in July 1965, when Papandreou was forced to resign because of a conflict with King Constantine over the control of the army and other matters, made a meaningful dialogue impossible. Nevertheless, Stephanos Stephanopoulos, Prime Minister from September 1965 to December 1966 (who had always been at loggerheads with the archbishop), agreed to hold secret talks with the Turks, based on the Acheson proposals.

The Plaza Report was noted by the Political Committee of the General Assembly and so can be said to have been approved to that extent by the UN. Moreover, on 18 December 1965 the Cyprus government succeeded in securing the adoption of resolution 2077 (XX) by the General Assembly which supported its claim for the 'unfettered' independence of Cyprus and discounted the Turkish claim to the right of intervention based on the Zürich and London treaties. The resolution, carried by 47 votes to 5 with 54 abstentions and 11 nations absent, called on all states to respect the sovereignty, unity, independence and territorial integrity of the island. Surprisingly, the Cyprus government did not demand a Security Council meeting to discuss the actual rejection of the Plaza Report. The five negative votes were cast by the USA, Turkey, Iran and Pakistan (all three CENTO members), and Albania.

In Cyprus meanwhile the two communities followed their antithetical directions. The Turkish Cypriot leadership, not content with keeping the two communities apart by persuasion, force, threats and killings, now set up regulations to keep them at a distance. A makeshift administration was set up in the main Nicosia-Kyrenia road enclave with representatives in other areas, a separate civil service, police force (the crescent and star replacing the republic's insignia) and radio station.

Consequently Turkish Cypriots abandoned many of their villages and gathered for 'self-protection' and the facilitation of partition in the more densely populated areas. According to UN figures around 25,000 so-called 'refugees' were forced to relocate in this manner. Greek Cypriots were not permitted to enter these areas nor were the Turks allowed to leave without permission from their leaders. Confined in such places without sufficient resources, the Turks survived as a 'separate' entity only with direct economic aid from Turkey (between £10 and £12 million annually). However, despite harassment from their leaders and pressure from armed gangs which had arrived from Turkey after 1963, a far greater number of Turkish Cypriots remained in government-controlled areas.

The Turkish demand for partition or, as a second best, the geographical separation of the two communities, never wavered. Glafkos Clerides, writing in 1966, explained:

A short analysis of all the proposals put forward by Turkey since the Turkish insurrection of December 1963, shows that the cornerstone of Turkish policy is either the immediate partition of the Island, or the preparation of the ground for such partition by demanding the creation in Cyprus of Turkish areas, under a so-called Turkish Cypriot Government in the form of a federal system; despite the fact that to bring about such a scheme would mean the compulsory uprooting of thousands of people, the creation of a tremendous refugee problem and the destruction of the economy of the Island. Turkey proposes a solution of the Cyprus problem for which there is no precedent in the world. Normally a federal state is created for the purpose of amalgamating into one state separate smaller ones. Cyprus has always been a unitary state. Turkey proposes to break up the unitary state by reshuffling the population on the basis of communal criteria to create predominantly Turkish areas, with the apparent intention of creating two federal states; but with the real intention of preparing the ground for partition, which today is physically impossible owing to the fact that the Greeks and Turks live side by side in the same villages and towns of the Island.[4]

Galo Plaza also pointed out in his report that he was reluctant to believe, as the Turkish Cypriot leadership claimed, in the 'impossibility' of the two communities learning to live together again in peace. He showed that in those parts of the island where movement controls had been relaxed and tensions reduced they were already proving otherwise. In fact a survey conducted on the damage caused to Turkish Cypriot properties induced the government to launch a rebuilding programme to encourage them to return to houses they had left during the fighting. Moreover contacts had already been established where they had been severed: commercial dealings for example had been restarted within days of the fighting. In fact there was in the economic sector an almost total unity and mutual dependence.

However, in order to counter the Turkish separatist moves the Greeks, having secured absolute control over the government, enacted legislation which incorporated most of Makarios' 13 proposed amendments to the 1960 constitution. On 28 May 1964 the police and gendarmerie were placed under a single command. On 1 June a conscription law created the national guard and called under arms more than 10,000 men. On 9 July the supreme judicial authority was incorporated in a single body, the supreme court. A new municipalities law was enacted in November. In March 1965 the Greek communal chamber was abolished and replaced by a ministry of education; communal courts were also abolished and their jurisdiction was transferred to the regular courts of the state. To smooth relations further, the Greeks in 1965 offered the Turkish Cypriots a Bill of Minority Rights.

In fact the structural and functional changes to the 1960 constitution had been directed towards establishing a unified state with unfettered independence. There was no intention of reverting to the conditions before December 1963. Plaza also emphasized that the problem of Cyprus could not be resolved by attempting to restore the situation before the outbreak of intercommunal strife, but that a new solution must be found consistent with the provisions of the UN Charter.

In 1965 Henry Labouisse, the new American Ambassador to Greece, prepared a five-point programme for the pacification of Cyprus over a six-month period. The terms were intended to satisfy the pride of the Turks and to improve their relative military position. Petros Garoufalias, the Greek Minister of Defence, who went to Cyprus in mid March to meet the Cypriot cabinet and present the Labouisse plan, returned empty-handed. Makarios, supported by Papandreou, maintained his unyielding stand and declared that he would never deviate from the line that the Cyprus question was exclusively a matter within the competence of the UN and 'cannot be the object of Greco-Turkish negotiations'.

It was around this time that the first news of an attempt to remove Papandreou appeared in the Press. In early April 1965 the Cypriot media carried the story that the king was searching for a way to overthrow the elected government, to form a cabinet of national unity and to close the Cyprus question on the basis of the Acheson plan. There was in fact such a conspiracy, and it had much to do with the Premier's strong stand on the Cyprus question. A deliberate plot brewing for weeks to oust him succeeded. On 15 July he was forced to resign, or perhaps was simply dismissed by King Constantine. According to Andreas Papandreou, 'Cyprus lay at the heart of the tragic political developments that led to the death of democracy in Greece'.

The Greek elections scheduled for 28 May 1967 were never held. On 21 April a small gang of junior army officers, under the leadership of George Papadopoulos and closely associated with the intelligence services of Greece and the USA, put into effect a NATO-elaborated contingency plan called Prometheus and thus plunged the country into a ruthless military dictatorship.

Following the coup many Cypriots feared that the large number of Greek troops in the island might attempt to overthrow Makarios and forcibly achieve *enosis*. In early August Papadopoulos, then Minister to the Prime Minister, visited Cyprus and tried to concert a plan for *enosis* with the island's government. At the same time the Greek leadership declared that 'Greece and Turkey are bound by the need to confront jointly the common enemy – communism – and to consider all outstanding differences of view as secondary to this primary interest'. Cyprus was soon to be auctioned, and leading the bidding were the two 'mother' countries.

On 9 September the Greek and Turkish delegations headed

by their two Premiers, Constantine Kollias and Suleyman Demirel, met at Kesan, a small Turkish village about 18 miles from the Greek border, and on the following day at Alexandroupolis in Thrace, Greece. Both countries had agreed that Cyprus must be integrated into the western defensive system, thus preserving the security of the Turkish mainland and of the island's Turkish Cypriots and nullifying the Communist danger from the north. The following issues are not at all certain:

> what percentage of the island's territory and how many military bases Turkey demanded in return for *enosis*;
> whether the Greeks offered Turkey the British sovereign base of Akrotiri;
> whether the Greeks offered territorial concessions in Thrace and elsewhere in return for *enosis*;
> whether the above proposals were also suggested to the Turks by Stephanopoulos in 1966.

In Cyprus meanwhile both sides were extending their fortifications and consequently, according to UNFICYP, over 600 shooting incidents took place during 1967. The Ayios Theodoros-Kophinou incidents of 15 November, in which 24 Turkish and 2 Greek Cypriots were killed, have been fully documented by an eye-witness, Brigadier Michael Harbottle, then chief of staff of UNFICYP, in his book *The Impartial Soldier*.

An acute crisis was caused by the incidents in these two villages. In Ankara the Grand Assembly met and decided to fight if necessary. Planes flew over Nicosia and 30 warships stood by in the channel separating the island from Turkey. In Ankara and Constantinople violent anti-Greek riots erupted, and the best units in the Turkish army were rushed to Alexandretta on the coast facing Cyprus. In Salonica, the principal port for garrisoning and supplying the Greek army on the island, there were unusual troop movements. Across the Evros river Turkish and Greek armoured units, guns at the port, faced each other.

The build-up by both countries continued. Papadopoulos, who for mainly personal reasons wanted peace, worked tirelessly to avoid such a confrontation. On 21 November he offered bilateral talks, an act contrary to the spirit of the Plaza proposals, but his offer was turned down while 80,000 people in Constantinople and 30,000 in Izmir demonstrated for war and blood donors volunteered at Turkish hospitals. In Athens air-raid shelters were being cleaned, and according to several reports Greek contingents received sealed battle orders.

Meanwhile peace initiatives to avert a war were forthcoming. U Thant for the UN sent a special envoy, Signor J. Rolz-Bennet, NATO sent Manlio Brosio, its Secretary-General, and President Johnson sent Cyrus Vance. Whilst the last was in Turkey President Sunay warned world leaders on 24 November that his country intended to solve the Cyprus problem 'once and for all'. Yet Demirel informed Kosygin at a Kremlin dinner on 20 September that, 'we are wholly and entirely guided by our desire for a peaceful solution of this problem'.

At midnight on 17 November Turkey delivered an ultimatum to Greece demanding that certain conditions should be agreed to instantly or its troops would land in Cyprus to defend the island's Turks. The five major demands were:

1 General Grivas should be recalled. To lower the temperature the Greeks decided on his immediate recall. He was flown to Athens on 19 November and on the next day resigned his supreme command of the Cyprus forces.

2 All Greek troops stationed in Cyprus since 1964 should be withdrawn. The withdrawal of this estimated 10,000 strong contingent began on 8 December. Since most of them were believed to be loyal to King Constantine he seriously thought of using them to stage a counter-coup in Greece on 13 December. Having failed he fled the country. The admittedly smaller number of Turkish troops that had infiltrated Cyprus since 1963 remained on the island.

3 An indemnity should be paid for the Turks killed and damages for the property destroyed.

4 Greek Cypriot organizations should be disarmed, including the national guard.

5 Pressure on the Turkish Cypriot community should cease.

Agreement on the above conditions and on several other issues was arrived at on 26 November. Cyprus was not invaded.

Turkey had triumphed and the agreed withdrawal of the Greek troops meant that Greece and the Greek Cypriots had lost an important bargaining card. In this political climate the Turkish Cypriots instituted on 28 December a separate administration which they named the Provisional Turkish Cypriot Administration. The UN was not informed until the day after and U Thant expressed his misgivings.

Even though intercommunal tensions eased after the clashes of 1967 the situation on Cyprus remained at an impasse. On the initiative of the Cyprus government the Cyprus question was again brought before the UN, where U Thant offered his good offices by proposing the commencement of direct negotiations between the island's two communities. The intercommunal talks began under his auspices in Beirut on 11 June 1968. Earlier, on 23 May, Denktash and Clerides met at the house of Osorio-Tafall, U Thant's special representative in Cyprus, for procedural discussions. Earlier still the Turkish leader met Criton G. Tornaritis in London for exploratory talks. The intercommunal talks were later extended, after the acceptance by the Security Council on 13 December 1971 of resolution no. 305, that Osorio-Tafall should offer the two negotiators his good services and that two constitutional experts, a Greek and a Turk, should also be present during the bilateral talks in an advisory capacity.

For six years the two negotiating teams met regularly. Even though agreement was reached on most matters, considerable differences divided the two sides over the authority to be vested in local government and the international guarantees to be given to the new constitutional order. Nikos Kranidiotis explains:

> The Turkish Cypriots maintained that local government must be left to separate central local government authorities deriving their powers and functions directly from the Constitution. In fact the Turkish Cypriot proposals aimed at establishing a federation, leading to geographical partition and creating a state within a state. The Greek Cypriot side agreed upon the need to establish local administration but would not accept any system that would provide for a state, which, while unitary in appearance, would in fact be run by three governments: a central government run jointly by

Greek and Turkish Cypriots, and two communal
governments, each exercising jurisdiction over its respective
community in the Republic.[5]

The chief stumbling block therefore seems to have been the
Turkish insistence on a separatist policy based on a federal
state composed of two communities. A breakthrough was very
nearly achieved in both 1972 and 1973 but it appears again that
Ankara suddenly objected. Partition under the euphemism of
federation had been its persistent objective.

Ioannis Christofides, the Cypriot Foreign Minister,
informed the UN General Assembly in November 1976 that the
Turkish Cypriots had plans to partition the island in 1963. He
quoted extracts from a secret document dated September 1963
bearing the signatures of Kutchuk and Denktash which
revealed planned self-segregation as the first step to partition.
In the following year Kemal Satir, a former deputy Prime
Minister of Turkey, publicly declared that 'Cyprus will be
divided into two sections, one of which will join Turkey'. A secret
document issued on 18 April 1964 by Ismet Inönü, the Turkish
Prime Minister, clearly laid out the partitionist plan of his
country which was named by him the 'Attila Plan'. This
scheme was proposed in 1965 by Kutchuk to the UN mediator
and appears in Plaza's report of 26 March 1965 to the UN
Secretary-General. The plan covered essentially the area which
Turkey occupied following its invasion of Cyprus in July 1974 –
the area coveted by Turkey for so many years.

Inönü also explained quite emphatically on 17 May 1964
that 'one day Greece will agree to a peaceful partition of Cyprus
with the help of NATO. As long as the Greeks refuse, the battle
will go on – Turkey will not recede in any hopeless position –
Turkey will use her right of intervention in the island'. On 8
September 1964 Inönü informed the National Assembly that
'officially we promoted the federation concept rather than the
partition thesis'. In fact geographical federation is simply a
disguised form of partition. In June of that year F.C. Erkin, the
Turkish Foreign Minister, stated in Athens that 'the radical
solution would be to cede one part of Cyprus to Greece and the
other, closest to the Turkish Asiatic coast, to Turkey'.

Turkey's intentions emerged once again on 1 February 1974

when, following a long parliamentary crisis after the elections of the previous autumn, the coalition government under Bülent Ecevit signed a protocol in which it declared that only 'federation' would be accepted in Cyprus. The Premier called once more for a 'federal solution' on 27 March. In April he firmly stated to the correspondent of *Le Monde* that the wish of his country was to obtain a 'federal solution' for the island. Furthermore in June Osman Olcay, the Turkish permanent representative to the UN, asked for a 'federal settlement' whilst addressing the Security Council.

Such official statements thwarted all efforts to reach a settlement in accordance with the previously accepted principles that the solution of the constitutional problem of Cyprus should be on the basis of an independent, sovereign and unitary state. Turkey, seeking a pretext to enforce its plans, set its invasion machine in motion. The opportunity soon appeared in the form of a *coup d'état* by the Greek junta and its proxies against President Makarios on 15 July 1974. Five days later Turkey invaded Cyprus.

The years since 1968 were notable for several other important events. Firstly, Makarios announced on 12 January 1968 that elections would be held during the following month. On 25 February he was re-elected president. He received 220,911 votes (95.45 per cent) and his opponent, a Nicosia psychiatrist Dr Takis Evdokas, leader of DEK (Democratikon Ethnikon Komma – Democratic National Party), received 8,577 (3.71 per cent). DEK (the predecessor of EOKA-B and ESEA) was organized by enosists in the latter part of the 1960s, and Evdokas began publishing *Gnomi (Opinion)*, a weekly newspaper that sharply criticized the government's policies and advocated *enosis* as the only guarantee against Communism. On 15 February Kutchuk was returned unopposed as Vice-President of Cyprus.

A second major event was the attempted assassination of the Greek 'military' leader. On 13 August 1968 A. Panaghoullis unsuccessfully tried to blow up the car of Papadopoulos. During the enquiries that followed curious links were revealed between Panaghoullis and the Cyprus government which led to the resignation of Polycarpos Georghadjis, a former EOKA district leader and at the time Minister of the Interior and

Defence. Georghadjis himself was mysteriously assassinated on 16 March 1970.

Thirdly, the Greek Cypriots found themselves plunged into a domestic political crisis. The government's policy of abandoning 'genuine *enosis*' for the 'attainable solution' of a peaceful, independent, sovereign Cyprus was opposed both by the extreme right of the island and by the junta in Greece. (By 1969 several terrorist organizations such as the National Front, the Akritas Group and the Enosis Youth Phinix had sprung up and claimed leadership in the *enosis* struggle.) By 1972 a new underground organization called EOKA-B was created and quickly infiltrated into the government, civil service, clubs and associations. Its political front ESEA (Epitropi Sindonismou Enotikou Agonos – Co-ordinating Committee for the Enosis Struggle), with Photis Papaphotis, ex-district EOKA leader, as its general secretary, had regular contacts with the island's senior churchmen and with the Greek embassy. The conspirators were both numerous and well armed.

Plots to assassinate Makarios became frequent. The first assault, coded Hermes, was made on 8 March 1970; power was to be seized by means of a coup. Grivas, reportedly disguised as a priest, returned to Cyprus in September 1971 to direct the anti-Makarios forces. Ankara, which in 1967 was instrumental in removing him from the island, did not raise a murmur in 1971.

In 1973 there were several armed clashes between the 'rebels' and the security forces. After the creation of EOKA-B the government in 1972 formed the Auxiliary Police (or Tactical Reserve) Force. Christos Vakis, the Minister of Justice, was kidnapped on 27 July. Another attempt was made on Makarios' life at Ayios Serghios on 7 October. Earlier, in August, police discovered machine-gun positions on the Nicosia-Troodos road and at Kokkinotrimithia, from which assassination attempts were to be made against Makarios. The president was not the only target. Since 1969 pro-*enosis* groups had embarked on a campaign of terrorism, raiding police stations to steal arms, bombing British military buildings and vehicles, shooting and wounding the chief of police and making several bomb attacks on government ministers and other political leaders. One such attack was outside Papaioannou's house on 14 October 1969. On the next day the AKEL leader accused the CIA of preparing a plan which entailed the assassination of progressive Members of Parliament, the arming of Greek and Turkish bands to provoke incidents, the overthrow of Makarios and the imposition of partition.

At the same time the Greek military government, subservient to foreign interests and for the sake of maintaining its power, followed a double policy in Cyprus. Though it officially supported the intercommunal talks it undertook a campaign to corrode the Cyprus state by financing and encouraging elements working to overthrow the island's legitimate government. The Athenian cabal (known popularly as the 'changing of the guard', Papadopoulos being replaced following the 'popular' rising of 16 November 1973 by the hidden strong man Brigadier Ioannides on 25 November) worked conscientiously for the virtual partition of Cyprus. Thus Papadopoulos told a Turkish reporter on 31 May 1971 that if Greece and Turkey came to a mutual argreement 'our children in Cyprus would also agree to bury their differences'.

As early as November 1967 the Pipenelis-Cyrus Vance talks seem to have proposed to partition the island. At the June 1971 NATO Foreign Ministers' Conference at Lisbon, the two countries by all accounts promised to split their differences and divide Cyprus. Relations between Papadopoulos and Makarios deteriorated and their meetings on 3-4 September 1971 proved futile. The Greek dictator was furious because the Cypriot president had visited the Soviet Union between 2 and 9 June of that year.

Makarios therefore had been under constant pressure from the mainland clique. Athens now insisted that he should dismiss ministers considered hostile to Greece. A provocative note dated 11 February 1972 demanded that a government of national unity should be formed and should include moderate representatives of Grivas. The president did not resist the pressure for long. A coup scheduled for 14 February was averted but on 5 May Spyros Kyprianou, the Foreign Minister, who had been the main target of the junta's hostility, resigned (his dismissal having been demanded since 1971) and in June the cabinet was reorganized. Soon afterwards Efstathios Lagagos was appointed Greek Ambassador to Cyprus.

After 1973 *enosis* adherents prepared such plans as Apollo, Gronthos and Aphrodite 3. The conspiracy was in full swing. In the spring and summer of 1974 EOKA-B intensified its activities. Police stations were raided and there were hundreds of bomb explosions. When Grivas died on 27 January George Karousos assumed command of the organization. However, by the end of February control of the movement apparently passed to Kikis Constantinou and Lefteris Papadopoullos. On 25 April EOKA-B was declared unlawful. Makarios reacted by sending a letter, dated 2 July but delivered the next day, to President Phaidon Ghizikis of Greece demanding, amongst other things, the withdrawal of Greek officers in the Greek contingent and national guard on the ground that they were plotting against the island's legal government. No reply was received.

By this time the plot coded Hermes was an open secret. On 3 July the Greek Foreign Minister S. Tetenes, his aides and several Greek officers resigned in disgust. On 5 July *Apoyevmatini*, a Nicosia newspaper, printed an account of the plot against Makarios, adding that the Greek officers and their EOKA-B henchmen planned to kill the president and put a puppet in his place. On 7 July Cypriot newspapers published the archbishop's letter under banner headlines. Surprisingly however nothing was done militarily to prevent it.

The main conspirators were:

In Greece:
the military strong man, Brigadier Demetrios Ioannides, who as colonel served in Cyprus between 1963 and 1964;
the chief of the armed forces, General Gregorios Mbonanos;
the chief of the army, Major-General Demetrios Galatsanos;
a majority of the top junta government officials.
Mbonanos and Galatsanos issued the final orders for the coup.

In Cyprus:
the chiefs of the Greek armed contingent and supreme command: Brigadier-General Michalis Georgitsis, Brigadier-General Andreas Kondilis and Major-General Pavlos Papadakis;
a few Greek Embassy top officials;
several EOKA-B members.

On 2 July, at the office of Mbonanos, the coup preparations

took their final shape. Those present were Mbonanos, Ioannides, Georgitsis and Papadakis. The last two were ordered to carry out these plans in Cyprus. In order to confuse the island's government, the political representative of Greece in Cyprus departed for the Greek capital on Friday 12 July.

The fateful day was Monday 15 July. The first announcement of the *coup d'état* came from the Cyprus Broadcasting Corporation at around 8 a.m. and it contained the following points:

1   The National Guard intervened on 15 July to stop internecine war between Greeks.

2   The main purpose of the National Guard is to maintain order.

3   The matter is an internal one among Greeks alone.

4   The National Guard is in control of the situation and Makarios is dead.

5   Anyone who puts up resistance will be executed at once.

Nicos Sampson, believed to be the fourth choice, was installed as president. Makarios however escaped and on 15 July confirmed reports that he was alive by broadcasting to his people from Paphos. The message, transmitted by the Free Cyprus Broadcasting Corporation, urged the entire Greek Cypriot population to continue its resistance against the dictatorship. From Paphos he was flown by helicopter to Akrotiri and then by RAF plane to Malta, where he spent the night at Valletta as the guest of the Mintoff government.

On 17 July Makarios arrived at RAF Lyneham, Wiltshire, and proceeded to have talks with Harold Wilson, the British Prime Minister, at 10 Downing Street and then at the Foreign and Commonwealth Office with James Callaghan. He was not only promised unqualified support at the UN but also that Her Majesty's Government would not recognize the island's 'existing' administration since he and none other was the acknowledged leader and elected President of Cyprus. The archbishop called for the restoration of his country's independence and sovereignty. The Americans however were not so accommodating. On 18 July Makarios was received in New York as archbishop and not as president. By the same title he was received by Kissinger in Washington on 22 July. Furthermore, on 19 July the USA fought hard at the Security Council to achieve two objectives:

> To allow the representative of the Sampson 'government' to speak on an equal basis with Makarios; and
> to prevent this body from reaching a decision which could have impeded a Turkish invasion.

Kissinger failed on the first but succeeded on the second and far more important issue.

In Turkey meanwhile there was a news black-out in its eastern regions and on 17 July two journalists were arrested in Mersin for trying to send out news of troop movements. Troop activity in the Mersin-Alexandretta districts had been evident since early June. Whitehall received a request from Turkey on 16 July for consultation with the government under the terms of Article 4 of the Treaty of Guarantee. Bülent Ecevit arrived on the following day. Ecevit appears to have proposed joint action by Anglo-Turkish forces to restore the status *ante bellum*. Wilson refused to use force, hoping that the crisis would be resolved diplomatically. Those who took part in the discussions of 17-18 July were Ecevit, Wilson, Callaghan, Hasan Isik, the Turkish Minister of Defence, Oguzhan Asiltürk, the Turkish Interior Minister and Joseph J. Sisco, the USA Assistant Secretary of State for Near Eastern and South Asian Affairs. During the next few days the last travelled extensively between the capitals of the three guarantor powers in an effort to restrain further warlike activities.

On the early morning of 20 July Turkey invaded Cyprus. The decision to invade was taken during the early evening of 15 July. 'The coup,' Ecevit recalled, 'was the green light for our invasion.' For this operation the full might of the Turkish military machine, supplied by America and NATO ostensibly to defend the country's and Allied interests, was used against Cyprus. A country with a population of around 40 million and an army of nearly 500,000 invaded an unprepared country with 630,000 inhabitants and an army comprising around 10,000 national guardsmen, the 1,000-man Greek contingent and approximately 5,000 others.

Turkey landed its troops in Kyrenia and its paratroopers

inside the Nicosia-Kyrenia road Turkish enclave and then bombed Nicosia and Famagusta. Churches, a mental institution, the Armenian higher school and hotels were destroyed. By 20 August around 200,000 Greek Cypriots were forced to abandon their homes and become refugees in their own country. Around 40 per cent of the island had been occupied. In economic terms the total assets under Turkish control amounted to:

70 per cent of the gross output;
65 per cent of the tourist accommodation;
87 per cent of the hotel beds under construction;
83 per cent of the general cargo handling (Famagusta);
56 per cent of the mining and quarrying output;
41 per cent of the livestock production;
48 per cent of the agricultural exports;
46 per cent of the plant production.

The Turks had at last realized their long-standing objective. Ecevit, hailed as the 'second Ataturk', at one time alleged that such intervention was made to protect the independence of the Republic of Cyprus and restore its constitutional order. On another occasion, through Osman Olcay, its permanent representative at the UN, Ankara supported the view that the aim of the invasion was to protect and liberate the island's oppressed Turkish minority.

It is by now universally accepted that the coup was not directed against the Turkish community, nor did Turkey bring to Cyprus peace other than 'the peace of the grave'. But as this naked act of aggression was bound to offend international public opinion, Turkey attempted to cover up her aims by invoking the legal fiction that her armies came to Cyprus in exercise of her rights under Article IV of the Treaty of Guarantee. This reads as follows:

In the event of a breach of the provisions of the present Treaty, Greece, Turkey and the UK undertake to consult together with respect to the representations or measures necessary to ensure observance to those provisions.
In so far as common or concerted action may not prove possible, each of the three guaranteeing Powers reserves the right to take action with the sole aim of re-establishing the

state of affairs created by the present Treaty.

Thus Article IV is clear and unambiguous. Turkey could not intervene unilaterally unless common or concerted action proved impossible after consultation among the three countries. As pointed out by Callaghan at the Geneva Conference on 13 August 1974, the required prior consultation between the three guaranteeing powers was to be completed on 23 July, three days after the Turkish invasion.

Even intervention should be limited to the 'sole aim of re-establishing the state of affairs created by the Treaty', which is the constitutional order of 1960 and nothing else. Not only did Turkey, in furtherance of her ulterior motives, avoid meaningful consultations but she also spared no effort to dismember Cyprus and destroy what she herself had guaranteed.

In the face of this gross breach of an international treaty, Britain and Greece avoided taking any action to protect the island. In fact Richard Crossman (a senior member of the Labour administration) recorded in his memoirs that in July of 1967 a paper on Cyprus came before the Cabinet in which it was suggested that if the Greek junta staged a coup against the government of Cyprus all British troops should stand aside. Although that policy was turned down, in effect it is what really happened in July 1974. To quote the words of the Select Committee on Cyprus which reported in 1976: 'Britain had the legal right, a moral obligation, and the military capacity to intervene in Cyprus during July and August 1974. She did not intervene for reasons which the Government refuses to give.'

At the time of the coup there were, according to the Ministry of Defence, some 3,000 troops in the sovereign base areas supported by considerable naval and air forces. Following the coup the garrison strength was increased to some 5,553 men, excluding a number of forces redeployed to the UN; a number of additional warships, including HMS *Hermes*, were diverted to the area and the air forces were also strengthened. Before the second invasion a further strengthening of British forces took place, including the deployment of Gurkha troops and Phantom aircraft. Other situations have demonstrated that the RAF can still respond effectively to an urgent military situation thousands of miles away.

The British Foreign Secretary suggested there was no moral obligation to intervene because the Treaty of Guarantee, though not formally abrogated, was in practice 'a dead letter'. The fact remains however that Britain had not honoured its signature and its obligation as a guarantor of the independence and territorial integrity of Cyprus. Furthermore all its actions point to collusion with and even capitulation to US foreign policy. Lord Caradon (formerly Sir Hugh Foot and last Governor of Cyprus) wrote in *The Times* on 17 April 1975 that, ' . . . it is not possible to uncover or detect any British influence or initiative other than that we should follow Dr Kissinger. We have followed him with devastating and shameful results and failed to honour the British obligation as guarantor of the Cyprus people'.

The tottering Greek cabal was certainly not ready to fight a war with Turkey over Cyprus. Inferior numbers plus less sophisticated weapons and above all general confusion would have meant national suicide. After an historic meeting in Athens on 23 July, the junta fell. Civilian government was returning – democracy, after seven years, had returned to Greece. The military and political heads attended that crucial meeting. General Mbonanos, who with Galatsanos had issued the final orders for the coup, proposed as Prime Minister Petros Garoufalias, an ultra-royalist. Yet by early afternoon Panayiotis Kanellopoullos, with George Mavros as his second-in-command, emerged as the favourite. However, by early evening, and owing mainly to Averoff, it was decided to recall Constantine Karamanlis from Paris. At 4 a.m. next day he was sworn in as Prime Minister by Archbishop Serafim. Mavros became the second most important figure in the government. This transition, on top of the other domestic and foreign difficulties, resulted in a brief period of complete inaction. Meanwhile Cyprus was burning.

As long ago as 1964 Acheson had attempted to partition the island. The double annexation of Cyprus would have meant the establishment of American and NATO bases there to serve the large western interests of the area. This solution would have filled the vacuum left by the British in the middle east. It was, as we have seen, rejected. Yet Acheson still persevered. In a speech at Salem College in North Carolina on 27 October 1966 he declared that a solution could be imposed on Cyprus by the use of superior arms. Acheson repeated more than once that 'there can be no isolation in a world of ceaseless power shifts, transformed environments and international tensions'.

Towards the end of 1973, at a well-attended seminar in Rome, that seasoned US diplomat Cyrus Vance warned that if there was another crisis in Cyprus his country would not attempt to stop the Turks. Those present included Averoff, Bitsios, Glafkos Clerides, President of the Cyprus House of Representatives, and Rauf Denktash. In 1964 and 1967 however the US managed to hold back the Turks after they had planned to invade Cyprus. Why not in 1974? Several possible reasons can be discerned:

1   The prolongation of the Cyprus conflict and the belief that the government was carrying out attrition tactics against the Turkish community led the US to decide that the problem could not be solved by the two communities. By not intervening in the coup of 1974 the Americans left the Turks to settle the problem unilaterally.

2   The Cypriot government's move towards non-alignment and hence away from the western sphere of influence, and its absolute reliance on the UN and non-aligned nations, induced the US to review its policy and tilt further towards the Turkish solution of permanently partitioning the island. The days when Cyprus served as the 'golden bridge between east and west', a phrase Makarios loved to use, were soon to be over.

3   The US also decided that the split within the pro-west Greek Cypriot right was irreparable. This would open the door to the pro-left elements which would therefore win any future election and thus ultimate control of the island. Cyprus would then become the Cuba of the Mediterranean. Ever since the Cypriot people had rejected the partitionist designs of America and NATO in 1964, Makarios had been marked down in Washington as a dangerous neutralist who flirted with the Communists and bought his arms from Prague, who opposed American policy towards Israel and who sheltered on his island a large and Communist-leaning labour and political movement. 'Cassocked Castro' became his informal designation in US diplomatic quarters. The long-term

American design was the removal of Makarios.

4   Turkey was growing impatient over the Cyprus impasse. The Turks in 1974 were better equipped with more up-to-date weapons. Hence they decided to settle the question once and for all. Ever since 1960 a faction of the Turkish military and political establishment had wanted to invade Cyprus. The carefully prepared nationalist upsurge of 1974 sealed the fate of the island.

5   In Greece the situation was very uneasy. Since 1973 the junta had been on the verge of collapse. Although loyal to the USA, the hysterical military leaders were prone to err on the side of national as opposed to purely American interests. The voice of the Greek anti-American populace, especially in the last few months before the coup, was becoming a decisive factor in US-Greek relations. Moreover, Greece had been badly hit by the energy crisis of 1973, and the discovery of significant quantities of oil off the island of Thasos in that year highlighted the question of Greco-Turkish claims to mineral rights under the Aegean seabed. The dispute over the two countries' respective continental shelves briefly raised the prospect of armed confrontation in April and May of 1974.

6   The ill-prepared Cypriot national guard was not capable of putting up any effective resistance if Turkey were allowed to intervene. The collusion of NATO-trained Greek and Turkish officers would see to that. From 1967 onwards Athens began to recall the non-political officers who formed the leadership of the Greek contingent in Cyprus. They were replaced with dedicated right-wingers who turned the national guard into an indoctrination centre where young recruits were taught the principles of Hellenic fanaticism. They were also encouraged at regular intervals to leave their arms lying around and have them stolen by the opponents of Makarios. Thus the national guard developed into a hostile institution, its main function being to erode the government's authority rather than to protect the island from a possible Turkish invasion. Cyprus was the victim of a concerted policy to subordinate its independence to the wishes of other nations.

7   The unsettled and dangerous middle east situation also

induced a more aggressive attitude by the Nixon-Kissinger and, since 9 August 1974, the Ford-Kissinger combinations to keep control of the island at all costs. The Yom Kippur war which broke out on 6 October 1973 (the fourth such war between several Arab states and Israel) transformed the whole middle east and international situation to an extent far beyond any of the previous Arab-Israeli conflicts.

8   During the crucial months of June and July the Soviet Union took up a 'non-active stance' over Cyprus, whilst in earlier years it prevented NATO's partitionist policies from taking concrete form. Was there collusion over spheres of influence by the two superpowers? Did the USSR expect a further weakening of NATO's south-eastern flank if Greece and Turkey eventually came to blows? Did she believe that if she helped Cyprus the extreme right would be the chief beneficiaries? Or was American and Turkish determination such that she expected a catastrophic confrontation if she intervened?

Hence the USA decided not to prevent the Turkish invasion. Although the Americans thought that the Greek Cypriots had a fair case their regional and international strategic policy dictated that they should support Turkey. The USA knew of the pending coup through the CIA but allowed it to happen and so can be accused of manipulating the whole Cyprus tragedy.

The USA's indecision and obsession with not antagonizing Ankara only served to give Turkey a free hand in Cyprus. Dr J.C. Campbell, an expert on European and middle eastern affairs, aptly remarked that 'American diplomacy was either an exercise in futility, or a well conceived and well executed exercise in deception'. Hefner, an ex-CIA official, disclosed some time after the coup that in 1973 the CIA spent $20 million in Cyprus, and $40 million in 1974. An American study mission report on 22 February 1974 clearly condemned US policy in Greece as 'faulty, ill-considered, short-sighted, and hopelessly dominated by military considerations'. A similar report concluded in September 1974 that 'US policy towards Cyprus seems to have been one of hasty improvisation which failed badly'. Senator Edward Kennedy constantly attacked the 'omissions' of American diplomacy over Cyprus and emphasized that 'the Turkish invasion has turned the island into a shambles'. Although the crisis of 1974 was only one in a series in the history of this tragic island, it was the greatest and most crucial because it threatened the destruction of Cyprus as a viable and independent state.

Meanwhile other countries limited themselves to expressions of sympathy and the passing of resolutions which Turkey completely ignored. It refused to comply either with resolution 353 of 20 July or with resolution 354 of 23 July of the Security Council, which among other things called for an immediate cease-fire, urged an end to foreign intervention and the withdrawal of all foreign troops and finally requested the three guarantor powers to start negotiations for a settlement. The Greek Cypriots complied with the cease-fire demand of 20 July but the Turks did not. Meeting no resistance they repeatedly violated it, thus realizing their objective of occupying about 37 per cent of Cyprus.

From the beginning of the invasion Turkey followed its prearranged and well-organized 'Attila Plan'. Attila was the notorious King of the Huns (*c*. 406-53) and is remembered for savagery, murder and arson. The aim of this plan was to exterminate the Greek population in the Turkish occupied areas; to alter the demographic status of Cyprus by the importation of Turks from the mainland; to ruin or usurp the sources of livelihood of the Greek Cypriots and to create such *faits accomplis* as would influence the solution of the Cyprus problem in favour of Turkey's objective. This objective is a *de facto* partition of the island under the guise of a loose federation, which would enable her for the present to exercise political and military control of the 'whole' territory but would lay the foundations for the possible annexation of the entire island.

In the meantime, under the pressure of public indignation, the junta in Greece was forced to resign on 23 July. On the same day the illegal government in Cyprus established by the coup found itself unable to stay in office and Sampson was replaced by Glafkos Clerides – the President of the House of Representatives.

A preliminary cease-fire was reached on 22 July, leading to the first Geneva Conference. The Foreign Ministers of the UK, Turkey and Greece held lengthy negotiations from 25 to 30

July. For Britain Callaghan proposed, amongst other things, direct intervention for the application of the cease-fire. For the Turks Professor Turan Günes proved to be uncompromising. No wonder Callaghan exploded on several occasions, shouting 'the prevailing state of affairs is unacceptable – you are mocking all of us'. For the Greeks George Mavros declared that 'Greek participation in the talks is meaningless since Turkish troops continue to break the cease-fire and thus conquer more and more territory'. Under such conditions there could be no equality at the bargaining table.

Nevertheless the three delegations recognized the importance of setting in motion measures to regularize the situation in the island, having regard to the international agreement signed at Nicosia on 16 August 1960 and to resolution 353 of 20 July 1974 approved by the Security Council. The participants declared that in order to stabilize the situation the areas controlled by opposing armed forces on 30 July at 22.00 hours Geneva time should not be extended. They called on all forces, including irregular ones, to desist from all hostile activities. A new meeting in which representatives of the two Cypriot communities would participate was also outlined. However, the Geneva Declaration signed at 9 p.m. on 30 July proved to be worthless.

The second Geneva Conference attended by Callaghan, Mavros and Günes, and on the following day by Clerides and Denktash, duly met on 8 August. Following heated arguments over the existence or non-existence of the 1960 constitution (Callaghan explained that he recognized only that of 1960), specific proposals for the settlement of the Cyprus problem were tabled by Clerides, Denktash and Günes. It became clear that Turkey had not gone to Geneva to negotiate but to issue an ultimatum – the acceptance immediately of either of its two plans, both based on Turkish administration of 34 per cent of the island's territory: in one case a single area in the north running from Limnitis on the west coast through Lefka, Morphou, the old city of Nicosia and ending at the old city of Famagusta, and in the other a smaller area in the north and five areas around the main towns. The second plan put forward by Günes had to be accepted by Greece and Cyprus on the spot. At

8 p.m. on 13 August Mavros and Clerides asked for 36 hours to consult their governments. Günes refused.

Callaghan explained that 36 hours' grace was justifiable and that all diplomatic avenues had not been fully explored. He accused Günes of being unreasonable. The latter not only disagreed but remarked later that his British counterpart was no more than a 'perfect telephone receptionist'. A furious Henry Kissinger explained that Callaghan's handling of the peace talks showed the dangers of letting 'boy scouts handle negotiations'.

At around 11 p.m. on 13 August Günes read the 'Kissinger Proclamation' to the delegates. It stressed:

1 The USA had been playing an active role in the current Cyprus negotiations.

2 The USA believed that the position of the Turkish community required considerable improvement and protection.

3 The Turkish community needed greater autonomy.

4 The parties at Geneva were negotiating on one or more Turkish autonomous areas.

5 The avenues of diplomacy had not been exhausted.

6 The USA therefore would consider a resort to military action unjustified.

The Geneva Conference broke down at 3 a.m. on 14 August. At 4.30 a.m. Turkish forces began operations which included the bombing of towns. Hence Turkey's prearranged tactics had triumphed. Its forces had occupied the area defined at Geneva plus another 3 per cent bringing it to 37 per cent, thus instituting the Attila or Sahin (Falcon) line, an artificial boundary separating the Greeks and Turks of Cyprus. The Attila II operation was thus completed.

On 14, 15, 16 and 30 August the Security Council issued new resolutions (numbers 357 and 361 – making eight since 20 July) calling for the immediate termination of military operations, the withdrawal of all foreign troops and the resumption of talks.

These recommendations were once more wholly disregarded by Turkey. Furthermore, on 1 November 1974 the General Assembly, by virtue of its resolution 3212 (XXIX) adopted by 117 votes in favour, none against and no abstentions, asked all countries to respect the sovereignty, independence, territorial integrity and non-aligned policy of the island and to refrain from any action or intervention against it. It also asked for urgent measures to be taken for the return to their homes, under conditions of safety, of all refugees. Finally it recommended the continuation of negotiations between the representatives of the two communities and expressed the hope that new efforts could be made to implement the recommendations of the above resolution.

This resolution was also ignored by the Turks. In fact the only agreement reached between the cease-fire of 16 August and the end of September was the one between Clerides and Denktash for the release of all prisoners of war. The agreement was signed on 20 September. However, the second phase of the Cyprus operation strained Turkey's relations with the UK, the USSR and finally the USA. On 22 August Turkey rejected Soviet proposals for a wider international conference. The US Congress voted repeatedly to cut off military aid to Turkey without however inducing Turkey to make any concessions of substance.

On 14 August Greece, in protest, withdrew its armed forces from NATO. Five days later, during a riot at the US Embassy in Nicosia by Greek Cypriots protesting at Washington's failure to put pressure on Turkey to halt its advances in the island, Rodger Davies, the US ambassador, and one of his employees Antoinette Varnava were killed. Revelations by the *New York Times* and *Washington Post* on 20 January 1976 have since shown that the CIA knew the identity of the gunmen, who were members of the outlawed EOKA-B. On 30 August the same CIA/EOKA-B combination made an attempt on the life of Dr Vasos Lyssarides, leader of EDEK, the Cypriot socialist party, personal physician to and confidant of Archbishop Makarios. His 'crimes' were those of demanding the return of Makarios and the end of foreign interference and aggression. Lyssarides escaped with minor injuries but one of his closest aides, Doros Loizou, was killed and several others were injured.

On 7 December 1974 Makarios returned to Cyprus. Almost half the total Greek population gathered in Nicosia on that day to welcome him. Addressing his people from the archbishopric, he declared a general amnesty for those who were involved in the July coup by saying 'I forgive them all for their sins' and also extended a hand of friendship to the Turkish community by repeating that talks were wanted 'for the bridging of our differences, for the finding of a solution to the Cyprus problem'.

Even though the intercommunal talks were resumed on 14 January 1975 the Turks used them as a pretext to gain time and bring about a new *fait accompli*. The Greek Cypriot leadership, under pressure from all sides, was forced on 10 February 1975 to make new proposals to the Turkish Cypriots aimed at preserving the unity and safeguarding the national sovereignty and territorial integrity of Cyprus. They conformed not only with the UN resolutions but with the joint communiqué issued in Vladivostok by Ford and Brezhnev, the US and Soviet leaders, on 24 November 1974.

These proposals were also intended to avoid upsetting the ethnological composition of the island, the forcible transfer of populations and the destruction of the economic and social life of the country, while at the same time providing the Turkish Cypriot community with a broad autonomy and self-administration within the framework of a strong government. The question of guarantees was not dealt with although it was stated that they should be 'effective and wide'.

The Turks responded by proclaiming a Turkish Federated State of Cyprus (TFSC) in the occupied area of the island on 13 February 1975. On the evening of the same day Denktash handed to Weckman-Munoz, the Secretary-General's special representative, a note containing a set of principles proposed by the Turkish Cypriot representative at the Cyprus talks on the constitutional aspects of the Cyprus problem. Later that evening Makarios issued a statement criticizing the Turkish Cypriot decision and adding that 'in the circumtances it is not possible to carry out constructive negotiations as provided by resolution 3212 (XXIX) of the UN General Assembly'.

The divergencies in the views of the two sides on settling the problem have been described as 'wider than the Aegean sea' – another Greco-Turkish irritant. A comparison of the first two proposals by each side (taken from the abortive meetings of January-February 1975) will suffice to illustrate this contention. Where the Greeks spoke of Cyprus being an 'independent sovereign republic', the Turks desired to see an 'independent and secular republic'. The Greeks wished that the 'constitution shall be that of a bicommunal multi-regional federal state', but the Turks demanded that 'there shall be made a constitution for a bicommunal and biregional federal state'. Denktash remarked on many occasions that 'the Turkish bizonal plan is a bitter pill for the Greeks to swallow'.

Thus from the Turkish point of view the only realistic solution was a federation composed of two ethnic groups. In their opinion the future political settlement of the Cyprus problem should be based on three principles:

a bizonal federation;
the establishment of a central government with limited powers;
the participation of the two national communities in the central government on an equal footing.

Ankara has · contended that the above principles were formulated in 'the light of the bitter experiences of the last twelve years'. Furthermore, 'these experiences have unmistakably shown that the two communities can, in future, only live side by side, and not intermingled with each other'. Yet for centuries the Greeks and Turks of the island lived together in mixed villages and mixed towns without any bloodshed. Together they were ploughing their fields and together they were harvesting their produce.

The Security Council met on 20 February 1975 to take up the complaint of the Greek Cypriot leadership about the proclamation of the TFSC in the northern part of the island. Resolution 367 adopted by consensus (without a vote) on 12 March expressed regret at the unilateral decision of the Turkish Cypriots. It also requested Dr Waldheim, the UN Secretary-General to convene new discussions under his personal auspices.

Accordingly talks took place in Vienna between 28 April and 3 May, as well as between 5 and 9 June 1975. However, no progress whatsoever was made since the Turkish side wished only to talk and not to negotiate.

The third and fourth rounds of talks took place in Vienna between 31 July and 2 August and in New York from 8 to 10 September. At the third round it was agreed that 9,000 Turkish Cypriots from the Greek-controlled southern part of the island should be allowed to rejoin their compatriots in the northern area and that the 10,000 Greek Cypriots already in the north should be allowed to stay and be joined by 800 of their relatives from the south. Other issues discussed included the jurisdiction of a federal government for the island. Clerides, the Greek Cypriot negotiator, told a press conference on 3 August that the Turkish Cypriot side had committed itself to produce by the end of August a comprehensive plan for solving all aspects of the Cyprus problem. However, no such plan having been submitted, the fourth round of talks in New York was adjourned on 10 September after a brief formal session, no date being set for future negotiations. The government of Cyprus made another recourse to the General Assembly on 16 September 1975. The assembly was also addressed by Makarios on 7 October.

Agreement on the resumption of the Cyprus talks was reached on 12 December 1975 by the Greek and Turkish foreign ministers, Dimitris Bitsios and Ihsan Sabri Caglayangil. They were held in Vienna from 17 to 21 February 1976. The communiqué issued at their conclusion stated that:

1   Clerides and Denktash had held 'substantive discussions on the territorial and constitutional issues'.

2   It had been agreed that an exchange of written proposals on both these issues would take place in Cyprus within the next six weeks.

3   The two negotiators would meet again in May 'with a view to establishing a common basis prior to referring the matter to mixed committees in Cyprus'.

It appears therefore that some progress towards a negotiated solution was achieved. The fifth round of talks were 'good, constructive and helpful' according to Denktash. However, Clerides resigned on 7 April, after admitting that he had made a secret 'procedural agreement' with Denktash without informing any member of the Greek Cypriot leadership.

The procedural agreement reached at the February

discussions laid down that the Greek side would be the first to submit recommendations for a settlement and that the Turks would then have ten days in which to consider them before submitting their own proposals. But when Clerides tried to fulfil the agreement by handing his co-negotiator a secret draft of the Greek proposals on 24 March, the latter reacted by disclosing publicly that he had received the draft and that he could not accept it. On the behaviour of the shrewd but highly unprincipled Denktash, a *Times* editorial recorded: 'There can be little doubt that his real aim in behaving as he did was to cause disarray on the Greek side and thus further delay any serious negotiation. He has already indicated that the replacement of Mr Clerides as negotiator by Mr Tasos Papadopoulos will entail a corresponding replacement of himself by a person with the same status.'[6]

The person chosen was Umit Süleyman Onan, then deputy speaker of the TFSC constituent assembly. The first meeting between these two London-trained lawyers took place on 27 May when they discussed humanitarian matters, principally the question of Greek Cypriots missing or living in the Turkish-controlled north of the island. At the time around 2,200 people were still unaccounted for.

The extent to which Cyprus had increased Turkey's defence spending was demonstrated on 1 December 1975 by the 1976 budget which showed a record outlay of nearly $3,000 million for defence expenditure – 240 per cent more than the sum budgeted for 1973-4 on the eve of the Cyprus war, 29 per cent of total spending, and approximately half the amount budgeted by Greece for the same period.

Presidential and parliamentary elections were held in the TFSC on 20 June 1976. In the presidential ones Denktash received 41,059 votes against 11,869 for Ahmet Midhat Berberoglou. In the parliamentary elections Denktash's national unity party won 30 out of the 40-seat legislative assembly. Nejat Konuk was named Prime Minister.

The Greek Cypriots also held elections on 5 September. While the pro-Makarios parties (Democratic Front, AKEL and EDEK) campaigned on a policy of non-alignment in the international sphere and of a long-term struggle over the Turkish occupation of northern Cyprus, the Democratic Rally led by Glafkos Clerides stood for a pro-western policy, arguing that only the USA and the EEC could exert pressure on Turkey to make the necessary concessions for a Cyprus settlement. Owing to the majority electoral system and bloc voting for the three-party alliance the Democratic Rally, which polled 24.1 per cent of the total vote, failed to win a single seat. The Democratic Front won 21 seats, AKEL 9 and EDEK 4. The remaining one was captured by Tasos Papadopoulos who stood as an independent.

More by design than by chance, Makarios received a letter from Denktash dated 9 January 1977 suggesting a meeting between them. They had not met since December 1963. The meeting took place on UN neutral ground on 27 January. Makarios stated later that the objective was 'to find common ground for a package deal'. Thus the accusation that Makarios has proved to be a barrier to a just solution of the Cyprus problem should be utterly refuted.

Denktash announced after this historic event that such fundamental aspects of the Cyprus question as the central administration, a federal system and the territorial issue were discussed. In fact the atmosphere of the discussions had been friendly and a step had been taken towards a resumption of the intercommunal talks deadlocked for about a year. The meeting was thus described as a 'breakthrough'.

A second meeting between them, attended by Kurt Waldheim, took place (again in Nicosia) on 12 February 1977. It was agreed that the intercommunal talks, suspended since February 1976, should be resumed. It appears that agreement was reached on four key guidelines:

1 The aim was to establish an independent, non-aligned, bi-communal federal republic.

2 The size of the territory under the administration of each community would be negotiated in the light of economic viability, productivity and property rights.

3 Questions of principle such as freedom of movement, freedom of settlement and property rights would be open to discussion, taking into account the fundamental principle of a bi-communal federal system and certain practical difficulties which might arise for the Turkish Cypriot community.

4   The powers and functions of the central federal government
would be such as to safeguard the unity of the country having
regard to its bi-communal character.

Describing the decision to resume the talks as 'a new
breakthrough, a new spirit in the right direction', Waldheim
added that the two sides had 'for the first time shown a
willingness to enter talks on substantive issues, notably the size
of the areas to be controlled by each community and the
constitutional nature of any agreed political settlement'. The
ill-informed optimists believed that a settlement would soon
come about. The pessimists, on the other hand, saw the talks as
not only a deceit and a betrayal but as a disaster.

In an effort to make some progress towards the solution of the
Cyprus problem, which he described as one of those 'perennial
festering sores which threaten world peace', President Carter of
the USA despatched Clark Clifford, a former Defence Secretary
and veteran White House confidant, on a nine-day exploratory
fact-finding trip to Europe beginning on 16 February. On his
return to the USA Clifford informed the House of
Representatives international relations committee on 10
March that 'with good faith on both sides a Cyprus settlement
is definitely possible before the end of 1977'.

It was announced by a UN spokesman on 8 March that the
sixth round of the intercommunal talks would begin in Vienna
on 31 March. The talks between Papadopoulos and Onan
which ended on 7 April took place under the chairmanship of
Waldheim and then in the later stages under Dr Javier Perez de
Cuellar.

In presenting their proposals on the territorial issue the
Greek Cypriots linked them to certain general principles:

1   The constitution of the Cyprus Republic shall provide for
the establishment of a bi-communal federal state, the Federal
Republic of Cyprus, which shall be a federation and not a
confederation, and shall

(a) preserve the sovereignty, independence and territorial
integrity of the Cyprus Republic;

(b) ensure that the Federal Republic of Cyprus shall be the
sole subject of international law, to the exclusion of its
constituent parts;

(c) preserve the unity of the country.

2 In the Federal Republic of Cyprus and its constituent parts the fundamental human rights and liberties, as set out in the international conventions ratified by the republic, shall be safeguarded.

3 Particular and without prejudice to the generality of the above, for every citizen of the republic

(a) there shall be the right of free movement throughout the territory of the republic and freedom of residence in any place in which he may choose to reside;

(b) his life, security and liberty shall be safeguarded and his private and family life shall be respected and his home shall be inviolable;

(c) his right to property shall be respected and safeguarded;

(d) his right to work, practise his profession or carry on his business in any place he chooses shall be assured.

According to the map presented by Papadopoulos, 20 per cent of the total area of Cyprus would remain under Turkish Cypriot administration. In the preparation of the map account was taken of the guidelines agreed between Makarios and Denktash in February on population, viability, productivity and land ownership. The Turks, on the other hand, were talking of a weak central government to rule a strong bi-communal Cyprus and there were no territorial concessions. Thus although some progress had been made in clarifying positions, there was no hope of bridging the gap between the two sides in that round of negotiations. In accordance with the communiqué issued at the end of the talks, Papadopoulos and Onan met again in Nicosia on 26 May and 3 June, but without making any further progress.

The widely contested Turkish general election on 5 June 1977 failed to provide a strong government. Ecevit and Demirel both failed to hold a government together. However, on 5 January 1978 the former unveiled his new administration and promised that a Cyprus settlement was at the top of his government's agenda. Turkey however faced graver problems. The state apparatus virtually ceased functioning, anarchy ruled in every sphere of social life; bribery and fraud were rampant; education had come to a halt; unemployment was running at over 20 per cent and inflation had trebled from 17 per cent in the early 1970s to well over 50 per cent in 1978.

Meanwhile the embittered Cypriots went through another ordeal. Archbishop Makarios died of a heart attack on 3 August 1977 at the age of 63. He was buried after five days on a mountain peak overlooking the Kykko monastery after a funeral service in Nicosia attended by nearly 200 representatives from more than 50 countries. Makarios had a unique multi-layered authority: spiritually as archbishop, communally as Ethnarch of Cyprus, nationally as unchallenged president and internationally as an acknowledged leader of the Commonwealth and the Third World and an apostle of non-alignment and world peace. Since 1950 Makarios had symbolized everything that was Cyprus. His life was the history of the island. His dominance was paramount and he was worshipped and loved by all, both at home and abroad.

His premature death revived fears of renewed conflict in Cyprus. These fears however have not materialized. Spyros Kyprianou, Foreign Minister from 1960 to 1972 and President of the House of Representatives since September 1976, who had automatically become acting president on the archbishop's death, was nominated on 13 August as the agreed candidate of the four main political parties for the election which would have been held on 10 September. On 31 August he was elected unopposed to serve the remainder of Makarios' five-year term of office due to expire in February 1978. On 26 January 1978 he was returned unopposed for a full five-year term. When nominations closed Kyprianou was the only candidate and the election which would have been held on 5 February was cancelled. Mr Clerides (leader of the Democratic Rally) had withdrawn his candidature on 16 December 1977 apparently because of the kidnapping on 14 December of Kyprianou's son by members of EOKA-B. He was released four days later.

The long-awaited Turkish proposals were handed to Waldheim on 13 April 1978 in Vienna. The procedural agreement reached when he met President Kyprianou and Denktash in January was that detailed and comprehensive proposals should be given to him, and that he should then hold consultations with both sides to establish whether or not they formed a basis on which he would be justified in recommending the resumption of the intercommunal talks, suspended since April 1977. Instead Waldheim was given a 34-page outline of the 'main aspects' of the Turkish proposals and told that the full text would not be made available until the talks were reconvened.

The Cyprus government rejected these proposals as 'completely unacceptable' since they in no way formed a basis for the resumption of the intercommunal talks. President Kyprianou said at a press conference on 19 April that they amounted to an attempt to 'legalize and consolidate the *faits accomplis*' and that acceptance of such proposals 'would mean a decision to commit suicide'.

The US Congress had finally decided to lift the partial embargo on arms supplies to Turkey, but with rigorous conditions which would tie future military aid and sales to substantial progress toward a solution of the Cyprus problem. Meanwhile the waters of Congressional arguments were somewhat muddied by an 'open message' on the future of Varosha (the new Famagusta) put out by Denktash on 20 July (the fourth anniversary of the Turkish invasion of Cyprus) which included proposals for an interim administration.

President Kyprianou denounced the proposals and responded on 24 July with a formula of his own according to which all Turkish troops would withdraw from the area, freeing Varosha from occupation so that the city's legal inhabitants could return to their homes and properties under the policing and security control of the UN. When this counter-proposal was accepted, the UN had moved in and the refugees had started to return, 'the Greek Cypriot side will at once be ready for negotiations on an open agenda under the auspices and guidance of the UN'.

In November 1978 the USA submitted to the two sides proposals for the resumption of the intercommunal talks. The 12-point plan, prepared jointly by the USA, the UK and Canada, was entitled 'framework for a Cyprus settlement'. Although the document included positive elements it was riddled with inconsistencies.

From April 1978 to May 1979 no conclusive move towards a solution of the Cyprus problem was made because of the failure of the Turkish Cypriot side to submit concrete proposals. The UN Secretary-General and his Special Representatives in Cyprus, first Dr Perez de Cuellar and then Dr Galindo Pohl, tried to lead the two sides to the negotiating table. Their efforts finally proved productive and a Kyprianou-Denktash meeting took place at which a ten-point agreement was reached on 19 May 1979:

1   The intercommunal talks should resume on 15 June.

2   The basis for the talks would be the Makarios-Denktash guidelines of 12 Feburary 1977 and the UN resolutions relevant to the Cyprus question.

3   There should be respect for the human rights and fundamental freedoms of all citizens of the republic.

4   The talks would deal with all territorial and constitutional aspects.

5   Priority would be given to reaching agreement on the resettlement of Varosha under UN auspices simultaneously with beginning consideration by the interlocutors of the constitutional and territorial aspects of a comprehensive settlement. After agreement on Varosha had been reached it would be implemented without awaiting the outcome of the discussion on other aspects of the Cyprus problem.

6   All should abstain from any action which might jeopardize the outcome of the talks, and special importance would be given to initial practical measures by both sides to promote goodwill, mutual confidence and the return to normal conditions.

7   The demilitarization of the Republic of Cyprus was envisaged, and matters relating thereto would be discussed.

8   The independence, sovereignty, territorial integrity and non-alignment of the republic should be adequately guaranteed against union in whole or in part with any other country and against any form of partition or secession.

9   The intercommunal talks would be carried out in a continuing and sustained manner, avoiding delay.

10   The intercommunal talks would take place in Nicosia.

On 15 June 1979 George Ioannides (who succeeded T. Papadopoulos) and Umit S. Onan met at the Ledra Palace Hotel in the UN controlled area. The meeting, chaired by Perez de Cuellar, was also attended by Galindo Pohn and his deputy Remy Gorgé. After only four meetings the talks were suspended, the two major sticking points being the acceptance or rejection of a bizonal or bicommunal federal state and the Varosha issue.

In an effort to break the deadlock Waldheim in 1980 proposed various alternative formulae for the resumption of the talks. In July of that year the Turkish Cypriot side rejected a Libyan mediation move. However, in the same month Waldheim's Special Representative in Cyprus Hugo Gobbi held an intensive round of consultations with both sides with the express purpose of reconvening the intercommunal talks. The two sides eventually agreed to resume the talks without advance commitments or preconditions and to explain their positions on all issues at the conference table. It was also agreed that the meaning of controversial terms such as 'bizonality' and 'security' would be determined during the detailed discussions to follow.

Ioannides and Onan duly met under the chairmanship of Gobbi on 9 August. At the inaugural meeting Gobbi read a statement by Waldheim outlining the latter's understanding of the common ground between the two sides and setting out the subjects to be discussed. These included the resettlement of Varosha by its Greek Cypriot inhabitants under UN auspices, practical measures to promote goodwill and mutual confidence, and constitutional and territorial issues. The statement also stressed that the talks were being resumed on the basis of the high-level agreements of February 1977 and May 1979. His understanding, he said, was that both sides supported a 'federal solution of the constitutional aspect and a bizonal solution of the territorial aspect'. Again the talks proved abortive. On 10-11 September 1980 a five-member National Security Council led by General Kenan Evren overthrew the civilian government of Suleyman Demirel.

In 1981 expectations that during the summer there might at last be a step forward in the Cyprus negotiations had been fuelled both by official statements and by press speculation. A report in the British *Sunday Times* on 24 May hinted that a solution based on the broad outlines set out below was on the cards:

1   Cyprus was to be divided into two autonomous zones in loose confederation.

2   The Turkish-controlled northern part was to be reduced in size from the post-1974 total of 40 (in fact, 37) per cent to 28 per cent. Thus Famagusta would be handed back.

3   The bulk of the refugees would be relocated, with approximately 70 per cent going back to the Famagusta district. The rest of the refugees were expected to accept compensation for the loss of their homes and land and could stay in the south.

4   For a trial period before a final deal was signed Famagusta would be opened up but would be under temporary UN control.

On the same day that the above article was published, the people of the Greek-controlled south went to the polls to elect a new House of Representatives. Seven parties and six independent candidates contested the election. In a turn-out of 95 per cent the results were:

Party	Leader	Votes	Percentage	Seats
Progressive Party of the Working People (AKEL)	E.Papaioannou	95,302	32.779	12
Democratic Rally (DESY)	G.Clerides	92,733	31.895	12
Democratic Party (DEKO)	S.Kyprianou	56,705	19.503	8
Unified Democratic Union of the Centre (EDEK)	V.Lyssarides	23,770	8.176	3
Pan-Cyprian Renewal Party (PAME)	Ch. Sofianos	8,106	2.788	–
Centre Union Party (CUP)	T.Papadopoulos	7,964	2.739	–
New Democratic Front (NEDEPA)	A.Michaelides	5,582	1.920	–
		290,162	98.800	35

Independent candidates received 0.2 per cent of the total

number of valid votes. The electorate totalled 308,511 of which 1,505 are Maronites, 1,114 Armenians and 256 Latins.

In the Turkish-controlled north, elections were held on 28 June. Comparing the results with those of the previous election we find:

	1976	1981
For Denktash as 'president'	76 per cent	51.7 per cent
For the 'assembly' of the TFSC and Denktash's National Unity Party	53 per cent	42.6 per cent

The parties which increased their power at the expense of the NUP were the Communal Liberation Party (CLP) and the Republican Turkish Party (RTP), which stood against economic or political integration of the occupied areas with Turkey and against Denktash's partitionist policy and called for a solution of real federation which would safeguard the unity of Cyprus. Omitting the votes of the mainland settlers, who constitute around 25 per cent of the population, it becomes evident that the overwhelming majority of the native Turkish Cypriot population voted against Denktash and his policies.

Meanwhile a new cycle of talks was in progress. On 6 May 1981 the priority issue was the 'resettlement of Varosha'. The two sides at the intercommunal talks then met on 2 June in Nicosia and made a 'general reappraisal' of the situation and of the ground covered so far in the negotiations, which had been going on since September 1980. The talks resumed on 8 July and there was a further meeting on 15 July. On 5 August the Turkish Cypriot side (for the first time) presented its proposals on the territorial aspect and also put forward proposals on the constitutional issues involved. The latter were the same as those submitted on 21 January 1981. Further talks took place later in August and in September. Although it is widely believed that the intercommunal talks are still the best available means of negotiating a solution, a settlement is still remote.

Greece went to the polls on 18 October. After 50 years of mainly conservative (and at times ultra-right) rule, the Greeks elected an unmistakably left-wing government. The long-awaited *allaghi* (change) had arrived. The full results were:

Party	Votes	Percentage	Seats
Panhellenic Socialist Movement (PASOK)	2,725,395	48.06	172
New Democracy (ND)	2,033,774	35.86	115
Communist Party of Greece (KKE)	619,296	10.92	13
Others	292,476	5.16	0
	5,670,941	100.00	300

The new government was headed by Andreas Papandreou. Its programme was the subject of a three-day parliamentary debate on 22-4 November, at the conclusion of which the government won a motion of confidence by 172 votes to 113. In his statement to parliament Papandreou emphasised that the Cyprus question was 'primarily one of foreign occupation' and was 'a vital national issue' for Greece, which 'had a legal right and a duty actively to support the Cypriot people's struggle for the withdrawal of all foreign troops, for the safeguarding of free settlement and movement and for the shaping of a constitutional charter which, while consolidating the unity and independence of the Republic of Cyprus, will give equal rights and obligations to all the citizens, to both the Greek Cypriots and the Turkish Cypriots'.

President Kyprianou flew to Athens for talks on 22 October, on 11 December, in January and February 1982 and then Papandreou visited Cyprus from 27 February to 1 March. These visits revealed that 'a complete identity of views' on the Cyprus question existed between two leaders.

Meanwhile an 'evaluation' was prepared by the UN Secretary-General, Dr Kurt Waldenheim, and was presented formerly at the intercommunal talks on 18 November. As reported, this 'evaluation' involved a negotiating basis allocating 70% of the area of the island (excluding a federal district) to the Greek Cypriots and 30% to the Turkish Cypriots, but with the Turkish Cypriots taking some 40% of the jobs in the public sector. Furthermore, it was also understood that the presidency would rotate between the two communities on an annual basis and there would be a six-member federal council in which four seats would be reserved for the Greek Cypriots and two for the Turkish Cypriots; each community would retain a large degree of veto power over major legislative and constitutional changes.

Nothing transpired from the 'proposals'. On 13 February 1983, Spyros Kyprianou (gaining more than the necessary 50% of the vote on the first round) was re-elected as President of Cyprus for a further five-year period. Kyprianou stood as the candidate of the Democratic Co-operation (DEKO and AKEL) on the basis of a 'minimum programme' of co-operation as agreed in April 1982. The results of the election were as follows:

	No. of votes	% of votes
S. Kyprianou	173,791	56.54
G. Clerides	104,294	33.93
V. Lyssarides	29,307	9.53
	307,392	100.00

On 15 February, Kyprianou urged the US to work for a withdrawal of Turkish troops from Cyprus as a step towards re-uniting the island. The President emphasised that Greek Cypriots had already made a large concession to Turkish Cypriot desires of autonomy by agreeing in principle to the idea of a 'bi-regional' federation'.

On 13 May, the UN General Assembly passed a resolution calling for a withdrawal of all 'occupation forces' from Cyprus. The resolution said that such a move was vital to a speedy and mutually acceptable solution to the Cyprus problem and endorsed Kyprianou's call for a complete demilitarisation of the island. The resolution was endorsed by a vote of 103 to 5 with 20 abstentions. Joining Turkey in opposing the measure were Pakistan, Malaysia, Somalia and Bangladesh.

Denktash, the Turkish Cypriot leader, responded three days later by indicating that he would declare the northern part of the island an independent state. As we shall see below, he carried out his threat on 15 November.

A further initiative was undertaken by the UN Secretary-General Mr Perez de Cuellar on 8 August when he submitted a document to the Cyprus government and the Turkish Cypriot leadership. He had undertaken to make a series of soundings in order to facilitate further discussion of the Cyprus problem. In a statement on 19 September, Kyprianou announced that the Cyprus government had accepted the UN Secretary-General's personal effort and his method of approach, which aims at leading, through successive phases of soundings, to the formulation of a framework for an overall solution of the Cyprus problem. The President promised to hand the text containing the Greek Cypriot position to the Secretary-General on 30 September.

Once again all efforts were thwarted. On 15 November the occupied part of Cyprus was declared an independent state. This move was in contravention of all UN resolutions and was duly greeted with world-wide condemnation. Three days later, UN resolution 541/83 urged the international community not to recognise any Cypriot state other than the Republic of Cyprus. This resolution was adopted with 13 votes in favour, one against (Pakistan) and one abstention (Jordan).

Later in the month, the 48-nation Commonwealth Summit in New Delhi not only condemned the illegal Turkish action to declare a separate state but decided to set up a five-nation action group (made up of ministers or top officials from Australia, Guyana, India, Nigeria and Zambia), to work with the UN to try and solve the Cyprus problem.

The year 1984 opened very briskly. On 11 January, a framework for a comprehensive settlement of the Cyprus problem had been submitted to the UN Secretary-General by President Kyprianou. This framework was also explained to Mrs Thatcher during her meeting with Kyprianou on 18 January at 10 Downing Street.

It appears that these top-secret proposals included the following:

1. A Turkish Cypriot administration retaining control of 25% of a demilitarised island. In return the towns of Famagusta and Morfou should be returned to Greek Cypriot control;

2. A phased demilitarisation of Cyprus. First the Turkish occupation forces and Turkish settlers from the mainland should go. Then the Greek and Turkish forces legitimately on the island under the 1960 Constitution would be withdrawn. At that stage the Cyprus National Guard and the Turkish Cypriot Security Force would be disbanded. A UN force composed of men from countries not directly involved in the Cyprus problem would then take charge of defence, internal security and some sensitive policing;

3. The failed treaty of guarantee of independence signed by Greece, Turkey and the UK would be replaced by a new international treaty specifically excluding those powers. The new guarantors would have to accept that they could only act collectively;

4. A federal council of Ministers containing 30% Turkish Cypriots;

5. The President would be a Greek Cypriot and the Vice-President a Turkish Cypriot;

6. The two communities would be equally represented in a new supreme court;

7. Although the Greek Cypriots preferred a single chamber legislature, they would accept a two-tier system with a lower house based on population ratios and an upper house biased towards the minority;

8. The proposals insist that there must be full freedom of movement, settlement and ownership of property across the whole island. Refugees who wished to return to their homes and businesses within areas controlled by the other community would be free to do so.

Again, all efforts proved abortive. Instead of replying, as promised, to the personal initiative of the UN Secretary-General, Mr Denktash announced on 10 April that he would organise a referendum on 19 August for the approval of the constitution of his illegal state and in addition go ahead with general elections in November. Furthermore, it was announced on 17 April that Turkey had formerly accredited an Ambassador to the occupied areas and had received the credentials of an Ambassador from the occupied areas in Ankara.

On the same date, President Kyprianou presided over a meeting of leaders or representatives of all political parties. Unanimous verdicts were reached on all subjects under discussion. It was also agreed to meet again on 24 April, to proceed to Athens for meetings with the Greek leadership and then on to New York to put the problem before the UN Security Council.

Thus, it can safely be said that since UDI Mr Denktash has proposed a much slower and more limited approach to reunification. Initially, he wants 'talks about talks' concerning the reopening of Nicosia airport (now a UN base), and the possible return (under UN control) of Greek Cypriot refugees to a small part of Famagusta.

On the other hand, President Kyprianou's framework remains the only comprehensive plan on offer. Greek Cypriots stress that a final, lasting and just solution to the Cyprus problem could be found if the principle of the unity of the state was accepted on the basis of the treaty of guarantee. The personal initiative of the UN Secretary-General is also of unique importance and should be used at least as the basis of a conference paper and as a guideline for immediate sincere negotiations aimed at preserving the unity and independence of the Republic of Cyprus.

* * *

On 11 May 1984 the Security Council adopted Resolution 550 on Cyprus by a vote of 13 in favour to one against (Pakistan), with one abstention (United States). The first four points in it make a fitting conclusion to this book. The Security Council stated that it:

1. Reaffirms its Resolution 541 (1983) and calls for its urgent and effective implementation.

2. Condemns all secessionist actions, including the purported exchange of ambassadors between Turkey and the Turkish Cypriot leadership, declares them illegal and invalid and calls for their immediate withdrawal.

3. Reiterates the call upon all states not to recognize the purported state of the 'Turkish Republic of Northern Cyprus' set up by the secessionist acts and calls upon them not to facilitate or in any way assist the aforesaid secessionist entity.

4. Calls upon all states to respect the sovereignty, independence, territorial integrity, unity and non-alignment of the Republic of Cyprus.

References

Chapter 1
1. C.D. Cobham, *Excerpta Cypria* (1908), page 55.
2. *The Sieges of Nicosia and Famagusta in Cyprus* (1903), page 10.
3. *Excerpta Cypria*, page 107.
4. Ibid., page 95.
5. Ibid., page 119.
6. *A History of Cyprus* (4 volumes), Volume 4 (1952), page 1.
7. *Cyprus* (1965), page 79.
8. *Excerpta Cypria*, page 201.
9. *Journal of a Tour in the Levant* (3 volumes), Volume 2 (1820), page 583
10. *Excerpta Cypria*, pages 452-3.

Chapter 2
1. *GB and the Cyprus Convention Policy of 1878* (1934), page 164.
2. ADD. MS. 39131. Folio 11.
3. Ibid., Folio 23.
4. *The New Turkey* (1938), page 42.
5. CMD. 2057 (1878), Volume 82, pages 3-4.
6. Ibid., page 5.
7. Parliamentary Debates. 3s. Volume 241. Col 1781.
8. ADD. MS. 39021, Foiio 144.
9. ADD. MS. 39026, Folio 303.
10. Parliamentary Debates. 3s. Volume 241. Cols 1753 and 1773.
11. G.C. Thompson: *Public Opinion and Lord Beaconsfield, 1875-1880* (2 volumes), Volume 2 (1886), page 490.
12. Parliamentary Debates. 3s. Volume 241. Col 1782.
13. *GB and the Cyprus Convention Policy of 1878* (1934), page 3.

Chapter 3
1. ADD. MS. 39025, Folios 110-111.
2. ADD. MS. 39032, Folios 194-195.
3. CO. 67/18/805.
4. ADD. MS. 44337, Folio 425.
5. CO. 67/106/14506.
6. Parliamentary Debates. 4s. Volume 31. Cols 684-685.
7. Ibid., Volume 75. Col 1527.
8. Ibid., Volume 108. Cols 641 and 643.
9. CO. 67/149/38671.
10. CMD. 3996. 1907-1908. Volume 71, page 985.

412   *References*

11. *The Unification of Greece 1770-1923* (1972), page 255.
12. Volume 173 (1891), pages 453-454.
13. ADD. MS. 44477, Folio 299.
14. Volume 173 (1891), page 447.
15. CO. 67/241/41397H.
16. Ibid.
17. CO. 67/158/8142.

Chapter 4
1. CO. 67/174/42788S.
2. FO. 800/172, page 16.
3. FO. 371/2273/152129.
4. FO. 371/2273/153141.
5. 75. HC. Deb. 5s. Col 5.
6. *The Vindication of Greek National Policy, 1912-1917* (1918), page 77.
7. *The 19th Century*, Volume 79. (1916), pages 240-241 and 252.
8. CO. 67/192/37309.
9. *Oxford Pamphlets*, No. 39 (1914), page 25.
10. *Cyprus Trusts in British Justice* (1919), pages 3-5.
11. CO. 67/192/31495.
12. *The Cyprus Cause* Official Correspondence (1920), page 10.
13. CO. 67/199/63192.
14. FO. 371/10222/10845, pages 67-68.
15. 127. HC. Deb. 5s. Cols 709-710.
16. CO. 67/187/46085.

Chapter 5
1. *The Cyprus Cause* (1924), page 10.
2. CO. 67/226/20.
3. CMD. 3477. 1929-1930. Volume 23, pages 16 and 18.
4. 219. HC. Deb. 5s. Cols 2668-2669.
5. *Orientations* (1937), page 553.
6. 254. HC. Deb. 5s. Col 232.
7. *Orientations* (1937), page 570.
8. *AKEL: The Communist Party of Cyprus* (1971), pages 17-18.
9. *Orientations* (1937), page 587.
10. CO. 67/230/1
11. CO. 67/239/41268.
12. CO. 67/243/98555/1.

Chapter 6
1. 264. HC. Deb. 5s. Col 1808.
2. CO. 67/243/98555/1.

Chapter 7
1. *The Orphaned Realm* (1951), page 208.
2. CO. 67/243/98555/11.

3. CO. 67/243/98555/1.
4. CO. 67/288/90197.
5. 349. HC. Deb. 5s. Col 1285.
6. *Fabian Colonial Bureau* (1941), page 7.
7. *The People of Cyprus Accuse GB* (1949), page 4.
8. CO. 67/288/90197.
9. CO. 67/252/19898.
10. *Cyprus Challenge* (1956), page 118.
11. *United Empire*, Volume 40, No 4, page 178.

Chapter 8
1. FO. 371/29846/R.198/198/19.
2. FO. 371/29902/R.5676/5676/19.
3. FO. 371/29846/9775.
4. FO. 371/29846/9775.
5. CO. 67/318/90625.
6. 126. HL. Deb. 5s. Cols 1024-1025.
7. Ibid., Cols 1032-1033.
8. *Cyprus Challenge* (1956), page 138.
9. FO. 371/43755/4175.
10. 410. HC. Deb. 5s. Col 194.
11. *Cyprus Challenge* (1956), page 92.

Chapter 9
1. 420. HC. Deb. 5s. Cols 300 and 302.
2. 431. HC. Deb. 5s. Col 2343.
3. 448. HC. Deb. 5s. Cols 1231-1232.
4. *The Crown Colonist*, Volume 19, No. 206, (January 1949), page 46.
5. 458. HC. Deb. 5s. Col 363.
6. FO. 371/78423/1022.
7. *The Contemporary Review*, Volume 171, No. 978, pages 338-9.
8. *United Empire*, Volume 40, No. 4, page 182.
9. FO. 371/29846/9775.
10. *Cyprus Challenge* (1956), page 10.
11. FO. 371/78425/1022.

Chapter 10
1. *Reminiscences of EOKA's struggle 1955-1959* (1961), page 22.
2. Dusan J. Djonovich: UN Resolutions, Series 1: General Assembly.
   Volume 5, 1954-1956 (1973), page 121.
3. 527. HC. Deb. 5s. Cols 1229-1230.
4. American Foreign Policy, 1950-1955. Basic Documents, Volume 1,
   Parts I-IX (1957), page 1707.
5. 531. HC. Deb. 5s. Cols 504, 508 and 509.

Chapter 11
1. CMD. 9594. 1955-1956. Volume 41, page 13.

2. 547. HC. Deb. 5s. Col 34.
3. American Foreign Policy, 1950-1955. Basic Documents, Volume 11, Parts X-XX (1957), page 2276.
4. 540. HC. Deb. 5s. Col 1936.
5. 562. HC. Deb. 5s. Col 1268.
6. 573. HC. Deb. 5s. Col 780.
7. Sir. Hugh Foot: *A Start in Freedom* (1964), page 163.
8. 573. HC. Deb. 5s. Col 871.

Chapter 12
1. American Foreign Policy, 1958. Current Documents (1962), pages 569-70.
2. 600. HC. Deb. 5s. Cols 621, 622 and 630.
3. CMD. 680. 1958-1959. Volume 30, page 238.

Chapter 13
1. *Pointing the Way, 1959-1961* (1972), pages 162-3.
2. *Canadian Institute of International Affairs*, Volume 24 (February 1965), No. 4, page 7.
3. *Current History*, Volume 48, New Series (May 1965), page 274.
4. 626. HC. Deb. 5s. Col 1635.
5. 626. HC. Deb. 5s. Col 1717.

Chapter 14
1. *Krisimes Ores (Critical Hours)*, pages 143-4.
2. *Democracy at Gunpoint* (1973), pages 136-7.
3. Ibid., page 140.
4. *Middle East Forum*, Volume 42 (Winter 1966), No. 1, page 11.
5. *The Cyprus Problem* (1975), pages 28-29.
6. *The Times*, 15 April 1976, page 15.

Appendix 1 *Cyprus Through the Years*

*c.*7000–3000BC	Neolithic (or new Stone) Age
*c.*3000–2500BC	Calcolithic Age
*c.*2500–2000BC	Early Bronze Age
*c.*2000–1500BC	Middle Bronze Age
*c.*1500–1050BC	Late Bronze Age: Settlement of Mycenaean Greeks
1050–58BC	Early Iron Age: Settlement of Phoenicians
8th–5th centuries BC	The established city kingdoms stood up well to the invasions and rule of some of the rising great empires – Assyrians, Egyptians and Persians
332–323BC	Alexander the Great freed the island and its kings retained their sovereignty. A power struggle between Alexander's successors, Antigonus and Ptolemy, followed for nearly 30 years.
294–58 BC	The Ptolemaic Period. Administrative unity was established by means of quasi-military control. The governor had the title of 'strategos' (general) of the island. He was both the civil administrator and the chief of the armed forces. The petty kingdoms were abolished. Generally speaking, the relatively peaceful conditions of the island during the greater part of Ptolemaic rule resulted in an expanding population and prosperity.
58BC–AD330	The Roman Period. Of special importance were the introduction of Christianity in AD45-6 and the massive Jewish rebellion of AD115-6.
330–1191	Cyprus became part of the Byzantine Empire.

The period was above all characterized by
the autocephaly of the Cypriot Orthodox
Church, the Arab raids between the 7th and
10th centuries and the destructive earthquakes of 332 and 342.

1191   Cyprus came into the hands of Richard I
                  ('Coeur-de-Lion'), King of England. He sold
                  the island to the Order of the Knights
                  Templar.

1192–1489   The Lusignan period.
                  Economically, socially, politically and
                  culturally, Cyprus was horizontally divided
                  into two separate and distinct sections. At
                  the apex was the feudal class, mostly of French
                  origin, and the foreign merchants, the vast
                  majority being Italian, who resided in the
                  island; at the bottom were the local Greek
                  inhabitants who were mostly serfs and
                  labourers.
                  The ruling class belonged to the Catholic
                  Church and the Greeks to the Orthodox
                  Church.
                  The ruling élite spoke mostly French and the
                  masses spoke Greek.
                  The part played by the Lusignans in building
                  up the civilization of Cyprus was negligible.
                  From 1374 to 1464 Famagusta was ruled by
                  the Genoese Republic.

1489–1571   The Venetian occupation.
                  Most of the people remained serfs to the
                  nobles and devoid of any rights whatsoever.
                  Venice drew considerable tribute from the
                  island and therefore conditions deteriorated
                  rapidly.
                  The period was marked by total
                  disinterestedness on the part of the rulers.

1571–1878   The Ottoman occupation.
                  Cyprus had been made into an eyālet or
                  beglerbegilik, with Muzaffar Pasha as the
                  first governor.
                  A major contribution towards the welfare of

the native Greek population was the Ottoman
decision to abolish the Roman Catholic
hierarchy and to restore the Orthodox Church
of Cyprus under its archbishop. This prelate
was made representative of his community
vis-à-vis the Ottoman government as the
ethnarch or head of the Greek community.
Turkish rule was marked by growing decay
and impoverishment. Trade dwindled,
productivity decreased and the population
showed a marked decline.
Revolts by both groups of the population
occurred at regular intervals. Those of 1680-
87, 1745, 1764-6 and 1833 were of particular
importance. These risings were put down by
force of arms.

1878-1960   The British occupation
At a time of extreme fear for its own security
and existence, Turkey ceded Cyprus to
Britain in 1878. In 1914 the island was
annexed and after all rights and claims to
the island were renounced by Turkey in 1923,
Cyprus became a Crown Colony in 1925.
The 'key' to the continents of Europe, Asia
and Africa remained a British possession for
82 years. Despite the many difficulties faced
by the new administration, the island proved
a strategic, political, economic and
commercial gain.
Of the many problems which Britain had to
face, perhaps the most perplexing was the
agitation by the Greek inhabitants for the
union of Cyprus with Greece. The Hellenic
ideal was much older than the British
occupation. Modern Panhellenism silently
grew under centuries of foreign domination.

1960-   The Cyprus Republic.
The Zürich-London Agreements of February
1959 finally set up the Cyprus Republic – the
99th member state of the United Nations.

Appendix 2 *British Personnel*

Administrators

1878 Garnet Wolseley
1879 Robert Biddulph
1886 Henry Bulwer

1892 Walter Sendall
1898 William Haynes Smith

High Commissioners

1900 William Haynes Smith
1904 Charles King-Harman
1911 Hamilton Goold-Adams

1915 John Clauson
1920 Malcolm Stevenson

Governors

1925 Malcolm Stevenson
1926 Ronald Storrs
1932 Reginald Stubbs
1933 Herbert Palmer
1939 William Battershill
1941 Charles Woolley

1946 Reginald Fletcher, Lord Winster
1949 Andrew Wright
1954 Robert Armitage
1955 John Harding
1957 Hugh Foot, later Lord Caradon

Appendix 3 *Ottoman Sultans (1566–1924)*

Selim II	1566–1574	Mahmoud I	1730–1754
Murad III	1574–1595	Osman III	1754–1757
Mohammed III	1595–1603	Mustapha III	1757–1774
Ahmed I	1603–1617	Abdul Hamid I	1774–1789
Mustapha I	1617	Selim III	1789–1807
Osman II	1618–1622	Mustapha IV	1807–1808
Mustapha I	1622–1623	Mahmoud II	1808–1839
Murad IV	1623–1640	Abdul Mejid I	1839–1861
Ibrahim	1640–1648	Abdul Aziz	1861–1876
Mohammed IV	1648–1687	Murad V	1876
Suleiman II	1687–1691	Abdul Hamid II	1876–1909
Ahmed II	1691–1695	Mohammed V	1909–1918
Mustapha II	1695–1703	Mohammed VI	1918–1922
Ahmed III	1703–1730	Abdul Mejid II	1922–1924 (caliph only)

The sultanate was abolished and Turkey became a republic in October 1923. The Moslem religion was disestablished and the caliphate abolished in March 1924.

Appendix 4 *Greek Monarchs (1833–1967)*

1833–1862 Otto, Prince Otto of Bavaria
1863–1913 George I, Prince William of Denmark
1913–1917 Constantine I
1917–1920 Alexander
1920–1922 Constantine I
1922–1923 George II
1924–1935 'Republic'
1935–1944 George II
1944–1946 'Regency'
1946–1947 George II
1947–1964 Paul I
1964–1967 Constantine II

The monarchy was abolished by the Greek junta.

Appendix 5 *Orthodox Archbishops of Cyprus*

Kyprianos	1810–1821
Joakim	1821–1824
Damaskinos	1824–1827
Panaretos	1827–1840
Joannikios II	1840–1849
Kyrillos I	1849–1854
Makarios I	1854–1865
Sofronios II	1865–1900
Kyrillos II, Papadopoulos	1909–1916
Kyrillos III, Vasiliou	1916–1933
Vacancy – Leontios Leontiou of Paphos Topoteretes	1933–1947
Leontios Leontiou	1947 (June-July)
Makarios II, Myriantheus	1947–1950
Makarios III, Moskou	1950–1977 (3 August)
Chrysostomos I	1977 (12 November)

The latter was Bishop of Paphos from July 1973 and acted as *locum tenens* after the death of Archbishop Makarios.

Appendix 6 *Population of Cyprus*

Year	Greek	Turkish
1490	100,000	–
1570	150,000	–
1572	85,000	20,000
1664	60,000	18,000
1745	55,000	18,000
1777	60,000	20,000
1825	80,000	25,000
1841	92,000	30,000
1881	138,000	45,000
1901	183,000	51,000
1931	277,000	64,000
1946	361,000	81,000
1960	443,000	104,000
1975 (estimated)	496,000	117,000

Official Census 1960

Greek	442,521
Turkish	104,350
Armenians	3,628
Maronite	2,708
British	3,351
Latins	2,796
Others	18,261
	577,615

Bibliography

My research was based firstly on extensive library work, especially at the Public Record Office, British Museum Reading Room and at the Universities of London and Athens, where unpublished documents, manuscripts, reports and other primary and secondary materials were consulted; and, secondly, on lengthy interviews and discussions with political and organization leaders, clergymen, journalists and other informed laymen who have lived through the recent years of Cypriot history.

UNPUBLISHED SOURCES:

A. *Colonial Office Documents 1878-1953*

CO 67/1-373	Original Correspondence	Cyprus
CO 68/1-16	Acts	Cyprus
CO 69/1-69	Sessional Papers – Administrative Reports	Cyprus
CO 70/1-43	Government Gazettes	Cyprus
CO 456/1-68	Miscellanea – Blue Books of Statistics	Cyprus
CO 512/1-33	Register of Correspondence	Cyprus
CO 516/1-7	Register of Out-Letters	Cyprus
CO 537/23-24, 693-701, 1245.	Supplementary Despatches	Cyprus
CO 700/1-16	Maps and Plans	Cyprus
CO 883/2-8	Confidential Print – Mediterranean Dept.	
CO 926/1-39, 72-139	Original Correspondence – Mediterranean Dept.	

B. *Foreign Office*

FO 78/2764-2829, 3373, 3613, 4092, 4197, 5181, 5246.
  General Correspondence – Turkey.

FO 195/1-2647   *Embassy and Consular Archives – Turkey. (relevant sections only)*

FO 329/1-16   *Embassy and Consular Archives – Turkey: Cyprus.*

FO 371/1-to date.   *General Correspondence: Political (Southern). Too numerous to list – relevant sections only to 1953.*

FO 421/31-33   *Cyprus Confidential Print, 1878-1880.*

FO 800/63, 79, 172, 240 *Various private collections – Ministers and Officials.*

C. *War Office (WO) Defence (DEFE) Admiralty (ADM) PRO.*

WO 147/6   Private Collections – Wolseley Papers
WO 169/1336-7,
   15878-84.   War Diaries – Middle East Forces 1939-45.
DEFE 2/1471, 1653-4 Combined Operations & Headquarters Records,
                           1939-50
ADM 121/55   Cyprus Correspondence, 1878-1883
PRO 30/57/1, 77,
   80, 91.   Kitchener Papers

D. *Cabinet (CAB) and Prime Minister Office Papers (PREM).*
   CAB 37/2/32   List of Cabinet Papers 1880-1914:
                           Revenue of Cyprus 1880
   CAB 37/89/83   List of Cabinet Papers 1880-1914:
                           Condition of Cyprus 1907
   CAB 41/36/2, 49   Cabinet Letters in the Royal Archives:
                           Cyprus and Greece – session of, 1914-1915.
   CAB 65/17-19   War Cabinet Minutes (Conclusions) 1941.
   PREM 3/113   Operational Papers: Cyprus 1941-1943
   PREM 3/211/1-16   Operational Papers: Greece Miscellaneous 1941-44
   PREM 3/212/1-14   Operational Papers: Greece Miscellaneous 1944-45
   PREM 3/213/1-17   Operational Papers: Greece Miscellaneous 1944-45
   PREM 3/214   Operational Papers: Supplies to Greece 1940-41
   PREM 8/224   Correspondence & Papers 1945-1951. Visit of the
                           Greek Prime Minister to London 1946
   PREM 8/740   Correspondence & Papers 1945-1951. Future of
                           Cyprus 1945-1948.
   PREM 11/178-180,
      452-3   Correspondence & Papers 1952-1954: Greece.

E. *Manuscripts*
   Beaconsfield Papers – relevant folios.
   Dilke Papers – relevant folios.
   Gladstone Papers – relevant folios.
   Grey Papers – relevant folios.
   Layard Papers – relevant folios.
   Salisbury Papers – relevant folios.

PUBLISHED SOURCES:
I. *Official Documents.*
A. *Parliamentary Papers/Records.*
   1. *Debates* – Commons & Lords 1875-1983 (Hansard)
   2. *Command Papers* (CMD).
      2930 (1881)   Correspondence respecting the Affairs of Cyprus
      3091 (1881)   Further Correspondence respecting the Affairs of Cyprus
      3996 (1908)   Correspondence relating to the Affairs of Cyprus.
      7662 (1948-49)   Universal Declaration of Human Rights (UN)
      9075 (1953-54)   Statement on Defence, 1954.

9169 (1953-54) The Colonial Territories.
9300 (1953-54) Cyprus on the Agenda of the United Nations.
9429 (1954-55) The Bagdad Pact.
9708 (1955-56) Correspondence exchanged between the Governor
      and Archbishop Makarios.
9594 (1955-56) The Tripartite Conference on the Eastern
      Mediterranean and Cyprus.
  42 (1956-57) Constitutional Proposals for Cyprus – Lord Radcliffe.
124 (1956-57) Defence: Outline of Future Policy.
455 (1957-58) Cyprus: Statement of Policy.
566 (1958-59) Discussion on Cyprus in NATO.
679 (1958-59) Conference on Cyprus: Documents signed and
      initialled at Lancaster House, 19/2/1959.
680 (1958-59) Conference on Cyprus: Final Statements at the
      Closing Plenary Session at Lancaster House,
      19/2/1959.
1093 (1959-60) Cyprus: Draft Treaty, Constitution, Exchange of
      Notes etc.
1252 (1960-61) Treaty concerning the Establishment of the Republic
      of Cyprus.
1253 (1960-61) Cyprus: Treaty of Guarantee. Nicosia 16/8/1960
  331 (1975-76) Report from the Select Committee on Cyprus 8/4/1976
6579 (1975-76) Report from the Select Committee on Cyprus. HMG
      Reply August 1976.

B. *Other Documents*
  a. UN Resolutions. 14 volumes, 1946-1974
  b. Public Papers of the Secretaries-General of the UN. 8 volumes,
      1946-1971
  c. Documents on International Affairs 1955-1963 – Royal Institute of
      International Affairs (RIIA).
  d. Current British Foreign Policy, 1970-1972
  e. A Decade of American Foreign Policy: Basic Documents 1941-1949
  f. American Foreign Policy. Basic (Current) Documents. Volume I etc.,
      1950-1967 – Department of State, Washington.

II. *Unofficial*
In order to keep the bibliography to a manageable length, periodical and
newspaper articles have been excluded.
  (1)   The main *periodical-journals* consulted were:
        *Keesings Contemporary Archives, Contemporary Review, International
        Affairs* (R.I.I.A.), *The Economist, ISC Conflict Studies, The Annual
        Register, Facts on File, Journal of Hellenic Studies, Balkan Studies, Cyprus
        Today, Foreign Affairs* (New York), *The Washington Papers* and *The
        Atlantic Papers.*
  (2)   The main newspapers consulted were:
        GB – *The Guardian, The Times, Sunday Times* and *The Observer.*

USA – *New York Times, New York Herald Tribune, Washington Post*.
GREECE – *Apogevmatini, Acropolis* and *Kathimerini*.
CYPRUS – *Eleftheria, Phileleftheros, Haravgi, Agon, Ta Nea* and *Cyprus Mail*.

(3)   Some of the *BOOKS* consulted were:
Note – One * denotes books in Greek, titles translated.
Two ** denote books in French, titles translated.

Adams, T.W. *US Army Area Handbook for Cyprus* (US Government Printing Office, Washington DC, 1964)
Adams, T.W. *AKEL: The Communist Party of Cyprus* (Hoover Institution Press, USA, 1971)
Adams, T.W. & Cottrell, A.J. *Cyprus between East and West* (Johns Hopkins Press, Baltimore USA, 1968)
Alastos, D. *Cyprus Guerrilla: Grivas, Makarios and the British* (Heinemann, London, 1960)
Alastos, D. *Cyprus in History: A Survey of 5,000 years* (Zeno, London, 1976)
*Anastasiadou, I. *Venizelos and the Greco-Turco Friendship Pact of 1930* (Athens, 1982)
Arnold, P. *The Cyprus Challenge* (Hogarth, London, 1956)
Attalides, M.A. (ed) *Cyprus Reviewed* (Nicosia, 1977)
Attalides, M.A. *Cyprus: National and International Politics* (Q Press, Edinburgh, 1979)
*Averof-Tositsa, E. *A History of Missed Opportunities. Cyprus 1950-1963*, 2 volumes (Athens, 1981)
Baker, S.W. *Cyprus as I saw it in 1879* (Macmillan, London, 1879)
Balfour, J.P.D. *The Orphaned Realm: Journeys in Cyprus* (Percivall Marshall, London, 1951)
Barker, D.R. *Grivas: Portrait of a Terrorist* (Cresset, London 1959)
Bitsios, D.S. *Cyprus: The Vulnerable Republic* (Institute for Balkan Studies, Salonica, 1975)
*Bitsios, D.S. *Beyond the Frontiers 1974-1977* (Athens, 1982)
Byford-Jones, H. *Grivas and the story of EOKA* (Robert Hale, London, 1959)
Carver, M. *Harding of Petherton* (Weidenfeld & Nicolson, London, 1978)
Casson, S. *Ancient Cyprus: Its Art and Archaeology* (Methuen, London, 1937)
Cesnola, L.P.Di *Cyprus: Its Ancient Cities, Tombs and Temples* (John Murray, London, 1877)
Cobham, C.D. *Excerpta Cypria* (C.U.P., 1908)
*Constantinidou, G.M. *The history of Cyprus from ancient times to the English occupation* (Larnaca, 1910)
*Constantinidou, K.A. *The 1878 British Occupation of Cyprus* (Nicosia, 1930)
Coufoudakis, V. (ed) *Essays on the Cyprus Conflict* (Pella, New York, 1976)
Couloumbis, Th.A & Hicks, S.M. (eds) *US Foreign Policy Towards Greece and Cyprus: The clash of Principle and Pragmatism* (Centre for Mediterranean Studies, Washington DC, 1975)
Crawshaw, N. *The Cyprus Revolt: An account of the struggle for union with Greece* (Allen & Unwin, London, 1978)

**Crouzet, F. *The Cypriot Conflict, 1946-1959* 2 volumes (Bruylant, Brussels, 1973)

*Dekleris, M.E. *The Cypriot Question, 1972-1974. The Last Opportunity* (Athens, 1981)

**Dendias, M. *The Cypriot Question from historical and international points of view* (Paris, 1934)

Denktash, R.R. *The Cyprus Triangle* (Allen & Unwin, London, 1982)

Durrell, L.G. *Bitter Lemons* (Faber & Faber, London, 1959)

*Dzelepy, E.N. *The Cypriot problem and its conspirators* (Athens, 1975)

Ehrlich, T. *Cyprus, 1958-1967* (O.U.P., 1974)

Engin, A. *The Voice of the Cypriot Turks* (Istanbul, 1964)

Engin, E. & Girneli, Y. *Cyprus Question* (Worker's Voice Publications, London, 1980)

Erim, I.N. *Reminiscences on Cyprus* (Ankara, 1974)

Foglietta, U. *The Sieges of Nicosia and Famagusta in Cyprus* (Waterlow & Sons, London, 1903)

Foley, C.M. *Island in Revolt* (Longmans, London, 1962)

Foley, C.M. *Legacy of Strife: Cyprus from Rebellion to Civil War* (Penguin Books, London, 1964)

Foley, C.M. & Scobie, W.I. *The Struggle for Cyprus* (Hoover Institution Press, Stanford, California, 1975)

Foot, F.L. *Emergency Exit* (Chatto & Windus, London, 1960)

Foot, H.M. *A Start in Freedom* (Hodder & Stoughton, London, 1964)

Foot, M.M. & Jones, M. *Guilty Men, 1957* (Victor Gollancz, London, 1957)

*Gregoriade, S. *Greece, Turkey, Cyprus 1830-1979* (Athens, 1979)

*Grivas, G. *Reminiscences of EOKA's Struggle, 1955-1959* (Athens, 1961)

Grivas, G. *Guerrilla Warfare and EOKA's Struggle* (Trans. A.A. Pallis, Longmans, London, 1964)

Gunnis, R. *Historic Cyprus* (Methuen, London, 1936)

*Garoufalias, P.E. *Greece & Cyprus. Tragic Mistakes – Missed Opportunities, 1964-1965* (Athens, 1982)

*Hackett, J. & Papaioannou, H.I. *History of the Orthodox Church of Cyprus* 3 vols. (Athens, 1923-1932)

Harbottle, M. *The Impartial Soldier* (O.U.P., 1970)

Harbottle, M. *The Blue Berets* (Leo Cooper, London, 1971)

Hill, G.F. *A History of Cyprus* 4 Vols. (C.U.P., 1940-1952)

Home, G.C. *Cyprus then and now* (J.M. Dent, London, 1960)

*Honthrokoukis, D.N. *The hidden side of Turkey* (Athens, 1978)

Hunt, D. *On the Spot. An Ambassador Remembers* (Peter Davis, London, 1975)

Hunt, D. *Footprints in Cyprus. An illustrated history* (Trigraph, London, 1982)

*Ierodiakonou, L. *The Cyprus Question* (Athens, 1975)

Jeffrey, G.E. *Cyprus under an English King in the 12th century* (W.J. Archer, Nicosia, 1926)

Karageorghis, V. *Cyprus. From the Stone Age to the Romans* (Thames & Hudson, London, 1982)

*Kakaounaki, N. *2650 Days of Conspiracy* 2 vols. (Athens, 1976)

*Katri, Y.A. *The Birth of Neofascism: Greece 1960-1974* (Athens, 1974)

*Katsi, A. *From Independence to the Turkish Invasion* (Limassol, 1977)

*Kepiades, G.I. *Reminiscences of the 1821 Tragedy in Cyprus* (Alexandria, 1888)

*Kitsiki, D. *Greece and the Foreign Powers, 1919-1967. From the Archives of the Greek Foreign Ministry* (Athens, 1977)

*Kranidiotis, N. *Cyprus in the Struggle for Freedom* (Athens, 1958)

*Kranidiotis, N. *A thorny course: Archbishop Makarios III* (Nicosia, 1977)

*Kranidiotis, N. *Difficult Years: Cyprus, 1950-1960* (Athens, 1981)

*Kyprianos (Archimandrite) *Chronological History of Cyprus* (Nicosia, 1933)

Kyriakides, S. *Cyprus: Constitutionalism and Crisis Government* (University of Pennsylvania Press, Philadelphia, 1968)

*Kyrris, C.P. *Cyprus between East and West Today* (Nicosia, 1964)

*Kyrou, A.A. *Dreams and Reality. Years of Diplomatic Life, 1923-1953* (Athens, 1972)

Lang, R.H. *Cyprus* (Macmillan, London 1878)

Lee, D.E. *GB and the Cyprus Convention Policy of 1878* (Harvard University Press, USA, 1934)

Le Geyt, P.S. *Makarios in Exile* (Nicosia, 1961)

*Loizides, S. *Luckless Cyprus: 1910-1980* (Athens, 1980)

Luke, H. *Cyprus under the Turks, 1571-1878* (Humphrey Milford, London, 1921)

Luke, H. *Cyprus: A Portrait and an Appreciation* (George G. Harrap, London, 1965)

Macmillan, H. *Riding the Storm, 1956-1959* (Macmillan, London, 1971)

Macmillan, H. *Pointing the Way, 1959-1961* (Macmillan, London, 1972)

Maier, F.G. *Cyprus from the earliest times to the present day* (Elek, London, 1968)

*Markezinis, S.B. *Reminiscences, 1972-1974* (Athens, 1979)

Markides, K.C. *The Rise and Fall of the Cyprus Republic* (Yale University Press, New Haven and London, 1977)

Mayes, S. *Cyprus and Makarios* (Putman, London, 1960)

Mayes, S. *Makarios: A Biography* (Macmillan, London, 1981)

*Mirianthopoulos, K.I. *Hadjigeorgagis Kornesios. Dragoman of Cyprus, 1779-1809* Nicosia, 1934)

Mogabgab, Th.A.H. *Supplementary Excerpts on Cyprus*, 3 parts (Nicosia, 1941-45)

Nutting, H.A. *I saw for myself: The aftermath of Suez* (Hollis and Carter, London, 1958)

Orr, C.W.J. *Cyprus under British Rule* (Robert Scott, London, 1918)

*Panayotacos, C.P. *In the front line of defence* (Athens, 1980)

Papadopoullos, Th. *Social and Historical data on Population, 1570-1881* (Nicosia, 1965)

*Papageorgiou, S. *Makarios: the Heroic Struggle* (Athens, 1976)

*Papageorgiou, S. *Cyprus Storm, 1955-1959* (Nicosia, 1977)

*Papageorgiou, S. *Zedros: Life and Death of the Revered Cypriot Hero Gregoris Avxentiou* (Athens, 1978)

*Papageorgiou, S. *From Zurich to Attila* (Athens, 1980)

Papandreou, A. *Democracy at Gunpoint: The Greek Front* (Penguin Books, London, England, 1973)

*Petrakides, S.M. *Extracts from the Contemporary History of Cyprus, 1931-1952* (Larnaca, 1952)

*Pikros, Y.P. *Venizelos and the Cypriot Question* (Athens, 1980)
**Politis, J.N. *Cyprus: The Legend, the Epic, the Tragedy* (Paris, 1959)
Polyviou, P.G. *Cyprus: The Tragedy and the Challenge* (London, 1975)
Polyviou, P.G. *Cyprus in search of a Constitution, 1960-75* (Nicosia, 1976)
Polyviou, P.G. *Cyprus: Conflict & Negotiation 1960-80* (G. Duckworth, London, 1980)
*Protopsaltis, E.G. *Cyprus in the struggle of 1821* (Athens, 1971)
*Psycharis, S.P. *Backstage Diplomacy* (Athens, 1975)
*Psycharis, S.P. *70 Critical Days* (Athens, 1976)
Purcell, H.D. *Cyprus* (Ernest Benn, London, 1969)
Rabinowicz, O.K. *A Jewish Cyprus Project* (Herzl Press, New York, 1962)
Rossides, Z.G. *The Problem of Cyprus* (Athens, 1957)
Rio, A.F. *The Four Martyrs* (Burns & Lambert, London, 1856)
Salih, I. *Cyprus: The Impact of Diverse Nationalisms on a State* (University of Alabama Press, USA, 1978)
*Sarris, N. *The Other Side: A Political Chronology of the Cyprus Invasion* (Athens, 1977)
*Servas, P. *The Cypriot Tragedy* (Athens, 1975)
*Servas, P. *The Cyprus Question: Responsibilities* (Athens, 1980)
*Solomonidou, L.S. *Vivid Recollections: Cyprus 1974* (Athens, 1977)
*Spyridakis, K. *Studies, Lectures, Speeches, Articles*, 2 vols., 5 parts (Nicosia, 1972-1974)
Spyridakis, K. *A Brief History of Cyprus* (Nicosia, 1974)
Stegenga, J.A. *The UN Force in Cyprus* (Ohio State University Press, USA, 1968)
Stephens, R. *Cyprus, a place of arms* (Pall Mall, London, 1966)
Stern, L. *The Wrong Horse. The Politics of Interaction and the Failure of American Diplomacy* (Times Books, New York, 1977)
Storrs, R. *Orientations* (Nicholson & Watson, London, 1937)
Surridge, B.J.A. *A Survey of Rural Life in Cyprus* (Nicosia, 1930)
*Tarsoulli, A. *Cyprus*, 2 vols. (Athens, 1955-1963)
**Tenekides, G. *Cyprus: Recent history and perspectives for the future* (Nagel, Paris, 1964)
*Tenekides, G. & Kranidiotis, Y. *Cyprus: Its History, Problems and the Struggles of its People* (Athens, 1981)
*Terlexi, P. *Diplomacy and Politics of the Cyprus Problem: Anatomy of a Mistake* (Athens, 1971)
*Theodoulou, Ch.A. *Positions from the International and Cypriot Political Life 1957-1970* (Nicosia, 1971)
Tornaritis, C.G. *Cyprus and its Constitutional and Other Legal Problems* (Nicosia, 1980)
*Tsalakos, G. & Kranidiotis, Y. *Makarios: The way others saw him* (Athens, 1980)
Vanezis, P.N. *Makarios: Faith and Power* (Abelard-Schuman, London, 1972)
Vanezis, P.N. *Makarios: Pragmatism v Idealism* (Abelard-Schuman, London, 1974)
Vanezis, P.N. *Cyprus: The Unfinished Agony* (Abelard-Schuman, London, 1977)

Vanezis, P.N. *Makarios: Life and Leadership* Abelard-Schuman, London, 1979)

*Vlachou, A. *Ten Years of the Cypriot Question* (Athens, 1980)

Volkan, V.D. *Cyprus: War and Adaptation* (University Press of Virginia, Charlottesville, USA, 1979)

Waldheim, K. *The Challenge of Peace* (Weidenfeld & Nicolson, London, 1980)

Woodhouse, C.M. *British Foreign Policy since the Second World War* (Hutchinson, London, 1961)

Woodhouse, C.M. *The Struggle for Greece, 1941-1949* (Hart-Davis MacGibbon, London, 1976)

Woodhouse, C.M. *Karamanlis: The Restorer of Greek Democracy* (Clarendon Press, Oxford, 1982)

*Xanthopoulos-Palama, H. *Diplomatic Triptych* (Athens, 1979)

*Xyde, A.G. Linardato, S. & Hadjiargiri, K. *Makarios and his Allies* (Athens, 1972)

Xydis, S.G. *Cyprus: Conflict and Conciliation, 1954-1958* (Ohio State University Press, USA, 1967)

Xydis, S.G. *Cyprus: Reluctant Republic* (Mouton, The Hague, 1973)

*Zannetos, F. *Cyprus, 1821-1830* (Athens, 1930)

*Zannetos, F. *History of Cyprus from the English Occupation to the Present*, 2 vols. (Larnaca, 1910-1911)

*Zighdis, J.G. *For Democracy and Cyprus. Four months of struggle in the USA* (Athens, 1975)

Index